Ethical Challenges of AI in Academia

Jesús Miguel Muñoz Cantero, Ana M.ª Porto Castro,
Eva M.ª Espiñeira Bellón, and M.ª Josefa Mosteiro García (eds.)

Ethical Challenges of AI in Academia: Impact and Implications for Higher Education

PETER LANG
Berlin · Bruxelles · Chennai · Lausanne · New York · Oxford

Bibliographic Information published by the Deutsche Nationalbibliothek
The Deutsche Nationalbibliothek lists this publication in the Deutsche Nationalbibliografie; detailed bibliographic data is available online at http://dnb.d-nb.de.

Library of Congress Cataloging-in-Publication Data
Names: Muñoz Cantero, Jesús Miguel editor | Porto Castro, Ana María editor| Espiñeira-Bellón, Eva María, 1976- editor | Mosteiro García, María Josefa, 1973- editor
Title: Ethical challenges of AI in academia : impact and implications for higher education / Jesús Miguel Muñoz Cantero, Ana M.ª Porto Castro, Eva M.ª Espiñeira Bellón, M.ª Josefa Mosteiro García (eds.).
Description: Berlin ; New York : Peter Lang, [2026] | Includes bibliographical references.
Identifiers: LCCN 2025045174 (print) | LCCN 2025045175 (ebook) | ISBN 9783631941263 hardcover | ISBN 9783631941270 pdf | ISBN 9783631941287 epub
Subjects: LCSH: Education, Higher—Technological innovations | Artificial intelligence—Educational applications
Classification: LCC LB1028.44 .E84 2026 (print) | LCC LB1028.44 (ebook) | DDC 371.33/4—dc23/eng/20260128
LC record available at https://lccn.loc.gov/2025045174
LC ebook record available at https://lccn.loc.gov/2025045175

The preparation of this book was supported by the Secretaría Xeral de Universidades of the Xunta de Galicia, within the framework of research on academic integrity in the Galician University System.

ISBN 978-3-631-94126-3 (Print)
ISBN 978-3-631-94127-0 (ePDF)
ISBN 978-3-631-94128-7 (ePUB)
DOI 10.3726/b23085

Published by Peter Lang GmbH, Berlin (Germany)

info@peterlang.com

This publication has been peer reviewed.

www.peterlang.com

No legacy is so rich as honesty.

William Shakespeare

Contents

Figures xv
Tables xvii
Acknowledgements xix
Prologue xxi
Introduction xxv

Educational Personalisation in the Age of Artificial Intelligence: Opportunities and Ethical Challenges 1
Jorge Soto Carballo, Antonio Bernal Guerrero and Antonio R. Cárdenas Gutiérrez
Identity and Human Destiny in the Algorithmic Age: Educational Challenges in the Face of the Technodigital Revolution 1
Artificial Intelligence in Education: Opportunities and Ethical Challenges 8
Integration of AI in Higher Education: Cultivating Entrepreneurial Potential as a Path to Educational Personalisation 18

The Use of Artificial Intelligence in Higher Education Institutions in Portugal – Ethical Challenges and Opportunities 31
Ana Pedro and Lucília Nunes
The Use of AI in Higher Education: Between Challenges and Opportunities 32

AI – a Question of Purpose, Not Intentionality 33
AI as a Tool to Support Research, Not a Substitute for Human Thinking 35
The Use of AI in Higher Education Institutions in Portugal: What Reality? International Framework 36
AI and the Portuguese Higher Education Reality – What Has Been Done? 38
Final Considerations 47

Artificial Intelligence in the Literature Review: Ethical Issues 51
Silvana Stremel and Jefferson Mainardes
Introduction 52
The Importance of the Literature Review 52
Integrating AI Tools into the Literature Review 56
Ethics and Integrity in the Use of AI Tools for Literature Reviews 59
Conclusion 62

IAgiarism: Ethical and Academic Challenges in the Age of Artificial Intelligence 67
Jesús Miguel Muñoz Cantero, Eva M.ª Espiñeira Bellón and María Cristina Pérez-Crego
Introduction 67
Objectives 69
Method 70
Population and Sample 70
Instruments 72
Data Collection Procedure 72
Technical Analysis of the Instruments 72
Data Analysis 73
Results 78
Conclusions 84

Scientific Retractions: Historical Evolution, Ethical Challenges and the Role of Artificial Intelligence 89
Jesús Miguel Muñoz Cantero, Ana M.ª Porto Castro, M.ª Josefa Mosteiro García and Enelina Mª Gerpe Pérez
Scientific Retractions and Artificial Intelligence (AI) 89
Impact of Retractions on the Scientific Community and Scientific Integrity 91
Evolution of Scientific Retractions and Their Relation to the Use of Artificial Intelligence 93
Main Causes of Misbehaviour Leading to Retraction 96
Scientific Misconduct 96
Unintentional Errors 97
Contextual Factors 98
Inappropriate Use of AI 100
Conclusions 102
AI Use Declaration 103
Acknowledgements 103

Excellence and Academic Integrity in the Age of Artificial Intelligence: An Ibero-American Perspective 111
Jean G. Guerrero-Dib, Luz H. Godina-Silva and Ana C. Muñiz-Pérez
Introduction 111
The State of Academic Integrity in Higher Education Institutions in Ibero-America 112
Literature Review 116
Generative Artificial Intelligence Tools 116
Detection Tools for AI-generated Text 121
Concept and Functionality 121
Culture of Academic Integrity 122
Analysis of Policies for AI Usage in Higher Education 124
Sample 124
Methodology 126
Results and Findings 129

Conclusions and Future Work: A Critical Review of Institutional Responses 137
Institutional Response and Regulatory Frameworks 137
Faculty: Expectations and Support 137
Student Responsibilities and Ethical Considerations 138
Institutional Commitment to Academic Integrity 138
Recommendations for Moving Forward 139
Acknowledgement 139

Generative AI as a Catalyst for Innovation and Teaching Improvements: Challenges and Opportunities 147
Eva María Olmedo Moreno and Jorge Expósito López
Introduction 148
New Epistemological, Normative and Practical Scenarios 151
Transformation of the Teaching Role as Both a Challenge and an Opportunity 155
GenAI Tools for Establishing New Teaching and Innovation Models in University Classrooms Through Co-Intelligence 157
Elements for Reflection and Improvement: Opportunities for Innovation with GenAI 162
Conclusion 167
Statement on Use of AI 167

The Impact of Generative AI on Academic Texts: Changes in Scholarly Communication and Integrity 169
Rubén Comas Forgas, Alex Glynn and Carmen Touza Garma
Introduction: Academic Publishing, Setting a Definition 169
Phase 1. Pre-1940s: Learned Societies and the Gentlemanly Ethos 170
Phase 2. 1940s–1980s: Expansion, Professionalisation, and the Rise of Commercial Publishing 171
Phase 3. 1980s–Present: Digital Transformation, Open-access, and the Commercial Oligopoly 171
Ethics in Scientific Communication: A Historical Analysis 172

Seventeenth and Eighteenth Centuries: The Foundations of Scientific Publishing and Early Ethical Concerns 173
Nineteenth Century: Institutionalisation of Science and Ethical Dilemmas 173
Twentieth Century: Fraud, Conflicts of Interest, and Replication Crises 174
Twenty-first Century: Open Science, Retractions, and New Challenges 175
A New Era: Opportunities and Perils of AI in Academic Publishing 176
Opportunities in Academic Publishing 176
Perils of AI in Academic Publishing 177
Policies on AI Use in Academic Publishing 179
Norms and Guidelines for AI in Academic Publishing 181
Undeclared and Unethical Use of AI in Academic Publishing: Evidence and Research 182
Prevalence of Undeclared AI Use in Academic Publishing 182
Detection Challenges and AI-assisted Writing Patterns 183
Ethical Implications of Undeclared AI Use 183
Commercial Exploitation and Paper Mills 184
Conclusions 185
AI Use Declaration 187
Acknowledgements 187

Criteria for Assessing the Impact of Generative AI on Students' Dissertation Defences 195
Cinta Gallent-Torres, Mercè Morey López and Pilar Ezpeleta-Piorno
Introduction 195
Literature Review 199
Study Approach and Methodological Framework 201
Reflections and Rationale for Assessment Criteria 202
Our Proposal 204
Discussion 209
Conclusions and Prospective 213
Acknowledgements 215

Spanish Early Career Researchers and Research Integrity: Main Controversies and Artificial Intelligence 223
Blanca Rodríguez-Bravo and David Nicholas
Introduction 223
Objectives and Methodology 225
Results Analysis 227
Controversial Behaviours and Practices in the Process of Scientific Communication 227
Artificial Intelligence (AI): The Last Disruptor 239
Conclusion 242

Artificial Intelligence in Higher Education: Limitations and Potential in the Teaching-Learning Process 247
Viviana Elizabeth Jiménez Chaves, Claudia Spinzi, Perla Sosa de Wood and Andrea Paola Riego Esteche
Introduction 247
Methodology 252
Informants, Inclusion and Exclusion Criteria 252
Data Collection Instrument 253
Validation of the Instrument 253
Data Collection Procedure 254
Data Analysis 254
Results Analysis 254
Discussion and Conclusion 256

Artificial Intelligence in Music Composition: Ethical and Academic Challenges in the Classroom 267
Rocío Chao Fernández and Vicente Castro Alonso
Theoretical Framework 267
Objectives 271
Methodology 271
Research Approach and Design 271
Instrument 273
Participation 273
Data Processing and Analysis 274
Results 276

Perceptions and Challenges of AI in Musical Composition 276
Educational Applications of AI in Music Teaching 277
Challenges and Dilemmas in Music Education: Creativity and Digital Literacy 279
Discussion and Conclusions 281

Academic Integrity or Artificial Intelligence? Towards a Preventive Culture in Sweden 289
Christophe Premat
Introduction 289
Background 292
Previous Studies and Theoretical Framework 295
Data and Method 299
Findings 301
Discussion 309
Limitations of the Study 314
Conclusion 314

AI-assisted University Training for Educators: Plagiarism, Ethics, and Research Skills Development 321
José Sánchez-Santamaría, María José Galván-Bovaira, Natalia Hipólito-Ruiz and Carmen Carmona-Rodríguez
Introduction 322
Working Hypotheses, Research Questions, and Objectives 324
Method 324
Results 326
Research Skills in Initial Educator Training 326
The European Framework for Researchers: ResearchComp ... 328
Proposals of AI-driven Research Skills in University Training ... 331
Ethical and Plagiarism Implications of the Use of AI in Research Skills Training 341
Conclusions 345

Figures

Figure 1: Network of categories and codes of the student body ... 77
Figure 2: Teacher category and code network ... 78
Figure 3: Number of articles found in 'Google Scholar' and 'Google Académico' using the terms 'academic integrity' (English) and 'integridad académica' (Spanish) ... 113
Figure 4: Historical development of AI in education ... 150
Figure 5: EU Artificial Intelligence Act: risk levels ... 153
Figure 6: Examples of precision education and adaptive learning systems that use GenAI ... 154
Figure 7: GenAI tools and their application to different phases academic research paper elaboration: planning, development and communication ... 159
Figure 8: Do you think AI can create technological dependence in students? ... 254
Figure 9: Do you think AI can create privacy and data security issues for students? ... 255
Figure 10: Do you think AI can enrich educational content and make it more interactive and engaging for students? ... 256
Figure 11: Research design ... 272
Figure 12: Alignment of content analysis categories and codes ... 275
Figure 13: Frequent word associations with the pronoun 'I' ... 303
Figure 14: Relationships between key concepts in students' answers regarding the use of ChatGPT ... 306
Figure 15: The European Competence Framework for Researchers ... 329

Tables

Table 1: Identification of Codes of Ethics or Conduct and Disciplinary Regulations in university subsystem 42
Table 2: Identification of Codes of Ethics or Conduct and Disciplinary Regulations in Polytechnic Subsy 43
Table 3: Categories and codes emerging from student and teacher data analysis 75
Table 4: Causes leading to the retraction of scientific articles 101
Table 5: Examples of studies conducted at Ibero-American Universities 114
Table 6: Descriptive synthesis of the universities comprising the sample 125
Table 7: Synthesis of the general aspects of the documents 126
Table 8: Synthesis of institutional aspects 131
Table 9: Summary of aspects related to faculty 134
Table 10: Summary of aspects related to students 136
Table 11: Assessment criteria for the oral defence of the TFT 206
Table 12: Signals for detecting AI use in the oral defence of the TFT based on the six assessment criteria 208
Table 13: Description of the sample of participants 274
Table 14: Frequent words for the answers on the question of the utility of the self-study course 301
Table 15: Frequent words for the answers of the students reflecting on the use of ChatGPT 305

Table 16: Linguistic patterns in responses on ChatGPT citation practices 308
Table 17: Working hypotheses, research questions, and objectives 325
Table 18: Example of abstract thinking 330
Table 19: Selection of AI tools for literature review and formulating research questions 333
Table 20: A selection of AI tools for methodological design and data analysis 335
Table 21: A selection of AI tools for dissemination and communication and collaboration 336
Table 22: AI tools and their relation to ResearchComp (I) 337
Table 23: AI tools and their relation to ResearchComp (II) 339

Acknowledgements

The content of this book is the result of the effort and collaboration of researchers from different parts of the world who have dedicated their time, knowledge, and experience to reflecting on the ethical and academic challenges posed by artificial intelligence in higher education.

Our deepest gratitude goes to the authors of this collective work, whose commitment to research and academic integrity has made it possible to build a volume with a global perspective. The diversity of approaches, institutions, and countries represented in these pages reflects the international dimension of a debate that transcends borders and educational systems, providing a rich and nuanced vision of the impact of artificial intelligence on teaching, learning, and research.

We would also like to express our appreciation to the Secretaría Xeral de Universidades of the Consellería de Cultura, Educación e Universidade of the Xunta de Galicia, and particularly to its Secretary General, Dr José Alberto Díez de Castro, for his strong support of research within the Galician University System (SUG). His leadership has been instrumental in developing in-depth studies on academic plagiarism and integrity in higher education, fostering the consolidation of an inter-university research team.

This effort has enabled collaboration among scholars from universities in Spain, Portugal, Brazil, Mexico, Paraguay, Sweden, the United Kingdom, the United States, and other countries. Thanks to their contributions, this work offers a comparative analysis of ethical and academic dilemmas across different educational contexts, identifying common challenges and diverse strategies to address the use of artificial intelligence in academia.

Finally, we would like to highlight that the preparation of this book has been a process of academic dialogue and exchange, integrating different disciplinary and cultural perspectives. We hope that this collaborative effort will serve as a significant contribution to the debate on academic integrity and the ethical use of artificial intelligence, providing valuable insights and tools for the future of higher education in a globalised context.

Prologue

> The illiterate of the 21st century will not be those who cannot read or write, but those who cannot learn, unlearn, and relearn.
>
> ALVIN TOFFLER

We live in a time of radical change. Artificial intelligence (AI) has burst into our lives with the force of a wave that cannot be stopped. It is not a recent invention, but its impact certainly is. In just a few years, it has gone from being a technical curiosity to becoming a constant presence in our daily lives. It speaks to us from our mobile phones, suggests what to watch or buy, assists us in our searches, even makes decisions on our behalf, often without us realising it. And although it fascinates us, it also makes us uneasy. In the field of higher education, this concern becomes particularly acute: What is the point of teaching certain content if a machine can generate it? How do we assess learning if students can delegate their tasks to an AI?

This technology is advancing steadily, and often imperceptibly. It is already with us, present in the simplest of actions such as requesting a song or writing a message. Its usefulness is undeniable. It saves us time, simplifies processes, and automates tasks. Yet it also compels us to stop and ask ourselves: Are we truly prepared to live with it without losing control?

The uncertainty of the future should not paralyse us. As with previous technological revolutions, fear is understandable, but not inevitable. The key lies in our attitude: we can resign ourselves to being mere spectators, or we can embrace the challenge of becoming protagonists of change. AI can be a powerful tool, but it must be guided by robust principles. Otherwise, its development may follow paths that we have not consciously chosen.

We cannot predict everything that is to come, but we can start to shape it. The decisions we make today will set the direction for the years to come. That is why it is urgent to establish clear ethical criteria. If we do not set limits, we run the risk of giving in too much. AI already influences our consumption decisions, our opinions, our habits, sometimes without us even realising it. We cannot allow the wires to become our veins, nor AI our brain. We must learn to look carefully, and to distinguish between when we are making choices and when we are being guided.

Learning to live with AI is not only a technical issue but also a cultural and ethical one. It involves understanding its logic but also about recognising our responsibility. Amid so many promises of efficiency and speed, there are aspects we must not neglect: intellectual property, originality, and honesty. Many students already use programmes such as ChatGPT to write papers. Can we still speak of authorship in the same terms? What happens to the creator's rights if the content has been generated by a machine?

Current laws barely address these issues. They are designed for a previous era. Although they recognise the author's right simply by the act of creation, they do not offer clear answers about what happens when the creation comes from software. Who, then, is the author? The person who gave the instructions? The company that developed the algorithm? No one? The lack of regulation opens fertile ground for confusion and conflict. If we do not address it in time, it will be too late.

AI is here to stay, and we still do not know its full scope. It is like an expanding ocean, full of currents whose destinations remain unknown. Yet the truth is that we are already navigating it. We cannot turn our backs on this reality or anchor ourselves to old paradigms. We need a new perspective, an open, critical, and constructive attitude.

This book, which I have the privilege to introduce, brings together expert voices that explore this issue from the context of higher education. Each chapter is an invitation to think, to debate, and to imagine, because universities, now more than ever, need to rethink and reimagine themselves. Not to lose their essence, but to defend it with intelligence, ethics, and honesty.

We are moving between two eras: one in which knowledge was almost exclusively the result of human effort, and another in which technology multiplies our capabilities but also blurs our boundaries. It is up to us to ensure that this transition does not mean giving up, and that we do not forget what is essential: the value of free thought, the integrity of knowledge, and the dignity of education.

Pilar Martínez Clares
Professor at the University of Murcia
26 June 2025

Introduction

In recent years, artificial intelligence (AI) has evolved from a technical innovation to a transformative force across all areas of society. Higher education, as a cornerstone of knowledge and innovation, is strongly impacted, facing both challenges and opportunities. Universities face the task of integrating AI into their systems while preserving core educational values like academic integrity, ethics, and equity. This book, *Ethical Challenges of AI in Academia: Impact and Implications for Higher Education*, brings together experts from diverse backgrounds to explore how AI is changing education on both global and local levels, often referred to as 'glocal impact'.

This book provides a comprehensive exploration of AI's impact on higher education. It addresses topics such as personalised learning and the ethical dilemmas surrounding AI-assisted plagiarism, highlighting key issues for both students and educators. Through case studies, theoretical insights, and research, the chapters invite readers to engage with the challenges and opportunities presented by this technology.

The book opens with a focus on the transformative potential of AI in higher education. In *Educational Personalisation in the Age of Artificial Intelligence: Opportunities and Ethical Challenges*, Jorge Soto Carballo, Antonio Bernal Guerrero, and Antonio R. Cárdenas Gutiérrez explore how AI-powered personalised learning can support critical thinking, creativity, and student autonomy. Their contribution highlights the need for a humanistic and ethically grounded approach that reinforces the educator's role.

This is followed by *The Use of Artificial Intelligence in Higher Education Institutions in Portugal – Ethical Challenges and Opportunities*, where Ana Pedro and Lucília

Nunes examine how Portuguese universities are responding to the rapid emergence of AI. They reflect on institutional strategies, the impact of new European legislation, and the role of critical thinking in shaping ethical academic practices.

The following chapters focus on AI's impact on ethics and integrity in academia, particularly in areas such as authorship, plagiarism, and academic standards. Silvana Stremel and Jefferson Mainardes, in *Artificial Intelligence in the Literature Review: Ethical Issues*, discuss the growing use of AI tools in literature reviews, stressing the importance of transparency, human oversight, and the development of ethical guidelines. Meanwhile, in *IAgiarism: Ethical and Academic Challenges in the Age of Artificial Intelligence*, Eva María Espiñeira-Bellón and María Cristina Pérez-Crego analyse the phenomenon of AI-assisted plagiarism. Drawing on research conducted in a Galician university, they propose preventive strategies including student training, detection tools, and pedagogical reform.

In *Scientific Retractions: Historical Evolution, Ethical Challenges and the Role of Artificial Intelligence*, Jesús Miguel Muñoz Cantero, Ana M.ª Porto Castro, M.ª Josefa Mosteiro García, and Enelina Mª Gerpe Pérez explore how AI is reshaping the retraction process in academic publishing. They highlight its role in detecting misconduct and improving transparency while addressing broader systemic challenges.

This analysis is followed by *Excellence and Academic Integrity in the Age of Artificial Intelligence: An Ibero-American Perspective*, where Jean G. Guerrero-Dib, Luz H. Godina-Silva, and Ana C. Muñiz-Pérez examine institutional policies across Ibero-American universities and propose strategies to strengthen academic integrity in the digital era.

As the book progresses, it explores how AI is transforming teaching innovation, academic communication, and evaluation. In *Generative AI as a Catalyst for Innovation and Teaching Improvement: Challenges and Potentialities*, Eva María Olmedo Moreno and Jorge Expósito López highlight how GenAI is influencing curriculum design, pedagogical approaches, and regulatory adaptation in university classrooms. Rubén Comas-Forgas, Alex Glynn, and Carmen Touza Garma, in *The Impact of Generative AI on Academic Texts: Changes in Scholarly Communication and Integrity*, analyse how generative technologies are reshaping academic writing, balancing democratisation with concerns over linguistic standardisation and ethical authorship.

A complementary perspective is offered in *Criteria for Assessing the Impact of Generative AI on Students' Dissertation Defences*, by Cinta Gallent-Torres,

Mercè Morey López, and Pilar Ezpeleta-Piorno. The authors propose criteria to detect the influence of AI in students' oral presentations and promote strategies to safeguard authenticity in academic discourse.

In *Spanish Early Career Researchers and Research Integrity: Main Controversies and Artificial Intelligence*, Blanca Rodríguez-Bravo and David Nicholas present longitudinal insights from early career researchers, revealing how increasing pragmatism and performance pressures intersect with evolving perceptions of AI's ethical risks and potential.

The final chapters illustrate the practical application of AI in diverse educational contexts. In *Artificial Intelligence in Higher Education: Limitations and Potential in the Teaching-Learning Process*, Viviana Elizabeth Jiménez Chaves and colleagues investigate the case of Paraguay, identifying both ethical concerns and AI's benefits for personalisation, feedback, and engagement. Rocío Chao Fernández and Vicente Castro Alonso, in *Artificial Intelligence in Music Composition: Ethical and Academic Challenges in the Classroom*, explore trainee teachers' views on AI's creative and educational potential, while also acknowledging its ethical challenges.

In *Academic Integrity or Artificial Intelligence? Towards a Preventive Culture in Sweden*, Christophe Premat analyses how Stockholm University is responding to AI's influence on academic conduct by promoting transparency, student engagement, and preventive policies.

Finally, *AI-Assisted University Training for Educators: Plagiarism, Ethics and Research Skills Development*, by José Sánchez-Santamaría and his colleagues, considers how AI can support the development of research skills in teacher education. The authors advocate for a critical and ethically responsible use of AI, anchored in European research frameworks and academic integrity.

This book aims to shed light on the challenges and opportunities of AI in higher education and encourage informed discussion, helping educational institutions design responsible and effective strategies for integrating these technologies into their processes. Each chapter, with its unique focus and contributions, provides valuable insights into AI's impact on teaching, research, and academic integrity.

Jesús Miguel Muñoz Cantero. A Coruña
March, 2025

Educational Personalisation in the Age of Artificial Intelligence: Opportunities and Ethical Challenges

Jorge Soto Carballo[1]*, Antonio Bernal Guerrero*[2] *and Antonio R. Cárdenas Gutiérrez*[3]

ABSTRACT

This chapter explores the ethical challenges and educational opportunities posed by artificial intelligence (AI), focusing on its transformative impact on human identity and learning processes. From a critical and humanistic perspective, it examines the implications of AI-powered personalised education, acknowledging both its potential benefits and the associated risks of dehumanisation, standardisation, and diminished autonomy. The authors advocate for a reflective integration of AI that upholds fundamental rights, fosters critical thinking, and reinforces the teacher's role in a digital society. In higher education, AI is presented as a tool to enhance entrepreneurial potential by cultivating skills such as creativity, leadership, and problem-solving, within an ethically governed and socially just framework.

Keywords: artificial intelligence, educational ethics, personalised learning, digital identity, educational entrepreneurship

Identity and Human Destiny in the Algorithmic Age: Educational Challenges in the Face of the Technodigital Revolution

Even more precisely, who or what will they become? The question of identity has been collectivised within contemporary intellectual discourse and avant-garde cultural debates. However, this intrinsic curiosity now revolves inexorably around a pressing inquiry into our evolutionary trajectory – into the next stage of a transformative process that, in accordance with the prevailing dynamic paradigm, positions us within a continuous and ever-changing cosmic flux. The past and present recede in the face of the uncertainty, anticipation, or enthusiasm elicited by an indeterminate

[1] University of Vigo, Spain. https://orcid.org/0000-0002-6768-4078

[2] University of Seville, Spain. https://orcid.org/0000-0002-0387-9538

[3] University of Seville, Spain. https://orcid.org/0000-0002-8799-2860

future – one that, to some extent, we are already actively shaping. At the core of this conceptual labyrinth lie 'posthumanism' and 'transhumanism'.

Or, as some eminent champions of the digital revolution – such as Raymond Kurzweil (2012) – proclaim, will we transcend the biological foundation that defines us, based on the premise that the biological component is not an essential aspect of human nature? The American inventor has predicted the imminent emergence of artificial intelligence indistinguishable from the human mind – that is, possessing self-awareness and emotional depth. This 'singularity', as described by the expert in artificial intelligence, would enable the transcendence of the limitations imposed by our biological bodies and brains, marking a rapid and exponential increase in intelligence as a distinguishing factor compared to previous technological milestones, such as writing.

Although its societal integration remains limited, the reality is that scientific advancements are increasingly enhancing the capacity for control over human development. Scientific and technological progress elicits unequivocal opposition from certain sectors, primarily due to concerns about its potential degenerative impact on humanity – often overlooking the substantial benefits it has generated across various domains, including medicine, communications, agriculture, and economics. While it is acknowledged that reducing material dependencies may facilitate deeper self-awareness, the collective advocacy for a return to nature – an idealised 'life in the woods', as envisioned by Henry David Thoreau in *Walden* (1854) – however evocative, appears fundamentally unfeasible in a world where the population has already surpassed eight billion and is projected to exceed ten billion by the end of this century.

Human destiny appears inextricably intertwined with technological progress; thus, the fundamental question is not whether to embrace it, but rather what form of development should be pursued.

Human identity undergoes transformation in a manner that is often imperceptible. Our contemporary existence bears little resemblance to that of our relatively recent ancestors. Advances in nutrition, pharmaceuticals, biomedical prosthetics – both external and internal – transportation, recreational activities, and information and communication technologies have collectively reshaped the human experience, constructing a vastly different landscape from that of previous generations.

Amid these profound shifts, we remain central, even as brain-computer interfaces transition from speculative fiction to empirical reality. Voice-based interaction with televisions, refrigerators, or computers constitutes only a marginal indicator of the profound technological transformations that lie ahead.

In 2022, at the Giardini of the Venice Biennale, Ai-Da participated in a poetry recital – one of several that took place that year. The act of listening to the verses of a distinguished poet is, in itself, unremarkable, as their reception naturally varies depending on individual literary preferences. However, what distinguishes this event is that Ai-Da is a robot. More precisely, Ai-Da is a humanoid robotic artist with the capability to compose poetry, draw, paint, and sculpt, among other creative tasks.

Ai-Da possesses a remarkable capacity: it processes and stores extensive historical data on literature and art, endowing it with an exceptional level of cognitive potential. Ai-Da functions as an artificial intelligence-based system for the autonomous generation of artistic content. Its creator, Aidan Meller, a British gallerist and art dealer, anticipates that any perceived disparity between Ai-Da's works and those produced by human artists will soon be eradicated – suggesting, ultimately, that Ai-Da's artistic output may even surpass that of human creators.

In Barcelona, as in other regions globally, a socially assistive robot designed to support elderly individuals living alone has been developed: ARI. This robotic system is programmed to detect emergency situations, issue medication reminders, interact through facial and voice recognition, and facilitate video communication. Furthermore, it can be remotely controlled by family members and caregivers, enhancing its integration into daily caregiving practices.

These advancements signal the emergence of a transformative era. The integration of artificial intelligence into human life is no longer a theoretical prospect but an ongoing and accelerating phenomenon.

At first glance, artificial intelligence may appear to function solely as a provider of answers, in contrast to the Socratic method, which is predicated on inquiry – to paraphrase Eilenberger (2025). Enthralled by its advantages, some scholars have even proposed the development of a political algorithm designed to govern the common good, administer justice, and enhance social well-being, with the ultimate goal of eliminating corruption.

From a critical perspective, the humanist César Antonio Molina cautions: 'What a beautiful naivety!' (2023, p. 351). A statement that warrants reflection.

Éric Sadin (2023) critiques the concept of a 'spectral life' shaped by our increasing technological integration. He contends that the notion of human-machine complementarity is a constructed fiction that merely channels the delegation of our capacity to formulate truths and engage in lived experience to technical systems. In response to this era of the metaverse and generative artificial intelligence, the necessary course of action must be political.

> In opposition to the spectral, we must affirm our full presence in the world and the richness of sensory experience. In resistance to the ascendancy of algorithmic normativity, we must champion the exercise of human reason and agency, defending our right – while upholding the inalienable respect for human plurality – to autonomously shape the course of our individual and collective destinies. In defiance of the artificial generation of language and symbols devoid of vitality, we must foster, in myriad forms, the creative impetus that ought to propel us forward each day (pp. 235–36).

The French philosopher's appeal to the community, shaped by the technophobia inherent in his diagnosis of contemporary society – closely linked to his critique of capitalism and its systemic structure – is, in many ways, representative of those who perceive the impact of current technological artefacts on humanity as transcending concerns about health, life expectancy, or the economic organisation of society. Indeed, their influence extends to deeper domains: desires, emotions, love, artistic creation, sentiments, belief systems, spatial and temporal perception, freedom, and destiny.

Education is also profoundly affected – an essential process that shapes human identity, to paraphrase Kant's famous dictum. The reasons for concern are substantial. In his final work, Bauman (2017) portrayed a landscape dominated by anxiety and fear. Are we witnessing the consolidation of a new form of totalitarianism, masked by the alluring promises of artificial intelligence, robotics, and algorithmic governance?

Concerns about the existential risks posed by automation to humanity are not confined to philosophers and scholars from various disciplines. This growing apprehension has been institutionalised through the recent establishment of key research centres, including the Future of Humanity Institute (University of Oxford), the Centre for the Study of Existential Risk (University of Cambridge), and the Machine Intelligence Research Institute, formerly known as the Singularity Institute for Artificial Intelligence (Berkeley).

However, science itself is not inherently responsible for any wrongdoing. It holds no more culpability than any admired work of art. As a fundamental component of the humanities, science both emerges from human culture and actively shapes it (Nussbaum, 1997). Science should not be positioned in opposition to humanity. Perhaps the defining characteristic of our era is that, for the first time in history, science and technology are advancing independently of human deliberation. This raises critical concerns about our capacity for adaptation and critical analysis in guiding the trajectory of this progress – progress that, in its most genuine form, cannot exist without humanity.

We must not relinquish our capacity for reflection, despite the increasing temptation toward passive acceptance. The exercise of critical thinking and self-governance demands sustained effort and ongoing vigilance. There is no freedom without intellectual struggle.

Amid both opportunities and risks, biotechnology and information technology continue their expansion. Jean Twenge (2018), a professor at San Diego State University, argues that the identity crisis in the digital age has intensified, as technology fosters unprecedented modes of identity construction and self-expression – offering both emancipatory potential and new constraints. The so-called 'Me Generation' frequently constructs its identity within online environments, adapting to the demands of a carefully curated public persona rather than fostering authentic self-expression. While this phenomenon is not entirely novel, the growing influence of social media has significantly magnified its associated risks.

The new modes of production driven by artificial intelligence (ChatGPT, Gemini, MusicLM, DALL-E 3, among others) are reshaping the ways in which we think, reason, and create. This is not merely an auxiliary technology but rather a paradigm shift that reconfigures cultural frameworks and ways of life. Indeed, identifying stable patterns that enable us to comprehend both reality and ourselves within this hyper-technological society is becoming increasingly complex (Bernal, 2021).

The erosion of confidence in the pursuit of meaning in reality is closely linked to the delegitimisation of any reference to truth, as all existing interpretations are elevated to an equivalent status. The exponentially growing volume of information has facilitated unprecedented global access to knowledge. However, in the absence of effective mechanisms for discernment, this proliferation has simultaneously heightened uncertainty due to the material impossibility of processing such vast amounts of data.

A distinct ecology of disinformation further compounds this complexity; this phenomenon extends beyond inadvertent or erroneous misinformation to include deliberately engineered narratives serving ulterior motives: 'Almost every time information is generated, the possibility of disinformation arises' (López, 2023, pp. 2–3). Hyper-information not only complicates our understanding of historical origins but also undermines our ability to anticipate the future, shape individual and collective aspirations, and define personal and communal trajectories. Consequently, the construction of identity is becoming increasingly precarious.

In response to the massive influx of data, electronic algorithms have become fundamental instruments for processing information and generating knowledge. The pervasive and continuous interconnectivity across various media and networks has given rise to what is now known as the Internet of Things – an ecosystem in which the erosion of privacy and autonomy is often disregarded as an insignificant trade-off. Consequently, individuals become embedded within an expansive and increasingly complex system – one that remains elusive yet is expected to provide solutions and guidance for decision-making regarding personal concerns and future projections.

Where, then, should the boundaries for algorithmic application be established? Efficiency – an intrinsic characteristic of artificial intelligence systems capable of processing vast amounts of data at unprecedented speeds – should not be the sole criterion when dealing with human-centred decision-making. When ethical implications are at stake, efficiency alone is insufficient as a guiding principle. As Pasquale (2020) argues, the mechanistic treatment of individuals by algorithmic systems results in a dehumanising effect, paradoxically reducing human agency to an operational function while treating automated systems as if they possessed human-like agency.

Navigating the intricate balance between the promises of technological advancement and the concerns it raises, Helga Nowotny (2022) advocates for a digital humanism. She underscores the necessity of preserving the notion of the future as an open and indeterminate horizon. In this regard, the greatest risk lies in uncritically accepting the premise that algorithms can predict the future with deterministic certainty. Contingency and uncertainty, however, are fundamental anthropological constructs that must be safeguarded if human identity is to be preserved. Reflecting on the implications of algorithmic governance, Nowotny cautions: 'If we place excessive trust in algorithmic predictions, we risk reverting to a deterministic worldview in which all outcomes are preordained, leaving us at the mercy of our own reverence for computational forecasting' (p. 184).

The Mexican essayist Juan Villoro (2024), after critically exploring the digital sphere, concludes that outright rejection is not the most constructive approach:

> Coexisting with the digital world – our pocket-sized cave –, assimilating it, and repurposing it within a new framework is more beneficial than denying its presence. This is not only due to its vast array of practical applications but also because the reciprocal exchange between the real and the virtual enhances both dimensions of experience. Every avant-garde movement fundamentally constitutes a critical appropriation of a preceding paradigm (p. 311).

The extent to which we can successfully coexist with the digital world largely depends on the quality of education we cultivate. Addressing the risk of allowing our existence to drift toward distraction and cognitive passivity – an inclination significantly reinforced by artificial intelligence – requires an educational approach that prioritises the development of cognitive faculties that define human intelligence.

The emergence of generative artificial intelligence has initiated a process of detachment from what is most fundamental to our nature. The increasingly sophisticated texts generated by ChatGPT and similar models progressively disengage us from our most essential faculty: the ability to produce language. This detachment may, in turn, erode our natural right to autonomous self-determination. '*What we need is to speak in the first person, not in the form of uninterrupted postings on platforms of expressivity*' (Sadin, 2023, p. 187).

The pervasive use of digital tools may be undermining our capacity for sustained attention (Patino, 2020). Platforms characterised by constant interruptions – tweets, notifications, e-mails, and instant messages – disrupt cognitive processes and, to an uncertain extent, impair our ability to engage in complex intellectual tasks. Continuous exposure to such distractions not only affects attention span but also influences overall cognitive development (Hari, 2022).

If educational paradigms are restricted exclusively to socio-emotional competencies, we risk neglecting the intellectual cultivation essential to critical reasoning. L'Ecuyer (2021) warns that ignorance is increasingly being valorised as a social norm. If the preservation of human dignity remains a priority, education must undergo a rigorous reassessment of how technological advancements are integrated into learning processes.

Historically, education has been a fundamental driver of human evolution; today, it assumes an unprecedented level of significance. We turn to it with hope, recognising it as both a force for resilience and transformation, continuity and innovation. In the formation of our identities, we necessarily seek to recover the most valuable aspects of our intellectual and cultural heritage while embracing the courage required for progressive advancement. What is at stake is not merely personal development but also the very survival of our societies (Bernal et al., 2025).

Education, inherently complex and rich in intellectual, emotional, and relational challenges, must develop within a framework that demands systemic responses, all while safeguarding the significance of individuality – an achievement secured through sustained effort. The commitment to education, both individually and collectively, is not spontaneous; it requires continuous attention and cultivation. Identifying the most effective strategies to foster this commitment in an increasingly hyperconnected society remains an urgent collective challenge. As Arana (2024) aptly reminds us, education cannot treat individuals as mere objects to be moulded but must recognise them as active, thinking subjects.

Artificial Intelligence in Education: Opportunities and Ethical Challenges

The impact of artificial intelligence (AI) on education is generating a broad and complex debate that encompasses both its potential benefits and the risks associated with its implementation. From personalised learning to the automation of teaching tasks, automated technologies present themselves as tools with substantial transformative potential. However, their integration into educational systems is not exempt from ethical and pedagogical dilemmas that must be addressed with rigour, as the rapid emergence of AI across various domains of social life – particularly within the educational ecosystem – has generated a complex network of opportunities and challenges that demand a coordinated and global ethical response.

Years ago, in 1996, UNESCO published Learning: The Treasure Within, widely known as the Delors Report, which envisioned education as a necessary utopia and a driving force for equity, development, and peace. This document established a holistic vision of education grounded in four pillars: learning to know, learning to do, learning to live together, and learning to be. Although it was conceived in a context prior to the explosion of artificial intelligence, its conceptual framework remains a vital reference point for understanding the current challenges of education in the digital age. At the end of the twentieth century, education faced the challenge of adapting to globalisation, emerging technologies, and transformations in the labour market.

Today, the rise of AI raises even deeper questions regarding access to knowledge, learning autonomy, values-based education, and the role of the teacher. The four pillars of the Delors Report have guided global educational policy for decades, yet artificial intelligence now compels a critical reassessment of these principles. Beyond these pillars, the Delors Report identified a series of fundamental tensions within education – many of which have acquired new dimensions with the advent of AI. The tension between the global and the local raises concerns about how to ensure personalised and culturally relevant education in a world increasingly dominated by centralised AI platforms. The dichotomy between tradition and modernity compels us to reflect on how to integrate AI without disregarding pedagogical methods that have proven effective. The relationship between the short- and long-term invites us to consider the importance of preparing students for an uncertain future without hastily implementing unregulated technologies. Likewise, the tension between competition and equity highlights the risk that AI may exacerbate educational inequalities due to the digital divide. Finally, the interplay between the material and the spiritual reminds us that education must not become a purely technological process, but rather continue to nurture critical and ethical citizens.

Remaining within the educational framework proposed by Delors and focusing on the era of artificial intelligence, several proposals can be drawn for an educational model that leverages the potential of this technology without compromising its fundamental values. From a critical standpoint, it is necessary to reformulate curricula to include training in AI, digital ethics, and computational thinking from early educational stages. Likewise, we must ensure that all educational institutions have access to advanced technologies without generating new social divides. More importantly, it is essential to foster critical thinking and creativity, preventing AI from replacing the development of intellectual autonomy. Instead, it should promote lifelong learning by serving as a tool for the continuous training of both teachers and students.

In light of the aforementioned, we can observe how intelligent technologies have radically transformed access to information, facilitating unprecedented access to massive volumes of data while simultaneously introducing challenges related to misinformation and cognitive dependency. As a result, education must prioritise digital literacy, critical thinking, and the capacity to discern reliable information from algorithmically generated content. The proliferation of educational chatbots and AI assistants has proven useful in personalising learning, but students must develop the skills to critically assess their responses and avoid passive acceptance of information. On another front, AI is displacing traditional jobs while creating new opportunities in fields such as robotics, data science, and programming. In response to this reality, education should focus on developing skills that are not easily replaced by AI, such as creativity, complex problem-solving, and interdisciplinary collaboration. Certain methodologies, such as project-based learning with AI, can enhance the development of practical competencies in programming and data analysis, preparing students for a constantly evolving labour environment. Nevertheless, we must question whether educational training should be exclusively aligned with market demands or if, conversely, it should uphold its mission of cultivating a critical and autonomous citizenry.

At present, AI can be regarded as a new educational utopia, with the potential to democratise access to knowledge and personalise learning. However, this utopia will only be beneficial if managed ethically and conscientiously. The primary risk lies in reducing education to a pedagogical dynamic devoid of relational meaning, where instructional systems are governed by algorithmic logics and optimised for efficiency rather than aimed at forming critical, creative, and socially committed citizens. The key, therefore, lies in finding a balance between technological innovation and core ethical-pedagogical principles, ensuring that AI does not replace the essence of human learning but rather enhances it. The education of the future should not be defined by algorithms, but guided by humanistic principles that enable the effective use of AI while preserving the fundamental goal of learning: to foster autonomous, reflective individuals capable of transforming the world.

Therefore, the use of AI in education requires a regulatory framework that ensures its safe and equitable implementation. In this context, it is crucial for governments and educational institutions to establish clear policies governing the use of AI in classrooms, to validate trustworthy tools, and to ensure the proper training of educators in this domain. The ethical development of artificial intelligence systems necessitates the incorporation of normative frameworks that guide technological implementation toward humanistic, inclusive, and responsible ends. To address these challenges, several countries have introduced guidelines promoting the responsible use of AI. Australia, in particular, has established a set of ethical principles intended to guide the development and implementation of AI systems in alignment with core values. These eight ethical principles constitute a voluntary and aspirational framework that advocates for the design, development, and deployment of AI systems grounded in values such as human well-being, equity, privacy protection, reliability, and explainability. These principles emphasise the necessity for AI to respect human rights and diversity while also ensuring mechanisms for oversight and accountability, especially when such technologies significantly impact individuals or communities. In doing so, they support an ethical and context-sensitive approach that mitigates risks related to discrimination, opacity, or dehumanisation in automated environments and complements existing legal frameworks with standards of social responsibility and algorithmic justice.

In this emerging context, and reviewing the initial steps in AI regulatory development, mention must be made of the Beijing Consensus (UNESCO, 2019), the result of an international conference organised by UNESCO and the Government of the People's Republic of China. This event represents a turning point in the reflection on intelligent technologies in education, emphasising that their integration must be carried out from a humanistic perspective focused on equity, human rights, and inclusion. This vision aligns with a fundamental ethical imperative: to ensure that technological development does not supplant the profound relational nature of education, but rather contributes to the enhancement of human capabilities and the preservation of teacher-student interaction as the irreplaceable core of the educational process. In this vein, recent developments in AI raise critical issues concerning the respect for fundamental rights. Algorithmic discrimination, model opacity, and the extensive use of surveillance technologies have triggered alerts about the potential to replicate – or even exacerbate – structural inequalities. The European Commission (2021), for its part, has identified such risks in various contexts, including personnel selection, credit granting, and risk prediction in judicial settings. Added to this is the threat of algorithmic opacity, which undermines the principle of explainability and erodes public trust in AI systems (PwC & OdiseIA, 2022). These concerns are not merely technical but are deeply ethical and political, as they directly influence how societies configure their systems of justice, rights protection, opportunity distribution, and education – and, by extension, how they shape the holistic development of their citizens.

The emergence of generative artificial intelligence (GenAI) introduces new layers of complexity to the ethical debate. These technologies, capable of autonomously generating textual, visual, and auditory content, redefine the boundaries between the human and the artificial, between created knowledge and simulated knowledge. UNESCO (2024), in its guidance on GenAI in education and research, warns of the risks of depersonalisation, thought homogenisation, and the erosion of ethical judgement, while also proposing pedagogical strategies and normative frameworks to ensure a responsible, equitable, and culturally sensitive use of these technologies. In this context, the report Artificial Intelligence and Education: Guidance for Policy-makers (UNESCO, 2021) offers a roadmap for the critical implementation of AI in educational systems. Rather than celebrating unrestricted automation, the guide underscores the need to prevent algorithmic bias, promote gender equity, prepare teachers and citizens for the cultural and cognitive shifts entailed by these technologies, and design public policies that incorporate international best practices. The document is aligned with the United Nations Sustainable Development Goals (SDGs), particularly Goal 4, which seeks to ensure inclusive, equitable, and quality education for all.

In the same vein, the Recommendation on the Ethics of Artificial Intelligence (UNESCO, 2021) represents a normative milestone by establishing the first international ethical framework of universal scope. With a focus on human dignity, this Recommendation articulates principles such as transparency, justice, accountability, and human oversight, and it sets forth concrete guidelines for implementation, including ethical impact assessments, the participation of multiple stakeholders, and special attention to global inequalities. From a philosophical and methodological perspective, some studies (Alonso-Rodríguez, 2024) advocate for an ethical framework grounded in the principles of beneficence, non-maleficence, autonomy, justice, and explainability. These studies caution against the confusing overlap of principles and call for a coherent articulation between professional ethics in teaching and the design of educational technologies. Within this framework, it becomes evident that the role of educators must be redefined in the age of intelligent platforms – not merely as technical facilitators but as guardians of the humanistic meaning of education. The proposal for ethical governance of AI requires not only legal norms but also an institutional commitment to the formation of a critical citizenry capable of understanding, questioning, and transforming the intelligent systems shaping both public and private life.

In the specific domain of training, UNESCO has developed two core competency frameworks focused on teachers and students. Regarding students, the AI Competency Framework for Students (2024) proposes a model of critical digital literacy rooted in principles of social justice and sustainability. The AI Competency Framework for Teachers (2024), in turn, establishes a training pathway encompassing five dimensions, ranging from ethics to pedagogical innovation. Both instruments position AI education not as mere technical training but as a formative process aimed at fostering digital citizenship, ethical reflection, and social transformation. This represents, therefore, an epistemological and axiological commitment that moves away from a technicist view to embrace a comprehensive understanding of both learners and educators.

Despite the growing presence of intelligent technologies in education, few countries have defined clear reference frameworks for teacher training in this area – an issue of considerable concern. This gap leaves many educators without the necessary tools to address the challenges and opportunities posed by AI in their pedagogical practices. Traditionally, the classroom has been a space where direct interaction between teachers and students formed the foundation of the learning process. However, algorithmic solutions have introduced a third actor into this equation: automated systems that process information, generate content, and provide predictive analytics to inform decision-making. This transformation demands a redefinition of the teacher's role and the competencies they must develop to ensure the ethical and effective use of technology in the classroom. For this reason, UNESCO has developed the AI Competency Framework for Teachers (UNESCO, 2024), an initiative aimed at equipping educators with essential tools to harness AI's potential without losing sight of their central role in shaping future generations. This model represents a crucial step forward. Its objective is not merely to train teachers in technological usage but also to promote a humanistic approach to the future of education

This competency-based approach to AI outlines fifteen skills organised into five core dimensions:

- Human-centred mindset: It is essential that educators adopt a critical perspective on the integration of AI in education. Technology must serve learning and not replace the role of the teacher.
- AI ethics: Ethical principles must be applied in the use of AI, ensuring the protection of students' privacy and equitable access to digital tools.
- Foundations and applications of AI: Educators must understand the basic concepts of AI and its impact on education, which will enable them to select and use appropriate tools in their classrooms.
- Pedagogy with AI: AI should be strategically integrated into teaching processes to enhance the learning experience without dehumanising education.
- AI for professional development: The continuous professional development of teachers can benefit from AI, enabling personalised learning and professional collaboration.

This competency model also establishes three progression levels to guide teachers' development in AI use. The first level, Acquire, focuses on basic AI literacy, providing essential knowledge about its functioning and applications in education. The second level, Deepen, involves teachers learning to critically evaluate AI tools and effectively integrate them into their pedagogical practices. Finally, the third level, Create, represents the most advanced stage, fostering innovation in teaching and the development of new methodologies that harness AI's capabilities without compromising ethics or educational equity.

Based on the arguments presented, and in contrast to techno-utopian visions that advocate for the accelerated adoption of AI as a solution to structural educational challenges, various voices have called for a more critical approach – one oriented toward preserving the integrity of educational purposes and emphasising the learner as a moral and cognitive agent in the formative process.

In 2024, the European Union approved the first comprehensive international law regulating the development, commercialisation, and use of artificial intelligence systems within its jurisdiction. This regulation adopts a risk-based approach, classifying AI systems according to their potential threat to fundamental rights, safety, and democratic values. Particularly relevant for the educational and ethical spheres is the prohibition and strict regulation of AI uses deemed unacceptable, such as social scoring systems or subliminal manipulation techniques. Moreover, the regulation imposes stringent technical and organisational obligations for high-risk systems, including those employed in education and career guidance, aiming to ensure transparency, traceability, human oversight, and algorithmic non-discrimination. This framework reflects a normative intent to harmonise technological progress with the protection of human dignity, equity, and fundamental values, positioning Europe as a global benchmark for ethical AI governance.

Within this scenario, the analysis of studies such as the Report from the Observatory for Educational Innovation and Digital Culture (ODITE, 2025) becomes especially relevant. This document systematically examines the implications of AI in contemporary education and focuses on three core dimensions: risks, benefits, and personalised learning. It highlights fundamental concerns regarding equity, privacy, and teacher autonomy in relation to AI's educational integration. The report not only warns against uncritical technological adoption but also advocates for a critical, ethical, and contextualised vision of AI in education, placing human agency, social justice, and pedagogical meaning at the centre.

The results of the meta-analysis included in the report reveal an optimistic trend in perceptions of AI in education, with 92.19% expressing confidence in its benefits and opportunities, compared to only 42.19% acknowledging its risks and challenges (Muñoz et al., 2025). This discrepancy in the attention given to risks suggests the need to balance the narrative and delve deeper into the ethical implications of AI use. One of the most pressing concerns is the potential commodification of education and the subordination of pedagogical processes to market-driven logics, which may reduce teaching to a model based on efficiency and automation, rather than prioritising critical thinking and the holistic development of learners (Muñoz et al., 2025). Similarly, although AI-powered personalised learning appears promising, it could result in hidden standardisation, where educational pathways are constrained by algorithms rather than tailored to the individual needs of students. In this context, it becomes essential to approach AI through a critical lens, ensuring its use in education adheres to robust ethical principles and a humanistic vision of learning. As the ODITE report notes, 'the goal is not to humanize AI, but to humanize education' (Muñoz et al., 2025, p. 35). Artificial intelligence must be understood as a means to enhance teaching – not to replace the teaching profession or reduce education to mechanised processes.

Based on these considerations, it can be assumed that artificial intelligence (AI) is rapidly transforming education, redefining the relationship between teachers and students and generating new dynamics in teaching and learning processes. However, this does not imply that computational intelligence should be seen as a substitute for traditional instruction, but rather as a tool that, when appropriately used, can enrich the learning experience and reinforce the role of teachers in society. As this new digital architecture of knowledge continues to evolve, educators will have the responsibility to remain updated and to lead the educational transformation with a critical, ethical, and human-centred vision. Only in this way can technology become a true ally of learning rather than an obstacle to quality education.

In a society increasingly permeated by the presence of artificial intelligence across various spheres of everyday life, it becomes imperative to reconsider the concept of convivencia – harmonious coexistence – as a core component in the holistic formation of individuals. This emerging technological agent has radically altered forms of human interaction, enabling more fluid global communication while simultaneously raising complex issues such as the proliferation of misinformation, the intensification of ideological polarisation, and the reproduction of discrimination through opaque algorithms. In response, education emerges as a privileged space to promote the ethical and critical use of these emerging technologies. In particular, AI-driven educational personalisation systems – if not designed with equity criteria – risk exacerbating existing socio-economic inequalities. Therefore, it is essential to promote respect for diversity, foster conscious management of digital identity, and cultivate an understanding of the impacts of algorithmic biases in order to build a digital citizenship committed to social cohesion and sustainable human development.

Aligned with this perspective, the learning of 'being' – as a fundamental dimension of comprehensive education – requires deep reflection on the effects that artificial intelligence may have on the construction of personal identity and individual development processes. Excessive reliance on AI-based tools can lead to uncritical delegation in decision-making, thereby undermining students' autonomy, creativity, and reflective capacity. Consequently, education must not merely integrate AI as an instrumental resource; it must also take on the challenge of reinforcing ethics, self-regulation, and personal agency in the use of technology. While adaptive learning represents an opportunity to tailor educational pathways, it is essential that students retain an active and conscious role in constructing their own knowledge, thereby avoiding a passive submission to automated decisions that could blur the emancipatory purpose of education.

The integration of computational processes with autonomous learning capabilities into the educational field represents a structural transformation that challenges both the aims of education and the means through which it is delivered. Far from being a mere technological tool, this new digital architecture of knowledge introduces ethical, epistemological, and pedagogical challenges that must be addressed from a reflective approach centred on human dignity. In this context, it is essential that education not be limited to incorporating technological innovations, but rather articulate a reflective framework that ensures the centrality of the learner, equity in access, the protection of fundamental rights, and the construction of an autonomous digital citizenship. Likewise, teacher training becomes a strategic pillar to ensure an ethical and transformative implementation of AI. The competency framework in artificial intelligence, developed by international organisations such as UNESCO, constitutes a relevant starting point, but it remains insufficient unless accompanied by inclusive public policies, coherent regulatory frameworks, and sustained institutional commitment. AI, understood as a tool in the service of the common good, demands ethical governance that prevents the uncritical automation of educational processes and strengthens the relational, critical, and emancipatory dimensions of education.

The promise of intelligent technologies as tools for personalisation, efficiency, and knowledge access can only be fully realised if they are framed within a horizon of educational justice and social sustainability. This not only entails defining universal ethical principles, but also guaranteeing material conditions that prevent digital divides from becoming new forms of exclusion. Ultimately, the challenge is not merely technological but profoundly pedagogical: to redefine the meaning of education in the age of artificial intelligence without relinquishing its humanistic foundations.

In conclusion, the challenge does not solely lie in incorporating AI into educational systems, but rather in transforming those systems from a perspective grounded in epistemic justice, social responsibility, and human dignity. In a context marked by technological acceleration and cultural volatility, the ethics of algorithmic systems must not be reduced to a mere regulatory addendum; instead, it must become the very foundation of all educational and political action. Only then will intelligent platforms avoid becoming instruments of dehumanisation and instead serve as tools that advance a more free, just, and consciously responsible humanity

Integration of AI in Higher Education: Cultivating Entrepreneurial Potential as a Path to Educational Personalisation

The emergence of artificial intelligence (AI) is driving a profound transformation in higher education, generating unprecedented opportunities for both educators and students (Chiu, 2023; Galdames, 2025). However, its integration also raises a series of critical questions, particularly regarding its incorporation into university learning processes. In this regard, recent studies have examined AI's role in higher education from diverse perspectives (Vera, 2023; Mahmudi et al., 2023; Michel-Villarreal et al., 2023; Jaboob et al., 2025; Jain & Raghuram, 2025). The existing body of research suggests that AI is becoming a versatile tool, capable of facilitating innovative methodologies that enhance both teaching and learning (Popenici & Kerr, 2017).

Despite prevailing uncertainties regarding the application of AI in educational contexts (Al-Marzouqi et al., 2024), there is consensus that it presents substantial pedagogical potential for personalised learning. AI is reshaping higher education by enabling more efficient and adaptive learning personalisation. Consequently, AI has become a fundamental component in the development of personal learning environments (PLEs), which are conceptualised as the integration of tools, processes, information sources, activities, connections, and strategies that individuals employ in their learning, both independently and collaboratively (Castañeda & Adell, 2015). In this context, AI constitutes a significant advancement in optimising tools and strategies for the configuration of PLEs, including chatbots and intelligent tutoring systems.

Entrepreneurship has been established as a fundamental competency for addressing the challenges of the twenty-first century, characterised by globalisation, digital transformation, and economic uncertainty. Entrepreneurial education extends beyond business creation, fostering key transversal skills such as creativity, problem-solving, and decision-making in dynamic and complex environments (Gibb, 2002). These competencies are critical in continuously evolving contexts, where adaptability and innovation are essential drivers of social, cultural, economic, and personal development (Neck & Corbett, 2018).

Empirical research has demonstrated that entrepreneurship education in higher education fosters the development of a proactive, autonomous, and responsible mindset (Kuratko, 2005; Carpenter & Wilson, 2022). Furthermore, educational policies have increasingly acknowledged its relevance, integrating entrepreneurship into higher education curricula as a strategic approach to enhancing critical thinking and independent decision-making (Fayolle & Gailly, 2015; Carpenter et al., 2022). In this context, entrepreneurship is not merely a mechanism for job creation but also a catalyst for social and economic transformation, equipping individuals with the competencies required to navigate and contribute to an ever-changing global landscape.

In this study, we conceptualise entrepreneurial education in relation to *entrepreneurial potential*, defined as the set of capabilities and predispositions that enable individuals to design, create, plan, and manage personal projects that foster their development and generate added value in various domains of life. This perspective extends beyond the concept of *entrepreneurship education*, which is traditionally associated with training for business and venture creation (Erkkilä, 2000; Rodrigues, 2023), and is more closely aligned with *enterprise education*. The latter encompasses a broader scope, as it focuses on the development of transferable skills applicable to lifelong learning and adaptive decision-making in diverse contexts (Pepin, 2012; Yasin & Khansari, 2021).

Although entrepreneurial education has yet to be fully established beyond economic and productive fields, its integration into higher education has prompted a paradigmatic shift in the understanding and advancement of entrepreneurship-related learning. This evolving framework extends beyond professional development, fostering skills that are essential not only for the employability of university students but also for their personal and social growth in an increasingly complex and dynamic environment.

The cultivation of entrepreneurial potential through AI is emerging as a transformative educational paradigm that enables the design of personalised learning trajectories aligned with students' abilities, interests, and aspirations. In this context, there is broad scientific consensus that entrepreneurial potential is structured around five core dimensions, which not only define entrepreneurial capacity but can also be reinforced through AI-driven interventions. These dimensions include creativity, motivation, leadership, personal agency, and problem-solving (Newman et al., 2019).

The integration of AI as a pedagogical tool for developing entrepreneurial potential expands the opportunities for strengthening these dimensions of entrepreneurial identity, promoting a more adaptive, data-informed, and learner-centred approach to entrepreneurship education.

This section explores how the integration of AI into educational processes contributes to the development of entrepreneurial potential. AI serves as a catalyst for creativity by providing access to novel sources of inspiration and facilitating the generation of innovative solutions (Moura, 2024). A key contribution of AI to creative processes is its ability to generate new ideas through three fundamental mechanisms: recombining known concepts in novel ways, exploring possibilities across diverse conceptual spaces, and implementing transformations that lead to the emergence of original ideas (Boden, 1998).

AI has attracted considerable interest as a tool for enhancing creative processes, particularly during the ideation phase. Recent studies indicate that AI plays a significant role in creative design, improving the quality of outcomes while reducing cognitive load (Chandrasekera et al., 2024).

The integration of AI into higher education has attracted growing scholarly attention, particularly regarding its effects on student motivation. A recent study by Hmoud et al. (2024) analysed the impact of ChatGPT on students' motivation in academic tasks. Through a qualitative investigation, five primary motivational categories were identified: task enjoyment, perceived effort, outcome evaluation, perceived relevance, and interaction with AI. The findings indicate that ChatGPT fosters a more engaging learning experience, enhancing motivation through its interactive nature and its capacity to facilitate meaningful academic interactions. The study concludes that generative AI can serve as an effective pedagogical tool, not only by fostering student motivation but also by improving academic performance.

Another study investigated the determinants of higher education students' motivation for the sustained use of ChatGPT in language learning through a quantitative approach. The results suggest that initial exposure to ChatGPT influenced students' perceptions of autonomy, competence, social relatedness, and perceived challenges in its use. Moreover, autonomy and social relatedness were found to be key predictors of students' competence in utilising ChatGPT for learning, as well as critical factors in their motivation for continued engagement. Among these, autonomy emerged as the most influential factor, demonstrating the strongest impact on student motivation (Annamalai et al., 2025).

Similarly, a mixed-methods study examining motivation and cognitive development highlights that intelligent tutoring systems and learning analytics contribute to improving student interaction and reinforcing motivation (Elbadiansyah et al., 2024). Furthermore, it is essential to emphasise that machine learning algorithms enable AI-driven educational platforms to personalise content based on individual learning needs, offering adaptive pathways aligned with students' progress and proficiency levels. This adaptive approach enhances motivation by allowing learners to advance at their own pace while encountering challenges calibrated to their abilities.

The intersection of AI and leadership constitutes an emerging field of study that remains underexplored within the context of higher education. Nevertheless, recent research has begun to examine this relationship, emphasising its implications for leadership development and management. Sposato (2024), for instance, investigates the role of AI in leadership processes and organisational practices through a qualitative study based on a comprehensive literature review and conceptual analysis. The findings underscore the necessity of integrating technical proficiency with emotional intelligence to effectively navigate AI-driven transformations. This shift necessitates a paradigm change in leadership models, fostering the design of personalised leadership training programmes grounded in proactivity, talent management, and ethical considerations.

A particularly relevant area of inquiry concerns the application of AI in leadership decision-making. AI's capacity to aggregate, process, and analyse vast datasets in real time enables leaders to make evidence-based decisions. In the domain of educational leadership, Wang (2021) argues that effective decision-making hinges on a balance between AI-assisted data analysis and human judgement informed by ethical values. While AI enhances efficiency and accuracy in information processing, its implementation in educational settings must be complemented by leaders' intuition, experience, and ethical principles. In this regard, AI should not be perceived as a substitute for human leadership but rather as a strategic resource that augments the cognitive capacities of educational leaders, enabling them to make more informed and adaptive decisions in complex and evolving environments. The insights derived from this research can be extrapolated to other leadership contexts.

As in the field of leadership, the dimension of self-regulation has not been widely explored in relation to the use of AI in higher education. In this regard, empirical studies linking these two constructs remain limited. An exception is the research conducted by Rodríguez-Ruiz et al. (2025), which examined the relationship between self-control, self-esteem, and self-efficacy in the use of AI tools among university students. Through a cross-sectional study involving students enrolled in education- and psychology-related programmes, the findings revealed that lower levels of self-control were associated with a higher frequency of AI use.

Additionally, both self-control and self-efficacy were positively correlated with the utilisation of AI tools for clarifying doubts, engaging in social interactions, and assisting with academic tasks. Conversely, higher levels of self-esteem were found to reduce the likelihood of students relying on AI due to a decreased need for mediated social interaction. These findings underscore the complex interplay between psychological factors and AI adoption in educational settings, suggesting that self-regulation competencies may influence students' engagement with AI-driven learning technologies.

Within the domain of problem-solving, it is essential to recognise that problems are addressed through an interrelated combination of cognitive, metacognitive, affective, and social processes. While extensive research supports the role of AI in cognitive problem-solving, there remains limited empirical evidence on its influence on the social and affective dimensions of this process. An exploratory literature review conducted by Joksimovic et al. (2023) highlights this gap, emphasising the need for further investigation.

Regarding university students, a study by Urban et al. (2024) compared the use of ChatGPT between a control group and an experimental group. The findings indicated that this tool significantly enhanced self-efficacy in problem-solving tasks and improved the quality, depth, and originality of generated solutions. Furthermore, participants who utilised ChatGPT perceived the task as less cognitively demanding and easier to complete. However, its use did not increase task engagement or intrinsic motivation.

The integration of AI into higher education constitutes an emerging field of study that presents both opportunities and challenges in the personalised development of students' entrepreneurial potential. While AI enables the adaptation of learning processes to individual needs, numerous research gaps and unexplored dimensions persist.

One of the primary challenges in this area is the uneven scholarly attention given to the different components of entrepreneurial potential. While dimensions such as creativity and motivation have been extensively examined, others, such as leadership and self-regulation, remain underexplored. This imbalance underscores the need for more comprehensive research that encompasses all the critical factors involved in entrepreneurial competency development.

It is crucial to avoid a technophilic perspective on AI in education – that is, assuming that its implementation will inherently lead to positive outcomes without critically assessing its limitations. Although AI facilitates personalised learning and enhances access to relevant information, it is imperative to evaluate the actual efficacy of its applications and the potential risks of fostering technological dependencies that may hinder students' autonomous development.

Thus, a critical approach is essential when leveraging AI to enhance entrepreneurship education. While AI has the potential to be a powerful tool for fostering entrepreneurial competencies, its impact largely depends on the pedagogical strategies through which it is implemented. Existing studies on its effectiveness remain preliminary, and their findings are not yet conclusive, highlighting the necessity for further rigorous and systematic research.

Furthermore, although AI offers significant opportunities for learning personalisation and the cultivation of entrepreneurial skills, there is still a considerable need to explore how to implement it efficiently. AI integration in educational contexts should extend beyond its technical functionality to consider its pedagogical and cognitive implications, ensuring that personalised learning strategies effectively contribute to students' meaningful development.

Finally, the ethical implications of AI in higher education are a crucial consideration. The deployment of algorithms for personalised learning raises significant concerns regarding privacy, equity, and transparency in educational processes. Therefore, it is imperative to establish regulatory frameworks and ethical guidelines that promote the responsible use of AI, mitigate algorithmic biases, and ensure that its application genuinely supports the comprehensive development of university students.

Bibliography

Alonso-Rodríguez, A. M. (2024). Hacia un marco ético de la inteligencia artificial en la educación [Towards an Ethical Framework of Artificial Intelligence in Education]. *Teoría de la Educación. Revista Interuniversitaria, 36*(2), 79–98. https://doi.org/10.14201/teri.31821

Al-Marzouqi, A., Salloum, S. A., Al-Saidat, M., Aburayya, A., & Gupta, B. (Eds.). (2024). *Artificial intelligence in education: the power and dangers of ChatGPT in the classroom* (Vol. 144). Springer Nature.

Amabile, T. M., & Pratt, M. G. (2016). The dynamic componential model of creativity and innovation in organizations: Making progress, making meaning. *Research in organizational behavior, 36*, 157–183. https://doi.org/10.1016/j.riob.2016.10.001

Annamalai, N., Bervell, B., Mireku, D. O., & Andoh, R. P. K. (2025). Artificial intelligence in higher education: Modelling students' motivation for continuous use of ChatGPT based on a modified self-determination theory. *Computers and Education: Artificial Intelligence, 8*, 100346. https://doi.org/10.1016/j.caeai.2024.100346

Arana, J. (Dir.). (2024). *El futuro de la identidad humana a debate. Protagonistas de la polémica sobre el transhumanismo*. Tecnos.

Bauman, Z. (2017). *Retrotopia*. Polity Press Ltd.

Bernal, A. (2021). Shaping identities in a hyperconnected world: Notes for the refutation of 'pedagogical levity'. In J. M. Muñoz-Rodríguez (Ed.), *Identity in a hyperconnected society* (pp. 3–13). Springer.

Bernal, A., Santos, M. A., & Azqueta, A. (2025). Liderazgo transformador de la educación para un mundo nuevo. In C. Naval & A. Bernal (Eds.), *La educación transformadora, luces y sombras*. EUNSA.
Boden, M. A. (1998). Creativity and artificial intelligence. *Artificial Intelligence, 103*(1–2), 347–356. https://doi.org/10.1016/S0004-3702(98)00055-1
Carpenter, A., & Wilson, R. (2022). A systematic review looking at the effect of entrepreneurship education on higher education student. *The International Journal of Management Education*, *20*(2), 100541. https://doi.org/10.1016/j.ijme.2021.100541
Castañeda, L., & Adell, J. (2015). *Entornos de aprendizaje: Claves para el ecosistema educativo en red* [Learning environments: Keys to the networked educational ecosystem]. Ed. Marfil.
Chandrasekera, T., Hosseini, Z., & Perera, U. (2024). Can artificial intelligence support creativity in early design processes? *International Journal of Architectural Computing, 0*(0), 1–15. https://doi.org/10.1177/14780771241254637
Chiu, T. K. F. (2023). The impact of Generative AI (GenAI) on practices, policies and research direction in education: a case of ChatGPT and Midjourney. *Interactive Learning Environments*, *32*(10), 6187–6203. https://doi.org/10.1080/10494820.2023.2253861
Colombelli, A., Loccisano, S., Panelli, A., Pennisi, O. A. M., & Serraino, F. (2022). Entrepreneurship Education: The Effects of Challenge-Based Learning on the Entrepreneurial Mindset of University Students. *Administrative Sciences*, *12*(1), 10. https://doi.org/10.3390/admsci12010010
Comisión Europea. (2021). Ethics guidelines for trustworthy AI. Publications Office of the European Union. https://digital-strategy.ec.europa.eu/en/library/ethics-guidelines-trustworthy-ai
Delors, J. (1996). La educación encierra un tesoro: Informe a la UNESCO de la Comisión Internacional sobre la Educación para el Siglo XXI. Ediciones UNESCO.
Department of Industry, Science and Resources. (2021). Australia's AI ethics principles. Australian Government. https://www.industry.gov.au/publications/australias-artificial-intelligence-ethics-principles/australias-ai-ethics-principles
Eilenberger, W. (2025). *Espíritus del presente. Los últimos años de la filosofía y el comienzo de una nueva ilustración 1948–1984*. Taurus.
Elbadiansyah, S., Sain, Z. H., Shehu Lawal, U., Chansa Thelma, C., & Luqman Aziz, A. (2024). Exploring the role of artificial intelligence in

enhancing student motivation and cognitive development in higher education. *TechComp Innovations: Journal of Computer Science and Technology, 1*(2), 59–67. https://doi.org/10.70063/techcompinnovations.v1i2.47

Erkkilä, K. (2000). *Entrepreneurial education: Mapping the debates in the United States, the United Kingdom, and Finland.* Garland Publishing.

Fayolle, A., & Gailly, B. (2015). The impact of entrepreneurship education on entrepreneurial attitudes and intention: Hysteresis and persistence. *Journal of Small Business Management, 53*(1), 75–93. https://doi.org/10.1111/jsbm.12065

Galdames, I. S. (2025). *Impact of artificial intelligence on higher education: A literature review.* In A. Abreu, J. V. Carvalho, A. Mesquita, A. Sousa Pinto, & M. Mendonça Teixeira (Eds.), *Perspectives and trends in education and technology. ICITED 2024* (Lecture Notes in Networks and Systems, Vol. 859). Springer, Cham. https://doi.org/10.1007/978-3-031-78155-1_35

Gibb, A. A. (2002). In pursuit of a new 'enterprise' and 'entrepreneurship' paradigm for learning: Creative destruction, new values, new ways of doing things and new combinations of knowledge. *International Journal of Management Reviews, 4*(3), 233–269. https://doi.org/10.1111/1468-2370.00086

Hari, J. (2022). *El valor de la atención*. Península.

Hmoud, M., Swaity, H., Hamad, N., Karram, O., & Daher, W. (2024). Higher education students' task motivation in the generative artificial intelligence context: The case of ChatGPT. *Information*, *15*(1), 33. https://doi.org/10.3390/info15010033

Jaboob, M., Hazaimeh, M., & Al-Ansi, A. M. (2025). Integration of generative AI techniques and applications in student behavior and cognitive achievement in Arab higher education. *International Journal of Human–Computer interaction*, *41*(1), 353–366. https://doi.org/10.1080/10447318.2023.2300016

Jain, K. K., & Raghuram, J. N. V. (2024). Gen-AI integration in higher education: Predicting intentions using SEM-ANN approach. *Education and Information Technologies*, *29*(13), 17169–17209. https://doi.org/10.1007/s10639-024-12506-4

Joksimovic, S., Ifenthaler, D., Marrone, R., De Laat, M., & Siemens, G. (2023). *Opportunities of artificial intelligence to support complex problem-solving: Findings from a scoping review. Computers and Education: Artificial Intelligence, 4*, 100138. https://doi.org/10.1016/j.caeai.2023.100138

Kuratko, D. F. (2005). The emergence of entrepreneurship education: Development, trends, and challenges. *Entrepreneurship Theory and Practice, 29*(5), 577–598. https://doi.org/10.1111/j.1540-6520.2005.00099.x

Kurzweil, R. (2012). *La singularidad está cerca*. Lolabooks.

L'Ecuyer, C. (2021). *Conversaciones con mi maestra*. Espasa.

López García, G. (Ed.). (2023). *Ecología de la desinformación y su impacto en el espacio público*. Peter Lang.

Mahmudi, A. A., Fionasari, R., Mardikawati, B., & Judijanto, L. (2023). Integration of artificial intelligence technology in distance learning in higher education. *Journal of Social Science Utilizing Technology, 1*(4), 190–201. https://doi.org/10.70177/jssut.v1i4.661

Miao, F., & Cukurova, M. (2024). AI competency framework for teachers. UNESCO. https://doi.org/10.54675/ZJTE2084

Miao, F., Holmes, W., Huang, R., & Zhang, H. (2021). Inteligencia artificial y educación: Guía para las personas a cargo de formular políticas. Organización de las Naciones Unidas para la Educación, la Ciencia y la Cultura (UNESCO). https://unesdoc.unesco.org/ark:/48223/pf0000373764

Michel-Villarreal, R., Vilalta-Perdomo, E., Salinas-Navarro, D. E., Thierry-Aguilera, R., & Gerardou, F. S. (2023). Challenges and opportunities of generative AI for higher education as explained by ChatGPT. *Education Sciences, 13*(9), 856. https://doi.org/10.3390/educsci13090856

Molina, C. A. (2023). *¿Qué hacemos con los humanos?*. Deusto.

Moura, F. T. (Ed.). (2024). *Artificial intelligence, co-creation and creativity: The new frontier for innovation* (1st ed.). Routledge.

Muñoz, J. M., Lorenzo, N., Suñé, X., & Prats, M. À. (Coords.). (2025). Inteligencias conectadas: Cómo la IA está redefiniendo el aprendizaje personalizado. Observatorio de Innovación Educativa y Cultura Digital (ODITE), Asociación Espiral, Educación y Tecnología. https://ciberespiral.org/es/odite/

Neck, H. M., & Corbett, A. C. (2018). The scholarship of teaching and learning entrepreneurship. *Entrepreneurship Education and Pedagogy, 1*(1), 8–41. https://doi.org/10.1177/2515127417737286

Newman, A., Obschonka, M., Schwarz, S., Cohen, M., & Nielsen, I. (2019). Entrepreneurial self-efficacy: A systematic review of the literature on its theoretical foundations, measurement, antecedents, and outcomes, and an agenda for future research. *Journal of Vocational Behavior, 110*, 403–419. https://doi.org/10.1016/j.jvb.2018.05.012

Nowotny, H. (2022). *La fe en la inteligencia artificial. Los algoritmos predictivos y el futuro de la humanidad*. Galaxia Gutenberg.

Nussbaum, M. C. (1997). *Cultivating humanity: A classical defense of reform in liberal education*. Harvard University Press.

OdiseIA & PwC. (2022). GuIA de buenas prácticas en el uso de la inteligencia artificial ética. Observatorio del Impacto Social y Ético de la Inteligencia Artificial.

Parlamento Europeo. (2023). Artificial Intelligence Act: Proposal for a regulation laying down harmonized rules on artificial intelligence. European Union. https://eur-lex.europa.eu/legal content/EN/TXT/?uri=CELEX%3A52021PC0206

Pasquale, F. (2020). *New laws of robotics*. Belknap Press.

Patino, B. (2020). *La civilización de la memoria de pez. Pequeño tratado sobre el mercado de la atención*. Alianza Editorial.

Pepin, M. (2012). Enterprise education: a Deweyan perspective. *Education+ Training*, *54*(8/9), 801–812. https://doi.org/10.1108/00400911211274891

Popenici, S. A., & Kerr, S. (2017). Exploring the impact of artificial intelligence on teaching and learning in higher education. *Research and practice in technology enhanced learning*, *12*(1), 22. https://doi.org/10.1186/s41039-017-0062-8

Reglamento (UE) 2024/1689 del Parlamento Europeo y del Consejo de 13 de marzo de 2024 relativo a normas armonizadas en materia de inteligencia artificial (Ley de inteligencia artificial) y por el que se modifican determinados actos legislativos de la Unión. Diario Oficial de la Unión Europea, L, 2024/1689. https://eur-lex.europa.eu/eli/reg/2024/1689/oj

Rodrigues, A. L. (2023). Entrepreneurship education pedagogical approaches in higher education. *Education Sciences*, *13*(9), 940. https://doi.org/10.3390/educsci13090940

Rodríguez-Ruiz, J., Marín-López, I., & Espejo-Siles, R. (2025). Is artificial intelligence use related to self-control, self-esteem and self-efficacy among university students? *Education and Information Technologies*, *30*, 2507–2524. https://doi.org/10.1007/s10639-024-12906-6

Runco, M. A., & Acar, S. (2021). Divergent thinking as an indicator of creative potential. *Creativity Research Journal*, *24*(1), 66–75. https://doi.org/10.1080/10400419.2012.652929

Sadin, É. (2023). *La vida espectral*. Caja Negra.

Sposato, M. (2024), 'Leadership training and development in the age of artificial intelligence', *Development and Learning in Organizations*, Vol. 38 No. 4, pp. 4–7. https://doi.org/10.1108/DLO-12-2023-0256

Thoreau, H. D. (1854). *Walden; or, life in the woods*. Ticknor and Fields.
Twenge, J. (2018). *iGen*. Atria.
UNESCO. (2019). Consenso de Beijing sobre la inteligencia artificial y la educación. Organización de las Naciones Unidas para la Educación, la Ciencia y la Cultura. https://unesdoc.unesco.org/ark:/48223/pf0000368303
UNESCO. (2021). Recomendación sobre la ética de la inteligencia artificial. https://unesdoc.unesco.org/ark:/48223/pf0000373434
UNESCO. (2021). Inteligencia artificial y educación: Guía para las personas a cargo de formular políticas. Organización de las Naciones Unidas para la Educación, la Ciencia y la Cultura. https://unesdoc.unesco.org/ark:/48223/pf0000377071
UNESCO. (2022). Recomendación sobre la ética de la inteligencia artificial (SHS/BIO/PI/2021/1). Organización de las Naciones Unidas para la Educación, la Ciencia y la Cultura. https://unesdoc.unesco.org/ark:/48223/pf0000381137
UNESCO. (2024). AI competency framework for students. United Nations Educational, Scientific and Cultural Organization. https://doi.org/10.54675/JKJB9835
UNESCO. (2024). Marco de competencias en inteligencia artificial para docentes. Organización de las Naciones Unidas para la Educación, la Ciencia y la Cultura. https://unesdoc.unesco.org/ark:/48223/pf0000388909
UNESCO. (2024). Guía para el uso de IA generativa en educación e investigación. Organización de las Naciones Unidas para la Educación, la Ciencia y la Cultura. https://www.unesco.org/es/open-access/cc-sa
Urban, M., Děchtěrenko, F., Lukavský, J., Hrabalová, V., Svacha, F., Brom, C., & Urban, K. (2024). *ChatGPT improves creative problem-solving performance in university students: An experimental study. Computers & Education, 215*, 105031. https://doi.org/10.1016/j.compedu.2024.105031
Vera, F. (2023). Integration of artificial intelligence technology in higher education: Exploring faculty members' experience. *Transformar, 4*(3), 17–22.
Villoro, J. (2024). *No soy un robot. La lectura y la sociedad digital*. Anagrama.
Vinuesa, R., Azizpour, H., Leite, I., Balaam, M., Dignum, V., Domisch, S., Felländer, A., Langhans, S. D., Tegmark, M., & Fuso Nerini, F. (2020). El papel de la inteligencia artificial en la consecución de los Objetivos de Desarrollo Sostenible. Nature Communications, 11, 233. https://doi.org/10.1038/s41467-019-14108-y

Wang, Y. (2021). Artificial intelligence in educational leadership: A symbiotic role of human-artificial intelligence decision-making. *Journal of Educational Administration*, *59*(3), 256–270. https://doi.org/10.1108/JEA-10-2020-0216

Yasin, N., & Khansari, Z. (2021). Evaluating the impact of social enterprise education on students' enterprising characteristics in the United Arab Emirates. *Education+ Training*, *63*(6), 872–905. https://doi.org/10.1108/ET-04-2020-0076

The Use of Artificial Intelligence in Higher Education Institutions in Portugal – Ethical Challenges and Opportunities

Ana Pedro[1] *and Lucília Nunes*[2]

ABSTRACT

In a world that is constantly changing, characterised by scientific and technological advances that promise to profoundly transform the way we think, act and decide, higher education is facing significant new challenges that are forcing it to rethink its role in society.

This is the case with the growing use of AI in higher education which, in addition to the countless benefits and opportunities it brings, poses a series of ethical challenges (privacy, algorithmic bias, teacher preparation, digital inclusion, transparency and democracy) that require a greater capacity for reflection, training, adaptation and innovation.

Are Portuguese higher education institutions prepared to adequately face this new irreversible scenario that AI represents in their academic life? What strategies are they using to respond to these new challenges? Are we witnessing a new paradigm in education that demands profound changes in the (traditional) role of the teacher and (finally) allows for a more personalised approach to teaching and learning?

In this chapter we will explore both the ethical challenges and opportunities of using AI in Portuguese higher education institutions, discuss their strategies for including AI in curricula; analyse its impact on the teaching-learning process and whether it contributes to the improvement and benefit of students, as well as the role of critical thinking in the use of new AI-based academic tools. We will also analyse the relationship with academic and scientific integrity and authorship. We'll consider the publication of the EU Regulation on Artificial Intelligence (Regulation (EU) 2024/1689 of the European Parliament and of the Council of 13 June 2024), which creates harmonised rules on artificial intelligence, and we'll see how each institution has developed strategies to meet the challenge of AI.

We will conclude that the use of AI in the Portuguese higher education context has numerous advantages in terms of the personalisation of learning, the new role of the teacher and the development of critical thinking as a higher-order skill that allows for the appropriate and ethical use of AI. It is therefore essential to debate and analyse the impact and consequences of the use of AI in higher education institutions, as well as what strategies they have adopted for its ethical and responsible use to guarantee the common good of humanity.

Keywords: artificial intelligence, Portuguese higher education, ethics

1 Work carried out at CLLC — Center for Languages, Literatures, and Cultures, funded by FCT (Ref. UID/04188/2025). Funding DOI: https://doi.org/10.54499/UID/04188/2025 within the scope of the UID/004188/Center for Languages, Literatures and Cultures Project. (UID/04188/2025). DOI do financiamento: https://doi.org/10.54499UID/04188/2025.

2 Instituto Politécnico de Setúbal. Portugal

The Use of AI[3] in Higher Education: Between Challenges and Opportunities

It is an incontrovertible fact that artificial intelligence (AI) is redefining human reality. Debating the role of technology in contemporary society and reflecting on how technological changes impact human experience is therefore an absolutely essential task (Floridi, 2014). In the context of higher education, the transformative impact of AI on research can represent a significant ethical challenge to academic integrity, as it emerges as an instrument that redefines the traditional paradigms of scientific research, with profound implications in terms of its epistemological and ethical foundations, leading to new hermeneutics or substantial resignifications in terms of how knowledge is produced.

This radical rethinking of traditional paradigms changes not only the way we think about research, but also what we consider to be knowledge. However, these changes in thinking are necessarily accompanied by a set of ethical complexities, insofar as AI (e.g. GPT Chat) is an ambivalent tool that carries inherent dilemmas in relation to its potential. It is in this sense that we can say that the use of GPT Chat in scientific research is not without its ethical challenges, as it brings with it a detail of the utmost importance: can be used either honestly or fraudulently. Technologies are therefore subject to misuse by their users. Hence the relevance of considering a human-centred approach to AI, the establishment of ethical formats for such tools, the promotion of ethical and responsible use of AI, academic and scientific

---

3 In this work, we have adopted the definition of AI created by the European Commission, according to which: '*Artificial intelligence (AI) systems are software (and possibly also hardware) systems designed by humans that, given a complex goal, act in the physical or digital dimension by perceiving their environment through data acquisition, interpreting the collected structured or unstructured data, reasoning on the knowledge, or processing the information, derived from this data and deciding the best action(s) to take to achieve the given goal. AI systems can either use symbolic rules or learn a numeric model, and they can also adapt their behaviour by analysing how the environment is affected by their previous actions. As a scientific discipline, AI includes several approaches and techniques, such as machine learning (of which deep learning and reinforcement learning are specific examples), machine reasoning (which includes planning, scheduling, knowledge representation and reasoning, search, and optimization), and robotics (which includes control, perception, sensors and actuators, as well as the integration of all other techniques into cyber-physical systems)*' (High-Level Expert Group on Artificial Intelligence, 2019, p. 6).

integrity, the importance of informing and raising awareness of the ethical implications and the preservation and defence of human rights associated with the use of these tools.

It is an incontrovertible fact that artificial intelligence (AI) is redefining human reality. Debating the role of technology in contemporary society and reflecting on how technological changes impact human experience is therefore an absolutely essential task (Floridi, 2014). In the context of higher education, the transformative impact of AI on research can represent a significant ethical challenge to academic integrity, as it emerges as an instrument that redefines the traditional paradigms of scientific research, with profound implications in terms of its epistemological and ethical foundations, leading to new hermeneutics or substantial resignifications in terms of how knowledge is produced.

This radical rethinking of traditional paradigms changes not only the way we think about research, but also what we consider to be knowledge. However, these changes in thinking are necessarily accompanied by a set of ethical complexities, insofar as AI (e.g. GPT Chat) is an ambivalent tool that carries inherent dilemmas in relation to its potential. It is in this sense that we can say that the use of GPT Chat in scientific research is not without its ethical challenges, as it brings with it a detail of the utmost importance: can be used either honestly or fraudulently. Technologies are therefore subject to misuse by their users. Hence the relevance of considering a human-centred approach to AI, the establishment of ethical formats for such tools, the promotion of ethical and responsible use of AI, academic and scientific integrity, the importance of informing and raising awareness of the ethical implications and the preservation and defence of human rights associated with the use of these tools.

AI – a Question of Purpose, Not Intentionality

It is a fact that databases can be subject to bias by the humans who set them up through the creation of deepfakes and fake news, the dissemination of racial prejudice and hate speech, as well as the use of data and images without consent. In this sense, the answers it generates are not necessarily correct: therefore, they cannot automatically be considered true without first carrying out a careful act of verification. It is only the human who can attribute the character of truth to the answers provided. But what often confuses and confounds the human mind is its tendency to anthropomorphise, in this case, AI, thinking that it has a moral conscience and, as such, that AI systems feel, think, lie or are racist. We forget, however, that although AI has no intention of lying, it can nevertheless be easily used or manipulated to do so. However, if it had intentionality – something that AI is far from having – we know that lies only exist when there is intentionality to lie with the clear intention of deceiving, in other words, to make people believe something that is false.

It is therefore important to remember that, although AI responds and acts apparently as if it were conscious from a human perspective, it cannot distinguish between right and wrong, true and false, nor is it governed by ethical principles. In other words: '… there are important differences between reproducing human-like behaviours, intelligent by definition but perhaps not entirely rational, and achieving rational behaviour based on principles' (Cozman & Neri, 2021, p. 22). AI doesn't even deal with the concept of truth or the concept of right and wrong: it has no intentionality whatsoever, only purpose. Its purpose – not its intentionality[4] – is to create and return to us a standard response to the requests we make of it. Nothing more. It is devoid of life-based wisdom, incapable of identifying the subtleties of implicit knowledge, of recognising irony and appropriating its meaning, of critical or creative thinking. It only acts for the purpose of collecting information from the databases it processes via the Internet, which consequently leads it to reproduce any cognitive bias found in that information, reinforcing cultural, gender or ethnic stereotypes and prejudices, as we have already mentioned.

Like Foucault's pendulum[5], the use of AI in an academic context brings with it both benefits, potential and new challenges, as well as disadvantages, risks and limitations, because, on the one hand, it can support students in their research by offering information on specific topics, suggesting bibliographic reference sources, providing summaries of academic articles, translating texts in real time from one language to another, helping to generate ideas for researchers' work, reviewing and editing their texts or helping to check the quality and accuracy of their information, improve academic

---

4 Searle, J. (1999). *Intencionalidade. Um ensaio da filosofia da mente*. Relógio D'Água.
5 Eco, U. (2016). *O Pêndulo de Foucault*. Gradiva.

writing in terms of grammatical correctness, word suggestion and content analysis (coherence and cohesion of the text, identifying redundancies and inconsistencies and assessing the quality of the argument), allowing more structured and coherent texts to be developed, on the other hand, on the other side of the coin, the truth is that it enables new forms of plagiarism and academic fraud to emerge, particularly when Chat GPT is used uncritically to write academic papers (Cotton et al., 2023; Ellis & Slade, 2023) and there is an excessive dependence on it to carry out research work, which may constitute a misuse of AI (Bostrom; Yudkowsky & Pablo 2012). In addition, it provides incomplete or even false content that can possibly confuse students in their academic tasks, it lacks cultural sensitivity, it is unable to fully understand the context and the user's intention, it does not recognise less popular languages, it lacks the capacity for critical and creative analysis, which can limit the development of skills such as critical thinking, and it is unable to assess the quality of the argument and the originality of the text (Gallent-Torres, Zapata-González, & Ortego-Hernand, 2023;Vincent-Lancrin & van der Vlies, 2020). It follows that AI is first and foremost a tool to support the development of researchers' intellectual independence, and not a substitute for personal effort and critical thinking.

AI as a Tool to Support Research, Not a Substitute for Human Thinking

The assistance that AI can provide in the creation of content (written text) for research work is to support or aid the activity of constructing the text; not to replace critical thinking or the reflection or writing process. We must therefore not forget that the authorship of texts is always human (Perfeito et al., 2023), although we can recognise the contribution of AI in carrying out some of these tasks. Although AI is useful, it is no substitute for the experience or specialised knowledge of a teacher or researcher, so the solid knowledge they have is essential for judging the veracity of the information presented and for detecting false or incorrect information.

AI is nothing more than a tool to inspire creativity, a support to help generate ideas, but it will never replace the researcher's or even the writer's experience of thinking, nor the exercise of critical and ethical thinking (Perfeito et al., 2023; Reyes Palau, 2023). AI is not a substitute for humans. It is therefore extremely important that universities encourage the creation of training spaces with a strong ethical-scientific component that combines Aristotelian practical wisdom (phronesis) with academic integrity, which is the place par excellence for ethical-critical reflection on the use and results generated by AI.

When analysing the teaching and education component, the National Ethics Council for the Life Sciences considered that 'it is desirable that the teacher is increasingly a mediator rather than a holder of knowledge (…) the role of the teacher should be to promote critical and reflective thinking in relation to the quality of information'[6]. They also emphasised that the use of AI in an academic environment has the challenge of increasing complexity in the evaluation and detection of fraud. The development of algorithms and generative language chatbots could 'jeopardise the integrity and even the capacity of the education system. In fact, what may even be at stake is the organisation of the education system from the outset, adapting teaching models and forms of assessment. One way or another, it's crucial to develop fraud detection tools that are not only robust but also adaptable'.[7]

The Use of AI in Higher Education Institutions in Portugal: What Reality? International Framework

Because access to technologies is unlikely to be equitable, we are also facing the potential for increasing inequality in education. In other words, not all schools and not all students will have similar access to advanced AI tools. If equitable access is not guaranteed, it could increase the performance gap between students from different socio-cultural backgrounds. This is a realisation that leads to a damaging risk of exacerbating inequalities.

As with any tool that handles or manages large amounts of data, there are risks of data leaks or misuse, which is why it is essential to guarantee data security and privacy measures. The EU Regulation on Artificial Intelligence[8] has created

6 Conselho Nacional de Ética para as Ciências da Vida (2024). Livro Branco. Inteligência Artificial (IA): inquietações sociais, propostas éticas e orientações políticas. p. 52. Available in https://www.cnecv.pt/pt/publicacoes/monografias/livro-branco-inteligencia-artificial-ai-inquietacoes-sociais-pro

7 Idem, p. 53.

8 Regulation (EU) 2024/1689 of the Parliament and of the Council of 13 June 2024

harmonised rules on artificial intelligence. Also, if students become accustomed to using AI to generate content and do so uncritically, they may jeopardise their own critical thinking skills as well as their training to formulate opinions.

From another perspective, educators can help promote the ethical use of AI, 'by incorporating conversations about the fragilities of AI models and their ethical use into their lectures. This can help students comprehend the potential consequences of AI-generated plagiarism and the negative effects on their own learning resulting from their excessive employment. They can also encourage students to use AI tools responsibly and openly, such as employing them as aids in idea generation instead of replacements for creating original work'.[9]

Ethical issues have been raised in various international documents, which we consider relevant to point out:

1. 'Ethical Guidelines for Trustworthy AI'[10], by the High-Level Expert Group on Artificial Intelligence, published in 2019;
2. 'The ethics of artificial intelligence: Issues and initiatives'[11], European Parliament in 2020;
3. 'Recommendation on the Ethics of Artificial Intelligence'[12] from UNESCO, in 2023;
4. 'Ethics and governance of artificial intelligence for health: guidance on large multi-modal models' from WHO in 2024.
   Some aspects are still unclear, such as the impact of energy consumption on the use of AI, and how this can exacerbate global inequalities and environmental costs.[13] Of the most recent developments, we highlight two elements:

---

9 Hoernig, S.; Pereira, P.; Ilharco, A.; Pereira, R. (2024) *Report. Generative AI and Higher Education: Challenges and Opportunities.* Em https://www.ipp-jcs.org/wp-content/uploads/2024/09/Report-AI-in-Higher-Education-IPP-1.pdf

10 Comissão Europeia, Direção-Geral das Redes de Comunicação, Conteúdos e Tecnologias, *Orientações éticas para uma IA de confiança*, Serviço das Publicações, 2019, https://data.europa.eu/doi/10.2759/2686

11 European Parliament. (2020). The ethics of artificial intelligence: Issues and initiatives. Panel for the Future of Science and Technology. Available in https://www.europarl.europa.eu/RegData/etudes/STUD/2020/634452/EPRS_STU(2020)634452_EN.pdf

12 UNESCO (2023). Recommendation on the Ethics of Artificial Intelligence. Available in https://www.unesco.org/en/articles/recommendation-ethics-artificial-intelligence

13 'IA pode triplicar consumo de energia elétrica no mundo nos próximos anos, aponta estudo da Deloitte', 13 December 2024. ('AI could triple the world's electricity

5. In February 2025, the publication of the 'Guidelines on prohibited artificial intelligence (AI) practices, as defined by the AI Act'[14] provide an overview of AI practices considered unacceptable due to their potential risks to European values and fundamental rights. The AI Act aims to promote innovation and ensure high levels of safety and human rights protection by categorising AI systems into different risk categories, including prohibited, high-risk and those subject to transparency obligations;
6. The AI Summit, which took place in Paris on 10 and 11 February 2025, culminated in the signing of the 'Declaration on Inclusive and Sustainable Artificial Intelligence for People and the Planet', signed by sixty countries, including Portugal. This Declaration reinforces the need to make AI accessible and safe, promoting its development in an ethical and transparent manner.

AI and the Portuguese Higher Education Reality – What Has Been Done?

Evidently, the national academic community[15] has been studying the subject – this universe[16] has 41,361 teachers and 446,028 students, with around 79% of teachers and more than 80% of students in public higher education,

---

consumption in the coming years', according to a study by Deloitte)'The year 2024 was marked by the growth in the use of generative artificial intelligences. Texts, images, audio and videos have been generated to exhaustion from different applications and devices. But what most users don't know is that each message sent to chats requires a huge amount of processing capacity from data centres – physical servers with supercomputers – and generates a silent but dangerous long-term environmental cost'.

14 Commission publishes the Guidelines on prohibited artificial intelligence (AI) practices, as defined by the AI Act. | Shaping Europe's digital future. The guidelines specifically address practices such as harmful manipulation, social scoring and remote biometric identification in real time, among others.

15 In Portugal, the higher education network is made up of ninety-seven institutions, 'of which 34 are public, 61 private and 2 military and police public schools. There are 5,460 cycles of study on offer, and in the 2022/2023 academic year the HE system had 446,028 students'. Direção-Geral Do Ensino Superior (2024) O Ensino Superior Em Portugal 2021/2023. P. 15.

16 PORDATA. Teachers in public higher education 32749 and in private higher education 8612. DGES – Direção-Geral do Ensino Superior (2024) O Ensino Superior em Portugal 2021/2023. p. 15. 'In the 2022/2023 academic year, the 446,028 higher education

which includes[14] universities in the university subsystem and twenty institutions in the polytechnic subsystem. Therefore, we analyse the documents, official sites and documents of this thirty-four higher education institutions.

Since 2023, courses and conferences have been held on Artificial Intelligence in Higher Education, threats and opportunities for the teaching-learning process. In one format or another – workshops, conferences, seminars, lectures, short courses, etc. – they are explicitly concerned with ethically rethinking the future of education with AI.

Some publications report on the activities, proposals and challenges considered, such as 'Artificial Intelligence in Education – Threats and opportunities for the teaching-learning process', documenting an event that 'sought to open a space for discussion that would provide some reflection on this new reality and discuss the impact that these new artificial intelligence (AI) platforms will have on current educational models. It is also important to understand how education should position itself in the face of the proliferation of this type of AI tool and what the implications of this new reality are from a pedagogical point of view'.[17]

We note the proposal to create a curricular unit that cuts across[18] several courses, presented at the National Congress of Pedagogical Practices in 2023. Some institutions have already given their opinion from a pedagogical[19] point

students were distributed 80.6% in public higher education (35,997 students), with 50.1% in universities (2,235,64) and 30.5% in polytechnics (135,833)'.

17 Oliveira, L.; Pinto, M. (Org.) (2023). *A Inteligência Artificial na Educação – Ameaças e oportunidades para o processo ensino-aprendizagem*. Escola Superior de Media Artes e Design, Instituto Politécnico do Porto ISBN: 978-989-35125-1-7. Em https://edicoes.ipp.pt/index.php/books/catalog/view/99/213/602, p.3.

18 Rebelo (E.) (2023) Como lidar com o uso da inteligência artificial no Ensino Superior? Livro de Atas do CNaPPES 2023, https://hdl.handle.net/10216/158403 The author proposes the creation of a new transversal skills curricular unit, 'based on the knowledge and use of artificial intelligence (the proposal for which is presented here, but which has not yet been implemented), aimed at students from the various engineering degrees at the Faculty of Engineering of the University of Porto, although its frequency could be extended to students from other degrees and masters from different higher education institutions (and to Erasmus and international students)'. (p. 160)

19 This was the case with the Instituto Superior Técnico – it argued that AI should be used by teachers and students, as well as generative AI tools such as ChatGPT, considering that they have a pioneering role to play in 'exploring the application of AI tools, of which generative language models are examples, in a wide variety of areas, namely

of view and the ethics committees of the HEIs have also given their opinion[20] and others, such as the University of Aveiro[21], have created curricular units for the 3rd cycle of the University of Aveiro called Transversal and Transferable Skills, approved by the Scientific Council in September 2021 (see deliberation no. 69/CC/2021). There are several competence modules, among which we would like to highlight Ethics in Research.

In the forms used by ethics committees to review research projects, parts relating to the use of AI have already been identified, specifically with questions on self-assessment[22].

Despite political intentions and institutional specificities, there are clear concerns about scientific integrity, for example about authorship and referencing. It is important to remember that AI tools cannot generate content from scratch but are based on a training process that uses existing (and copyrighted) content. As these tools do not have legal personality, authorship must always be associated with a human creator who can be attributed and held

---

in training our students for emerging work methodologies in engineering, science and technology'. The document drawn up by the REFlet commission is available at https://conselhopedagogico.tecnico.ulisboa.pt/informacoes

20 This was the case with the Ethics Committee of the Polytechnic Institute of Setúbal, Opinion nº 103/04/2024, Questões Éticas na Utilização da Inteligência Artificial no Ensino Superior.

21 https://www.ua.pt/pt/edua/transversal-and-transferable-competences

22 See, for example, Request for an Opinion/Form from the IST Ethics Committee (CE-IST). Ethics Committee – Ata 1/2023 (09 de fevereiro de 2023) Minute 1/2023 (09 February 2023). Artificial intelligence [a.] Does your research involve the development, installation and/or use of artificial intelligence-based systems? [b.] Does the AI system/technique have the potential to stigmatise or discriminate against people (e.g. on the basis of sex, race, ethnic or social origin, age, genetic characteristics, disability, sexual orientation, language, religion or belief, membership of a political group, or membership of a national minority)? [c.] Does the AI system/technique interact with, replace, or influence human decision-making processes (e.g. likely to affect human life, health, well-being, or human rights, or economic, social, or political decisions)? [d.] Does the AI system/technique have the capacity to cause negative social (e.g. on democracy, media, labour market, freedoms, educational options, mass surveillance) and/or environmental impacts, either through its intended applications or plausible alternative uses? [e.] Does the AI to be developed/used in the project raise any other ethical issues not covered in the previous paragraphs (e.g. subliminal, covert, or deceptive AI, AI that is used to stimulate addictive behaviours, realistic humanoid robots, etc.)?

accountable. In other words, on the one hand, good referencing practices include transparency and specificity regarding the use of AI tools, and on the other hand, authors are fully responsible for the content of their writings.

Concerns are also commonly expressed about learning and the development of critical thinking, as people are not always able to validate content and may take AI misconceptions and hallucinations for granted. On the other hand, many institutions lack the infrastructure and resources to effectively implement AI technologies. In addition, if the risk of fraud and plagiarism increases, opportunities (and challenges) can also be identified to change assessment methodologies and rethink other ways of gauging student knowledge, without resorting exclusively to written production (as generative AI may be used without being referenced, in fraudulent behaviour that goes unnoticed).

Considering that one of the dimensions of action available to HEIs is to establish a code of ethics or ethical conduct, this component is also accompanied by the disciplinary matrix. A framework for sanctioning improper behaviour is a measure associated with responding adequately to fraud when it occurs. That's why we researched the existence and date of the instruments that can support behaviour – whether the Code of Ethics and/or Conduct or the Student Disciplinary Regulations.

The vast majority of HEIs have a code of ethics and/or ethical conduct or similar designation – more specifically, 92.8% of HEIs in the university subsystem and 95% of HEIs in the polytechnic subsystem.

All HEIs have a disciplinary statute or regulation – the majority (80%) of HEIs have a singular thematic regulation; 20% (7 HEIs) have the student disciplinary statute included in the institution's statutes (in a title, chapter, or annex). In some cases, the date of their publication or approval is well before the widespread appearance of AI tools, i.e. before 2022.

Of the documents from all the HEIs, 35% (12) are from the last 5 years (between 2019 and 2023); 62% (21) are from the last 10 years (2013–2023); 32% (11) are more than 10 years old. This is a potentially critical aspect that requires updating, making the statutes or disciplinary regulations more adjusted to the new realities.

Analysing by subsystem, at university level the range of disciplinary regulations varies between 2010 and 2024, and only at one HEI was it published in 2024.

Table 1: Identification of Codes of Ethics or Conduct and Disciplinary Regulations in university subsystem

HEI	Code of Ethics/Conduct	Disciplinary Regulation
ISCTE	Código de Conduta Académica, Regulamento n.º 25/2017 – Código de Conduta Ética na Investigação, Despacho nº 86/2016	Regulamento Disciplinar de Discentes, Deliberação n.º 2246/2010, 6 de dezembro
UA	Carta de conduta dos estudantes, Deliberação CPedagógico 2008	Regulamento Disciplinar dos Estudantes Despacho (extrato) n.º 14355/2013
UAb	Código ético, Despacho nº 80/2023	Alterações ao Regulamento Disciplinar dos Estudantes da Universidade Aberta. Despacho n.º 12678/2024, de 23 de outubro
UAç	Código de Ética da UAç, Despacho n.º 9795/2015	Despacho n.º 9143/2017 – Regulamento Disciplinar dos Estudantes
UAlg	Código de Ética da UAlg, Despacho n.º 2131/2020	Regulamento n.º 487/2015 – Regulamento Disciplinar dos Estudantes
UBI	Código de Integridade Académica da UBI, 2018	Regulamento n.º 766/2019 Regulamento Disciplinar dos Estudantes da UBI
UC	Código de Ética, Conduta e Integridade da UC, Regulamento n.º 498/2023	Regulamento n.º 400/2019, Regulamento Disciplinar dos Estudantes da UC
UÉ	Código de Ética da Universidade de Évora, Despacho n.º 89/2023	Despacho n.º 59/2019 Regulamento Disciplinar dos Estudantes da UÉ
UL	Código de Conduta da UL, Despacho n.º 4573/2020	Despacho n.º 6441/2015 Regulamento disciplinar dos estudantes da UL
UMa	Código de Conduta da UMa, Regulamento n.º 575/2010	Regulamento disciplinar dos alunos da UMa, 2010
UMinho	Código de Conduta Ética da UMinho, Deliberação CGeral 18/2020	Despacho RT-80/2019 Regulamento Disciplinar dos Estudantes da UMinho

HEI	Code of Ethics/Conduct	Disciplinary Regulation
UNL	Código de Ética da UNL, Despacho n.º 15464/2014	Regulamento n.º 679/2020, Regulamento Disciplinar dos Estudantes da UNL
UP	Código Ético de Conduta Académica, 2017 Declaração de Princípios sobre Integridade Académica, 2011	Despacho nº GR.03/07/2011 Regulamento Disciplinar dos Estudantes da UP
UTAD	----	Regulamento n.º 468/2011 Regulamento Disciplinar dos Estudantes da UTAD

In the polytechnic subsystem, the range of publication of disciplinary regulations varies between 2009 and 2024, with 5 HEIs between 2023 and 2024.

Table 2: Identification of Codes of Ethics or Conduct and Disciplinary Regulations in Polytechnic Subsy

IES	Código de Ética/Conduta	Regimento/Regulamento disciplinar
IPBeja	Código de Conduta Ética do IPBeja, 30 novembro 2023	Estatuto disciplinar do estudante do IPBeja – homologado presidente 2012
IPB	Código de Conduta do IPB, Despacho n.º 3009/2022	Regulamento n.º 113/2014 de 19 de março – Regulamento disciplinar dos estudantes do IPB
IPCA	Código de Conduta do IPCA, Despacho n.º 8643/2020	Regulamento n.º 677/2016 Regulamento Disciplinar dos Estudantes do IPCA
IPCB	Código de Conduta Ética, Despacho N.º 68/2022	Regulamento disciplinar dos estudantes do IPCB 26.02.2020
IPC	Código de Ética e Conduta do IPC, Versão 02, 10.10.2022	Despacho n.º 5655/2023 de 17 de maio Regulamento disciplinar dos estudantes do IPC
IPG	---	Título III dos Estatutos do IPG. Estatuto disciplinar dos estudantes. Despacho n.º 48/2008

(Continued)

Table 2: *(Continued)*

IES	Código de Ética/Conduta	Regimento/Regulamento disciplinar
IPL	Código de Conduta do IPL, Despacho n.º 12394/2023 de 4 dezembro	Estatutos do IPL – Despacho Normativo n.º 20/2009, de 21 de maio
IPLei	Código de Conduta do Instituto Politécnico de Leiria. Regulamento n.º 1331/2024 de 20 de novembro	Alterações aos Estatutos do Instituto Politécnico de Leiria – Estatuto disciplinar dos estudantes. Despacho Normativo n.º 6/2024
IPP	Código de Ética do IPP, Despacho n.º 8047/2021	Despacho Normativo n.º 35/2008 de 21 março Alterado Estatuto em 2024
IP Porto	Código de Boas Práticas e de Conduta, Despacho n.º 11171/2020	Despacho Normativo n.º 10/2024 de 10 de abril – Estatuto do IPP. Estatuto disciplinar dos estudantes no art.º 46º
IPSantarém	Código de Ética e de Conduta, Despacho n.º 2434/2023	Regulamento n.º 309/2023 Regulamento Disciplinar dos Estudantes e a Carta de Direitos e Garantias dos Estudantes do IP Santarém
IPS	Código de Ética e Conduta, Despacho n.º 9382/2022	Despacho nº 13714/2016 de 15 de novembro Regulamento disciplinar dos estudantes do IPS
IPT	Código de boas práticas e de conduta do IPT, Despacho n.º 5124/2022	Despacho Normativo n.º 9/2021 de 4 de março- Anexo III aos estatutos
IPVC	Código de Ética do IPVC, Despacho n.º 4690/2020	Regulamento n.º 552/2014 de 15 dezembro, Regulamento Disciplinar dos Estudantes do IPVC
IPV	Código de Boas Práticas e de Conduta, Despacho n.º 11534/2022	Despacho Normativo n.º 12-A/2009 de 27 de março. Secção II
ESEnfC	Código de conduta da Escola Superior de Enfermagem de Coimbra 2010	Regulamento interno de aplicação disciplinar dos estudantes, 2009

IES	Código de Ética/Conduta	Regimento/Regulamento disciplinar
ESEL	Código de Conduta da ESEL, 2024	Regulamento Disciplinar do Estudante, 2012
ESEP	Código de Conduta Ética, Regulamento n.º 29/2022	Regulamento de aplicação do estatuto disciplinar do estudante, 2021
ENIDH	Código de Ética e de Conduta, Despacho nº 1578/2024	Regulamento n.º 214/2015, de 4 de maio, Regulamento disciplinar dos estudantes
ESHTE	Código de Ética e Conduta da ESHTE, 2023	Despacho Normativo n.º 13/2021, de 6 de maio – Título VI – Estatuto Disciplinar dos Estudantes

We believe it is important to update disciplinary regulations to correctly answer facing situations that may arise in the current reality and not fall into regulatory gaps or omissions.

In just over two years, we have found many AI functionalities available at HEIs, including examples of information and availability of generative AI tools (Universidade do Porto digital[23] provides tools based on generative AI, which it presents and compares for the information and availability of the academic community), the adoption of generative AI in the classroom (Universidade Nova de Lisboa, the Nova Information Management School, was the first to provide teachers and students with access to Microsoft Azure OpenAI technology in a classroom context) or the use of a virtual assistant (example of the Universidade do Minho portal).

Far beyond ChatGPT, there are also automatic transcriptions, interactive annotation tools, meeting summaries (as provided by Zoom Colibri FCCN, a service that FCT makes available to all higher education institutions in Portugal for videoconferencing).

[23] UPortodigital – 'Sistemas de Inteligência Artificial generativa. Fique a conhecer algumas das ferramentas baseadas em Inteligência Artificial (IA) generativa, com potencial utilização na comunidade académica da U.Porto. Utilizam tecnologias avançadas que auxiliam na criação de novos conteúdos e também na execução de tarefas rotineiras. Baseiam-se em padrões e estruturas que são aprendidas usando grandes quantidades de dados. Destas ferramentas, com versões gratuitas ou subscrições pagas com mais potencialidades, destacamos algumas com maior notoriedade como o Copilot da Microsoft, ChatGPT da OpenAI, Gemini da Google e Claude da Anthropic'.

It is important to delve deeper into learning theories in chatbot[24], research, to explore theoretical starting points, as well as ontological aspects and epistemological assumptions.

We believe that the impact of chatbots on higher education is currently an emerging area of research – with studies[25] carried out on chatbots or their use in specific areas[26]. 'Until now, AI in education has focused on intelligent tutorial systems. However, more recently, with the expansion of digital data and the development of the field of learning analytics, also known as educational data mining, AI aims to use the growing amounts of digital data from education to better understand learning processes and make inferences about students and the contexts in which they learn (Baker, 2019)'.[27]

Overall, the opportunities associated with AI in higher education include personalised learning methods, reduced workload for teachers, the possibility of greater objectivity and fairness in assessing progress, and improved access and inclusion opportunities for students with special needs.

The National Artificial Intelligence Agenda will be presented in 2025, with the vision being 'to ensure that by 2030 Portugal has a robust artificial intelligence ecosystem, based on ethics and scientific excellence, which promotes social well-being and boosts the productivity and competitiveness

---

24 McGrath, C., Farazouli, A. & Cerratto-Pargman, T. Generative AI chatbots in higher education: a review of an emerging research area. *High Educ* (2024). https://doi.org/10.1007/s10734-024-01288-w

25 Zheng, B. (2024). Chatbots baseados em inteligência artificial: um protótipo para uma instituição de ensino superior. Tese de Mestrado Análise de Dados e Sistemas de Apoio à Decisão. Instituto Superior de Contabilidade e Administração de Coimbra. http://hdl.handle.net/10400.26/51653; Salgado dos Santos, R. (2024) Tradução e comunicação institucional: uma ferramenta virtual para o futuro do IPB. Mestrado em Tradução. Escola Superior de Educação de Bragança. http://hdl.handle.net/10198/30759

26 Baptista, D. (2024). Oportunidades e desafios da inteligência artificial na produção de textos em língua portuguesa. In Simões, V. et all (Organiz) *Comunicação, Cultura e Sociedade: diálogo luso-brasileiro sobre os desafios do século XXI.* Universidade de Aveiro. http://hdl.handle.net/10773/42321 Algumas estratégias pedagógicas que podem ser utilizadas no contexto da aprendizagem da Escrita para ambiente web.

27 Machado, H.; Silva, S. (2024). Desafios Sociais e Éticos da Inteligência Artificial no Século XXI. UMinho Editora. p.77. https://ebooks.uminho.pt/index.php/uminho/catalog/book/130

of the Portuguese economy'[28]. Portugal enacted the Strategy for the Digital Transformation of Public Administration 2021–2026, which aims to harness the potential of the vast volume of data accessible to the Public Administration to improve public services, support better decision-making and enhance transparency. The Portuguese government is concluding its National Artificial Intelligence Agenda, which is expected to be officially[29] presented in middle 2025, as part of the Digital National Strategy, outlines the country's strategic approach to AI, aiming to build a robust and innovative AI ecosystem in Portugal.

Final Considerations

We conclude that the use of AI in the context of Portuguese higher education presents great advantages regarding the personalisation of learning, the new role of the teacher, and the development of critical thinking as a higher-order skill that allows for appropriate and ethical use of AI.

It is therefore essential to debate and analyse the impact and consequences of the use of AI in higher education institutions, as well as what strategies for its ethical and responsible use that guarantees the common good of humanity.

Bibliography

Anderson, A. & Ferreira, J. (2023). Ética e integridade acadêmica na Pós-Graduação em Educação em tempos de Inteligência Artificial. *Periódico Horizontes* – USF – Itatiba, SP – Brasil – e023032. https://doi.org/10.24933/horizontes.v41i1.1620

Baptista, D. (2024). Oportunidades e desafios da inteligência artificial na produção de textos em língua portuguesa. In Simões, V. et all (Organiz) *Comunicação, Cultura e Sociedade: diálogo luso-brasileiro sobre os desafios do século XXI*. Universidade de Aveiro. http://hdl.handle.net/10773/42321

28 Portugal. https://digital.gov.pt/estrategias/estrategia-digital-nacional/o-estado/10-agenda-nacional-de-inteligencia-artificial

29 A public consultation process was launched, including public sessions in Lisbon, Évora and Porto in January 2025, led by the Agency for Administrative Modernisation. Citizens and organisations can also submit contributions online, ensuring transparency and inclusivity. For more information https://participa.gov.pt/base/home

Bostrom, N., Yudkowsky, E., & Pablo, T. (2012). A ética da inteligência artificial. *Fundamento, 1* (3), 201–226. Em https://periodicos.ufop.br/fundamento/article/view/2270Comissão de Ética do Instituto Politécnico de Setúbal, Parecer nº 103/04/2024, Questões Éticas na Utilização da Inteligência Artificial no Ensino Superior.
Comissão Europeia, Direção-Geral das Redes de Comunicação, Conteúdos e Tecnologias (2019). *Orientações éticas para uma IA de confiança*, Serviço das Publicações, https://data.europa.eu/doi/10.2759/2686
Conselho Nacional de Ética para as Ciências da Vida (2024). *Livro Branco. Inteligência Artificial (IA): inquietações sociais, propostas éticas e orientações políticas*. CNECV. P. 52. Disponível em https://www.cnecv.pt/pt/publicacoes/monografias/livro-branco-inteligencia-artificial-ai-inquietacoes-sociais-pro
Cotton, D. Cotton, P. & Shipway, P. (2023). Chating and cheating: ensuring academic integrity in the era of ChatGPT. *Innovations and Teaching International*, 61(2), 228–239. Doi: oi.org/10.1080/14703297.2023.2190148
Cozman, F., Plonski, G. & Neri, H. (2021). *Inteligência artificial: avanços e tendências*. Universidade de São Paulo. Instituto de Estudos Avançados. DOI: https://doi.org/10.11606/9786587773131
Eco, U. (2016). *O Pêndulo de Foucault*. Gradiva.
Ellis, A. R., & Slade, E. (2023). A New Era of Learning: Considerations for ChatGPT as a Tool to Enhance Statistics and Data Science Education. *Journal of Statistics and Data Science Education*, 31(2), 128–133. https://doi.org/10.1080/26939169.2023.2223609
Ethics Committee of the Polytechnic Institute of Setúbal (2024). Opinion nº 103/04/2024, Questões Éticas na Utilização da Inteligência Artificial no Ensino Superior.
European Parliament. (2020). The ethics of artificial intelligence: Issues and initiatives. Panel for the Future of Science and Technology. Em https://www.europarl.europa.eu/RegData/etudes/STUD/2020/634452/EPRS_STU(2020)634452_EN.pdf
European Commission (2024). Commission publishes the Guidelines on prohibited artificial intelligence (AI) practices, as defined by the AI Act. | Shaping Europe's digital future
Floridi, L. (2014). *The Fourth Revolution. How the Infosphere is Reshaping Human Reality*. Oxford University Press.
Gallent-Torres, C., Zapata-González, A., & Ortego-Hernando, J. (2023). El impacto de la inteligencia artificial generativa en educación superior: una

mirada desde la ética y la integridad académica. *RELIEVE, Investigación y Evaludácion Educativa 29*(2), art. M5. http://doi.org/10.30827/relieve.v29i2.29134

Hoernig, S.; Pereira, P.; Ilharco, A.; Pereira, R. (2024) *Report. Generative AI and Higher Education: Challenges and Opportunities.* Em https://www.ipp-jcs.org/wp-content/uploads/2024/09/Report-AI-in-Higher-Education-IPP-1.pdf

Higher Technical Institute | Instituto Superior Técnico Reflexão Sobre Ensino e Formação na era dos Large Language Models – Relatório Comissão REFLeT

Higher Technical Institute | Instituto Superior Técnico Ethics Committee (CE-IST). Ethics Committee – Ata 1/2023 (09 de fevereiro de 2023) Minute 1/2023 (09 February 2023).

McGrath, C., Farazouli, A. & Cerratto-Pargman, T. Generative AI chatbots in higher education: a review of an emerging research area. *High Educ* (2024). https://doi.org/10.1007/s10734-024-01288-w

Oliveira, L.; Pinto, M. (Org.) (2023). A Inteligência Artificial na Educação – Ameaças e oportunidades para o processo ensino-aprendizagem. Escola Superior de Media Artes e Design, Instituto Politécnico do Porto ISBN: 978-989-35125-1-7. Em https://edicoes.ipp.pt/index.php/books/catalog/view/99/213/602

Perfeito, M. *et al.* (2023) Quais tensões ou conflitos circundam o uso da inteligência artificial para a produção escrita nas pesquisas em educação? *Educação em Debate*, Fortaleza, ano 45, n.º 90, 1–17.

Portugal. Direção-Geral Do Ensino Superior (2024) O Ensino Superior Em Portugal 2021/2023. ISBN: 978-972-741-178-8

Rebelo (E.) (2023) Como lidar com o uso da inteligência artificial no Ensino Superior? Livro de Atas do CNaPPES 2023, https://hdl.handle.net/10216/158403

Regulation (EU) 2024/1689 of the Parliament and of the Council of 13 June 2024. Regulamento – UE – 2024/1689 – EN – EUR-Lex

Reyes Palau, N. (2023). Inteligencias artificiales en la formación del pensamiento crítico en Ciencias Sociales. *Maestro y Sociedad*, 20(4), 1023–1029. https://maestroysociedad.uo.edu.cu/index.php/MyS/article/view/6263

Salgado dos Santos, R. (2024) Tradução e comunicação institucional: uma ferramenta virtual para o futuro do IPB. Mestrado em Tradução. Escola Superior de Educação de Bragança. http://hdl.handle.net/10198/30759

Searle, J. (1999). *Intencionalidade. Um ensaio da filosofia da mente*. Tradução: Madalena Poole da Costa. Relógio D'Água.

Steffen Hoernig, Paulo Trigo Pereira, André Ilharco e Regina Pereira (2024) *Report. Generative AI and Higher Education: Challenges and Opportunities.* Em https://www.ipp-jcs.org/wp-content/uploads/2024/09/Report-AI-in-Higher-Education-IPP-1.pdf

UNESCO (2023). Recommendation on the Ethics of Artificial Intelligence. Disponível em https://www.unesco.org/en/articles/recommendation-ethics-artificial-intelligence

Universidade do Porto UPortodigital – Sistemas de Inteligência Artificial generativa.

Vincent-Lancrin & van der Vlies, 2020, Trustworthy artificial intelligence (AI) in education: promises and challenges. *OECD Education Working Paper* No. 218 By Stéphan Vincent-Lancrin (OECD) and Reyer van der Vlies (OECD) https://www.oecd.org/content/dam/oecd/en/publications/reports/2020/04/trustworthy-artificial-intelligence-ai-in-education_f1a7c415/a6c90fa9-en.pdf

WHO (2024). Ethics and governance of artificial intelligence for health: guidance on large multi-modal models. Em https://www.who.int/publications/i/item/9789240084759

Zheng, B. (2024). Chatbots baseados em inteligência artificial: um protótipo para uma instituição de ensino superior. Tese de Mestrado Análise de Dados e Sistemas de Apoio à Decisão. Instituto Superior de Contabilidade e Administração de Coimbra. http://hdl.handle.net/10400.26/51653.

Artificial Intelligence in the Literature Review: Ethical Issues*

Silvana Stremel[1] *and Jefferson Mainardes*[2]

ABSTRACT
This chapter explores the contributions of artificial intelligence (AI) tools to the literature review process and their ethical implications. The main AI tools specifically designed for literature review were classified into three groups: a) tools for retrieving scientific literature (Semantic Scholar); b) tools based on citation mapping (Litmaps, Connected Papers, Research Rabbit, Inciteful); and c) tools for literature search, information synthesis, and research questions (Elicit, Scite.ai, Consensus.app, ChatPDF).

We argue that AI tools are valuable for conducting literature reviews and fostering innovation in this process. However, these tools should be used as a complement to research procedures, under human supervision. Despite the advantages of using AI tools in literature reviews, some limitations are also noted, such as restricted free access, the predominant use of English, and the need for specific knowledge to operate these tools effectively. We emphasise that the responsible use of AI in literature reviews requires a critical analysis of its ethical and social implications, as well as clear descriptions of how AI-based tools were employed in the research. Among the ethical concerns raised about using AI in academic writing are questions of authorship responsibility, plagiarism, academic integrity, and transparency. The chapter advocates the ethical and responsible use of generative AI tools and emphasises the importance of developing ethical guidelines for AI use by educators, researchers, and students. It is essential that these guidelines include specific topics related to literature review.

Keywords: literature review, artificial intelligence, research ethics, responsible AI, ethical guidelines

* To survey the literature on the topic, the Portal de Periódicos da Capes (Capes Journal Portal) was used, which gave access to the Taylor & Francis Online, SpringerLink, Sage Journals and ScienceDirect databases. In addition, the following AI-supported literature search tools were consulted: Semantic Scholar, Research Rabbit and Inciteful. The selection of texts that supported the discussion was carried out by the author based on their contributions to the analysis of the theme. The author is fully responsible for the content, intellectual contributions and interpretations.

1 Federal Technological University of Paraná (UTFPR). https://orcid.org/0000-0002-3110-2005

2 State University of Ponta Grossa (Brazil). https://orcid.org/0000-0003-0401-8112

Introduction

The advancement of artificial intelligence (AI) has been transforming the way research is conducted across various fields of knowledge. Numerous studies have been published regarding the potential applications of AI in qualitative research (Longo, 2020; Morgan, 2023). In particular, some studies highlight how AI-based tools can potentially support literature review processes, expanding the possibilities for obtaining, synthesising, and analysing knowledge production on a given topic (Atkinson, 2024; Bolaños et al., 2024; Foley et al., 2025; Pan et al., 2023; Wagner et al., 2022).

Researchers now have access to new methodological approaches to optimise one of the most fundamental and labour-intensive stages of research. AI's ability to process large volumes of information can make literature reviews faster and more efficient (Wagner et al., 2022). However, integrating AI tools into literature reviews requires researchers to assume essential reflective responsibilities from an ethical and research integrity perspective (Foley et al., 2025).

Although AI offers significant advantages for literature reviews, it remains a complementary methodological strategy that does not replace the human role in processing and interpreting data. Thus, the ethical use of AI tools in research involves concerns related to transparency and accountability (Foley et al., 2025; Wagner et al., 2022). Responsible use entails describing how AI tools were employed in the research, including their limitations and biases, as well as explaining how data were generated and used (Resnik & Hosseini, 2024).

In this chapter, we explore the possibilities of integrating AI tools into literature reviews and discuss the ethical issues involved in using such tools. We argue that ethics and integrity are essential aspects of scientific research and that the ethical use of AI tools is a topic that must be addressed at all levels of education, from basic education to higher education.

The Importance of the Literature Review

The literature review is a fundamental step in any academic or scientific research. According to Hart (2001): 'The literature review is integral to the success of academic research. A major benefit of the review is that it ensures the researchability of your topic before "proper" research commences' (p. 13). The author defines literature review as:

> The selection of available documents (both published and unpublished) on the topic, which contain information, ideas, data and evidence written from a particular standpoint to fulfil certain aims or express certain views on the nature of the topic and how it is to be investigated, and the effective evaluation of these documents in relation to the research being proposed (p. 13).

There is no consensus on the term 'literature review' among scholars. Some authors refer to it as the 'state of the art' or 'state of knowledge'. Among those who use the term 'literature review', some researchers advocate for the systematic literature review (Cherry et al., 2023; Gough et al., 2017; Torgerson, 2003; Zawacki-Richter et al., 2020) and others support the integrative review (Kimberly & Knippenberg, 2020; Toronto & Remington, 2020). A common point among these approaches is the need to conduct an exhaustive search of existing research on the topic in order to present a synthesis of the knowledge already developed in the field.

The systematic literature review is a rigorous and structured method for collecting, evaluating, and synthesising available evidence on a given topic or research question (Torgerson, 2003). Unlike a traditional review, which may be broader and more subjective, the systematic review follows a specific protocol, which includes:

1. **Clear definition of the research question**: The process begins with the formulation of a well-defined research question that guides the entire review.
2. **Inclusion and exclusion criteria**: A set of criteria is established to determine which studies will be included in the review, ensuring that only relevant and high-quality research is considered.
3. **Comprehensive search**: A systematic search is carried out across multiple academic databases to identify all relevant studies, minimising selection bias.
4. **Critical appraisal**: The included studies are evaluated for methodological quality, which helps assess the reliability of the evidence.
5. **Synthesis of results**: Data from the selected studies are synthesised, often using statistical methods (meta-analysis) to combine results.
6. **Transparency and reproducibility**: The process is documented in detail, allowing other researchers to replicate the review, which increases its transparency and credibility.

7. **Practical implications:** The results of a systematic review can inform clinical practices, public policies, and future research, as they provide a comprehensive and evidence-based overview of the topic.

The 'Preferred Reporting Items for Systematic Reviews and Meta-Analyses' (PRISMA) statement was developed to guide systematic literature reviews. The PRISMA 2009 statement included a 27-item checklist recommended for reporting systematic reviews, as well as an 'Explanation and Elaboration' document providing additional guidance and examples for each item.

The PRISMA 2020 update was developed primarily for systematic reviews of studies evaluating the effects of health interventions, regardless of study design. However, the checklist items are also applicable to reviews assessing other types of interventions (such as social or educational interventions), and many items are relevant for systematic reviews with other objectives (such as assessing aetiology, prevalence, or prognosis).

PRISMA 2020 is intended for use in systematic reviews that include summaries (e.g. meta-analyses or other forms of statistical synthesis) or even in cases where summarisation is not possible (e.g. when only one eligible study is identified). The PRISMA 2020 checklist is also relevant for mixed-methods systematic reviews (including both quantitative and qualitative studies), but reporting guidelines specific to the synthesis and presentation of qualitative studies should also be consulted (Page et al., 2022).

The integrative literature review is a type of review that aims to synthesise and integrate evidence from different studies on a specific topic, allowing for a more comprehensive understanding of the issue at hand. This approach is particularly useful in areas where there is a diversity of research, theories, or methodologies. The main characteristics and objectives of the integrative review are as follows:

a. **Breadth of sources:** Unlike a systematic review, which focuses on studies with specific methodological rigour, the integrative review can include a variety of study types – such as qualitative, quantitative, and theoretical – providing a more holistic view of the topic.
b. **Knowledge synthesis:** Its primary goal is to integrate findings from different studies in order to offer a more complete and diverse understanding of the subject, identifying patterns, contradictions, and gaps in the existing knowledge.

c. **Exploration of complex topics:** It is especially useful for complex or emerging topics, where multiple perspectives and approaches are needed for in-depth analysis.
d. **Focus on critical reflection:** The integrative review goes beyond simply describing existing studies; it also involves a critical reflection on how these studies relate to one another and what their impact is on the field of knowledge.
e. **Contribution to policy and practice:** The results of an integrative review can inform professional practices, health policies, and guidelines, as well as highlight areas in need of further research.
f. **Flexible structure:** The integrative review does not follow a protocol as rigid as that of a systematic review, allowing for greater flexibility in approach and study selection.

The importance of the literature review can be summarised in the following points:

a. Contextualisation of the topic: The literature review allows researchers to situate their topic within a broader context, helping them identify what has already been studied on the subject.
b. Identification of gaps: Through the review, researchers can identify areas that have not yet been sufficiently explored or questions that require further investigation, thus justifying the relevance of their study.
c. Metatheory: The literature review helps researchers understand which theoretical and epistemological perspectives have been used in previous studies on the topic.
d. Methodology: It allows researchers to identify the methods used in earlier studies, aiding them in selecting or adapting the most suitable methodology for their own research.
e. Meta-analysis or meta-synthesis of data: The review enables the synthesis of findings from different studies.
f. Avoiding redundancy: The literature review helps prevent duplication of efforts, ensuring that researchers do not repeat studies unnecessarily.
g. Hypothesis development: Based on the analysis of existing literature, researchers can formulate stronger and more well-founded hypotheses.

h. Credibility: A well-conducted literature review demonstrates academic rigour and enhances the credibility of the research by showing that the researcher is well-informed on the topic.

In summary, the literature review is an essential component that enhances the quality and relevance of research.

Integrating AI Tools into the Literature Review

The advantages of using AI-powered tools in literature reviews include mapping existing research, quickly identifying relevant articles related to the research topic, generating concise summaries, and processing large volumes of data efficiently. In addition to generative AI chatbots such as ChatGPT (Morgan, 2023), there are specific tools designed for literature review. It is important to note that not all these available tools are entirely free.

Several studies have described AI-based tools that support literature reviews (Bolaños et al., 2024; Foley et al., 2025; Santana et al., 2024). Additionally, initiatives such as the Systematic Review Toolbox[3] provide an open, free, and searchable catalogue of tools and guidance articles that assist researchers in various tasks within systematic reviews and the broader process of research evidence synthesis (Johnson et al., 2022).

Given the diversity of AI tools available, we present a selection of those that may be useful for literature review, based on recommendations from the aforementioned studies and our own research experience with such tools. We have selected and described nine relevant AI-based tools that can contribute to literature review processes, organising them into three groups:

a. Tools for Retrieving Scientific Literature
   - Semantic Scholar[4]: A free scientific literature search platform that identifies semantically similar articles. Researchers enter a search term, and the platform returns a list of articles with accessible metadata (publication details, authors, abstracts, access via publisher), along with functionalities such as citations and related articles.

---

3 More information on the Systematic Review Toolbox can be found at https://www.systematicreviewtools.com

4 For Semantic Scholar, visit: https://www.semanticscholar.org

b. Tools Based on Citation Mapping
   - Litmaps[5]: With some free features, this platform uses citation networks to find and recommend articles. Given a particular article, the tool generates a map of the most relevant related articles. The map can be navigated to observe the most cited articles, the most recent ones, and the relationships between them through citations.
   - Connected Papers[6]: This tool uses visual graphs to display relevant studies through citation networks. The free version allows a limited number of graph generations per month. The resulting map allows users to explore connections between articles, the most cited papers, and publication timelines. Additionally, it offers functionalities such as filters, metadata exploration, and the ability to identify the most frequently cited articles within the graph (highlighting influential studies in the field) as well as the articles that have cited those in the graph (showing more recent, potentially relevant works).
   - Research Rabbit[7]: A free platform for literature mapping based on citation networks. By selecting one or more articles, the tool finds similar works related to the research topic. It functions like a 'Spotify for literature' (Foley et al., 2025), allowing users to create research collections and explore recommendations for related works. Additionally, users can view publication metadata and visual citation network maps generated by the tool.
   - Inciteful[8]: A free tool designed to support literature discovery. It offers two main features: 'discover' and 'literature connects'. In the discover mode, by providing a reference article, the tool generates a network of articles related to the topic based on citation links, displaying a connection map of the literature. Users can apply filters and add additional articles of interest to the graph. It also provides insights such as recent papers from leading authors, key institutions, and top journals. In the literature connects mode, users can input two articles and examine the connections between them through existing literature.

---

5 Find Litmaps at: https://www.litmaps.com
6 Connected Papers can be accessed here: https://www.connectedpapers.com
7 Discover Research Rabbit at: https://researchrabbitapp.com
8 Access Inciteful at: https://inciteful.xyz

c. Tools for Literature Search, Information Synthesis, and Research Question Analysis
   - Elicit[9]: With some free features, this AI-powered research assistant finds relevant articles based on a query or search term, using semantic similarity. The generated results display the most relevant articles and allow users to create a table that summarises key information (such as methodology, results, and conclusions). The columns of this summary can be customised according to the researcher's interests. The platform also enables users to upload PDFs for data extraction and generates a summarised response to the query based on information from the articles.
   - Scite.ai[10]: A platform with limited free features for testing. Using smart citations, which display the citation context and indicate whether an article provides supporting or contrasting evidence, Scite.ai allows researchers to track literature relevant to their interests. It also offers the Assistant, which answers research questions with concise summaries of recent academic literature, allowing users to explore the sources included in the response.
   - Consensus.app[11]: With some free functionalities, this search engine processes research queries and locates relevant answers within academic articles. The tool provides a summarised text response and references the articles used as sources.
   - ChatPDF[12]: A free tool that leverages AI models to extract information from PDF documents, facilitating article comprehension. It generates summaries of content and allows users to interact via chat to explore the content of the articles.

Despite the advantages of using AI tools in literature reviews, some drawbacks can be highlighted: a) Most tools are not entirely free, making access more difficult for students and researchers; b) These tools perform better and are more user-friendly in English, often to the detriment of other languages;

9 Elicit: Explore at https://elicit.org
10 Scite.ai: Learn more at https://scite.ai
11 Consensus.app: Find it at https://consensus.app
12 ChatPDF: Visit https://www.chatpdf.com

c) Using them effectively requires AI literacy, as researchers need to grasp their limitations and potentialities – essential for their critical, reflective, and responsible use.

Based on Foley et al. (2025), several reflective responsibilities for researchers using AI to explore the literature can be emphasised: a) Clearly discussing how AI tools are used; b) Demonstrating awareness of how AI influences the interpretation of literature review data; c) Including a specific section on reflexivity that addresses how decisions about AI tool outputs influenced the development of knowledge on the research topic; d) Maintaining political awareness of the dominance of publishing environments by research from the Global North, since AI tools often overlook research from economically disadvantaged regions due to limited funding for open-access publication; e) Maintaining an informed perspective on the commercial dynamics of AI tool development and academic publishing, recognising potential biases introduced by AI. Open-access, indexed journal publications have a higher likelihood of being read and cited and, therefore, of being identified as relevant in AI tool mapping; f) Understanding the historical nature of the data used to train AI. This includes awareness of potential biases regarding current debates that may not have been addressed in previous research – and, therefore, may not yet be 'learned' by AI models.

Ethics and Integrity in the Use of AI Tools for Literature Reviews

The use of AI in research raises concerns related to ethics and scientific integrity, including honesty, accuracy, transparency, and responsibility. While AI does not require a significant change in the ethical norms of science, it does call for the scientific community to develop specific guidelines for its appropriate use (Resnik & Hosseini, 2024).

Broadly speaking, several studies have examined the implications of using AI in the development of academic writing and the conduct of doctoral-level research (Anik et al., 2025; Dwivedi et al., 2024; Hosseini et al., 2023; Parker, 2024). Among the ethical concerns raised regarding the use of AI in academic writing, the following stand out:

a. Authorship responsibility: There is an ongoing debate about whether AI tools should be considered authors, given that they cannot be held morally or legally accountable for the content they generate. Hosseini et al. (2023), along with other scholars such as Moffatt and Hall (2024) and Dwivedi et al. (2024), argue that AI systems should not be listed as authors, as they do not meet fundamental authorship criteria (such as responsibility). These researchers contend that moral responsibility is exclusive to human beings, implying that, despite their technical capabilities, AI tools cannot fulfil the ethical obligations of authorship (Dwivedi et al., 2024).
b. Plagiarism and academic integrity: The use of AI may raise concerns about plagiarism, as some AI tools aggregate and synthesise existing content. This can call into question the originality of the work and the accountability of authors for content generated with the assistance of AI. In academic settings, the term *AI-giarism* or *AIgiarism* has emerged to describe a new form of academic dishonesty involving plagiarism related to AI. It primarily refers to the improper use of AI tools by students and researchers to produce academic work (Chan, 2024). This is a widely debated topic, as generative AI outputs may replicate or paraphrase existing content without properly attributing the original sources (Dwivedi et al., 2024).
c. Transparency: Transparency regarding the methods and tools used is essential to ensure research integrity and rigour. Concealing the use of AI tools may compromise the integrity of the research by omitting key aspects of how the work was developed (Hosseini et al., 2023). The use of AI tools and software can be acknowledged in the body of the text and references, described within the methodological section of the research, or explicitly stated in a dedicated section that includes a statement disclosing the use of generative AI and AI-assisted technologies in the manuscript writing process.
d. Some editorial policies, such as those of Elsevier and Springer Nature, now require authors to clearly disclose whether AI tools were used and the extent to which they contributed to the writing of the text (Dwivedi et al., 2024). It is worth noting that prohibiting the use of AI tools may encourage their clandestine use, preventing the academic community from being properly educated about responsible practices that preserve research integrity (Hosseini et al., 2023).

As publications discussing AI-related ethical issues grow in number, several systematic literature reviews have been conducted to organise and synthesise key concerns and debates (Giarmoleo et al., 2024), either in general or centred on specific themes (An et al., 2024; Andrade-Hidalgo et al., 2024; Biagini, 2025; Bond et al., 2024; Memarian & Doleck, 2023; Mouta et al., 2024). Among the specific topics, the following stand out:

a. AI literacy (Biagini, 2025): AI is no longer just a tool, but an essential part of the evolving digital ecosystem. In this context, the swift integration of AI across various sectors has led to a crucial demand in education: Artificial Intelligence (AI) literacy. AI literacy encompasses a broad set of competencies that include both technical knowledge of AI mechanisms and the ability to apply AI responsibly in different contexts, as well as to critically evaluate its social impacts and ethical implications. These skills are essential for effective interaction with AI systems and for making informed decisions about their application in the broader digital landscape (Biagini, 2025).
b. AI in education (An et al., 2024; Mouta et al., 2024) and AI in higher education (Bond et al., 2024; Memarian & Doleck, 2023): These studies focus on education policies and practices related to the use of AI to support teaching, learning, and educational processes. It is essential to establish ethical frameworks to guide the development and implementation of AI in educational settings. This requires participatory processes involving various stakeholders, such as students and teachers (Mouta et al., 2024). According to An et al. (2024), educational institutions must understand and develop ethical guidelines for AI in education from the users' perspectives, ensuring its sustainable and responsible integration.
c. AI in academic writing (Andrade-Hidalgo et al., 2024): A recurring theme in discussions on the use of AI in academic writing is the development of strategies to regulate its use in order to preserve academic integrity. It is essential to adopt ethical values when using AI tools and to review the outputs they generate, as AI does not replace human judgement (Andrade-Hidalgo et al., 2024).

In light of the broader debate surrounding ethical issues and the use of AI in educational and scientific contexts, we outline below some guidelines for literature review processes. Keeping up with this ongoing debate is essential for critically analysing the potential ethical implications of using AI in the search and synthesis of scholarly literature.

Like any type of research, conducting a literature review with AI involves ethical and integrity-related issues. In general, researchers need to:

- Specify which AI tools were used and how they were incorporated into the research report.[13]
- Indicate how the data obtained through AI was verified.
- Clarify the human contribution to the research process, as literature reviews generated solely by AI tools tend to be limited and potentially biased.
- Clearly indicate whether AI-generated automatic translations were used.

Conclusion

AI tools offer valuable support for conducting literature reviews and promoting innovation in this process. However, they should be used to complement research procedures and must operate under human supervision.

The ethical and responsible use of AI has been widely debated. Upholding theoretical, epistemological, and methodological rigour – along with strict adherence to ethical standards – is essential to ensure the validity, reliability, and integrity of scientific research.

Developing competencies for using AI tools in general – and for AI-assisted literature reviews in particular – requires artificial intelligence literacy among teachers, researchers, and students. In our view, these competencies should be developed across all levels of education, starting from early schooling.

Several universities, academic institutions, and scientific associations have begun developing guidelines for AI use (Abella García & Fernández Mármol, 2024; European Union, 2024; Pontifical Catholic University of

---

13 The European Code of Conduct for Research Integrity (All European Academies [ALLEA], 2023) lists 'Hiding the use of AI or automated tools in the creation of content or drafting of publications' (p. 10) as one of the unacceptable practices of research.

Minas Gerais [PUC Minas], 2024). Alonso-Rodríguez (2024) advocates for the creation of an ethical framework for AI in educational research. Establishing guidelines for AI use is crucial, as they serve as reference points for faculty, researchers, advisers, and students. Additionally, given the growing number of AI tools specifically designed for literature review, we emphasise the importance of addressing their specific features in AI-related guidelines for literature review.

Bibliography

Abella García, V., & Fernández Mármol, K. (2024). *Docencia en la Era de la Inteligencia Artificial: Enfoques prácticos para docentes*. Universidad de Burgos. https://riubu.ubu.es/handle/10259/8868

Alonso-Rodríguez, A. M. (2024). Hacia un marco ético de la inteligencia artificial en la educación. *Teoría de la Educación. Revista Interuniversitaria*, *36*(2), 79–98. https://doi.org/10.14201/teri.31821

All European Academies. (2023). *The European Code of Conduct for Research Integrity – revised edition*. ALLEA. https://allea.org/wp-content/uploads/2023/06/European-Code-of-Conduct-Revised-Edition-2023.pdf

An, Q., Yang, J., Xu, X., Zhang, Y., & Zhang, H. (2024). Decoding AI Ethics from Users' Lens in Education: a systematic review. *Heliyon*, *10*(20), e39357, 1–14. https://doi.org/10.1016/j.heliyon.2024.e39357

Andrade-Hidalgo, G., Mio-Cango, P., & Iparraguirre-Villanueva, O. (2024). Exploring the Impact of Artificial Intelligence on Research Ethics – a systematic review. *Journal of Academic Ethics*, 1–18. https://doi.org/10.1007/s10805-024-09579-8

Anik, M. H., Raaz, S. N. C., & Khan, N. (2025). Embracing AI Assistants: unraveling young researchers' journey with ChatGPT in science education thesis writing. *International Journal of Artificial Intelligence in Education*, *35*, 225–244. https://doi.org/10.1007/s40593-024-00438-6

Atkinson, C. F. (2024). Cheap, Quick, and Rigorous: Artificial Intelligence and the Systematic Literature Review. *Social Science Computer Review*, *42*(2), 376–393. https://doi.org/10.1177/08944393231196281

Biagini, G. (2025). Towards an AI-Literate Future: a systematic literature review exploring education, ethics, and applications. *International Journal of Artificial Intelligence in Education*, 1–51. https://doi.org/10.1007/s40593-025-00466-w

Bolaños, F., Salatino, A., Osborne, F., & Motta, E. (2024). Artificial Intelligence for Literature Reviews: Opportunities and challenges.

Artificial Intelligence Review, *57*, 1–49. https://doi.org/10.1007/s10462-024-10902-3

Bond, M., Khosravi, H., De Laat, M., Bergdahl, N., Negrea, V., Oxley, E., Pham, P., Chong, S. W., & Siemens, G. (2024). A Meta Systematic Review of Artificial Intelligence in Higher Education: A call for increased ethics, collaboration, and rigour. *International Journal of Educational Technology in Higher Education*, *21*(4), 1–41. https://doi.org/10.1186/s41239-023-00436-z

Chan, C. K. Y. (2024). Students' perceptions of 'AI-giarism': investigating changes in understandings of academic misconduct. *Education and Information Technologies*, 1–22. https://doi.org/10.1007/s10639-024-13151-7

Cherry, M. G., Boland, A., & Dickson, R. (2023). *Doing a Systematic Review: a student's guide*. Sage.

Dwivedi, Y. K., Malik, T., Hughes, L., & Albashrawi, M. A. (2024). Scholarly Discourse on GenAI's Impact on Academic Publishing. *Journal of Computer Information Systems*, 1–16. https://doi.org/10.1080/08874417.2024.2435386

European Union. (2024). *A complete guide – The EU AI Act. 2024*. Onetrust DataGuidance.

Foley, K., McLean, C., De Zylva, R., Asa, G., Maio, J., Batchelor, S., Dzando, G., & Dimassi, A. (2025). Developing a critical imagination for how researchers can use artificially intelligent tools reflexively and responsibly during qualitative literature reviews. *International Journal of Qualitative Methods*, *24*, 1–17. https://doi.org/10.1177/16094069251316249

Giarmoleo, F. V., Ferrero, I., Rocchi, M., & Pellegrini, M. M. (2024). What Ethics Can Say on Artificial Intelligence: Insights from a systematic literature review. *Business and Society Review*, *129*(2), 258–292. https://doi.org/10.1111/basr.12336

Gough, D., Oliver, S., & Thomas, J. (2017). *An Introduction to Systematic Reviews*. Sage.

Hart, C. (2001). *Doing a literature review*. Sage.

Hosseini, M., Resnik, D. B., & Holmes, K. (2023). The Ethics of Disclosing the Use of Artificial Intelligence Tools in Writing Scholarly Manuscripts. *Research Ethics*, *19*(4), 449–465. https://doi.org/10.1177/17470161231180449

Johnson, E. E., O'Keefe, H., Sutton, A., & Marshall, C. (2022). The Systematic Review Toolbox: Keeping up to date with tools to support evidence synthesis. *Systematic Reviews*, *11*, article number 258, 1–8. https://doi.org/10.1186/s13643-022-02122-z

Kimberly, E., & Knippenberg, D. (2020). Creating High-Impact Literature Reviews: an argument for 'integrative reviews'. *Journal of Management Studies*, *57*(6), 1277–1289. https://doi.org/10.1111/joms.12581

Longo, L. (2020). Empowering qualitative research methods in education with artificial intelligence. In A. P. Costa, L. P. Reis, & A. Moreira (Eds.), *Computer Supported Qualitative Research: New trends on qualitative research* (WCQR2019) (pp. 1–21). Springer. https://doi.org/10.1007/978-3-030-31787-4_1

Memarian, B., & Doleck, T. (2023). Fairness, Accountability, Transparency, and Ethics (FATE) in Artificial Intelligence (AI) and Higher Education: A systematic review. *Computers and Education: Artificial Intelligence*, *5*, 100152, 1–12. https://doi.org/10.1016/j.caeai.2023.100152

Moffatt, B., & Hall, A. (2024). Is AI my co-author? The ethics of using artificial intelligence in scientific publishing. *Accountability in Research*, 1–17. https://doi.org/10.1080/08989621.2024.2386285

Morgan, D. L. (2023). Exploring the Use of Artificial Intelligence for Qualitative Data Analysis: The case of ChatGPT. *International Journal of Qualitative Methods*, *22*, 1–10. https://doi.org/10.1177/16094069231211248

Mouta, A., Pinto-Llorente, A. M., & Torrecilla-Sánchez, E. M. (2024). Uncovering Blind Spots in Education Ethics: Insights from a systematic literature review on artificial intelligence in education. *International Journal of Artificial Intelligence in Education*, *34*, 1166–1205. https://doi.org/10.1007/s40593-023-00384-9

Page, M. J., McKenzie, J. E., Bossuyt, P. M., Boutron, I., Hoffmann, T. C., Mulrow, C. D., Shamseer, L., Tetzlaff, J. M., Akl, E. A., Brennan, S. E., Chou, R., Glanville, J., Grimshaw, J. M., Hróbjartsson, A., Lalu, M. M., LI, T., Loder, E. W., Mayo-Wilson, E., McDonald, S., McGuinness, L. A., Stewart, L., Thomas, T., Tricco, A. C., Welch, V. A., Whiting, P., & Moher, D. (2022). A declaração PRISMA 2020: diretriz atualizada para relatar revisões sistemáticas. *Epidemiologia e Serviços de Saúde*, *31*(2), 1–20. http://dx.doi.org/10.1590/s1679-49742022000200033

Pan, S. L., Nishant, R., Tuunanen, T., & Nah, F. F.-H. (2023). Literature Review in the Generative AI Era – How to make a compelling contribution. *The Journal of Strategic Information Systems*, *32*(3), 1–4. https://doi.org/10.1016/j.jsis.2023.101788

Parker, J. L., Richard, V. M., Acabá, A., Escoffier, S., Flaherty, S., Jablonka, S., & Becker, K. P. (2024). Negotiating meaning with machines: AI's role in doctoral writing pedagogy. *International Journal of Artificial Intelligence in Education*, 1–21. https://doi.org/10.1007/s40593-024-00425-x

Pontifical Catholic University of Minas Gerais. (2024). *Código de Integridade acadêmica no uso do ChatGPT e outras formas de Inteligência Artificial Generativa*. PUC Minas.

Resnik, D. B., & Hosseini, M. (2024). The Ethics of Using Artificial Intelligence in Scientific Research: New guidance needed for a new tool. *AI and Ethics*, 1–23. https://doi.org/10.1007/s43681-024-00493-8

Santana, I. M., Souza, F. N., & Viana, H. B. (2024). Ferramentas de inteligência artificial na revisão de literatura: um estudo com base no tema das falácias lógicas. *Revista Tempos e Espaços em Educação*, *17*(36), 1–16. http://dx.doi.org/10.20952/revtee.v17i36.22252

Torgerson, C. (2003). *Systematic reviews*. Continuum.

Toronto, C. E., & Remington, R. (2020). *A step-by-step guide to conducting an integrative review*. Springer.

Wagner, G., Lukyanenko, R., & Paré, G. (2022). Artificial intelligence and the conduct of literature reviews. *Journal of Information Technology*, *37*(2), 209–226. https://doi.org/10.1177/02683962211048201

Zawacki-Richter, O., Kerres, M., & Bedenlier, S., Bond, M., Buntins, K. (2020). *Systematic Reviews in Educational Research: Methodology, Perspectives and Application*. Springer.

IAgiarism: Ethical and Academic Challenges in the Age of Artificial Intelligence

Jesús Miguel Muñoz Cantero[1]*, Eva M.ª Espiñeira Bellón*[2] *and María Cristina Pérez-Crego*[3]

ABSTRACT

Taking into account the findings of recent research, so-called 'intelligent plagiarism' – defined by the authors as the act of using AI and large amounts of data (big data) to automatically generate texts without relying on appropriate data sources – has become an emerging problem in the academic world.

This chapter analyses the main characteristics of IAgiarism and presents the results of a study conducted at a Galician university on the opinions of students and faculty regarding its key ethical and academic implications, as well as the measures that should be implemented to address this issue.

Based on the responses of 541 students and 297 faculty members, the main measures that could help prevent AI-assisted plagiarism are identified: first, raising student awareness and providing training are highlighted as the primary preventive strategies: second, the development and implementation of specific tools for detecting AI-generated assignments are recommended; third, changes in teaching and assessment methodologies are suggested, with faculty assuming a more active supervisory role. Finally, the study emphasises the need to focus on the consequences of such misconduct.

In terms of ethical and academic implications, the study also identifies specific competencies that should be fostered in academia to ensure the ethical use of AI: raising ethical awareness, promoting the responsible use and integration of AI, and developing critical thinking and analytical skills.

Keywords: artificial intelligence, plagiarism, preventive measure, ethical implications, academic implications

Introduction

Academic plagiarism has been defined as the 'partial or total misappropriation, with or without malice, of an idea or work, without acknowledging the original source' (Wilches-Visbal et al., 2022, p. 1). Such a situation is

[1] University of A Coruña, Galicia, Spain. https://orcid.org/0000-0001-5502-1771
[2] University of A Coruña, Galicia, Spain. https://orcid.org/0000-0001-7522-9406
[3] University of A Coruña, Galicia, Spain. https://orcid.org/0000-0001-5937-0047

considered a serious violation of scientific ethics (Pastor, 2018) that has become a problem in academia.

There is no doubt that the current incursion of generative artificial intelligence (GAI) in the educational and training domain has generated great concern regarding the delivery of academic assignments by university students (Perezchica-Vega et al., 2024), whereby the use of text generation capabilities to create content that appears to be original, but is actually based on copying and adapting existing material without proper sources, has been defined as intelligent plagiarism (Muñoz-Cantero & Espiñeira-Bellón, 2024), which involves the fraudulent use of technology and is attributed to the misuse of knowledge or ideas.

Thus, the main concerns today lie in identifying these actions and redefining teaching strategies to moderate or mitigate these risks (Williams, 2024), so that it is necessary for teachers to adapt their teaching methodologies, taking advantage of the benefits of GSI, but implementing measures to ensure that students develop critical and independent thinking skills (Holmes et al., 2019).

It is therefore necessary to analyse the main characteristics of IAgiarism that influence the key ethical and academic implications within the university context, to determine the specific skills that should be developed for the ethical use of generative AI, and to identify the main preventive measures to be implemented in this regard.

One of the aspects most frequently addressed in studies on preventive measures focuses on *training*. As García-Acuña et al. (2023) point out, all those involved in the implementation of generative AI in education – especially faculty and students – must be adequately trained in AI ethics.

Closely related to this is the need to strengthen *guidance and supervision by teaching staff*. Faculty should monitor and act as appropriate guides in the use of generative AI as a learning tool, teaching students to use it critically and encouraging reflection on its use.

Furthermore, studies that focus on institutional *academic integrity policies* highlight the importance of clearly defining in such regulations what constitutes improper use of generative AI tools, as well as specifying the consequences of such misconduct.

In addition to all of the above, the use of technological tools for plagiarism detection has emerged as an ally in preserving originality (Flores-Morales et al., 2024).

Therefore, it is essential for faculty to acquire new skills for working with AI while maintaining a focus on the added value that teachers bring to the teaching and learning process (Caldevilla-Domínguez, 2024).

Regarding the development of specific skills, *methodological changes* in classroom dynamics are highlighted. It is recommended that academic assignments require students to engage in reflective thinking, as such skills are considered difficult for AI tools to replicate. In addition, increasing the use of practical applications and real-life scenarios is suggested. In terms of assessment, faculty must ensure that evaluation tasks are appropriately designed so that they cannot be easily completed by generative AI (Espiñeira-Bellón et al., 2020).

Furthermore, in a world where AI integration has become widespread, faculty play a crucial role in reminding students of the effort required for genuine learning and understanding.

According to Téllez-Estrada and Valadez-Azúa (2025), this implies selecting or developing authentic tasks that foster creativity and the development of critical thinking, while providing the necessary support offered by generative AI tools.

For this reason, the role of faculty should focus on promoting the responsible use of technology by fostering ethical awareness in its application (Caldevilla-Domínguez, 2024). Teachers should help students use AI as one more tool in their learning process, ensuring that they employ it responsibly and are mindful of both its strengths and limitations.

Objectives

The general objective of this study is to analyse perceptions regarding the integration of generative artificial intelligence tools in the academic field and their pedagogical impact on the training of future educators and current university faculty.

The specific objectives of the study are as follows:

- To identify the main existing measures for preventing plagiarism assisted by generative artificial intelligence.
- To determine the key specific skills that should be developed to ensure the ethical use of generative artificial intelligence.

Method

Population and Sample

The target population of this study consists of students and faculty at the University of A Coruña who attended and taught undergraduate, master's, and doctoral programmes during the 2023/2024 academic year.

The sample was selected using a non-probabilistic, purposive, and convenience sampling method, based on the number of individuals who agreed to participate by providing their responses. The final data-producing sample consisted of 541 students and 297 faculty members.

The characteristics of the student body are as follows:

- Regarding gender, 70.4% of the students (n = 209) identify as female, 26.3% (n = 78) as male, 1.3% (n = 4) identify with other categories, and 2.0% (n = 6) prefer not to answer this question.
- Regarding the type of programme, 72.1% of the students are enrolled in undergraduate programmes, 17.8% in master's programmes, and 10.1% in doctoral programmes.
    i. The majority of undergraduate students are enrolled in Early Childhood Education (32.7%), Nursing (13.1%), Primary Education (9.3%), and Social Education (7.0%).
    ii. The majority of master's students are enrolled in the Master's Degree in Secondary Education Teaching, Baccalaureate, Vocational Training, and Language Teaching (42.9%). Other master's programmes, though less represented, include the Master's Degree in Terrestrial Biodiversity (6.1%), the Master's Degree in Artificial Intelligence (6.1%), and the Master's Degree in Advanced Research and Innovation Methods in Social Analysis (6.1%).
    iii. Among doctoral students, the largest groups are enrolled in the Information and Communication Technologies programme (13.3%), Computing (10.0%), Economic Analysis and Business Strategy (10.0%), Social and Behavioural Sciences (6.7%), and Social Sciences and Ageing (6.7%).
- Regarding the year of study, 48.6% of the students are in their first undergraduate year, and 22.4% are in their fourth year. Additionally, 14.5% are in their third year, 14.0% in their second year, and 0.5% in their fifth year. Most master's students are in their first year (67.9%), 13.2% are in their second year, 1.9% in their third year, and 17.0% did not answer. The majority of doctoral students are in their fourth year (26.7%).

The characteristics of the teaching staff are as follows:

- Regarding gender, half (50.0%) of the faculty identify as male (n = 88), a proportion similar to those who identify as female (n = 86; 48.9%). One person, representing 0.6% of the total, preferred not to answer this question, which is the same number and percentage as those who identify with another sex and/or gender.
- Regarding year of birth, most faculty members were born between the 1940s and 1980s: 40.9% between 1949 and 1968, and 36.9% between 1969 and 1980. The remaining percentage corresponds to those born after the 1980s.
- Regarding teaching experience, just over half of the faculty (55.6%) have between 11 and 20 years (27.8%) or more than 40 years (27.8%) of teaching experience. A further 18.2% have between 21 and 30 years of experience, 19.9% have between 1 and 10 years, and the remaining percentages correspond to those with less than 1 year (2.8%) and those with 31 to 40 years (3.4%).
- Regarding academic rank, most faculty members hold the position of Associate Professor (29.6%), Assistant Professor (15.3%), or Senior Lecturer (13.6%). The distribution for other ranks is as follows: Adjunct Lecturer (10.2%), Research Fellow (3.4%), Full Professor of University College (1.1%), Collaborating Lecturer (0.6%), Interim Lecturer (10.2%), Tenured Lecturer (2.8%), and Associate Professor of University College (1.7%).
- By field of knowledge, 44.9% of the faculty belong to the field of Social and Legal Sciences, 18.8% to Engineering and Architecture, 11.4% to Sciences and Health Sciences, and 13.6% to Arts and Humanities.
- Regarding teaching activity, the majority of faculty members teach undergraduate courses (82.4%). The degree programmes with the highest teaching load are Primary Education (12.5%), Early Childhood Education (7.4%), Law (6.8%), Speech Therapy (5.7%), and Social Education (5.7%).

Instruments

To collect the information, two ad hoc instruments were designed:

- Questionnaire on Attitudes and Perceptions regarding the Use of Artificial Intelligence in Higher Education_Students (CAPAI_S), aimed at understanding university students' perceptions of plagiarism and the use of artificial intelligence in teaching, its pedagogical impact on teacher training, and its relation to intelligent plagiarism.
- Questionnaire on Attitudes and Perceptions regarding the Use of Artificial Intelligence in Higher Education_Faculty (CAPAI_F), aimed at exploring university faculty members' perceptions and perspectives regarding the increasing integration of artificial intelligence in the academic field.

Both questionnaires include an initial section with questions on personal and academic information, followed by twenty items (for students) and twenty-three items (for faculty) measured on a Likert scale from 1 (strongly disagree) to 5 (strongly agree), with additional options for Don't know (DK)/No response (NR). The items are organised into six dimensions: Institutional Policies; Use of Artificial Intelligence in Higher Education; Originality and Ethics; Consequences and Prevention; Responsibility and the Future of Academic Writing; and Ethical Application and Pedagogical Impact.

Finally, both questionnaires also contain seven open-ended questions addressing topics related to Consequences, Prevention, Responsibility and the Future of Academic Writing; Reflection on Authorship and Originality; and the Ethical Impact of Artificial Intelligence in Higher Education/Future of Education and Artificial Intelligence.

Data Collection Procedure

The data collection instruments were distributed online to students and faculty members from various undergraduate, master's, and doctoral programmes between May and July 2024.

Technical Analysis of the Instruments

To validate the instruments, their validity was verified through expert judgement, involving members of the IA Network (Ibero-American Research

Network on Academic Integrity) and the Interuniversity Academic Integrity Group from the three universities that make up the Galician University System.

The reliability of the instruments was calculated through an internal consistency analysis using Cronbach's Alpha coefficient (Cronbach, 1951). The Cronbach's Alpha for the CAPAI_S questionnaire was .818, and for the CAPAI_F questionnaire it was .835.

Data Analysis

To analyse the responses to the open-ended questions in the questionnaires and to address the study's objectives, a methodological procedure with a qualitative approach was employed. This decision was made in order to understand and interpret the meaning that students and faculty members – participants in the phenomenon under study – expressed through their own narratives and reflections (Creswell & Clark, 2011).

Once the information provided by the students and faculty was compiled, it was reduced, organised, arranged, and interpreted. Prior to this, the information was coded through an inductive procedure by developing a hierarchical system of categories (Miles & Huberman, 1994; Miles et al., 2014). This process consisted of identifying the central theme of each paragraph or group of words with one or two keywords describing the key aspects of each topic. Additionally, to facilitate the later retrieval of each quotation or excerpt, labels were assigned to the emerging themes.

The data were processed using the qualitative data analysis software ATLAS.ti. This tool enables the researcher to establish links between emerging categories, record the frequency with which categories appear, and visualise the relationships among them, thus 'promoting the transparency, communication, reduction, and interpretation of empirical material, making the qualitative research process simpler and, at the same time, more rigorous and systematic' (Pérez-Ripossio, 2023, pp. 8–9).

As the data were analysed, a structure of the different thematic categories was developed. To build this structure, the criterion of relevance was considered, ensuring that the categories were coherent and appropriate in relation to the study's objectives and the information analysed (Herrera-Rodríguez et al., 2015).

To address the reliability of the procedure conducted in the study, the data analysis process is described, providing a clear record of the categories and analysis codes (Flick, 2014). The categories and codes obtained from the analysis are presented in the various figures and table included in this study. Furthermore, information from two types of informants – faculty and students – is provided and identified in the different results presented. Likewise, the findings have been contrasted with the existing literature to offer a more robust interpretation in relation to the study's theoretical framework (Miles et al., 2014).

Regarding the ethics of the research process, participants were informed about the data collection and processing procedures, which were carried out rigorously and with respect for the information obtained (Rebollo-Catalán & Jiménez-Cortés, 2018). The information collected was stored in an anonymous database, ensuring participants that no information allowing their identification would be disclosed in the results disseminated through scientific publications, thereby guaranteeing the confidentiality of their data. Additionally, the study received a favourable report from the Research and Teaching Ethics Committee of the University of A Coruña.

The analysis of students' and faculty members' responses regarding measures to prevent plagiarism arising from the use of artificial intelligence in higher education made it possible to identify key issues in their answers. Based on the content analysed, various categories and subcategories were established to group the proposed ideas. The main measures identified to prevent AI-assisted plagiarism include: training and awareness-raising; the implementation of detection tools; regulation through institutional policies and guidelines; faculty supervision; and consequences for the improper use of AI. In terms of specific skills needed to ensure the ethical use of artificial intelligence in the academic field, the following stand out: ethical awareness and responsible use; integration of and training in AI; and the development of critical analysis skills.

To ensure the rigour of the analysis, the main categories obtained from the data analysis are presented in Table 3.

Table 3: Categories and codes emerging from student and teacher data analysis

Categories	Subcategories	Codes	Definition
Measures	Training and awareness-raising	Training	Training for students and teachers on ethical use of AI and plagiarism.
		Ethical awareness	Raising awareness of originality, authorship and academic ethics.
		Cross-curricular training	Integration of training on the responsible use of AI in educational programmes.
	Implementation of tools	AI detection	Use of software or applications to identify AI-generated content.
		Software improvement	Optimisation of existing tools to detect AI-generated content.
	University policies and regulations	Control policies	Establishment of institutional regulations on the use of AI in higher education.
		Usage regulations	Clear definition of the limits and ethical ways of using AI in academic work.
		Legislative framework	Development of regulations that address the risks and challenges of using AI in education.
	Teacher monitoring	Teacher monitoring	Monitoring and adaptation of assessment strategies by teachers.
		Alternative assessment methods	Implementation of oral assessments, critical reflections, creative work, or activities that hinder the misuse of AI.
	Consequences	Sanctions	High disciplinary measures for inappropriate use of AI in academic work.
		Loss of grade	Reduction of marks or cancellation of the work if plagiarism with AI is detected.
		Future impact	Awareness of the academic and professional consequences of AI misuse in future careers.

(Continued)

Table 3: *(Continued)*

Categories	Subcategories	Codes	Definition
Skills	Ethical awareness and responsible use	Responsible use	Ability to use AI without compromising academic integrity.
		Critical thinking	Ability to evaluate AI-generated information and discern its quality.
		Ethical discernment	Understanding of when and how to use AI appropriately in academia.
		Academic responsibility	Commitment to authorship and intellectual honesty in academic work.
	AI integration	Correct use of AI	Use of AI as a tool in the development of academic content.
		Prompts	Ability to formulate appropriate questions to obtain useful information from AI.
		Help	Use of AI to support the development of academic tasks, without relying entirely on it.
	AI training	Teacher training	Training on how to use AI tools ethically and effectively by students.
		Teacher training	Training for teachers to integrate AI into teaching and detect plagiarism.
	Development of critical analysis skills	Critical analysis using AI	Development of skills to assess the veracity and relevance of AI information (sound ethical judgement).

The categories and codes emerging from the analysis of student data (Figure 1) and from the analysis of teacher data (Figure 2) are presented.

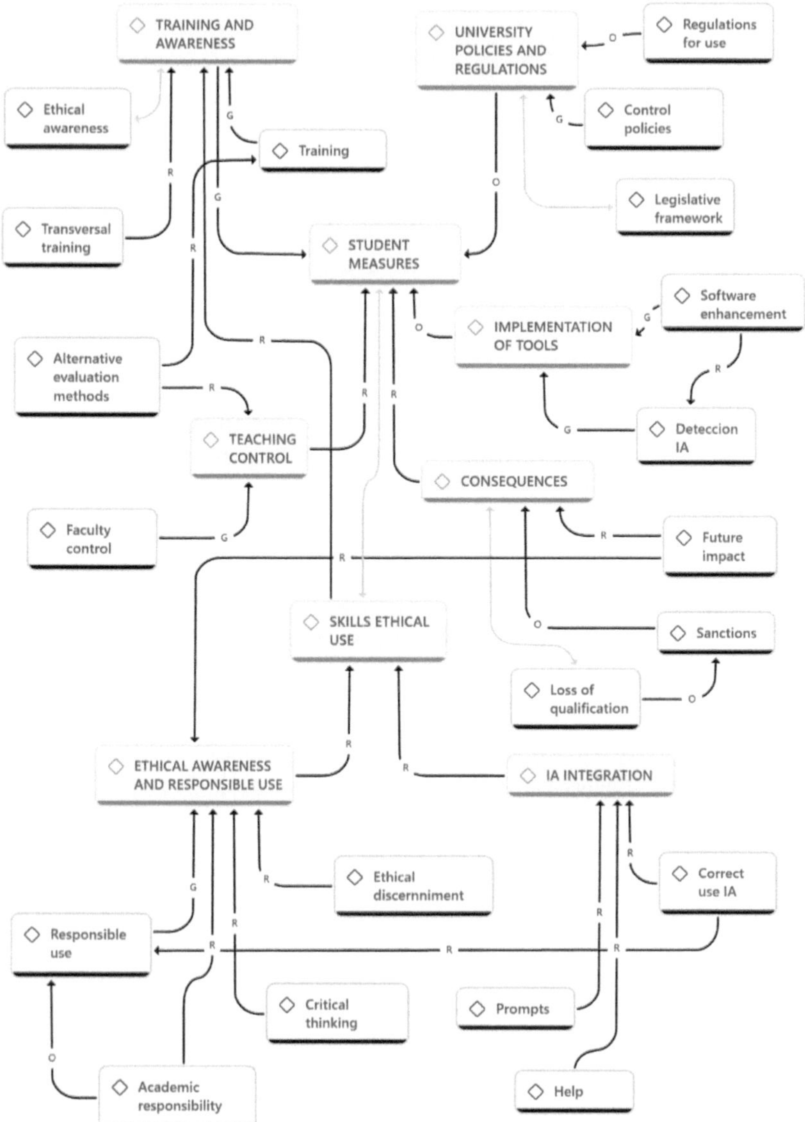

Figure 1: Network of categories and codes of the student body

Note: The connectors between the rectangles correspond to the following legend: N=is cause of, G=is part of, O=is a and R=is associated with.

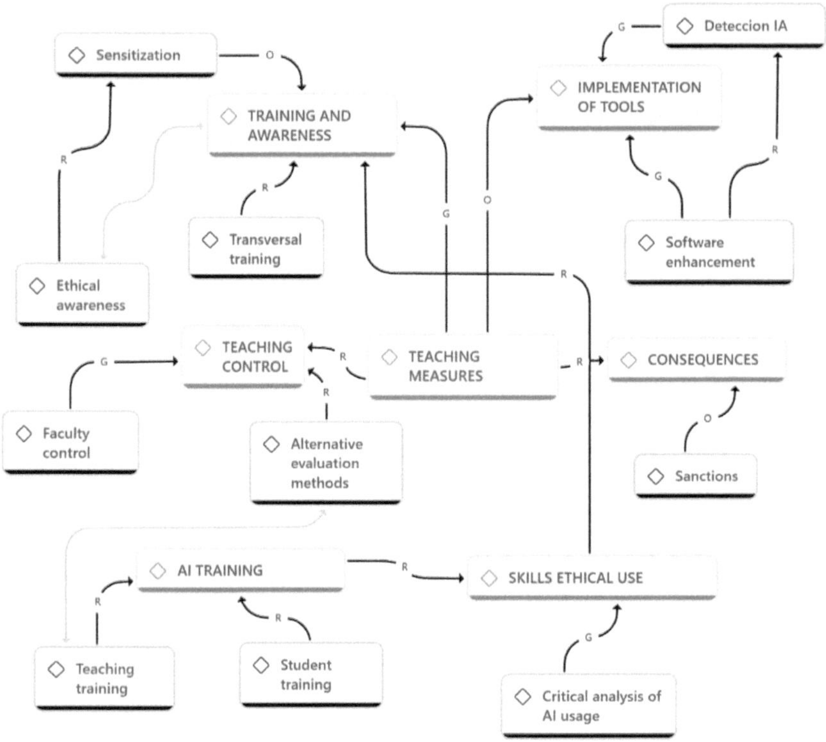

Figure 2: Teacher category and code network

Note: The connectors between the rectangles respond to the following legend: N=is cause of, G=is part of, O=is a and R=is associated with.

Results

The following section describes the results obtained, organised according to the measures that, in the opinion of students and faculty members, could be implemented to prevent AI-assisted plagiarism in higher education, followed by the specific skills that students and faculty believe should be developed to ensure the ethical use of AI in academia.

Measures That Could Be Implemented to Prevent AI-assisted Plagiarism in Higher Education According to Students

According to the students (N = 195), the measures that could be implemented to prevent AI-assisted plagiarism can be structured into several types: first, those aimed at training and raising awareness; second, those focused on the implementation of detection tools; third, those related to university policies and regulations; fourth, faculty oversight; and fifth, measures centred on consequences.

Words such as 'training', 'ethical awareness', 'AI detection', 'control policies', and 'usage regulations' are the most frequently mentioned in the responses, indicating the key areas where students believe more measures should be implemented.

A large percentage of student responses (N = 48; 24.61%) suggest measures related to training, awareness, and sensitisation on the ethical use of AI and the implications of AI-assisted plagiarism: 'training for teachers and students'; 'ethical awareness'; 'raising awareness about its importance, about the importance of authorship and originality of academic work, and the ethical principles involved', and similar comments.

The need to integrate ethical training and responsible use into educational programmes is also emphasised: 'responsible AI use courses; the problem is not the tool, it's how it's used'; 'education, education, and more education; for example, through talks with real testimonies from scientists, teachers, artists, and creators who have suffered plagiarism by AI'; 'first, plagiarism should be addressed from school education onwards; second, it could be included as cross-curricular content in all subjects or as a dedicated subject that covers this along with APA norms so that students learn to do their work correctly'; 'include information on AI use in course syllabi, establishing limits and ways to use it ethically while counteracting plagiarism', among others.

Secondly, 19.49% of the responses (N = 38) propose a more effective role for faculty in monitoring and controlling such situations: 'greater oversight'; 'teachers should correct assignments themselves and adapt tasks so that they're not just "write an essay about X"'; 'the best way to prevent it is to ask students questions about what they have written; that is, hold in-person defences of their papers'; 'assignments should require critical reflection that cannot be carried out by artificial intelligence'; 'provide more persistent support when students need it, teach them how to find reliable information sources, teach them how to cite properly', and 'seek alternative assessment methods', among others.

Thirdly (N = 34; 17.44%), the responses suggest the implementation of technological tools to detect and control the use of AI in academic work, such as specific programmes to identify AI-generated content or improve existing software: 'the creation, dissemination, and use of detection tools'; 'an app to identify plagiarism', and similar ideas.

A further 5.64% (N = 11) of the responses focus on explicitly outlining the consequences of such improper behaviours: 'probably the most effective measure would be the "fear" of facing serious consequences if it is discovered that AI was used to complete the assignment'; 'explain the serious consequences this will have for the student's future as an author'; 'strict penalties'; 'point deductions for plagiarised work', and similar comments.

Meanwhile, 3.08% (N = 6) of the responses suggest creating clear policies and regulations regarding the use of AI in higher education: 'a total ban on its use at all levels of education: higher, secondary, and lower'; 'ensure that students understand the institution's policies'; 'implement a policy that integrates AI citation (as if it were an additional author) whenever it is not possible to identify the human authors behind the AI-generated information'; 'first build a legislative framework that can evolve and address all the vulnerabilities or risks that may arise, since today we still do not know the magnitude and scope it may reach', among others.

Finally, it should be noted that eight students (4.10%) favoured multiple measures at once, with training and detection being the most common combinations. Additionally, forty-three students (22.05%) did not provide any measure, four students (2.05%) mentioned the difficulty of taking effective action, and three responses (1.54%) could not be classified in any of the previous categories due to the ambiguity of the answers provided.

Measures That Could Be Implemented to Prevent AI-assisted Plagiarism in Higher Education According to Faculty

According to the faculty (N = 131), the measures that could be implemented to prevent AI-assisted plagiarism can be structured into four main types: first, raising student awareness and providing training as the primary preventive measure; second, developing and implementing specific tools to detect AI-generated work; third, making changes to teaching and assessment methodologies, with faculty playing a supervisory role; and fourth, focusing on consequences.

A portion of the faculty responses (N = 33; 25.19%) suggest measures related to student training, awareness, and sensitisation on the ethical use of AI and the implications of AI-assisted plagiarism: 'inform students about the benefits and risks; identify in the classroom the biases and errors generated by AI by cross-checking other sources; teach the ethical implications and distinguish appropriate use from academic fraud'; 'the best measure would be to include training programmes so that students have the resources they need to conduct research and learn how to cite correctly'; 'raising student awareness about how to use AI ethically', and similar comments.

Secondly, 20.61% of the responses (N = 27) propose a more effective role for faculty in monitoring and controlling such situations: 'having students defend their work before a committee of experts; using oral exams instead of only submitting written assignments'; 'designing tasks that AI cannot solve because the material is not in its database (increasingly challenging); for example, practical cases based on topics covered in lectures that AI would not know'; 'short oral discussions about the work process and students' contributions; bringing back the value of spoken word'; 'reducing class sizes and combining oral and written assessments'; 'assigning more creative tasks, personal reflections, and data analysis', among others.

Thirdly (N = 24; 18.32%), the responses suggest implementing technological tools to detect and control the use of AI in academic work, such as specific programmes to identify AI-generated content or improve existing software: 'developing applications or anti-plagiarism platforms specifically designed for this purpose'; 'creating a programme that significantly detects AI use within an assignment'; 'designing a tool capable of accurately identifying whether a text was written by a human or by ChatGPT', and similar ideas.

Fourthly, 1.53% (N = 2) of the responses focus on explicitly outlining the consequences of such improper behaviours: 'severe disciplinary measures in cases of detected plagiarism'; 'clearly establishing the consequences for non-compliance with these principles'; 'regulating punitive or limiting consequences for its academic use'; 'academic and even financial penalties', among others.

Finally, it should be noted that seventeen faculty members (12.98%) favoured multiple measures at once, with training and faculty supervision being the most common combination. In addition, twenty-three faculty members (17.55%) did not provide any measure, and five responses (3.82%) could not be classified in any of the previous categories due to the ambiguity of the answers provided.

Specific Skills That Need to Be Developed to Ensure the Ethical Use of AI in Academia According to Students

According to students (N = 173), the specific skills that should be developed in academia to ensure the ethical use of AI can be grouped into two main areas: ethical awareness and the responsible use of AI, and AI integration.

In this regard, the words and phrases most frequently used by students include 'ethical awareness', 'knowing how to discern', 'responsible use', 'limits of use', and 'integrating AI into teaching', which reflect a clear concern for the proper and ethical use of AI in academic contexts.

Thus, the responses (N = 94; 54.33%) emphasise the importance of developing skills related to ethics, awareness, and the responsible use of AI in academic work, highlighting the need to discern when and how to use AI appropriately: 'understanding the consequences of misuse, knowing how to use it responsibly in academic work, knowing how to teach its use as a future teacher'; 'morality, proper citation'; 'ethical values'; 'knowledge of responsible use'; 'responsibility in creating assignments'; 'knowing how to use information responsibly, having critical thinking, cultural awareness, and sensitivity'; 'individual responsibility'; 'responsible use of information tools, the importance of giving credit'; 'critical and creative thinking'; 'idea generation', and similar comments.

Secondly (N = 43; 24.86%), the responses focus on the need to develop skills to integrate AI appropriately into academic activities and teaching, without compromising the integrity of the work or replacing student effort: 'skills and the ability to apply AI to detect sources and resources it uses for creation. Also, the skill to craft appropriate and effective prompts for the desired outcome'; 'AI tools have the potential to greatly change how many human tasks are carried out, including learning'; 'citing the AI used, not to generate content but to help find ideas and alternative approaches'; 'strengthening twenty-first-century skills and practising with AI tools in the classroom to reinforce human abilities (re-researching, reasoning, and reflecting)'; 'learning to use AI properly, developing original content based on AI-generated responses'; 'learning how to find information and shape it while retaining and understanding the content', among others.

Finally, it should be noted that twenty-seven students (15.61%) stated that they do not know what specific skills should be developed, reflecting a lack of training or knowledge on this topic, and nine responses (5.20%) could not be classified under the previous categories due to the ambiguity of the answers provided.

Specific Skills That Need to Be Developed to Ensure the Ethical Use of AI in Academia According to Faculty

According to faculty (N = 112), the specific skills that should be developed in academia to ensure the ethical use of AI can be grouped into two main areas: training and the promotion of critical analysis skills.

Thus, the responses (N = 43; 38.39%) emphasise the need for specific training for both faculty and students: 'training for faculty and students on AI tools; learning how to use ChatGPT, Gemini, or other tools so that, for example, they can be used as research and teaching assistants'; 'I consider it essential for faculty to be trained in these technologies, not only to detect plagiarism but also to make use of their potential for teaching purposes; it is also important to understand what they are and how they work to better explain to students the possible consequences of using them for unethical purposes'; 'knowledge of their applicability and ethical debate'; 'training in ethics'; 'training in values; academic vocation; professional honesty', and similar comments.

Secondly (N = 11; 9.82%), the responses focus on the importance of developing skills that enable a stronger ethical judgement regarding AI and critical analysis abilities: 'critical capacity and analytical thinking'; 'critical and reflective capacity'; 'metacognitive skills to discern the quality/appropriateness of the information generated'; 'understanding how these tools can serve as support while promoting critical thinking and the originality of students' work'; 'fundamentally cognitive component skills that foster critical thinking and ethics in academic work', among others.

Finally, it should be noted that twenty-one faculty members (18.75%) stated that they do not know what specific skills should be developed, reflecting a lack of training or knowledge on this topic; three faculty members (2.68%) mentioned both areas at once, and thirty-four responses (30.36%) could not be classified under the previous categories due to the ambiguity of the answers provided.

Conclusions

The faculty and students at the University of A Coruña, through this study, have focused on analysing perceptions regarding the integration of generative artificial intelligence (GAI) tools, identifying the main existing measures to prevent GAI-assisted plagiarism, and determining the key specific skills that should be developed to ensure the ethical use of GAI.

According to the participating faculty and university students, the main measures that could be implemented to prevent AI-assisted plagiarism can be grouped into several categories. In the opinion of both groups, raising student awareness and providing training should be the primary preventive measure, followed by measures focused on developing and implementing specific tools to detect AI-generated work and, finally, focusing on the consequences. These measures should be complemented by necessary changes in teaching and assessment methodologies, with faculty playing a supervisory role, as well as by the students' suggestion to create clear policies and regulations on the use of AI in higher education.

These measures are not so different from the results of previous analyses on academic plagiarism prior to the integration of GAI (Delgado-Salas et al., 2024; Muñoz-Cantero et al., 2024; Vargas-Morúa, 2021).

The analysis reveals that most participants consider training and awareness to be the main measures for preventing GAI-assisted plagiarism in higher education. However, given that a significant percentage suggest developing detection tools and implementing clear policies and regulations, it can be inferred that there is a need to establish a comprehensive strategy that combines education, technology, and regulation to effectively address the use of GAI in academic settings, in line with the findings of Amén-Mora et al. (2024), Gallent-Torres et al. (2023), and Guerra-Guerrero and Tass-Herrera (2024).

Regarding the specific skills that should be developed in academia to ensure the ethical use of GAI, students highlight the importance of developing ethical awareness and the responsible use of GAI, as well as its integration, while faculty focus on training and fostering critical analysis skills. The analysis of the responses shows a widespread concern for the development of ethical skills and the responsible use of GAI, especially in academic contexts (Niño-Carrasco et al., 2025). However, the dispersion of responses suggests a lack of consensus or clear information on which specific competencies are needed for the ethical use of AI – issues addressed by Chuñir-Panjon (2025) in relation to the integration of AI into teaching planning.

The results provided in this study deepen the understanding of GAI and its academic impact, both in the teaching and learning process and in relation to academic integrity and plagiarism (Caldevilla-Domínguez, 2024), as well as the role of faculty involvement in its prevention (Muñoz-Cantero & Espiñeira-Bellón, 2020).

Bibliography

Amén-Mora, P., Zavala-Baque, D. L., Moran-Lozano, N. S., & Intriago-Terán, A. B. (2024). Ethical and privacy challenges in the implementation of artificial intelligence in higher education. *Refereed Scientific Journal of Research in Communication, Marketing and Business, REICOMUNICAR,* 7(14), 613–628. https://doi.org/10.46296/rc.v7i14.0286

Caldevilla-Domínguez, D. (2024). Ethical uses of AI in the modern university: beyond plagiarism. *EDU REVIEW. International Education and Learning Review, 12*(1), 57–65. https://doi.org/10.62701/revedu.v12.5184

Chuñir-Panjon, J. (2025). Specific competencies for the integration of artificial intelligence in teacher planning. *Mamakuna, 24,* 80–92. https://doi.org/10.70141/mamakuna.24.1050

Creswell, J. W., & Clark, V. I. (2011). *Designing and conducting mixed methods research.* Sage.

Cronbach, L. J. (1951). Coefficient alpha and the internal structure of tests. *Psychometrika, 16,* 297–334. https://doi.org/10.1007/BF02310555

Delgado-Salas, J. A., Contreras-Paredes, E. I., Bravo-Cedeño, J. G., & Chico-Guzmán, B. A. (2024). Ethical dilemmas in higher education: an analysis of the challenges and responsibilities of academics and students. *Revista Social Fronteriza, 4*(4), e44325. https://doi.org/10.59814/resofro.2024.4(4)325

Espiñeira-Bellón, E. M., Mosteiro-García, M. J., Muñoz-Cantero, J. M., & Porto-Castro, A. M. (2020). Academic honesty as a criterion for the evaluation of university student work. *RELIEVE. Electronic Journal of*

Educational Research and Evaluation, 26(1), art. 2. http://doi.org/10.7203/relieve.26.1.17097

Flick, U. (2014). *Quality management in qualitative research.* Ediciones Morata.

Flores-Morales, J. A., Reyes-Quinteros, M. F. G., Contreras-Maguiña, A. P., & Luna-Román, E. A. (2024). Originality and Intellectual Honesty: Navigating the Waters of Plagiarism. *Journal of Climatology Special Issue Social Sciences, 24,* 2032–2038. https://doi.org/10.59427/rcli/2024/v24cs.2032-2038

Gallent-Torres, C., Zapata-González, A., & Ortego-Hernando, J. L. (2023). The impact of generative artificial intelligence in higher education: a look from ethics and academic integrity. *RELIEVE. Electronic Journal of Educational Research and Evaluation, 29*(2), 1–21. http://doi.org/10.30827/relieve.v29i2.29134

García-Acuña, L. T., Zambrano-Andrade, F. I., Acuña-Chong, M. G., & Acuña-Cumba, M. L. (2023). Opportunities and challenges in the application of artificial intelligence in higher education. *Refereed Scientific Journal of Research in Communication, Marketing, and Business, REICOMUNICAR, 6*(12), 255–282. https://doi.org/10.46296/rc.v6i12edespoct.0172

Guerra-Guerrero, C. O., & Tass-Herrera, B. (2024). Practical Applications of Generative Artificial Intelligence in Teaching: The Case of Multimedia Design Engineering. *European Public & Social Innovation Review, 9,* 1–20. https://doi.org/10.31637/epsir-2024-816

Herrera-Rodríguez, J. I., Guevara-Fernández, G. E., & Munster-de la Rosa, H. (2015). Designs and strategies for qualitative studies. A theoretical-methodological approach. *Gaceta Médica Espirituana, 17*(2), 120–134. https://revgmespirituana.sld.cu/index.php/gme/article/view/1015/pdf_56

Holmes, W., Bialik, M., & Fadel, C. (2019). *Artificial intelligence in education promises and implications for teaching and learning.* Center for Curriculum Redesign. https://discovery.ucl.ac.uk/id/eprint/10139722/

Miles, M., & Huberman, M. (1994). *Qualitative Data Analysis. An expanded sourcebook.* Sage.

Miles M., Huberman, M, & Saldaña, J. (2014). *Qualitative Data Analysis. A Methods Sourcebook.* Sage.

Muñoz-Cantero, J. M., & Espiñeira-Bellón, E. M. (2020). Teaching performance as a condition to avoid academic plagiarism. In E. De la Torre Fernández (ed.), *Contextos universitarios transformadores: Boas prácticas no marco dos GID* (pp. 421–434). Universidade da Coruña. https://doi.org/10.17979/spudc.9788497497756.421

Muñoz-Cantero, J. M., & Espiñeira-Bellón, E. M. (2024). Intelligent Plagiarism as a Misconduct in Academic Integrity. *Acta Médica Portuguesa, 37*(1), 1–2. https://doi.org/10.20344/amp.20233

Muñoz-Cantero, J. M., Espiñeira-Bellón, E. M., & Pérez-Crego, M. C. (2024). Measures to combat plagiarism in learning processes. *Education XX1. Revista de Facultad de Educación, 24*(2), 97–120. https://doi.org/10.5944/educxx1.28341

Niño-Carrasco, S. A., Castellanos-Ramírez, J. C., Perezchica Vega, J. E., & Sepúlveda Rodríguez, J. A. (2025). Perceptions of university students on the uses of artificial intelligence in education. *Fuentes Journal, 27*(1), 94–106. https://doi.org/10.12795/revistafuentes.2025.26356

Pastor, J. (2018). Plagiarism in publications. *Archivos de la Sociedad Española de Oftalmología, 93*(12), 571–572. https://doi.org/10.1016/j.oftal.2018.10.024

Pérez-Ripossio, R. N. (2023). Qualitative analysis with ATLAS. ti 22 in Social Sciences: New tools and concrete applications. *Perspectivas Metodologicas,* 1–10. https://ri.conicet.gov.ar/handle/11336/220799

Perezchica-Vega, J. E., Sepúlveda-Rodríguez, J. A., & Román-Méndez, A. D. (2024). Inteligencia artificial generativa en la educación superior: usos y opiniones de los profesores [Generative artificial intelligence in higher education: uses and opinions of teachers]. *European Public & Social Innovation Review, 9,* 01–20. https://doi.org/10.31637/epsir-2024-593

Rebollo-Catalán, A., & Jiménez-Cortés, R. (2018). The rigor of qualitative research to ensure its publication. *Aula Magna 2.0.* [Blog]. https://doi.org/10.58079/nesr

Téllez-Estrada, M. R., & Valadez-Azúa, R. (2025). Educational strategies facing the new challenges of Artificial Intelligence. *Revista Chicomoztoc,* 7(13), 227. https://doi.org/10.48705/kkwcbe86

Vargas-Morúa, E. (2021). Plagiarism: considerations for its prevention. *Espiga Magazine, 20*(41), 68–85. https://doi.org/10.22458/re.v20i41.3521

Wilches-Visbal, J. H., Castillo-Pedraza, M. C., & Pérez-Anaya, O. (2022). Plagiarism and predatory journals: an economic and ethical problem in public universities in Colombia. *Revista Cubana de Información en Ciencias de la Salud, 33,* e1911https://bit.ly/3e8GVfk

Williams, R. (2024). The ethical implications of using generative chatbots in higher education. *Frontiers in Education, 8,* 05-06. https://doi.org/10.3389/feduc.2023.1331607

Scientific Retractions: Historical Evolution, Ethical Challenges and the Role of Artificial Intelligence

Jesús Miguel Muñoz Cantero[1], *Ana M.ª Porto Castro*[2], *M.ª Josefa Mosteiro García*[3] *and Enelina Mª Gerpe Pérez*[4]

ABSTRACT
Scientific retraction is a fundamental mechanism for preserving the integrity of the scientific record by correcting errors, fraud, and misconduct. Its evolution has been driven by historical, ethical, and technological factors, adapting to the changing challenges of the scientific environment since its first documented occurrence in 1977. Today, artificial intelligence (AI) plays a transformative role in this process. Tools such as iThenticate and Retraction Watch use advanced algorithms to detect potential cases of dishonesty in academic papers and correct them in real time. However, technology does not function in isolation; factors such as the pressure to publish, academic competition, and questionable editorial practices continue to influence the phenomenon of retractions. This chapter first examines the phenomenon of retractions and the role of artificial intelligence. It then analyses their impact on the scientific community. Finally, it provides a brief overview of key developments explaining the evolution of scientific retractions. The fourth section explores the main causes of retractions and the central role of AI in managing them. The chapter concludes with final remarks and bibliographic references.

Keywords: scientific retraction, academic integrity, artificial intelligence, automated plagiarism, publication ethics

Scientific Retractions and Artificial Intelligence (AI)

Formally, the retraction of a scientific article indicates that it contains serious errors or falsified data that lead to its exclusion from the scientific record. This decision can be made either by the authors themselves or by

[1] University of A Coruña, Galicia, Spain. https://orcid.org/0000-0001-5502-1771
[2] University of Santiago de Compostela, Galicia-Spain. https://orcid.org/0000-0002-9410-5457
[3] University of Santiago de Compostela, Galicia-Spain. https://orcid.org/0000-0001-6354-3289
[4] University of Santiago de Compostela, Galicia-Spain. https://orcid.org/0000-0001-7560-4608

scientific journals when they discover substantial issues that invalidate the study's results. Retraction is, therefore, essential for maintaining the accuracy of the scientific record (Bhatt, 2021).

The impact of retractions on scientific research largely depends on the correct identification and management of the affected documents. According to COPE (2019), the retraction process involves registering the publication as retracted in scientific databases, along with a notice detailing the specific reasons for the retraction, which can range from serious errors and fraud to authorship disputes or ethical conflicts. This ensures transparency and traceability of errors, thereby strengthening the integrity of the scientific literature. Retracted articles remain in the records and are only removed in cases of severe ethical violations.

In this context, artificial intelligence, through the use of systems such as *Statcheck* for automated statistical review or *iThenticate* for detecting plagiarism (Casadevall et al., 2014; Májovský et al., 2023), has begun to play an essential role in the retraction process, enabling editors and reviewers to respond in a timely manner to different types of irregularities, allowing them to assess, categorise and flag inconsistencies in scientific papers and ensuring that informed decisions are made and the most appropriate level of action is determined for each situation (Májovský et al., 2023)

The scope of a retraction varies depending on the severity of the error, the nature of the issue, and its impact on the results. To address these different levels of severity, the scientific literature has established a hierarchical system of corrective actions ranging from minor corrections to complete retraction.

Among the different levels of action in the retraction of scientific articles, we have to point out, first of all, the *minor correction*, applicable when errors do not significantly compromise the conclusions of a paper. Today, AI-assisted natural language processing and statistical analysis tools make it possible to identify typographical errors, incorrect references and inconsistent data before an article is published, providing automatic recommendations to editors for quick and accurate corrections (Ramos et al., 2024).

When *errors* are more *serious*, but do not completely invalidate the study and its conclusions, a major correction or *erratum* is issued. In these cases, the required correction involves updating information that could affect the interpretation of the results, without requiring a full retraction. Machine learning systems have proven effective in detecting incorrect calculations or significant statistical deviations prior to publication, using advanced tools such as *DataRefiner* and *Manuscript Analyzer* (Koçak, 2024; Matthews & Ferriss, 2024; Scarlat, 2017).

In more complex cases, when *serious errors* are detected or fraud is proven, a full retraction is issued, which involves labelling the article as 'retracted', allowing access to the detailed explanation of the reasons behind the decision taken. According to Bhatt (2021), full retraction is crucial when an error compromises the validity of the results or scientific misconduct is detected. This process ensures transparency and continuous correction of the scholarly record, promoting more rigorous ethical standards in scientific research. Massive data analysis algorithms such as *iThenticate* and *CrossRef Similarity Check* have optimised this process by systematically reviewing and generating automatic alerts for journal editors.

Accessibility of retracted articles is a fundamental principle to ensure transparency of the whole retraction process. Scientific journals typically retain the original article along with the retraction notice for public access. As for AI systems applied to scientific databases, they generate automatic alerts and allow labelling of problematic publications, ensuring that researchers can be informed of their status before citing or using them in future studies (Liverpool, 2023; Resnik et al., 2015).

In some cases, retractions are complemented by additional sanctions for authors, including temporary or permanent bans from publishing in certain journals. In this regard, Redman et al. (2008) highlight the importance of strict notifications to warn the scientific community about the seriousness of certain cases. AI makes it possible to automate this process through auditing systems such as *Author Integrity Tracker*, which detects suspicious patterns and generates reports for ethics committees, promoting a more transparent management of sanctions associated with scientific misconduct (Matthews & Ferriss, 2024; Razack et al., 2021).

Impact of Retractions on the Scientific Community and Scientific Integrity

Having defined the significance and scope of retractions, it is crucial to analyse their impact on the scientific community. Retractions significantly affect both individual researchers and institutions, as well as the academic ecosystem as a whole. For authors, particularly lead authors, retractions can severely damage their professional reputation, limiting their future ability to publish and participate in research projects (Memon et al., 2023; Azoulay et al., 2015). Additionally, they may face professional barriers and a decline in citation rates (Foo & Tan, 2014; Sharma & Mukherjee, 2023).

From an institutional point of view, scientific journals experience credibility losses when they must retract articles. This particularly affects high-impact journals, which try to respond to this challenge by developing more rigorous editorial policies and internal audits (Fang et al., 2012; Steen et al., 2013), costly actions in terms of editorial time and resources, which do not always succeed in fully restoring confidence in peer review processes. Furthermore, from a systemic perspective, retractions negatively impact on the funding and development of specific research areas (Brainard & You, 2018; Hesselmann et al., 2017; Stern et al., 2014).

On the other hand, retractions of scientific articles are essential to maintain the integrity of the scholarly record and trust in the scientific literature. However, their effectiveness can be compromised by the persistence of post-retraction citations, i.e. when retracted articles continue to be cited, sometimes even more than before their correction. This problem suggests substantial deficiencies in indexing systems and adequate notification of researchers (Friedman, 1990; Korpela, 2010). According to Bar-Ilan and Halevi (2017) persistence occurs due to lack of adequate visibility of retractions and academic inertia, as researchers often cite studies without verifying their status, unintentionally contributing to the dissemination of incorrect information (Bornemann-Cimenti et al., 2016). In addition, inconsistent editorial policies and inadequate retraction notices hinder the effectiveness of corrections.

Artificial intelligence (AI) can play a key role in mitigating this situation. Specifically, advanced algorithms can analyse a large volume of data using platforms such as *PubMed* and *Google Scholar*, which are able to automatically detect citations of retracted articles and generate real-time alerts. Similarly, systems such as *CrossRef Similarity Check* or *Manuscript Analyzer* allow precise semantic searches to identify and tag compromised research (Hagberg, 2020; Tang, 2023).

Ultimately, a collaborative approach between institutions, publishers journal and technology developers would ensure more effective management of the scholarly record, preserving transparency and trust in scientific research.

Tackling the problem of retractions requires coordinated action based on three fundamental pillars:

1. Strengthening indexing platforms: improving the signalling of retracted articles through automatic alerts and more visible warning labels.
2. Ethics and reference management training: develop training programmes for researchers and editors on citation checking and the ethical implications of citing retracted articles (Teixeira da Silva & Al-Khatib, 2021).
3. Proactive editorial monitoring: using AI algorithms to scan databases, detect problematic references and alert journal editors prior to publication (Furman et al., 2012; Tang, 2023).

Evolution of Scientific Retractions and Their Relation to the Use of Artificial Intelligence

Scientific retraction has gone through different stages, each marked by different milestones that transformed the editorial policies of scientific journals and the management of academic integrity, evolving to adapt to the needs of a more open science, with more rigorous regulatory frameworks and advanced technologies that allow more accurate detection of errors and fraud. In other words, from the first documented cases to the current integration of artificial intelligence (AI), the management of retractions has been refined to ensure transparency and preserve scientific credibility.

Historically, the first documented scientific retraction is dated 1977 in the journal *Infection and Immunity*, setting a precedent in the formal correction of the academic record. In 1990, the first retraction for duplicate publication was documented, illustrating how the scope of retractions has expanded over time. Both events show how retractions have diversified over time. Here are some of the key moments in this evolution and their characteristics.

During the 1990s, the need for ethical regulation became particularly important, driven by scientific scandals that highlighted the vulnerability of the academic system in the absence of institutional controls. These efforts were consolidated through the development of international legal frameworks and regulatory codes such as the Declaration of Helsinki, aimed at protecting the rights of human beings in biomedical research and promoting ethical standards and norms in scientific research (Broad & Wade, 1982; Lamas et al., 2010). Simultaneously, technological advancements enabled the development of open-access scientific databases, a crucial step in enhancing the visibility and scrutiny of published research. A fundamental event in this decade was the creation of PubMed in 1996, an open-access database with more than nineteen million bibliographic references on biomedical literature, which centralised scientific information by providing immediate access to research carried out in the field of health and strengthened peer review. In this sense, as Dellavalle et al. (2007) point out, access to open data and the strengthening of transparency standards became crucial elements to prevent fraud and improve academic integrity.

In the last years of the twentieth century, the pressure to publish articles in high-impact journals intensified enormously, driving scientific practices that, sometimes, prioritised quantity over quality. Particularly striking cases such as that of John R. Darsee, a cardiology researcher at Harvard University, who falsified data in more than eighty of his publications, had a devastating impact on academic trust and were the trigger that led to substantial reforms in scientific practices, the development of stricter auditing policies and the creation of institutional systems that professionalised ethical oversight (Broad & Wade, 1982). Recognition of the vulnerability of science in the absence of adequate controls encouraged the development of specific regulations to prevent fraud and data manipulation in scientific research.

Subsequently, in the period between 2000 and 2010, there was an expansion of transparency and public auditing. In this decade, on the one hand, the creation in 2002 of *Retraction Watch,* a website that publishes retractions of academic articles and scientific research, marked a turning point in scientific transparency and, on the other hand, the cases of Scott S. Reuben and Robert A. Slutsky, which highlighted the deficiencies in the processes for detecting fraud in publications by traditional publishers (Fang et al., 2012).

Between 2010 and 2020, the processes for detecting plagiarism and methodological errors in articles by scientific journals improved significantly, by integrating advanced tools such as *iThenticate* and *CrossRef Similarity Check* focused on detecting plagiarism, or platforms such as *Statcheck* and *DataRefiner* that strengthen automated statistical review, allowing the detection of data manipulation (Wang et al., 2019). However, authors such as

Resnick et al. (2015) warn of two risks associated with relying exclusively on algorithms: one, that they can generate false positives, and the other, that they can lead to errors in editorial decision-making.

From 2020 onwards we are in a new phase of AI-based monitoring. The COVID-19 pandemic intensified the pressure to publish, affecting especially the biomedical field. Indeed, individual journals such as *The Lancet* and the *New England Journal of Medicine* experienced an increase in retractions due to accelerated reviews and incomplete editorial processes (Lancaster & Salasevicius, 2023). The use of advanced AI models, such as machine learning systems that can analyse large amounts of data, generate automatic alerts and detect inconsistencies before publication, can help to avoid this situation. However, challenges related to algorithmic bias and editorial accuracy are still present and therefore require human supervision (Inastrilla et al., 2024).

In short, the AI-driven future of scientific retractions is shaping up to be a scenario of increased transparency and accuracy, where technology and human engagement must act in synergy to preserve the integrity of scientific knowledge. The continuing evolution of AI promises to redefine retraction processes in scientific research. As advanced algorithms become more accurate and accessible, their ability to reduce the publication of fraudulent studies and to improve the early detection of errors is becoming established as a fundamental pillar of academic integrity. Indeed, platforms such as *CrossRef Similarity Check* or *Retraction Watch AI* have proven effective in detecting plagiarism and manipulated data, providing automatic alerts that inform editors and reviewers of these facts before journals publish problematic studies (Matthews & Ferriss, 2024).

It should also be recognised that a key feature of AI is its presence throughout the entire publication process of an article: from the peer review phase to its subsequent publication. In this sense, with adaptive learning systems, errors not detected during the initial review of the publication can be corrected through continuous audits, thus strengthening the accuracy of the scientific record. In the long term, the development of neural networks and predictive algorithms could redefine the scientific review process, ranging from plagiarism detection to the evaluation of complex studies in areas such as the humanities, thus strengthening the ethical and methodological commitment of academic research (Resnick et al., 2015). But for this to materialise, it will be essential to combine these technological tools with clear ethical policies and continuous training processes for researchers and reviewers.

Main Causes of Misbehaviour Leading to Retraction

In the scientific literature, article retraction is seen as an essential mechanism for correcting errors and maintaining the integrity of the scientific record. The causes of retraction are many and varied and range from scientific misconduct, unintentional errors, contextual factors to inappropriate use of AI. We now turn to a more detailed explanation of each of these four types of causes of retraction of a scientific article.

Scientific Misconduct

Scientific misconduct is one of the main causes of retraction in academic research, seriously affecting the credibility of published research findings and the integrity of the scientific record. According to Castillo (2014), approximately 70% of retractions in biomedical journals are precisely the result of author misconduct.

Among the most common forms of scientific misconduct is *plagiarism*, which accounts for about 21% of the reasons for retraction (Fang et al., 2012; Kohl & Faggion, 2023). Plagiarism is defined as 'the appropriation of ideas, processes or results presented in a publication without giving credit to the author of the publication' (Saldaña-Gastulo, et al., 2010, p. 64). With the increasing use of AI, the concept of 'Agiarism' arises, which is described as the misuse of artificial intelligence (AI)-based tools to generate content without proper attribution. For Gallent-Torres et al. (2023) the proliferation of AI-based text generation platforms has intensified the problem of academic plagiarism; these authors highlight in their study that the inappropriate use of AI tools creates additional challenges for scientific journals, especially those with less strict editorial policies; they also propose, to mitigate this risk, to establish standards of ethical use and rigorous editorial practices that include the training of reviewers and editors in AI-based plagiarism detection technologies.

Another misconduct is the *falsification of data*, understood as the alteration or fabrication of data to obtain desired or expected results.

The *buying and selling of academic papers* is another scientific misconduct. In their research Lancaster and Salasevicius (2023) reveal that paid advertising services for academic papers on Google are offered on 49% of the portals they analysed, despite the fact that this contradicts the search engine's policies. The commercial exploitation of these platforms represents a considerable challenge to the promotion of academic integrity, especially in vulnerable fields such as the humanities and education.

Finally, *undeclared conflicts of interest* constitute another critical dimension of scientific misconduct. Resnick et al. (2015) argue that AI-based technologies have begun to address this problem through automated verification systems that cross-check databases and alert editors to potential inconsistencies in conflict of interest declarations. The technology developed significantly improves the early detection of ethical problems that previously relied solely on manual review by editors and reviewers.

Unintentional Errors

Errors in scientific research represent another relevant cause of retraction. Unlike scientific misconduct, they are usually unintentional, although their consequences can seriously compromise the validity of published work.

Common errors include design flaws, incorrect data analysis and errors in the interpretation of results. Wray and Andersen (2018) note that approximately 51% of retracted articles in the journal *Science* were retracted due to honest errors, highlighting that inaccuracy in research does not always imply fraudulent intent. However, errors are not exclusively limited to flaws in methodological design; inaccurate data collection, the use of inappropriate measurement instruments, or statistical errors can also lead to erroneous conclusions. These errors, although often arising from unforeseen circumstances, are significant enough to warrant a retraction that safeguards the accuracy of the scientific record (Jalalzadeh et al., 2017).

In this context, artificial intelligence (AI) has transformed the way errors are handled in the scientific literature. Wren (2018) argues that algorithms are capable of detecting complex errors prior to publication and also, that they are essential in post-publication as they allow the detection of errors that traditional methods miss, minimising problems related to miscalculations and omissions. For example, advanced tools such as *DataRefiner* and

Manuscript Analyzer have proven to be very effective in identifying statistical anomalies and methodological errors (Matthews & Ferriss, 2024); their ability to process large amounts of data and generate automatic alerts has strengthened editorial oversight, reducing the incidence of errors that previously went unnoticed. However, some problems manifest themselves even after the initial review. In fact, authors such as Habibzadeh (2018) or Fang et al. (2012) state that, in many cases, problems arise when the original data are revised with new techniques or analytical models, revealing inconsistencies not detected in previous revisions. The incorporation of predictive analytics and automated verification systems thus becomes a key strategy to mitigate these risks (Diong et al., 2018).

It should also be considered that errors are not always attributable to researchers. The editorial process plays a fundamental role in scientific integrity, especially in the management of scientific articles in fast-paced digital publishing environments. In fact, between 10% and 15% of retractions are attributable to editorial errors, a figure that could decrease with better review and control practices (Moilan & Kowalczuk, 2016). In this regard, Espiñeira-Bellón et al. (2023) highlight the lack of uniform policies and the need to establish shared procedures among scientific journals to minimise editorial errors. Likewise, ethical training of editors and researchers is a key element to improve early detection and reduce the incidence of fraudulent publications and unintentional errors. Along the same lines, Gallent-Torres et al. (2023) recommend that journals adopt active monitoring policies through automated verification systems. Ramos et al. (2024) show that these technologies not only identify editorial problems before publication but can also generate real-time alerts that inform editors and reviewers of possible errors.

Contextual Factors

In the complex dynamics of scientific publishing, contextual factors such as the manipulation of the peer review process, pressure to publish or institutional incentives can create an environment that fosters breaches of scientific integrity and, consequently, the occurrence of retractions.

Thus, the manipulation of the process *peer review* becomes one of the causes of retraction. Authors and editors sometimes resort to mock reviews to ensure the publication of a study, highlighting the need for rigorous controls and oversight systems that combine technology and human review (Tang, 2023; Resnick et al., 2015). Platforms such as *Manuscript Analyzer* are helpful in identifying these practices prior to publication (Gallent-Torres et al., 2023). In some cases, the peer review process fails to detect significant errors or ethical issues prior to publication of a paper, which subsequently leads to the retraction of the article (Atlas, 2004). This deficiency may be exacerbated in environments where review processes rely excessively on automated systems without adequate human oversight, as Gallent-Torres et al. (2023) warn, pointing out that algorithmic review cannot always replace expert judgement. Today, it can be said that scientific culture has moved towards transparency. Along these lines, scientific journals have adopted stricter editorial policies that promote self-retraction and strengthen peer review processes, improving confidence in the scholarly record (Graham, 2023; Retraction Watch Database, 2022). Still, experts such as Oransky (2022) argue that further strengthening of control systems is needed to ensure the integrity of scientific output.

In other cases, the growing *pressure* on researchers *to publish* in high-impact journals can lead to ethical lapses and errors that result in retractions. A highly competitive environment, combined with the ability to manipulate metrics through advanced technologies, fosters questionable practices and compromises research quality (Ribeiro & Vasconcelos, 2018). The expression 'publish or perish' has become a key descriptor of this dynamic (Freijedo-Fariñas et al., 2024). The growth of so-called 'article mills' represents a significant threat to academic integrity. These entities produce spurious research on a large scale, challenging even the most prestigious journals and automated detection systems (Graham, 2023; Van Noorden, 2023). The development of databases such as *Retraction Watch* and the use of advanced data analysis technologies have significantly improved the detection of problematic research. Similarly, machine learning algorithms can predict future retractions by analysing full text and structured data (Modukuri et al., 2021; Zheng et al., 2024). However, their effectiveness depends on ethical implementation and integration with expert human review (Resnick et al., 2015).

Finally, *incentives and rewards for publishing* can compromise the scientific integrity of researchers, increasing the rate of retractions. The proliferation of AI-based text generation platforms has further complicated this scenario, as their inappropriate use facilitates the submission of academic papers without due methodological rigour or ethical authorship (Comas-Forgas et al., 2023). Today, some studies document that the growth of public databases such as *Retraction Watch* and the use of artificial intelligence systems account for malpractices that previously went unnoticed (Horbach & Halffman, 2018; Modukuri et al., 2021).

Inappropriate Use of AI

With the beginning of the new century, the phenomenon of retractions has been driven by the proliferation of technological tools and a scientific culture focused on greater transparency and editorial accountability Freijedo-Fariñas et al., 2024; Shuai et al., 2017).

Research errors are inevitable, but the possibility of mitigating them through advanced technologies offers an unprecedented opportunity to improve the accuracy and reliability of the scientific record. Artificial intelligence, applied from research design to editorial management, has established itself as a crucial tool for preventing and correcting errors, ensuring a more transparent and rigorous scholarly output. However, artificial intelligence (AI), while primarily used to mitigate errors, can also contribute to their production when used inappropriately or for unethical purposes. Recent studies suggest that some researchers use AI tools to generate data or text without proper attribution, which represents an emerging ethical challenge (Muñoz-Cantero & Espiñeira-Bellón, 2024).

Finally, post-publication review is a clear example of how AI is redefining the life cycle of a scientific article. Continuous audits using machine *learning algorithms* allow for the detection of errors that may have gone unnoticed during the initial review. This constant corrective capability ensures that the scholarly record is increasingly accurate and reliable. Machine learning algorithms facilitate the detection of anomalies in data and texts, improving the accuracy of the scholarly record. Examples include platforms such as *Retractions Wath* (Retraction Watch Data base, 2022) capable of issuing automatic alerts about possible errors or suspicious behaviour, or *CrossRef Similarity Check* and *PubPeer*, for real-time notification of possible problems detected in recent publications (Dinh et al., 2019; Modukuri et al., 2021). The use of platforms that allow automated data verification has become a key solution to avoid retractions. Requiring authors to share their raw data at the outset ensures more rigorous validation prior to publication. AI allows complex datasets to be audited and checked for anomalies, improving confidence in the results presented.

Table 4 summarises the main causes leading to the retraction of scientific articles according to the reviewed literature, describing their most notable characteristics.

Table 4: Causes leading to the retraction of scientific articles

Causes	Actions	Description	References
Scientific misconduct	Data Falsification	Alteration or invention of data to obtain desired results.	Castillo (2014); Fang et al. (2012)
	Plagiarism	Unauthorised use of ideas or text without proper attribution.	Comas-Forgas et al. (2023); Espiñeira-Bellón et al. (2023)
	IAgiarism	Misuse of AI to generate academic texts without attribution.	Muñoz-Cantero & Espiñeira-Bellón (2024)
	Buying and Selling Works	Marketing of academic work through web-based platforms.	Lancaster & Salasevicius (2023)
	Undeclared conflicts of interest	Failure to disclose financial or personal interests.	Resnick et al. (2015)
Unintentional errors	Methodological errors	Design flaws or incorrect data analysis.	Wray & Andersen (2018); Jalalzadeh et al. (2017)
	Errors of interpretation	Incorrect interpretation of results.	Habibzadeh (2018); Fang et al. (2012)
	Editorial errors	Technical problems such as layout errors or incorrect references.	Espiñeira-Bellón et al. (2023); Kowalczuk (2016)
Contextual factors	Peer Review Poor	Failure to detect errors and ethical issues before publication.	Atlas (2004); Gallent-Torres et al. (2023)
	Pressure to Publish	Competition to publish in high-impact journals.	Ribeiro & Vasconcelos (2018)
	Incentives and Rewards	Rewards that generate risky behaviour and quick publications.	Walsh et al. (2018)

(Continued)

Table 4: *(Continued)*

Causes	Actions	Description	References
Inappropriate use of AI	Automation of revisions	Use of AI to review scientific articles before publication.	Matthews & Ferriss (2024); Wren (2018)
	Automatic Text Generation	Automatic production of academic content by AI.	Moya & Eaton (2023); Bolshakov (2021)
	Algorithmic Monitoring	Error detection using advanced algorithms.	Ramos et al. (2024); Gallent-Torres et al. (2023)

Conclusions

The analysis of scientific retractions reveals that this phenomenon is multidimensional and driven by historical, technological and social factors.

As highlighted, the main causes of retractions range from scientific misconduct and methodological errors to structural factors such as pressure to publish or manipulation of editorial processes. These actions underline the need to improve institutional oversight, promote self-regulation and strengthen ethical auditing processes.

The historical trajectory of scientific retractions shows an evolution marked by the necessity to correct errors and uphold academic integrity. Traditional methods of reviewing scientific publications, primarily based on human intervention, have proven to be insufficient in adequately addressing this task, given the increasing volume of publications and the complexity of current studies. In this context, artificial intelligence has emerged as an essential tool to prevent retractions and reinforce transparency in the editorial process.

Advancements in artificial intelligence have marked a turning point, strengthening error, fraud and plagiarism detection processes. However, technology alone is not sufficient. Ethics training must evolve to include the responsible use of AI in scientific research. This requires equipping authors, reviewers, and editors with the skills to properly handle these tools, avoiding algorithmic biases and ensuring data privacy. Ethics must not only apply to human conduct, but also to the development and use of algorithms that affect the fate of scientific publications.

In this context, the future of scientific retractions is envisioned as a more transparent and proactive process, where artificial intelligence and human oversight work together to strengthen research quality. The ethical and strategic integration of these technologies represents a historic opportunity to reduce errors, prevent fraud and promote fairer and more reliable scientific enterprise.

Since the impact of retractions extends beyond academia – affecting public trust in science, funding, and public policies based on discredited research – it is essential to reinforce automated alert systems and ethical education for researchers. Ethical and technological commitment must be consolidated in the development of new editorial monitoring tools and in the promotion of a culture of scientific integrity. Only through the synergy between technology and human oversight can a more transparent, accurate and reliable academic record be guaranteed for future generations of researchers.

AI Use Declaration

This chapter was developed by Jesús Miguel Muñoz Cantero, Ana M.ª Porto Castro, M.ª Josefa Mosteiro García, and Enelina M.ª Gerpe Pérez with the support of generative artificial intelligence tools (ChatGPT-4o, OpenAI) to enhance the quality of writing and content structure. In accordance with recommendations on transparency in the use of artificial intelligence in academic writing, it is declared that AI was used as an assistive tool without replacing intellectual authorship or responsibility for the presented content. All final decisions regarding editing, validation, and review of the chapter remain exclusively with the authors.

Acknowledgements

Chapter elaborated within the framework of the support provided by the Secretaría Xeral de Universidades of the Consellería de Cultura, Educación e Universidade of the Xunta de Galicia, which has fostered research on academic integrity and the impact of artificial intelligence in higher education within the Galician University System (SUG) over the past years. This research has been developed under the project OTRI Universidade da Coruña, Administrative Record Reference: OTR0424

Bibliography

Atlas, M. C. (2004). Retraction policies of high-impact biomedical journals. *Journal of the Medical Library Association, 92*(2), 242–250. https://pubmed.ncbi.nlm.nih.gov/15098054/

Azoulay, P., Bonatti, A., & Krieger, J. L. (2015). The career effects of scandal: Evidence from scientific retractions. *Research Policy, 44*(8), 1510–1523. http://dx.doi.org/10.1016/j.respol.2017.07.003

Bar-Ilan, J., & Halevi, G. (2017). Post retraction citations in context: A case study. *Scientometrics, 113*(1), 547–565. org/10.1007/s11192-017-2242-0

Bhatt, B. A. (2021). Multi-perspective analysis of retractions in life sciences. *Scientometrics, 126*, 4039–4054. https://link.springer.com/article/10.1007/s11192-021-03907-0

Bolshakov, D. Y. (2021). *Analytics in the publication of a scientific journal. Science Editor and Publisher, 5*(2), 102–112. https://doi.org/10.24069/2542-0267-2020-2-102-112

Bornemann-Cimenti, H., Szilagyi, I. S., & Sandner-Kiesling, A. (2016). Perpetuation of retracted publications using the example of the Scott S. Reuben case: Incidences, reasons, and possible improvements. *Science and Engineering Ethics, 22*(4), 1063–1072. https://doi.org/10.1007/s11948-015-9680-y

Brainard, J., & You, J. (2018). *What a massive database of retracted papers reveals about science publishing's 'death penalty'.* Science. https://www.science.org/content/article/what-massive-database-retracted-papers-reveals-about-science-publishing-s-death-penalty

Broad, W., & Wade, N. (1982). *Betrayers of the Truth: Fraud and Deceit in the Halls of Science.* Simon & Schuster.

Casadevall, A., Steen, R. G., & Fang, F. C. (2014). Sources of error in the retracted scientific literature. *FEMS Microbiology Letters, 28*, 3847–3855. https://doi.org/10.1096/fj.14-256735

Casadevall, A., Steen, R. G., & Fang, F. C. (2014). Sources of error in the retracted scientific literature. *The FASEB Journal, 28*(10), 3847–3855. https://doi.org/10.1096/fj.14-256735

Castillo, M. (2014). The fraud and retraction epidemic. *American Journal of Neuroradiology, 35*(9), 1653–1654. https://doi.org/10.3174/ajnr.A3835

Comas-Forgas, R., Cerdà-Navarro, A., Touza Garma, C., & Moreno Herrera, L. (2023). Prevalence and factors associated with academic plagiarism in new students of Social Work and Social Education: an empirical analysis. *RELIEVE – Revista Electrónica De Investigación Y Evaluación Educativa, 29*(2). https://doi.org/10.30827/relieve.v29i2.29055

COPE (2019). Guidelines for managing the relationships between society owned journals, their society, and publishers. https://doi.org/10.24318/cope.2018.1.2

Dellavalle, R., Lundahl, K., Freeman, S., & Schilling, L. (2007). Journals should set a new standard in transparency. *Nature*, *445*, 364–364. https://doi.org/10.1038/445364a

Dinh, L., Cheng, Y.-Y., & Parulian, N. N. (2019). ReTracker: An open-source plugin for automated and standardized tracking of retracted scholarly publications. *Proceedings of the 2019 ACM/IEEE Joint Conference on Digital Libraries (JCDL)*, 406–407. https://doi.org/10.1109/JCDL.2019.00092

Diong, J., Butler, A., Gandevia, S., & Héroux, M. (2018). Poor statistical reporting, inadequate data presentation and spin persist despite editorial advice. *PLoS ONE, 13*(8). e0202121. https://doi.org/10.1371/journal.pone.0202121

Espiñeira-Bellón, E. Mª., Muñoz-Cantero, J. M., Porto-Castro, A. Mª., & Mosteiro-García, Mª. J. (2023). Perceptions and effectiveness of plagiarism detection mechanisms in Spanish, Portuguese and Ibero-American Social Science journals. *RELIEVE*, *29*(2), art. M2. https://doi.org/10.30827/relieve.v29i2.29097

Fang, F. C., Steen, R. G., & Casadevall, A. (2012). Misconduct accounts for the majority of retracted scientific publications. *Proceedings of the National Academy of Sciences, 109*(42), 17028–17033. https://doi.org/10.1073/pnas.1212247109

Foo, J., & Tan, X. (2014). Analysis and Implications of Retraction Period and Coauthorship of Fraudulent Publications. *Accountability in Research*, *21*, 198–210. https://doi.org/10.1080/08989621.2013.848799

Freijedo-Farinas, F., Ruano-Ravina, A., Pérez-Ríos, M. *et al.* (2024) Biomedical retractions due to misconduct in Europe: characterization and trends in the last 20 years. *Scientometrics*, *129*, 2867–2882. https://doi.org/10.1007/s11192-024-04992-7

Friedman, P. J. (1990). Correcting the literature following fraudulent publication. *Journal of the American Medical Association*, *263*(10), 1416–1419. https://doi.org/10.1001/jama.1990.03440100136019

Furman, J., Jensen, K. & Murray, F. (2012). Governing knowledge in the scientific community: Exploring the role of retractions in biomedicine. *Research Policy, 41*(2), 276–290.https://doi.org/10.1016/j.respol.2011.11.001

Gallent-Torres, C., Zapata-González, A., & Ortego-Hernando, J. L. (2023). The impact of generative artificial intelligence in higher education:

a look from ethics and academic integrity. *Relieve. Revista Electrónica de Investigación y Evaluación Educativa, 29* (2). https://doi.org/10.30827/relieve.v29i2.29134

Graham, F. (2023). Daily briefing: Record number of papers retracted in 2023. Nature. https://doi.org/10.1038/d41586-023-04035-w

Habibzadeh, F. (2018). Editorial Process and Peer Review. In P. Sahni & R. Aggarwal (Eds.), *Reporting and Publishing Research in the Biomedical Sciences*, 217–224. Springer. https://doi.org/10.1007/978-981-10-7062-4_21

Hagberg, J. (2020). The Unfortunately Long Life of Some Retracted Biomedical Research Publications. *Journal of Applied Physiology, 128*(5), 1381–1391. https://doi.org/10.1152/japplphysiol.00003.2020

Hesselmann, F., Graf, V., Schmidt, M., & Reinhart, M. (2017). The visibility of scientific misconduct: A review of the literature on retracted journal articles. *Current Sociology, 65*(6), 814–845. https://doi.org/10.1177/0011392116663807

Horbach, S., & Halffman, W. (2018). The ability of different peer review procedures to flag problematic publications. *Scientometrics, 118*(1), 339–373. https://doi.org/10.1007/s11192-018-2969-2

Inastrilla, C., Santana, M., Vera, D., Del Carmen Roche Madrigal, M., Urrutia, A., & Inastrilla, A. (2024). Systematic review on Artificial Intelligence in the editorial management of scientific journals. *EAI Endorsed Transactions on AI and Robotics, 3*, 1–6. https://doi.org/10.4108/airo.5643

Jalalzadeh, S., Abbasi, F., & Pashazadeh, F. (2017). 212: Scientometrics study of published retractions in PubMed. *BMJ Open*, 7(Suppl 2). https://doi.org/10.1136/bmjopen-2016-015415.212. https://doi.org/10.1136/bmjopen-2016-015415.212

Koçak, Z. (2024). Publication ethics in the era of artificial intelligence. *Journal of Korean Medical Science, 39*, e249. https://doi.org/10.3346/jkms.2024.39.e249

Kohl, C., & Faggion, C. (2023). A comprehensive overview of studies that assessed article retractions within the biomedical sciences. *Accountability in research, 31*(6), 557–575. https://doi.org/10.1080/08989621.2022.2154660

Korpela, K. M. (2010). How long does it take for the scientific literature to purge itself of fraudulent material? The Breuning case revisited. *Current Medical Research and Opinion, 26*(4), 843–847. https://doi.org/10.1185/03007991003603804

Lamas, E., Ferrer, M., Molina-Pérez, A., Salinas, R., Hevia, A., Bota, A., Feinholz, D., Fuchs, M., Schramm, R., Tealdi, J., & Zorrilla, S. (2010). A comparative analysis of biomedical research ethics regulation systems in Europe and Latin America with regard to the protection of human subjects. *Journal of Medical Ethics*, *36*, 750–753. https://doi.org/10.1136/jme.2009.035097.

Lancaster, T. E., & Salasevicius, M. (2023). An international comparison of the academic paper buying and selling industry. *Relief. Electronic Journal of Educational Research and Evaluation*, *29*(2), art. M3. https://doi.org/10.30827/relieve.v29i2.29227

Liverpool, L. (2023). AI intensifies fight against 'paper mills' that churn out fake research. *Nature*, *618*, 222–223. https://www.nature.com/articles/d41586-023-01780-w

Májovský, M., Černý, M., Kasal, M., Komarc, M., & Netuka, D. (2023). Artificial Intelligence Can Generate Fraudulent but Authentic-Looking Scientific Medical Articles: Pandora's Box Has Been Opened. *Journal of Medical Internet Research*, *25*, e46924. https://doi.org/10.2196/46924

Matthews, B. J., & Ferriss, J. (2024). Finding errors in the blink of AI: Use of an artificial intelligence tool to identify clinically important corrections to references cited by NCCN Guidelines for gynecologic malignancies. *Journal of Clinical Oncology*, *42*(16). https://doi.org/10.1200/JCO.2024.42.16_suppl.e13658

Memon, S. A., Makovi, K., & AlShebli, B. (2023). Characterizing the effect of retractions on scientific careers. *arXiv*:2306.06710 [cs.SI]. https://doi.org/10.48550/arXiv.2306.06710

Modukuri, S. A., Rajtmajer, S., Squicciarini, A., Wu, J., & Giles, C. L. (2021). Understanding and predicting retractions of published work. Retraction Watch Database. *SDUAAAI.* https://www.semanticscholar.org/paper/Understanding-and-Predicting-Retractions-of-Work-Modukuri-Rajtmajer/3dcba4fa5bc69966064f154d57ec68aa6234266f?utm_source=consens

Moilan, E. C., & Kowalczuk, M. K. (2016). Why articles are retracted: a retrospective cross-sectional study of retraction notices at BioMed Central. *BMJ Open*, *6* (11): e012047. https://doi.org/10.1136/bmjopen-2016-012047

Moya, B. A., & Eaton, S. E. (2023). Examining Recommendations for the Use of Generative Artificial Intelligence with Integrity from a Teaching and Learning Lens. *Relief. Electronic Journal of Educational Research and Evaluation*, *29*(2), art. M1. https://doi.org/10.30827/relieve.v29i2.29295

Muñoz-Cantero, J. M. & Espiñeira-Bellón, E. M. (2024). Intelligent Plagiarism as a Misconduct in Academic Integrity. *Acta Médica Portuguesa 37*(19), 1–2. https://doi.org/10.20344/amp.20233

Oransky, I. (2022). Retractions are increasing, but not enough. *Nature, 608* (7921), 9. https://doi.org/10.1038/d41586-022-02071-6

Ramos, S., Perez-Lopez, J. A., & Abreu, R. (2024). Bibliometric Analysis of Artificial Intelligence Trends in Auditing and Fraud Detection [Special issue]. *Corporate Governance and Organizational Behavior Review, 8* (2), 330–342. https://doi.org/10.22495/cgobrv8i2sip8

Razack, H. I. A., Mathew, S. T., Saad, F. F. A., & Alqahtani, S. (2021). Artificial intelligence-assisted tools for redefining the communication landscape of the scholarly world. *Scientometrics, 8*(2), 134–144. https://consensus.app/papers/artificial-intelligenceassisted-tools-for-redefining-razack-mathew/55ad74041c8e52cdafcb91a4656ed3c3

Redman, B., Yarandi, H., & Merz, J. (2008). Empirical developments in retraction. *Journal of the Medical Ethics, 34*, 807–809. https://doi.org/10.1136/jme.2007.023069

Resnick, D., Wager, E., & Kissling G. (2015). Retraction policies of top scientific journals ranked by impact factor. *Journal of the medical Library Association, 103*(3), 136–139. https://doi.org/10.3163/1536-5050.103.3.006

Retraction Watch Database (2022). *Retraction Watch: The Center For Scientific Integrity.* https://retractionwatch.com/retracted-studies

Ribeiro, M. D., & Vasconcelos, S. M. R. (2018). Retractions covered by Retraction Watch in the 2013–2015 period: Prevalence for the most productive countries. *Scientometrics, 114*(2), 719–734. https://doi.org/10.1007/s11192-017-2621-6

Saldaña-Gastulo, J. J., Quezada-Osoria, C., Pena-Oscuvilca, A., and Mayta-Tristan, P. (2010). High frequency of plagiarism in medical theses at a Peruvian public university. *Revista Peruana de Medicina Experimental y Salud Pública*, 27(1), 63–67.http://www.scielo.org.pe/scielo.php?script=sci_arttext&pid=S1726-46342010000100011

Scarlat, M. (2017). Erratum, corrigenda et emendatio or 'mistake, correction and amendment'. *International Orthopaedics, 41*, 1071–1072. https://doi.org/10.1007/s00264-017-3501-7

Sharma, K., & Mukherjee, S. (2023). The Ripple Effect of Retraction on an Author's Collaboration Network. *ArXiv*, abs/2310.05941. https://doi.org/10.48550/arXiv.2310.05941

Shuai, X., Rollins, J., Moulinier, I., Custis, T., Edmunds, M. and Schilder, F. (2017). A Multi-dimensional Investigation of the Effects of

Publication Retraction on Scholarly Impact. *Journal of the Association for Information Science and Technology, 68*(9), 2225–2236. https://doi.org/10.1002/asi.23826
Steen, R. G., Casadevall, A., & Fang F. C. (2013). Correction: Why has the number of Scientific Retractions Increased?. *PLoS ONE 8*(7). 10.1371/annotation/0d28db18-e117-4804-b1bc-e2da285103ac. https://doi.
Stern, A. M., Casadevall, A., Steen, R. G., & Fang, F. C. (2014). Financial costs and personal consequences of research misconduct resulting in retracted publications. *eLife*, *3*, e02956. https://doi.org/10.7554/elife.02956
Tang, B. L. (2023). Some Insights into the Factors Influencing Continuous Citation of Retracted Scientific Papers. *Publications*, *11*(4), 47, 1–14. https://doi.org/10.3390/publications11040047
Teixeira da Silva, J. A., & Al-Khatib, A. (2021). Ending the retraction stigma: encouraging the reporting of errors in the biomedical record. *Research Ethics, 17* (2), 251–259. https://doi.org/10.1177/1747016118802970
Van Noorden, R. (2023, 12 December). More than 10,000 research papers withdrawn in 2023, a new record. *Nature.* https://doi.org/10.1038/d41586-023-03974-8
Walsh, J. P., Lee, Y. N., & Tang, L. (2018). Pathogenic organization in science: Division of labor and retractions. *Research Policy, 47*(8), 1471–1482. https://doi.org/10.1016/j.respol.2018.09.004
Wang, C., Hsu, H. C. K., Bonem, E. M., Moss, J., Yu, S., Nelson, D., & Levesque-Bristol, C. (2019). Need satisfaction and need dissatisfaction: A comparative study of online and face-to-face learning contexts. *Computers in Human Behavior, 95*, 114–125. https://doi.org/10.1016/j.chb.2019.01.034
Wray, K. B., & Andersen, L. E. (2018). Retractions in Science. *Scientometrics, 117*(3), 2009–2019. https://doi.org/10.1007/s11192-018-2922-4
Wren, J. (2018). Algorithmically outsourcing the detection of statistical errors and other problems. *The EMBO Journal, 37*, 1–3. https://doi.org/10.15252/embj.201899651
Zheng, E.-T., Fu, H.-Z., & Fang, Z. (2024). Can ChatGPT predict article retraction based on Twitter mentions? *ArXiv.* https://doi.org/10.48550/arXiv.2403.16851

Excellence and Academic Integrity in the Age of Artificial Intelligence: An Ibero-American Perspective

Jean G. Guerrero-Dib[1], *Luz H. Godina-Silva*[2] *and Ana C. Muñiz-Pérez*[3]

ABSTRACT
In light of the challenging state of an emerging culture of academic integrity, the rise of generative artificial intelligence tools, and the limitations of current technologies to detect their involvement in academic deliverables such as essays, reports, presentations, and projects, a shared concern has arisen among faculty and institutions: how to 'protect' learning in university classrooms while ensuring both excellence and academic integrity. This chapter provides a comparative analysis of guidelines issued by select Ibero-American universities regarding the use of technology tools in teaching and learning processes and offers criteria and recommendations to strengthen the culture of academic integrity in a context increasingly shaped by the presence of artificial intelligence.

Keywords: academic integrity, artificial intelligence, generative artificial intelligence, policies for AI use, academic policies

Introduction

The study of academic integrity in Ibero-America remains in its early stages. This is evidenced by the limited number of published studies written in Spanish available in comparison to written and published in English. Similarly, efforts to develop robust standards and comprehensive academic integrity programmes are still scarce, both in terms of quantity and quality. While it is common to find universities that formally and fiercely stand against academic dishonesty, many fail to demonstrate a systematic and intentional approach to addressing it with adequate policies, resources and budget.

A notable exception is a recent initiative by a Mexican accrediting agency, which has encouraged universities to conduct diagnostics and implement

[1] Universidad de Monterrey, México, https://orcid.org/0000-0003-3150-9363
[2] Universidad de Monterrey, México, https://orcid.org/0000-0001-6475-6438
[3] Universidad de Monterrey, México, https://orcid.org/0009-0007-3918-2189

action plans to mitigate the concerning levels of academic dishonesty. Although the limited number of published studies generally reflect the situation of specific institutions, they consistently indicate that academic misconduct is still a significant problem within Ibero-American higher education. As reported in the following sections, between 52% and 90% of students at various universities admit having engaged in or witnessed breaches of academic integrity.

While the unethical use of generative artificial intelligence (GenAI) applications remains less prevalent compared to traditional forms of academic misconduct, its occurrence has doubled within just one year. This astonishing increase, coupled with the growing accessibility and use of AI technologies, presents a considerable challenge for higher education institutions. In response, many universities have instinctively issued policies to regulate the use of these tools in teaching and learning processes.

This chapter presents the findings of a comparative content analysis of publicly available regulations on the use of GenAI in eight prominent Ibero-American universities, comprising one from Argentina, one from Chile, one from Colombia, two from Spain, and three from Mexico. The results offer valuable insights for other institutions seeking to draft or update their own policies, providing practical guidance tailored to various stakeholders within the academic community.

Key findings include the identification of common institutional guidelines, the definition of faculty responsibilities, and the establishment of clear expectations for students. Additionally, the chapter provides actionable recommendations to help universities adopt a more systemic and forward-thinking approach to the integration and regulation of AI technologies in academic contexts.

In the following section, the chapter explores the current state of academic integrity culture in Ibero-American higher education institutions.

The State of Academic Integrity in Higher Education Institutions in Ibero-America

Numerous international studies have examined the prevalence of various forms of academic dishonesty from the perspectives of both students and faculty. Among the most notable are the ones conducted by Bowers (1964) and its replication by McCabe (2016) years later. However, no publications have been identified that specifically report on the state of academic integrity in higher education institutions across Ibero-America. Academic integrity – and conversely, the issue of academic dishonesty – has only recently begun to receive scholarly attention in the region.

The state of academic integrity in Latin America has been scarcely investigated (García-Villegas et al., 2016). In 2020, Ayala et al. conducted a quick review of articles and papers in scientific databases and electronic libraries such as Latindex and SciELO, finding only a very limited body of research. For this chapter, a similar effort was undertaken to examine the number of articles available over the years in 'Google Scholar' and 'Google Académico' using the search terms 'academic integrity' in English and 'integridad académica' in Spanish. The results obtained are shown in Figure 3.

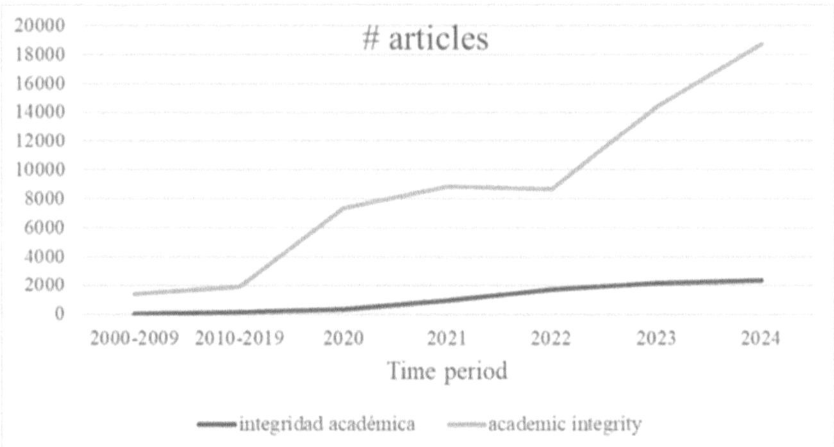

Figure 3: Number of articles found in 'Google Scholar' and 'Google Académico' using the terms 'academic integrity' (English) and 'integridad académica' (Spanish).

As shown in Figure 3, there are eight times more publications related to 'academic integrity' than to 'integridad académica' (18,700 vs. 2,340), and if current trends persist, this gap will likely continue to widen.

The studies that have been published primarily consist of isolated surveys and assessments conducted at universities in Portugal, Spain and Latin America. Table 5 provides examples of some of these studies.

Table 5: Examples of studies conducted at Ibero-American Universities

Country	Key Findings on Academic Dishonesty	Citation
Argentina	78% of students admitted to allowing peers to copy during an exam.	Ventura et al., 2012
Brazil	83% of students reported having cheated in exams or course assessments.	da Costa et al., 2006
Colombia	Over 90% of students acknowledged engaging in some form of academic fraud during university.	Martínez & Ramírez, 2018
Costa Rica	69% of students attributed their academic dishonesty to external factors.	Campos Céspedes & Solano Gutiérrez, 2012
Ecuador	70% of students reported having engaged in academic dishonesty.	Quispe & Ruiz, 2024
Mexico	52% of students perceived that their peers used unauthorised materials during exams, and 63% admitted to copying during tests.	Guerrero-Dib, 2020
Peru	81% of evaluated theses contained some form of plagiarism.	Saldaña-Gastulo et al., 2010
Portugal	62% of students admitted to having copied at least once.	Teixeira & de Fátima Oliveira Rocha, 2010
Puerto Rico	Up to 75% of students admitted to engaging in academically dishonest behaviour at least once.	Medina-Díaz & Verdejo-Carrión, 2005
Spain	Nearly 75% of students reported having allowed others to copy at least once.	Comas et al., 2011

As seems evident from the data, there have been few comprehensive efforts to synthesise the state of academic integrity in the Ibero-American region. Furthermore, most existing research focuses on assessing academic dishonesty rather than academic integrity itself. Notably, the second and most recent edition of the *Handbook for Academic Integrity* (Eaton, 2024) – the most comprehensive compilation effort on the subject – does not include a dedicated chapter on Ibero-America in its section on 'Global Perspectives on Academic Integrity' as it does for many other regions of the world. There is a clear need to expand research efforts to develop a more comprehensive understanding of academic integrity in Latin America to, as Ayala et al. (2020, p. 31) state, 'have a complete perspective of all of the issues around academic integrity in Latin America'.

Nonetheless, as part of this chapter, we present findings from an initiative led by the 'Federación de Instituciones Mexicanas Particulares de Educación Superior' (FIMPES) in the Mexican context which can serve as a sample of what is happening in the area. Since 2019, FIMPES, the most prestigious accreditation agency in Mexico has incorporated academic integrity requirements into its accreditation system (Federación de Instituciones Mexicanas Particulares de Educación Superior [FIMPES], 2023). These requirements compel affiliated universities to demonstrate their efforts in promoting academic integrity.

Firstly, FIMPES introduced a distinction in academic integrity, allowing affiliated institutions to formally showcase their commitment to integrity. This distinction consists of three levels, requiring institutions to administer a survey and develop an action plan aimed at enhancing their academic integrity culture by addressing identified areas for improvement.

Additionally, FIMPES incorporated an accreditation criterion requiring that affiliated institutions demonstrate that they 'possess the structures, policies, and procedures, and utilise assessment results to fulfil their Mission and Educational Model, ensuring continuous improvement in the promotion of academic integrity at all levels' (2023, p. 5).

As part of this initiative, institutions seeking the distinction in academic integrity gained access to the results of the eighth cohort of universities that administered the 'Academic Motivation and Integrity Survey' (Stephens, 2024). In this so-called administration, five Mexican universities participated, implementing the survey during the first semester of 2024. This instrument evaluates perceptions related to:

- Academic and Social Climate (e.g. emphasis on developing academic competence, perceptions of faculty as caring and fair);
- Academic Integrity Policies (e.g. whether policies are well-communicated, understood, effective, supported, fair, and enforced);
- Peer Norms (e.g. disapproval of cheating and perceptions of peer cheating behaviour);
- Moral Attitudes (e.g. tendencies to justify or minimise moral responsibility for cheating); and
- Engagement in Academic Misconduct.

On average, 66.3% of surveyed students admitted to having engaged in at least one form of academic dishonesty listed in the survey (compared to a maximum of 86% when considering all eight cohorts since 2019, in which fifty-six institutions have participated). Additionally, 23.8% of students reported using digital technologies to obtain assistance during a test or exam, compared to 28.5% when considering all prior survey administrations (Stephens, 2024).

In the last three administrations of the survey, students were also asked whether they had used artificial intelligence (AI) to write all or part of an assignment and submitted it as their own. Results indicate an accelerated increase – more than double – in this form of academic misconduct, with reported cases rising from a range of 11%-20% in the first trimester of 2023 to 18%-43% in the most recent administration (first trimester of 2024), undoubtedly the fastest-growing trend among academic misconduct behaviours (Stephens, 2024).

The next section will explore the concept of artificial intelligence, its applications across various industries – particularly in education – and the impact it is projected to have on the field.

Literature Review

This section briefly explores the concepts of AI and GenAI, as well as their applications in businesses and different industries. It focuses on the most common uses in education, highlighting their benefits, limitations, and risks. It also describes the degree of use reported by students and teachers in various research exercises. Finally, it explains what AI-generated text detection software is and how it works, as well as its performance and effectiveness according to various studies.

Generative Artificial Intelligence Tools

Artificial Intelligence

AI is a concept that has evolved since 1950, when the first article exploring the possibility of machines thinking was published (Turing, 2009). This evolution has been driven, among other factors, by the rapid growth of AI as a field of study in recent years. Currently, the term refers to the capacity of technological systems to simulate human intelligence, that is, to replicate mental functions and emulate human cognitive abilities (Posso Pacheco et al., 2025). AI operates by recognising patterns in large amounts of data, allowing systems to make inferences, build algorithms and mathematical models, and learn automatically and autonomously to facilitate decision-making – in essence, to perceive, understand, predict, and manipulate the world (Russell & Norving, 2021).

Generative Artificial Intelligence

GenAI refers to a specialised branch type of AI technology that creates new content – such as texts, images, audios and videos – based on the statistical probability of correctness, using large pre-fed and available datasets (Campbell, 2023). These outputs are obtained through concise, logical and precise prompt instructions alongside a reasonable degree of user interaction, whereby users evaluate and refine the generated outputs until the desired results are achieved (Goff, 2025).

Applications in Education and Others Fields

AI tools developed in recent years have materialised as sensors, geolocators, robots, voice recognition systems (Siri, Alexa), text, image, video, and code generators (IBM, 2025). Among the most widely used GenAI applications are ChatGPT and DALL-E by OpenAI; Microsoft Copilot; Google Gemini; Meta AI for Facebook, Messenger, Instagram, and WhatsApp; Perplexity AI; Midjourney; and Claude by Anthropic, among others (Marquis et al., 2024).

In educational settings, students frequently utilise these technologies to summarise information, request detailed explanations of complex topics – they have not fully understood-, search for data, brainstorm project ideas, improve their writing, design study strategies, translate texts into languages they do not master, and also, regrettably, to complete academic assignments effortlessly, gaining unearned benefits and hindering their learning.

For educators, AI applications prove valuable in instructional design, content creation, design of assessment tools, and the automation of feedback and grading processes – all aimed at individualised customising these basic teaching and learning processes (Cevallos Gamboa et al., 2025).

In the business domain and in other industries such as economics, law, manufacturing and medicine, among others, AI has been implemented in automatic voice recognition for customer enquiries and/or authentication in banking systems; in customer service via virtual agents or chatbots; in image recognition to support medical decision-making and/or the development of autonomous vehicles; in supply chain management to optimise inventories, schedule maintenance, and coordinate digital manufacturing through Internet of Things (IoT), pattern recognition and algorithm development; in weather forecasting; and in anomaly detection, among the most common applications (IBM, 2025).

Beyond these fields and for recreational uses, AI is also commonly used to request recipes, compose poems or songs, organise travel itineraries, craft jokes, and even seek advice and guidance on emotional challenges, among various other uses. AI has permeated all industries and will continue to do so in the future.

Benefits, Limitations, and Risks

The benefits of AI are evident, with some of the most notable including (Chowdhury & Sadek, 2012; Davenport, 2018):

- Reduced decision-making time. As previously mentioned, AI's ability to process vast amounts of data far exceeds human capability. AI tools collect, screen, and process information at a speed unmatched by any human, thereby enabling more informed decision-making in increasingly complex scenarios.
- Preservation of human knowledge for future applications. AI facilitates the effective and efficient documentation of human-generated knowledge across various sectors, organisational levels, and timeframes. This prevents the loss or distortion of information, which, in the absence of AI, would be confined to the individuals directly involved in its creation.
- Increased reliability of generated information. While it is impossible to guarantee absolute accuracy, AI's processing mechanisms allow for the integration of quantitative and qualitative data, establishing models and algorithms that, through statistical inference, produce results with a high probability of aligning with real-world scenarios.

However, AI also presents significant limitations and risks. Scholars (Devineni, 2024; Parycek et al., 2024; Selwyn, 2024) widely recognise several challenges inherent to the technology itself, including:

- Inaccuracy of generated information, as AI outputs are not always correct.
- Bias in results, stemming from the datasets used for training, which may not fully represent the reality of the user requesting the output.
- Inequitable access to AI technology. While many AI tools offer free versions with limited functionality, full access often requires payment, making them inaccessible to all populations.
- Concerns over intellectual property, data privacy, and security. AI interactions involve the sharing of personal data, which could lead to severe consequences if misused.
- Environmental, social, and human rights implications. AI systems require significant computational power, resulting in high energy and water consumption for data storage and processing. Additionally, the rapid obsolescence of hardware generates considerable electronic waste, posing further environmental challenges.

Use of GenAI in Academic Contexts by Students and Faculty

The use of GenAI grew exponentially following the release of the free version of ChatGPT in November 2022. This launch was a true game-changer, as it marked the first widely accessible GenAI tool that required neither specialised training nor advanced technological resources, enabling interactive dialogue for users.

Various studies (Sublime & Renna, 2024; Goff, 2025; Freeman, 2025) report that this technology has been widely adopted by students worldwide. Findings indicate that between 84% and 92% of university students employ GenAI tools for academic tasks. Students primarily use these tools to request explanations of concepts, summarise articles, brainstorm for research projects, structure their ideas, and improve their writing, among other academic activities – in essence, to save time and enhance the quality of their work.

In contrast, only 61% of teachers report using AI as a support tool in their teaching. Interestingly, 78% of teachers in Latin America view the advent of AI as an opportunity, and 96% anticipate using AI in the near future (Digital Education Council [DEC], 2025). Educators utilise AI for content creation, administrative tasks, enhancing student engagement with the course, and providing feedback, among other instructional purposes.

As is evident, students use AI more frequently than their professors, and it is reasonable to assume that younger students – digital natives – make even greater use of it than their older peers. Two key phenomena emerge from these observations: (1) GenAI is widely used – far more than adults initially imagined – and (2) students have an advantage over their professors; they possess greater expertise, are more familiar with AI features and capabilities, and are therefore more proficient with AI tools (Freeman, 2025).

Although 66% of teachers believe that incorporating AI into their teaching is essential to preparing students for future job markets, they tend to adopt a more cautious approach to integrating AI into their educational practices. Many cite a lack of time to explore its potential, uncertainty about its benefits, and concerns about potential negative impacts, among other reasons (DEC, 2025). This cautious and distant approach towards AI is perceived by students, as less than half (42%) believe their teachers are adequately prepared to address their AI-related queries (Freeman, 2025). Furthermore, only 47% of teachers consider themselves to have an adequate level of AI proficiency (DEC, 2025).

It is crucial to emphasise that the use of GenAI is not inherently unethical. As previously noted, AI is being increasingly employed across various professional fields, and graduates are expected to possess AI literacy. Given this reality and the benefits of GenAI, prohibiting its use would be both impractical and ¿naive? A more appropriate approach for educational institutions is to guide students in learning how to use GenAI ethically, as well as future technologies that will inevitably emerge (Weber-Wulff et al., 2023).

But what do we know about GenAI-mediated academic misconduct? How many students use it to complete assignments without genuinely seeking to learn? Undoubtedly, GenAI presents significant ethical dilemmas, including students utilising AI for academic work in ways that constitute various forms of academic fraud, such as authorship misrepresentation, fabrication of information, and lack of transparency (Gallent-Torres et al., 2023). Different studies (Freeman, 2025; Intelligent, 2023; Sullivan et al., 2023) report AI-mediated academic dishonesty rates ranging from 18% to 75%. Students admit to directly incorporating AI-generated outputs into their final submissions and/or using AI tools with considerable uncertainty as to whether doing so constitutes cheating. It is also interesting to know that, at least half of the students, believe that the improper use of these tools in coursework and exams creates a disadvantage for those who wish to learn and act with academic integrity (Goff, 2025).

The question that arises, then, is how educational institutions can promote the ethical use of these tools in support of learning and academic integrity. Only 36% of students report having received any form of institutional support in developing their AI literacy skills (Freeman, 2025). From a regulatory, punitive perspective, an instinctive response would be to severely sanction unethical use of GenAI, relying on AI-generated text detection tools, which will be explored in the following section.

Detection Tools for AI-generated Text

Concept and Functionality

AI-generated text detection tools are a type of software designed to identify whether a given text has been partially or entirely produced using generative artificial intelligence.

To determine whether a text has been authored by a human or AI, these tools (GPTZero, 2024):

1. Analyse linguistic and structural characteristics, such as paragraph structure, vocabulary usage, and overall writing style, to detect patterns more typical of machine-generated content than human writing;
2. Compare texts with others stored and indexed in extensive databases, similar to the approach used by text similarity detection tools; and
3. Calculate perplexity and burstiness – that is, how predictable the choice of vocabulary is (perplexity) and the variance in paragraph structure and length (burstiness) – as AI-generated texts tend to exhibit lower perplexity and burstiness.

In summary, while GenAI constructs grammatically correct sentences, human writers often incorporate more creative, subtle, and profound elements into their compositions, making their texts less predictable and uniform – in other words, more 'erratic'.

Accuracy, Precision and Reliability: Some of the most widely used free and commercial AI-generated text detection software includes Check For AI, Compilatio, Crossplag, DetectGPT, Go Winston, GPTZero, PlagiarismCheck, Turnitin, Writer, and Zero GPT (Weber-Wulff et al., 2023; Chaka, 2024).

Weber-Wulff et al. (2023) evaluated these and other GenAI detection tools based on accuracy, precision, and usability criteria. Their analysis involved various types of texts, ranging from those written entirely by humans – ensuring they had never been exposed to the Internet – to AI-generated texts modified using obfuscation techniques, such as paraphrasing, synonym substitution, and back-and-forth translation into different languages, either manually or by automated systems. Their conclusion was that these tools are neither precise nor reliable and, therefore, should not be used – as the stand alone proof – to determine whether a text has been written by a human or a GenAI tool. If used for this purpose, the authors argue, a student who has fully complied with academic responsibilities could be unjustly accused of misconduct, while a student who has improperly relied on AI tools to complete their assignments could evade detection and therefore sanction and 'a teachable moment'.

If prohibiting the use of GenAI is both impractical and undesirable, and if AI-generated text detection tools are unreliable, how can universities and other educational institutions uphold genuine learning, excellence, and academic integrity? The best available answer – until a better one emerges – is the long-standing recommendation of academic integrity experts (Bertram-Gallant, 2016; Bertram-Gallant & Guerrero-Dib, 2022; Bretag & Mahmud, 2016). Perhaps the most effective response to the evolving landscape of academic misconduct is to foster a culture of academic integrity that installs in students an ethical compass, guiding them to make responsible decisions both during their studies and later in their professional and civic lives (Guerrero-Dib, 2020; Guerrero-Dib et al., 2020; Guerrero-Dib et al., 2023).

Culture of Academic Integrity

Two main international standards can guide educational institutions in their efforts to build a culture of academic integrity. These are the Academic Integrity Rating System, developed by the International Center for Academic Integrity (ICAI), and the Academic Integrity Self-Evaluation Tool for Institutions, proposed by the European Network for Academic Integrity (European Network for Academic Integrity [ENAI], 2025).

Both frameworks follow a similar approach and recommend that educational institutions focus their efforts on different key areas (Bertram-Gallant & Guerrero-Dib, 2022):

1. Administrative Leadership and Support: Academic integrity should be a priority on the agenda of the Executive Committee, with its members actively involved in promoting it. Academic Integrity should be intentionally and consistently integrated into curriculum design and course outlines. Institutions should provide services and programmes that support student success. Additionally, a dedicated centre or specialised unit – with part-time or full-time personnel – should be responsible for coordinating institutional efforts on academic integrity. A specific budget should also be allocated for the operation of the academic integrity programme and staff.
2. Faculty Engagement and Support: Faculty members should receive training and guidance on academic integrity, with participation recognised as part of their professional development. They should play an active role in initiatives and bodies dedicated to promoting academic integrity, and their involvement should be formally acknowledged. Furthermore, course evaluations should consider the extent to which faculty members foster academic integrity in their teaching practices.
3. Student Engagement and Support: Students should have access to training and guidance on academic integrity and be encouraged to participate. A significant number of students should be actively involved in academic integrity initiatives and governance structures, with opportunities to assume meaningful leadership roles.
4. Staff Engagement and Support: Administrative and support staff should receive training and guidance on academic integrity, with participation acknowledged and rewarded. They should also play an active role in fostering a culture of academic integrity within the institution.
5. Education and Communication: Institutions should provide and promote accessible resources to raise awareness, educate, and train members of the academic community on academic integrity. These may include websites, tutorials, courses, workshops, events, ceremonies, campaigns, and other educational experiences.
6. Policies and Procedures: Institutions should establish clear and accessible regulations, including codes, policies, and procedures. These should be widely communicated, regularly reviewed and updated, and, most importantly, effectively enforced.

7. Research and Evaluation: Institutions should conduct ongoing research to assess the state of academic integrity, using findings as a basis for programme improvements. The effectiveness of various initiatives should be evaluated, and results should be transparently shared with the academic community.

The following section will present the findings of a study analysing how institutions have responded to the emergence of artificial intelligence in education through policies and procedures for AI usage. Additionally, recommendations will be provided for those who have yet to develop a strategy or wish to improve their existing one.

Analysis of Policies for AI Usage in Higher Education

The sample, method and analysis technique of the qualitative comparative analysis of the content of regulations on the use of artificial intelligence in eight Ibero-American universities is described next.

Sample

This study used a convenience sampling method. According to Gall et al. (2006), the aim of selecting a few representative cases is to gain a deeper understanding of the phenomenon under study, in this case, the regulations concerning the use of AI in higher education institutions. In order to obtain a comprehensive understanding of the progress made in establishing policies for the use of AI in Ibero-American educational institutions, the decision was made to analyse documents from universities that met the following criteria: (1) from Spanish-speaking countries; (2) a mix of both public and private; (3) with historical and cultural significance; (4) prominent positioning within their respective countries; and (5) national and regional influence and leadership.

Eight universities from five different countries meeting the aforementioned criteria were identified. It should be noted that some of the institutions included within a broader group, were not selected in this study due to the absence of publicly available AI usage regulations. A descriptive synthesis of the participating institutions is presented in Table 6, which highlights the strength and impact these institutions have, often extending beyond their national borders to international contexts.

Table 6: Descriptive synthesis of the universities comprising the sample

Country	Name	Foundation Year	Funding	National Ranking	Programmes	Faculty	Enrolled students
Argentina	Universidad de Buenos Aires (UBA)	1821	Public	1	663	15,954	115,993
Chile	Pontificia Universidad Católica de Chile (PUCC)	1888	Private	1	193	2,704	26,905
Colombia	Universidad de los Andes (UDLA)	1948	Private	1	171	1,168	16,133
Mexico	Universidad Nacional Autónoma de México (UNAM)	1551	Public	1	250	16,622	161,134
Mexico	Tecnológico de Monterrey (TECMTY)	1943	Private	2	118	6,013	47,049
Mexico	Universidad de Monterrey (UDEM)	1969	Private	20	46	466	11,290
Spain	Universidad Carlos III de Madrid (UC3)	1990	Private	7	189	2,402	20,870
Spain	Universidad Complutense de Madrid (UCM)	1293	Public	1	307	4,866	49,425

Note. Compiled with information from Quacquarelli Symonds [QS] Rankings (2025).

Methodology

The purpose of the study was to establish the aspects the sampled universities deemed relevant for guiding the use of AI within their educational community based on their AI usage policies. It employed content analysis, a research technique aimed at the objective and systematic description of the statements expressed in the documents under study (Gall et al., 2006).

The appropriate procedures were followed to carry out a content analysis with a comparative purpose, often referred to as benchmarking. The use of this formal analysis and comparison exercise, conducted with methodological rigour, is recognised as one of the most important tools for improvement. By comparing one's own activities with those occurring in leading organisations, best practices can be identified for implementation (Bhutta & Huq, 1999). A brief overview of the activities carried out in each stage of this study is presented below.

Identification of Documents

A search was conducted for the documents each institution had decided to publish to guide the proper use of AI tools within teaching and learning processes. Nine documents were identified and are listed in Table 7.

Table 7: Synthesis of the general aspects of the documents

Document name	Original name (in Spanish)	University	Year of publication	Audience	Citation
Framework for the Use of Artificial Intelligence in Teaching	*Marco para el uso de Inteligencia Artificial en docencia (dirigido a docentes)*	Pontificia Universidad Católica de Chile	2024	Faculty	(PUCC, 2024a)
Artificial Intelligence and Academic Integrity in Teaching Practice	*Inteligencia Artificial e Integridad Académica en la práctica docente*	Pontificia Universidad Católica de Chile	2024	Faculty	(PUCC, 2024b)
Guidelines for the Use of Generative Artificial Intelligence	*Lineamientos para el uso de inteligencia artificial generativa (IAG)*	Universidad de los Andes	2024	Faculty, students, researchers and staff	(UDLA, 2024)

Document name	Original name (in Spanish)	University	Year of publication	Audience	Citation
Guidelines for the Ethical Use of Artificial Intelligence/ Directed to Students of Tecnológico de Monterrey	*Lineamientos para el uso ético de inteligencia artificial dirigido a estudiantes del Tecnológico de Monterrey*	Tecnológico de Monterrey	2024	Students	(TECMTY, 2024a)
Guidelines for the Ethical Use of Artificial Intelligence/ Directed to Faculty of Tecnológico de Monterrey	*Lineamientos para el uso ético de inteligencia artificial dirigido a docentes del Tecnológico de Monterrey*	Tecnológico de Monterrey	2024	Faculty	(TECMTY, 2024b)
Guidelines for the Use of AI Tools in Teaching and Learning Processes	*Lineamiento de uso de herramientas de IA en procesos de enseñanza-aprendizaje*	Universidad de Monterrey	2025	Faculty and students	(UDEM, 2025)
Recommendations for the Use of Generative Artificial Intelligence in Teaching	*Recomendaciones para el uso de la inteligencia artificial generativa en la docencia*	Universidad Nacional Autónoma de México	2023	Faculty	(UNAM, 2023)
Recommendations for Teaching with Generative Artificial Intelligence	*Recomendaciones para la docencia con inteligencias artificiales generativas*	Universidad Carlos III de Madrid	2023	Faculty	(UC3, 2023)
Report and Recommendations on the Use of Generative AI	*Informe y Recomendaciones sobre el Uso de IA Generativa*	Universidad Complutense de Madrid	2023	Faculty	(UCM, 2023)

Concerning the University of Buenos Aires, it was not possible to identify a regulatory document regarding the use of IA tools. However, some evidence of how they are integrating AI into educational processes was found on their institutional website (Universidad de Buenos Aires [UBA], 2023, 2024a, 2024b), and it was included into the analysis.

Definition of Categories

Two previous exercises contributed significantly to the definition of the categories for the analysis: (1) Almaguer (2023) conducted a comparative study of AI usage policies at six international universities, and this benchmarking exercise provided initial insights, and (2) Muñiz (2024) performed a comparison – with a greater level of detail – of documents of two leading institutions that supported the final framework for analysis.

Through a thoughtful review of the documents generated by the universities in the sample, four key categories emerged. The categories derived into subcategories – specific elements included within the documents that delve into the specifications regarding the use of AI. The following list enumerates the categories and their corresponding subcategories.

1. General aspects of the documents: This category serves as an identification sheet for each document. It includes the following subcategories: (a) Document name; (b) Issuing institution; (c) Year of publication; (d) Audience; and (e) Citation (with the link for further consultation).
2. Institutional aspects: This category encompasses elements within the documents referring to characteristics of institutional influence and/or framing where or to whom the policy applies to. The following subcategories were defined: (a) Entire university community as the target audience; (b) Acceptance of AI use in academic work, (c) Conditions for using AI in academic work, (d) Conditions for providing information into AI apps; (e) Importance of incorporating AI into teaching and learning processes; (f) Options for AI use in disciplines and institutional settings; (g) Recognition of technical and ethical risks of AI usage; (h) Alignment to integrity, institutional values, and/or existing regulations in AI usage; (i) Ethical and informed use of AI; (j) Criteria for protecting personal data; (k) Verification of information generated by AI; (l) Bias in information generated by AI; (m) Ethical principles

for AI usage; (n) Support resources; (o) Responsibilities for faculty and students; and (p) Recommended uses for administrative staff.
3. Aspects related to faculty: This category identifies the attributes assigned to professors as part of their educational role within the institutions. Subcategories include: (a) Acknowledgement and declaration of the use of AI; (b) Training in AI tools; (c) Responsibilities in the use of AI; (d) Role of the professor; (e) Protection of intellectual property and copyrights; (f) Encouragement to design challenging activities and assessment instruments for students; (g) Clear and written rules by professors; (h) Reporting misuse of AI, and; (i) Use of AI for researchers.
4. Aspects related to students: This category encompasses elements attributed to students in each institution. Subcategories include: (a) Acknowledgement and declaration of the use of AI; (b) Training in AI tools; (c) Consequences of not adhering to policies; (d) Responsibilities in the use of AI; (e) Role of the student; (f) Protection of intellectual property and copyrights; (g) Reporting misuse of AI.

Systematic Review and Results Finding

This qualitative study, conducted as a content analysis, used the nine documents from the eight universities and the four categories (and their subcategories) to conduct a comparative analysis of the regulations, identifying common elements and the way they are approached, as well as the nuances and dissonant elements. The findings can be found in the next section.

Results and Findings

This section of the document presents the findings from the comparative exercise of the nine documents that constitute the sample. These findings are presented according to the four identified categories.

General Aspects of the Documents

The nine documents analysed are normative in nature and applicable across the entire institution, with publication dates ranging from 2023 to 2025. This reflects the urgency felt by universities to regulate the use of generative AI tools. It is undeniable that the amazing irruption of these technologies is driving innovation in teaching and learning processes.

Although the aim of the analysed documents is shared, each university, in accordance with its culture and existing internal regulations, has established different hierarchies of importance and approaches to the subject, which can be evidenced in the various types of documents. Four of these are presented in the format of guidelines, three are recommendations, one is a regulatory framework, and one is classified as a descriptive document. Another aspect of analysis is the identification of the intended recipients of the document. It has been found that six are specifically addressed to faculty members, two have a normative focus that encompasses students, faculty, and administrative staff, and one is directed exclusively to the student community. A descriptive synthesis of these results are presented in Table 6.

Institutional Aspects

This category identifies aspects that are addressed at an institutional level. A key aspect to highlight is that the existence of the documents analysed, in itself, communicates that it has been given a special importance to the topic at an institutional level. It should be noted that the absence of a specific mention of any aspect in this category does not imply its absence from the documents. Some aspects may be included in the following categories, as they appear associated with the functions and responsibilities of teaching practices or the role of the students.

All the documents studied state that universities approve a regulated use of various AI tools in academic work that forms part of the teaching-learning process. Five of the documents address, in more detail, specific conditions for their use. These regulations recognise that the integration of AI tools into academic life, in an ethical manner and for the benefit of student learning, is relevant and in line with the global technological advancements currently taking place in the world. In alignment with this, four of the documents include options for integrating AI tools into various areas and disciplines within institutional settings.

Another relevant subcategory in this analysis is the recognition of the technical and ethical risks associated with AI use. All universities issue warnings about potential dangers and pitfalls, such as, for instance, 'delegating value judgements or the resolution of ethical dilemmas to the tools' (Universidad de los Andes [UDLA], 2024). In response to such risks, the application of existing institutional regulations is proposed, such as Academic Regulations, Codes of Honour or Conduct, as well as principles and institutional values that guide actions in line with the university's foundational philosophy.

Moreover, emphasis is placed on the necessity of ethical and informed usage. Particular attention is given to the proper handling of personal and institutional data provided to AI apps (used in prompts), as it is noted that this could violate existing university policies. The regulations consulted also warn of the risks associated with bias and the questionable accuracy of information in materials or products created by generative tools, as clarified by the Pontificia Universidad Católica de Chile [PUCC] (2024b), 'replicating unverified information could promote misinformation among students and negatively affect their learning process'.

Finally, all institutions recognise the importance of providing support resources to their academic communities. However, only six of the documents detail specific materials available for learning and training in the use of these tools. A synthesis of the content in the documents for each of the subcategories relating to the institutions is presented in Table 8.

Table 8: Synthesis of institutional aspects

Subcategory	**PUCC (2024a)**	**PUCC (2024b)**	**UDLA (2024)**	**TECMTY (2024a)**	**TECMTY (2024b)**	**UDEM (2025)**	**UNAM (2023)**	**UC3 (2023)**	**UCM (2023)**
Entire university community as the target audience	X	X	X	X	X	X	X	X	X
Acceptance of AI use in academic work	X		X	X	X	X	X	X	X
Conditions for using AI in academic work		X		X		X	X	X	
Conditions for providing information to AI				X	X	X	X	X	X
Importance of incorporating AI into teaching and learning processes	X					X	X	X	X

(Continued)

Table 8: *(Continued)*

Subcategory	**PUCC (2024a)**	**PUCC (2024b)**	**UDLA (2024)**	**TECMTY (2024a)**	**TECMTY (2024b)**	**UDEM (2025)**	**UNAM (2023)**	**UC3 (2023)**	**UCM (2023)**
Options for AI use in disciplines and institutional settings						X	X	X	X
Recognition of technical and ethical risks of AI usage	X		X	X	X	X	X	X	X
Adherence to integrity, institutional values, and/or existing regulations in AI usage	X		X	X	X	X	X	X	X
Ethical and informed use of AI	X		X	X	X	X	X	X	X
Criteria for protecting personal data		X	X	X	X	X	X	X	X
Verification of information generated by AI		X	X	X	X	X	X	X	X
Bias in information generated by AI		X	X	X	X		X	X	X
Ethical principles for AI usage		X	X	X	X	X	X	X	X
Support resources	X		X	X	X		X	X	X
Responsibilities for faculty and students	X		X	X	X	X			
Recommended uses for administrative staff			X						

One important yet unaddressed aspect in the analysed documents is the process by which institutions define their AI usage regulations. The experiences of the Universidad de Buenos Aires (UBA) and the Universidad de Monterrey (UDEM) illustrate this process, as both institutions adopted collaborative and participatory approaches.

Such methods require time and dedicated spaces for learning and reflection. UBA, through its Centre for Innovation in Technology and Pedagogy, initiated discussions in 2022, resulting in the first AI integration guidelines by late 2024 and plans for resource dissemination in 2025 (UBA, 2023, 2024a, 2024b). UDEM followed a structured approach, beginning with a draft policy led by its Centre for Integrity, followed by multiple consultations with faculty, experts, and university authorities, including the President and representatives of the University Council (Universidad de Monterrey, 2024). These review and validation processes not only enhance the rigour and relevance of the policies but also generate interest in regulatory frameworks and cultivate a network of advocates who support their implementation.

Aspects Related to Faculty

The universities explicitly acknowledge that faculty members hold the primary responsibility and authority to approve or deny the use of AI tools in their classes. This responsibility is delegated because, as previously mentioned, institutions do not oppose the use of such tools; however, it is considered essential that specific aspects be taken into account to ensure that teaching practices align with the intended learning outcomes for students. This can only be achieved if the lecturer provides clear guidelines, ideally in writing, at the beginning of their courses or when publishing or requesting an academic assignment, especially considering that these rules may vary even from one activity to another.

In this category, it is remarkable the alignment in the criteria that universities deem essential for regulating the integration of AI into their teaching and learning processes. It is noticeable that the technological disruption, driven by the rise of AI tools, compels lecturers to modify their educational and instructional practices. There is also a huge consensus that it is essential for lecturers to redesign their courses, developing challenging, dynamic, and innovative activities and assessment tools for students, aligned with the new educational context.

A key request is that clear instructions must be provided to students on how to declare the use of AI in their academic work or assignments, with the expectation that lecturers do the same with their shared materials. It is also the lecturer's responsibility to ensure that students possess a basic understanding of how to use these tools ethically in their courses. In other words, lecturers cannot expect students to develop a reasoned judgement on the use of AI if they do not take the necessary steps to teach them.

Additionally, it is crucial that the information provided to students highlights the existing risks, such as the violation of intellectual property and copyrights. As pointed out by Tecnológico de Monterrey (2024b), 'it is important to bear in mind that ideas or writings published on these platforms become part of their database and lose their originality, becoming public domain information'. This could potentially violate other institutional regulations and trigger legal processes within the institutions and even in broader contexts.

Finally, it is noteworthy that only three documents formally specify that the misuse of these tools should be reported, although all recognise that academic integrity is a fundamental pillar for genuine learning and competency development, which is the ultimate goal of university work. A summary of the findings in the documents, for each of the subcategories related to teaching staff, is presented in Table 9.

Table 9: Summary of aspects related to faculty

Subcategory	**PUCC (2024a)**	**PUCC (2024b)**	**UDLA (2024)**	**TECMTY (2024a)**	**TECMTY (2024b)**	**UDEM (2025)**	**UNAM (2023)**	**UC3 (2023)**	**UCM (2023)**
Acknowledgement and declaration of the use of AI		X	X		X	X	X	X	X
Training in AI tools	X	X			X	X	X	X	X
Responsibilities in the use of AI	X		X		X	X	X	X	X
Role of the professor	X				X	X	X	X	X

Subcategory	PUCC (2024a)	PUCC (2024b)	UDLA (2024)	TECMTY (2024a)	TECMTY (2024b)	UDEM (2025)	UNAM (2023)	UC3 (2023)	UCM (2023)
Protection of intellectual property/ copyrights			X		X	X	X	X	X
Encouragement to design challenging activities and assessment instruments for students	X	X	X		X	X	X	X	X
Clear and written rules by professors	X	X	X		X	X	X	X	X
Reporting misuse of AI		X			X	X			
Use of AI for researchers			X						

Aspects Related to Students

The final category analysed addresses the aspects related to the responsibility of students when using AI tools. This category highlights the importance of students recognising their role and responsibilities within the teaching-learning process they experience within their university. Although just the Tecnológico de Monterrey has developed a specific document addressed – only – to students to raise awareness among them on this matter, this does not imply that the other institutions do not consider students as active participants in these regulations.

A key aspect is that students are compelled to familiarise themselves with the usage policies established by their professors for each course (whether it is permitted or not, and how it should be used for each assignment). And this knowledge will be valuable in order to avoid violations to academic integrity. The Pontificia Universidad Católica de Chile, Universidad Carlos III de Madrid, and Universidad de Monterrey inform their student community about the importance of being properly trained in the use of AI, so as to make the most of these tools while always complying with the established regulations.

In five of the documents reviewed, it is specified that students must indicate, cite, or declare whenever AI tools are used to generate content present in academic materials, whether under their own authorship or in collaboration with other peers.

Additionally, in relation to the risks outlined in the other categories, this category also emphasises the need to warn students about potential risks and ethical considerations. Failure to comply with these guidelines could lead to sanctions, particularly regarding violations of academic integrity. However, only two universities underline that improper use of AI should be appropriately reported through the relevant channels. A summary of the findings in the documents, for each of the subcategories related to students, is presented in Table 10.

Table 10: Summary of aspects related to students

Subcategory	**PUCC (2024a)**	**PUCC (2024b)**	**UDLA (2024)**	**TECMTY (2024a)**	**TECMTY (2024b)**	**UDEM (2025)**	**UNAM (2023)**	**UC3 (2023)**	**UCM (2023)**
Acknowledgement and declaration of the use of AI				X		X	X	X	X
Training in AI tools	X					X		X	
Consequences of not adhering to policies				X		X		X	
Responsibilities in the use of AI			X	X		X		X	X
Role of the student			X			X		X	X
Protection of intellectual property/ copyrights						X		X	
Reporting misuse of AI				X		X			

From the analysis, it is evident that all institutions recognise the disruptive emergence of AI tools and their impact on teaching and learning processes. The concern regarding ethical behaviour and academic integrity in the context of using these new technologies, without adequate reflection on the matter, is repeatedly emphasised. The findings also highlight the fundamental role of educators in creating meaningful learning experiences and the challenges posed by the integration of these tools for all stakeholders: institutions, students, but particularly for educators.

Conclusions and Future Work: A Critical Review of Institutional Responses

The introduction of GenAI into the educational landscape is a relatively recent phenomenon. As evidenced by the publication dates of the related documents, this field is evolving rapidly, demanding continuous adaptation and accelerated learning. Despite the apparent challenge of keeping the pace, it's essential that higher education institutions maintain openness to experimentation and knowledge acquisition.

Institutional Response and Regulatory Frameworks

Higher education institutions have predominantly responded to the rise of GenAI by establishing regulatory frameworks to govern its use. These policies typically define permissible actions, outline prohibited behaviours, and specify the consequences of violations. Additionally, they provide guidance for educators and students, offering criteria and directives to support decision-making.

Faculty: Expectations and Support

Universities actively encourage faculty members to engage with GenAI technologies, promoting familiarity and understanding of their functions, applications, and limitations. Educators are urged to critically explore how GenAI might be integrated into their teaching practices and disciplinary contexts. Institutions offer resources for faculty development, fostering a reflective approach towards their evolving roles as facilitators of student learning.

Bertram-Gallant (2025) highlights the necessity for instructors to adopt a critical and creative stance, adapting both instructional design and assessment methods to ensure their relevance and integrity. The recommendation is that any task susceptible to completion using GenAI should either be conducted under supervision or reconsidered altogether.

However, it is noteworthy that institutional guidelines often lack subject-specific recommendations. As Gallent-Torres et al. (2023) observe, faculty members are frequently left navigating an abstract set of principles. Furthermore, these policies generally fail to acknowledge the significant time and effort faculty members invest in understanding, applying, and regulating the use of GenAI in their pedagogical practices.

Student Responsibilities and Ethical Considerations

Students are expected to familiarise themselves with their instructors' specific guidelines regarding GenAI usage for assignments and assessments. Institutional policies emphasise that ignorance of these rules does not exempt students from accountability. Additionally, students are reminded that they bear full responsibility for the originality and accuracy of their submissions.

Universities also promote the responsible use of GenAI, encouraging students to adopt a critical mindset and remain transparent about their use of these technologies. Proper acknowledgement and citation of AI assistance are required, along with adherence to copyright regulations and the protection of sensitive data.

Although students often recognise the potential harm of unethical AI use (Bertram-Gallant, 2025), institutions must ensure that accessible resources are available to support students in navigating these ethical complexities. Clear guidance on appropriate AI use, transparency in application, and the consequences of misconduct should be readily provided.

Institutional Commitment to Academic Integrity

Dawson (2024) advocates for a shift in focus within higher education, urging institutions to prioritise the assurance of authentic student learning over the mere prevention of academic misconduct. This perspective is reflected in the recognition of GenAI as a catalyst for redefining the primary mission of higher education: the facilitation and certification of genuine learning.

To achieve this, universities are encouraged to foster engaging learning environments, implement competency-based curricula, modernise assessment methods, and develop comprehensive academic integrity initiatives. However, there is an evident tendency for institutions to delegate the bulk of the responsibility for GenAI adaptation to faculty members. Educators are often tasked with navigating technological advancements, revising instructional strategies, and establishing AI-related policies, all without adequate institutional support. Bertram-Gallant (2025) uses a compelling analogy to describe this challenge, likening it to a pilot being asked to redesign an aircraft mid-flight while ensuring a seamless passenger experience.

Recommendations for Moving Forward

To mitigate these challenges, higher education institutions should allocate dedicated resources to enhance faculty development in AI literacy. Additionally, targeted initiatives should be introduced to improve students' understanding of both the technical and ethical dimensions of GenAI. Beyond technological proficiency, universities must cultivate human-centric competencies such as critical thinking, problem-solving, ethical reasoning, and effective communication to ensure responsible AI usage (Goff, 2025).

Furthermore, institutions should conduct ongoing assessments of their AI policies, revising them based on empirical evidence and emerging best practices. These evaluations should include robust academic integrity frameworks, institutional leadership support, enhanced faculty and student training, and transparent communication. By fostering a culture of ethical AI use, universities can effectively navigate the challenges and opportunities presented by GenAI in education.

Acknowledgement

We would like to express our recognition to the global university community for its steadfast commitment and dedication to integrating artificial intelligence solutions into educational practices. The collective efforts in harnessing the potential of AI not only benefit our students but also contribute to the broader advancement of society. Their ongoing support and innovation are invaluable in shaping a future where technology enhances learning and the well-being of society. The authors acknowledge the use of ChatGPT (https://chat.openai.com/) to assist in the translation of this chapter from Spanish to English.

Bibliography

Almaguer, L. C. (2023). *Benchmark de normativas de IA en universidades del mundo*. Unpublished work. Universidad de Monterrey.

Ayala-Enriquez, P.; Franco-Perez, N.; Guerrero-Dib, J. G., Pizarro-Pucio, G. (2020). From moral awareness to academic integrity in Latin America. In T. Bretag (Ed.), *A Research Agenda for Academic Integrity* (pp. 28–39). Elgar Research Agendas.

Bertram-Gallant, T. (2016). Systems Approach to Going Forward. In T. Bretag (Ed.), *Handbook of Academic Integrity* (First, pp. 975–978). Springer.

Bertram-Gallant. T. (2025). Empowering Excellence: The Role of AI in Learning & Academic Integrity. XVII Assembly of the International Advisory Board for Students Affairs, Monterrey, México.

Bertram-Gallant, T. y Guerrero-Dib, J. G. (2022) AIRS 2.0, Pilot Webinar.

Bowers, J. W. (1964). Student Dishonesty and its Control in Colleges. (C. U. Bureau of Applied Social Research, Ed.), *Bureau of Applied Social Research*. New York, USA.

Bretag, T. y Mahmud, S. (2016). A Conceptual Framework for Implementing Exemplary Academic Integrity Policy in Australian Higher Education. In T. Bretag (Ed.), *Handbook of Academic Integrity* (1st ed., pp. 463–480). Springer.

Bhutta, K. S., & Huq, F. (1999). Benchmarking – best practices: an integrated approach. *Benchmarking: An International Journal*, 254–268.

Campbell, J. (2023). *Generative artificial intelligence*. Salem Press Encyclopedia of Science.

Campos Céspedes, J. & Solano Gutiérrez, W. (2012). Discurso atribucional de estudiantes inculpados por deshonestidad académica en una universidad pública costarricense. *Revista Electrónica Actualidades Investigativas en Educación*, 12 (2), 1–28.

Cevallos Gamboa, M. A., Tomalá De La Cruz, M. A., Aroni Caicedo, E. V., & Manzo Nazate, M. E. (2025). Análisis de la aplicación de la inteligencia artificial en la educación superior. Una revisión sistemática.

RECIMUNDO, 9(1), 29–37. https://doi.org/10.26820/recimundo/9.(1).enero.2025.29-37
Chaka, C. (2024). Reviewing the performance of AI detection tools in differentiating between AI-generated and human-written texts: A literature and integrative hybrid review. *Journal of Applied Learning and Teaching,* 7(1), 115–126. https://doi.org/10.37074/jalt.2024.7.1.14
Chowdhury, M., & Sadek, A. W. (2012). Advantages and limitations of artificial intelligence. *Artificial intelligence applications to critical transportation issues,* 6(3), 360–375.
Comas, R., Sureda, J., Casero, A., & Morey, M. (2011). La integridad académica entre el alumnado universitario español. *Estudios pedagógicos (Valdivia), 37*(1), 207–225. https://dx.doi.org/10.4067/S0718-07052011000100011
da Costa, I. C. B., Martins, M. S., Mata-Virgem, S. F., Rolim, C. E. C., Santana, L. R., Bataglia, P. U. R., Silvany Neto, A. M., & Pena, P. G. L. (2006). Má práctica por estudiantes de Medicina: Estudio piloto. *Gazeta Médica da Bahia,*76(2), 29–37.
Davenport, T. H. (2018). *The AI advantage: How to put the artificial intelligence revolution to work.* MIT Press.
Dawson, P. (2024). Validity matters more than cheating. *Assessment & Evaluation in Higher Education, 49*(7), 1005–1016. https://doi.org/10.1080/02602938.2024.2386662
Devineni, S. K. (2024). AI in data privacy and security. *International Journal of Artificial Intelligence & Machine Learning (IJAIML)*, 3(01), 35–49.
Digital Education Council. (2025, 20 January). Digital Education Council Global AI Faculty Survey 2025. https://www.digitaleducationcouncil.com/post/digital-education-council-global-ai-faculty-survey
Eaton, S. E. (Ed.). (2024). *Second handbook of academic integrity.* Springer.
European Network for Academic Integrity (2025). Academic Integrity Self-Evaluation Tool for Institutions. https://www.academicintegrity.eu/survey/management
Federación de Instituciones Mexicanas Particulares de Educación Superior (2023, 19 October). Sistema de Acreditación a través del Desarrollo y Fortalecimiento Institucional Versión 4.1. https://portal.fimpes.org.mx/acreditaciones
Freeman, J. (2025, 26 February). *Student Generative AI Survey 2025.* Higher Education Policy Institute. https://www.hepi.ac.uk/2025/02/26/student-generative-ai-survey-2025/

Gall, M. D., Gall, J. P., & Borg, W. R. (2006). *Educational research: An introduction* (8th ed.). Pearson.

Gallent-Torres, C., Zapata-González, A., & Ortego-Hernando, J. L. (2023). El impacto de la inteligencia artificial generativa en educación superior: una mirada desde la ética y la integridad académica. *RELIEVE. Revista Electrónica de Investigación y Evaluación Educativa, 29*(2), 1–21. https://doi.org/10.30827/relieve.v29i2.29134

García-Villegas, M., Franco-Pérez, N., and Cortés-Arbeláez, A. (2016). Perspectives on Academic Integrity in Colombia and Latin America. In T. Bretag (ed.), *Handbook of Academic Integrity* (pp. 161–180). Springer.

Goff, L. (2025, 03, 6–8) GenAI LEARN: Supporting Students Responsible Use of GenAI, 33rd International Center for Academic Integrity 2025 Annual Conference, Chicago, Illinois, USA.

GPTZero. (2024, 14 October). How AI Content Detectors Work to Spot AI. https://gptzero.me/news/how-ai-detectors-work/

Guerrero-Dib, J. G. (2020). *Relación entre la integridad académica universitaria y el comportamiento ético en el entorno laboral.* Instituto Tecnológico y de Estudios Superiores de Monterrey. https://hdl.handle.net/11285/636866

Guerrero-Dib, J. G., Portales, L. & Gallego, D. (2023). Academic Integrity as a Way to Promote Workplace Ethical Behaviour. In: Curtis, G. J. (eds.) *Academic Integrity in the Social Sciences. Ethics and Integrity in Educational Contexts*, 6. Springer, Cham. https://doi.org/10.1007/978-3-031-43292-7_11

Guerrero-Dib, J. G., Portales, L., & Heredia-Escorza, Y. (2020). Impact of academic integrity on workplace ethical behaviour. *International Journal for Educational Integrity, 16*(1), 2. https://doi.org/10.1007/s40979-020-0051-3

IBM, 2025. ¿Qué es la inteligencia artificial (IA)? https://www.ibm.com/mx-es/topics/artificial-intelligence

Intelligent. (2023, 23 January). Nearly 1/3 college students have used ChatGPT on written assessments. https://www.intelligent.com/nearly-1-in-3-college-students-have-used-chatgpt-on-written-assignments

Marquis, Y., Oladoyinbo, T. O., Olabanji, S. O., Olaniyi, O. O. and Ajayi, S. A. (2024). Proliferation of AI Tools: A Multifaceted Evaluation of User Perceptions and Emerging Trend (9 January 2024). *Asian Journal of Advanced Research and Reports* 18(1), 30–55. https://ssrn.com/abstract=4689091

Martínez, L. & Ramírez, E. R. (2018). Fraude académico en universitarios en Colombia: ¿Qué tan crónica es la enfermedad? *Educação e Pesquisa*, 44, 19 pp. http://www.scielo.br/pdf/ep/v44/1517-9702-ep-S1517-9702201706157079.pdf

McCabe, D. (2016). Cheating and Honor: Lessons from a Long-Term Research Project. In T. Bretag (Ed.), *Handbook of Academic Integrity* (First, p. 1097). Springer.

Medina-Díaz, M. del R. & Verdejo-Carrión, A. (2005). Encuesta acerca de la deshonestidad académica estudiantil en la Universidad de Puerto Rico, Recinto de Río Piedras. *Pedagogía, 38*(1), 179–204. https://revistas.upr.edu/index.php/educacion/article/view/19282

Muñiz, A. C. (2024). Comparativa de normativas de IA en dos universidades de Monterrey [Unpublished work]. Universidad de Monterrey.

Parycek, P., Schmid, V., & Novak, A. S. (2024). Artificial Intelligence (AI) and automation in administrative procedures: Potentials, limitations, and framework conditions. *Journal of the Knowledge Economy, 15*(2), 8390–8415. https://doi.org/10.1007/s13132-023-01433-3

Pontificia Universidad Católica de Chile. (2024a). *Marco para el uso de inteligencia artificial en docencia*. https://docencia.ia.uc.cl/wp-content/uploads/2024/06/Marco-para-el-Uso-de-Inteligencia-Artificial-en-Docencia_compressed-1.pdf

Pontificia Universidad Católica de Chile. (2024b). *Inteligencia Artificial e Integridad Académica en la práctica docente*. https://integridadacademica.uc.cl/wp-content/uploads/2024/11/02.-Inteligencia-Artificial-e-Integridad-Academica.pdf

Posso Pacheco, R. J., Posso Pacheco, E. E., & Salazar Ayala, J. J. (2025). La Inteligencia Artificial en la Educación: Propuesta de una Metodología de Enseñanza Integrada. *MENTOR Revista de investigación Educativa y Deportiva, 4*(10), 1–8. https://doi.org/10.56200/mried.v4i10.9501

Quacquarelli Symonds. (2025). *QS World University Rankings 2025: Top global universities*. https://www.topuniversities.com/world-university-rankings

Quispe, C. R. L., & Ruiz, O. E. B. (2024). Innovación Educativa: Estrategias efectivas en el aula para reducir la deshonestidad académica: Educational Innovation: Effective classroom strategies to reduce academic dishonesty. *LATAM Revista Latinoamericana de Ciencias Sociales y Humanidades, 5*(4), 1818–1835.

Russell, S. J., & Norvig, P. (2021). Artificial Intelligence: A Modern Approach (4th ed.). Pearson.

Tecnológico de Monterrey. (2024a). *Lineamientos para el uso ético de inteligencia artificial/dirigido a estudiantes del Tecnológico de Monterrey.* https://tec.mx/sites/default/files/repositorio/integridad-academica/lineamientos-eticos-alumnos-tec-de-monterrey.pdf

Tecnológico de Monterrey (TECMTY). (2024b). *Lineamientos para el uso ético de inteligencia artificial/dirigido a profesores del Tecnológico de Monterrey.* https://tec.mx/sites/default/files/repositorio/integridad-academica/lineamientos-ia-profesores-tec-de-monterrey.pdf

Turing, A. M. (2009). Computing Machinery and Intelligence. In: Epstein, R., Roberts, G., Beber, G. (eds) *Parsing the Turing Test*. Springer, Dordrecht. https://doi.org/10.1007/978-1-4020-6710-5_3

Saldaña-Gastulo, J. J. C., Quezada-Osoaria, C. C., Peña-Oscuvilca, A. & Mayta-Tristán, P. (2010). Alta frecuencia de plagio en tesis de medicina en una universidad pública peruana. *Rev Peru Med Exp Salud Pública, 27*(1), 63–67.

Selwyn, N. (2024). On the limits of artificial intelligence (AI) in education. Nordisk tidsskrift for pedagogikk og kritikk, 10(1), 3–14.

Stephens, J. (2024). The Academic Motivation and Integrity Survey Results from the April 2024 Administration at FIMPES.

Sublime, J. & Renna, I. (2024). Is ChatGPT Massively Used by Students Nowadays? A Survey on the Use of Large Language Models such as ChatGPT in Educational Settings. https://arxiv.org/html/2412.17486v1

Sullivan, M., Kelly, A., & McLaughlan, P. (2023). ChatGPT in higher education: Considerations for academic integrity and student learning. *Journal of Applied Learning & Teaching,* 6(1), 31–40. https://doi.org/10.37074/jalt.2023.6.1.17

Teixeira, A. A., & de Fátima Oliveira Rocha, M. (2010). Academic misconduct in Portugal: results from a large-scale survey to university economics/business students. *Journal of Academic Ethics*, 8, 21–41.

Universidad Carlos III de Madrid (UCM) (2023). *Recomendaciones para la docencia con inteligencias artificiales generativas*. https://ssii.ucm.es/file/informe-general-ia-generativa-uc

Universidad Complutense de Madrid (UCM) (2023). *Informe y recomendaciones sobre el uso de IA generativa*. https://ssii.ucm.es/file/informe-general-ia-generativa-uc

Universidad de Buenos Aires (2023, 29 de junio). La UBA capacita a docentes en Inteligencia Artificial. UBA Noticias. https://www.uba.ar/ubanoticias/noticias/15

Universidad de Buenos Aires (2024a, 24 de junio). La IA en el aula: percepciones y desafíos desde la mirada docente. UBA Noticias. https://www.uba.ar/ubanoticias/noticias/345

Universidad de Buenos Aires (2024b, 2 de diciembre). La UBA trabaja en la integración de la IA en la enseñanza. UBA Noticias. https://www.uba.ar/ubanoticias/noticias/540

Universidad de los Andes (2024). *Lineamientos para el uso de inteligencia artificial generativa (IAG)*. https://secretariageneral.uniandes.edu.co/images/documents/lineamientos-uso-inteligencia-artificial-generativa-IAG-uniandes.pdf

Universidad de Monterrey (2024). *Lineamiento de Uso de Inteligencia Artificial para procesos de enseñanza-aprendizaje.* Universidad de Monterrey. https://www.udem.edu.mx/sites/default/files/2025-04/LO-DIPRI-007-A-Lineamiento-Uso-de-Herramientas-de-Inteligencia-Artificial.pdf

Universidad de Monterrey (2025). *Lineamiento de uso de herramientas de IA en procesos de enseñanza-aprendizaje*. https://www.udem.edu.mx/es/comunidad/reglamentos

Universidad Nacional Autónoma de México (2023). *Recomendaciones para el uso de la inteligencia artificial generativa en la docencia*. https://iagenedu.unam.mx/docs/recomendaciones_uso_iagen_docencia_unam_2023.pdf

Ventura, A. C., Biagioni, F., Bozocovich, N. & Borgobello, A. (2012). Estudio exploratorio de prácticas académicas deshonestas en exámenes de estudiantes universitarios. IV Congreso Internacional de Investigación y Práctica Profesional en Psicología XIX Jornadas de Investigación VIII Encuentro de Investigadores en Psicología del MERCOSUR. Facultad de Psicología-Universidad de Buenos Aires, Buenos Aires.

Weber-Wulff, D., Anohina-Naumeca, A.; Bjelobaba, S., Foltýnek, T., Guerrero-Dib, J., Popoola, O., Šigut, P., & Waddington, L. (2023). Testing of detection tools for AI-generated text. *International Journal for Educational Integrity, 19*, 26, 1–39. https://doi.org/10.1007/s40979-023-00146-z

Generative AI as a Catalyst for Innovation and Teaching Improvements: Challenges and Opportunities

Eva María Olmedo Moreno[1] *and Jorge Expósito López*[2]

ABSTRACT

In the current era, we find ourselves navigating increasingly blurred boundaries between human and artificial intelligence (AI), paving the way to that which has come to be known as 'precision education' (Olmedo-Moreno et al., 2024). This paradigm emphasises personalisation in higher education, wherein generative artificial intelligence (GenAI) minimises the time allocated to mechanical tasks, thereby allowing greater focus on essential cognitive processes such as creativity and critical thinking.

However, significant concerns have arisen within educational institutions regarding the implementation of AI. UNESCO (2023) and the European Union (2023) underscore the need to regulate AI, given its ethical implications, as evidenced by the recent proposal put forth in the EU Artificial Intelligence Act. This legislation aims to ensure that AI systems operational within the EU are both safe and respectful of fundamental rights by adopting a regulatory framework that is predicated on risk assessment.

This law delineates four levels of risk, which are assessed on a scale ranging from unacceptable to low. Each level is subjected to regulations that are tailored towards their specific characteristics. Notably, educational or professional training is deemed a critical criterion with the absence of such training leading to the determination of unacceptable risk. In response to such regulatory frameworks, universities have formulated guidelines promoting best practice for AI use in both teaching and research. These guidelines advocate for the ethical and safe application of AI, fostering a reflective and pragmatic approach to learning. The integration of AI in higher education, not only, simplifies the personalisation of learning tailored towards individual needs, but, also, enhances the efficiency and accuracy of data collection and analysis, thereby facilitating more informed educational decisions. Nevertheless, AI integration is not devoid of challenges, such as the need to transform learning strategies and deliver comprehensive training to educators so that they adeptly wield AI tools.

1 mailto:emolmedo@ugr.es; University of Granada, Spain. https://orcid.org/0000-0003-0558-1513

2 University of Granada, Spain. https://orcid.org/0000-0001-9076-0377

Artificial intelligence is revolutionising teaching within higher education by refining curriculum planning and pedagogical methods to better meet the educational demands and personal and professional skills of students. This methodological shift allows for the development and enhancement of educational guides that incorporate new competencies such as digital literacy. Nonetheless, the deployment of AI is accompanied by challenges, including inconsistencies in its application and the need to establish standardised procedures that effectively integrate AI elements within educational materials (Expósito and Olmedo, 2024).

Moreover, AI advocates for dynamic and participatory teaching methods, both in physical and virtual settings, facilitated by the universal design for learning and elaboration of adaptable educational materials. However, the implementation of such active teaching methodologies necessitates the continuous professional development of educators and students and introduces risks such as privacy breaches and identity fraud, which brings about a need to use tools such as ChatGPT and reliable 'fact-checking' tools.

In the context of tutoring, GenAI aids in pinpointing learning deficits and crafting personalised learning activities for students with specific needs. Effective integration of GenAI into this process hinges on the proper training of educators and availability of suitable infrastructure.

In terms of assessment, GenAI refines evaluation methodologies, enabling deeper critical reflection and the customisation of evaluative materials. Although GenAI enhances both the correction and self-correction of assessments, it is crucial that the authenticity and validity of GenAI content is verified and that it is ensured that final evaluative decisions remain within the purview of educators.

Collectively, AI alleviates the mechanical burden associated with teaching and promotes a more innovative and personalised educational approach that is tailored to meet the individual needs of students and is congruent with hybrid learning models. While it is true that GenAI furnishes potent tools for customising and enhancing educational outcomes, a methodical and regulated approach is required to maximise its benefits and mitigate potential risks. The ongoing adaptation of educators and students to the nuances of GenAI is indispensable for making substantive advancements in this burgeoning field.

Keywords: GenAI, individualised education, precision teaching, innovation, improvement of higher education

Introduction

Higher education is at the cusp of profound change. Key moments throughout history include the shift from Plato's concept of the academy towards medieval universities, the Industrial Revolution with the advent of the printing press, the democratisation of universities in the twentieth century and, more recently, the transformation driven by advances in information communication technology. Each of these key turning points have marked significant shifts towards the development of competences in place of the mere accumulation of knowledge. Each and every one has been fundamental in explaining the transformation of the purpose and relevance of scientific work at university level.

Major milestones on the path towards the rise of artificial intelligence (AI, hereafter), starting in 1950 and continuing into 2024, also stand tall as key turning points in terms of change, with these markers precipitating others at an increasingly faster rate (see Figure 4). AI emerges as an enabling technology for the implementation of more efficient and innovative services. The quest for artificial general intelligence (AGI, hereafter), as a system with cognitive capabilities comparable to human ones, has been a long-standing goal in the field of artificial intelligence. Unlike specialised artificial intelligence (AI) systems that master specific tasks, such as speech recognition or computer vision, AGI aspires to possess human-like understanding and adaptability across a wide range of domains. Generative artificial intelligence (GenAI) and artificial general intelligence (AGI) represent two distinct approaches within the field of artificial intelligence. While GenAI focuses on the creation of new and creative content, AGI aims to develop systems with human-like cognitive capabilities that are flexibly applicable in a variety of areas.

Both types of AI present challenges and risks that must be considered when developing solutions based on this type of technology. It is, therefore, essential that knowledge-generating technology is subject to continuous and careful critical reflection. We must not allow decision-making and implementation to be left solely in the hands of artificial general intelligence (AGI) with the flagrant freedom to determine uncontested outcomes. Instead, it is crucial to ensure that human beings remain at the heart of the process. This implies that teachers and policy makers must be actively involved in evaluating the way in which these technologies influence educational processes and knowledge formation. In doing so, it can be ensured that GenAI be used as a tool that complements and enrichens the capabilities of humans, rather than replacing human judgement and ethics. In this way, education and learning will continue to be deeply humanistic and individual-centred processes. Such an approach will, not only, ensure a more ethical and responsible integration of technology, but, also, foster educational innovation that truly benefits society as a whole.

1 1950-1970: First Golden Age

The Term "artificial intelligence" was coined in 1956. Eliza, the first natural language chatbot, was created in 1966.

2 1980-1970: Second Golden Age

Deep Blue beats chess champion Kasparov in 1997, marking a milestone in AI capability.

3 2010-2018: Generalized application

AlphaZero teaches itself to play chess in 2018, demonstrating the autonomous learning potential of AI.

4 2022-Present: AI in Higher Education

OpenAI launches ChatGPT, generating mixed emotions and ushering in Generative AI in Education.

Figure 4: Historical development of AI in education
Source: Authors

In the specific context of education, society finds itself in an era in which the boundaries between human intelligence and artificial intelligence are becoming increasingly blurred, paving the way to that referred to as 'precision education' (Olmedo-Moreno, et al., 2024). This approach focuses on the personalisation of learning in higher education, shifting attention from minor details – not because they are unimportant, but because they fall under the remit of GenAI – to crucial and distinctively human aspects such as creativity, discovery, and critical and reflective thinking. AI not only facilitates the tailoring of learning to the individual needs of each learner, but, also, enhances data collection and analysis, which enables more informed and timely educational decisions. This frees teachers to focus more on developing the essential competencies required by students. However, the adoption of GenAI in educational settings presents significant challenges, as it requires a profound transformation of pedagogical and teaching strategies. For its successful integration, it is essential that specific training is provided to ensure the effective and safe use of these technologies, ensuring that the essence of educational process is maintained and enhanced, while maximising the potential of technological innovation for the benefit of personalised learning.

New Epistemological, Normative and Practical Scenarios

The widespread use of GenAI in educational environments is revolutionising both our perception of educational settings and the very definition of learning. This transformation impacts everything from planning and implementation models to methodologies, and from teaching dynamics to assessment processes. This evolution is often so profound that traditional epistemological principles no longer adequately support these processes or serve to justify the decisions underlying them. Thus, it appears essential that this new educational and formative model be developed from new principles and arguments.

Against this backdrop, it is crucial to explore the way in which GenAI adapts to formative processes in higher education, as its use expands, not only, in spatial and temporal terms, but, also, in terms of the diversity of educational content and resources. This adaptability makes GenAI particularly compatible with Universal Design for Learning (UDL), which allows for the creation of personalised educational processes that effectively meet all specific needs.

Thus, a new landscape in higher education emerges. A landscape that has, so far, received little consideration and promises to profoundly transform the way we teach and learn. This landscape rests on another fundamental principle of personalised learning. This second principle, together with the first, promotes what is called precision learning for individual persons, moments and situations. Learning that is tailored, personalised and precision-adjusted to the conditions and pace of individual students facilitates a more inclusive and accessible educational experience.

Another fundamental principle of GenAI that it is important to mention here pertains to the cumulative use of data to refine and optimise both processes and educational content. This principle parallels with traditional teaching models, emphasising the importance of implementing formative assessments that analyse both the processes and outcomes of learning.

Further, engagement in continuous assessment, not only, raises the quality of education, but, also, fosters and facilitates educational innovation through an evidence-based approach.

From an institutional perspective, one of the major concerns regarding GenAI use relates to its security and ethical implications. In this regard, UNESCO (2022) states that there is a need to regulate the ethical implications of GenAI. The EU published Regulation (EU) 2024/1689, known as the AI Act, as a pioneering step for the field at an international level. The aforementioned regulation aims to ensure that GenAI systems available on the European market and subsequently employed in the EU are safe and respectful of fundamental rights and EU values. The main tenet of the act is that GenAI be regulated based on its potential to harm society in line with a 'risk-based' approach. Accordingly, the greater the risk, the stricter the rules. As the first legislative proposal of its kind in the world, the act sets a global standard for the regulation of AI in other jurisdictions, similar to the General Data Protection Regulation, thus promoting a European approach to technology regulation on the global stage. This law establishes four levels of risk (unacceptable, high, limited and low). When determining unacceptable risk, the second most relevant criterion refers to 'educational or professional training, which can determine access to education and the professional course of a person's life (for example, exam scoring)' (see Figure 5).

Alongside this European law, universities are emerging with Best Practice Guides to orientate the use of AI by teachers, students and researchers. These guides express basic recommendations for responsible AI use in teaching and learning. They comprise guidelines on the ethical and safe use of this technology, as well as information about its misuse, risks and potential. The goal of this is to guide both students and teachers in the proper use of these technologies, promoting a more reflective and practical approach to learning that is also known as 'authentic learning'. Authentic learning refers to an innovative pedagogical model that emphasises meaningful educational experiences, which are situated in real or simulated contexts and linked to the professional and personal situations that may be faced by students throughout their professional lives. In higher education, authentic learning is especially relevant as it connects theory with practice, allowing students to solve real problems, reflect critically and develop practical competencies that are applicable to their immediate and future professional settings.

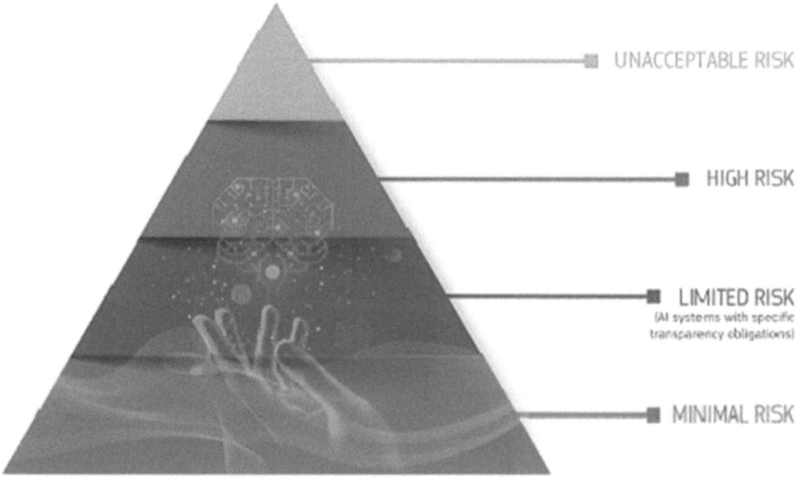

Figure 5: EU Artificial Intelligence Act: risk levels
Source: Regulation (EU) 2024/1689, AI Act

Generative artificial intelligence is revolutionising university teaching and its potential to enrichen authentic learning is gradually being unveiled. GenAI-based tools enable the creation of personalised educational scenarios, realistic simulations and dynamic case studies, at the same time as offering immediate feedback tailored to the progress of individual students. This allows university students to experience specific situations in controlled yet highly realistic environments, which enhances the relevance of learning and their motivation and commitment to it. The integration of GenAI in higher education improves the practical and creative application of complex concepts, while, also, fostering autonomy in decision-making.

Furthermore, the use of AI drives the development of advanced digital competencies and promotes an ethical and responsible digital citizenship. From this perspective, it not only provides deeper and more meaningful learning, but, also, prepares students to participate actively and competently in an increasingly digitalised society. Thus, GenAI tools designed to enhance adaptive learning systems use algorithms to provide personalised insights that help educators better understand individual and group learning processes.

This ability to personalise learning adds a new dimension to academia, which allows for more targeted and effective interventions (see Figure 6).

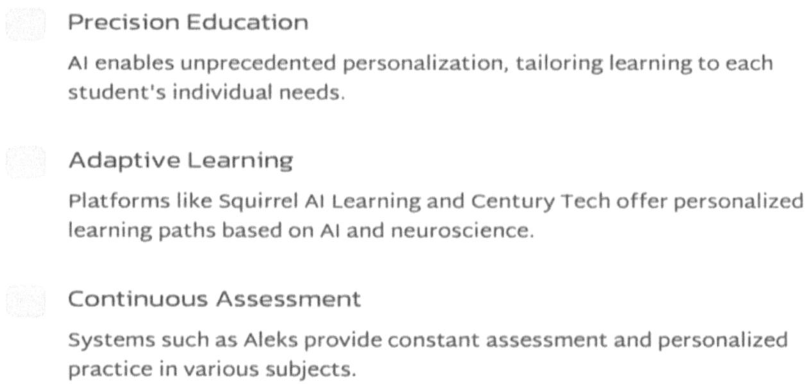

Figure 6: Examples of precision education and adaptive learning systems that use GenAI
Source: Authors

According to the Horizon11 report published by Educause (2023), artificial generative intelligence (AI) is emerging as the leading candidate to be the most influential educational technology over the coming years, due to its application in learning analytics and as a teaching tool. However, its use poses challenges, especially regarding the need to train teachers to use these tools effectively and responsibly in automated academic environments. Fredi Vivas (2023) highlights that these technologies are becoming so integrated that their presence often goes undetected. This underscores the importance of a conscious and prepared implementation of GenAI in higher education.

From a teaching perspective, teachers are on a journey, more or less together. Some are more advanced than others, but most perceive that we are coming towards the end of the track and are now peering into an abyss with an uncertain future. In this future, we glimpse disappointment, due to the high expectations placed on GenAI tools for teaching development not being met, in addition to excitement, driven by the belief that this resource will help us to move forward faster and boost our creativity.

Transformation of the Teaching Role as Both a Challenge and an Opportunity

The advent of artificial generative intelligence (GenAI) in the educational field is feeding a significant transformation in the traditional role assumed by teachers. In traditional models, which still prevail in many university learning practices, teachers act as transmitters of knowledge and are responsible for imparting information and ensuring that students assimilate it correctly. However, with the integration of GenAI into educational processes, this view is shifting towards a more facilitative approach to learning that is based on guiding and mentoring students, especially in environments where personalisation and adaptation are crucial. In this case, the inherent usage characteristics and potential of these elements means that their application requires teachers to adopt the role of learning facilitators. This means that knowledge provision is substituted as their main goal for the creation of an environment in which students can explore and discover knowledge for themselves. Throughout this process, the opportunity emerges to find a friendly face in the new role of teacher, as GenAI use frees up time and resources making it an element that facilitates and relieves the burden of teaching tasks by handling the more routine and repetitive aspects of this labour. This allows teachers to concentrate on activities of greater cognitive and pedagogical value, such as critical and creative skill development in students.

In this transition from the role of knowledge transmitter to learning facilitator, teachers are expected to adopt a more humane and personalised approach to education. This involves adapting both teaching materials and teaching pace to the individual learning levels and styles of students. Moving away from the traditional 'one size fits all' approach, teachers have the opportunity to act as mentors, providing personalised support and guidance. This adaptation of teaching, not only, improves provision, but, also, fosters a more inclusive learning environment that is responsive to the unique needs of individual students. This more personalised and tailored approach to individual student needs takes us a step closer towards that known as Universal Design for Learning (UDL).

This transition also supports teachers to adopt a role that is closer to that assumed by counsellors and mentors. It enables them to devote more time to resolving complex issues, stimulating critical thinking and fostering problem-solving. Additionally, teachers are supported to facilitate the development of soft skills such as communication, collaboration and self-management, all of which are crucial in the twenty-first century. Nonetheless, this transformation is not without challenges, as it requires teachers to be trained in the use of both GenAI tools and innovative pedagogies that maximise the potential of these technologies. In turn, it provides the opportunity to radically rethink what it means to teach and learn, while promoting a more collaborative and less hierarchical approach to education.

Thus, the integration of GenAI in education is, not only, changing the role of the university teacher from knowledge transmitter to learning facilitator and guide, it is also offering a wide range of benefits when it comes to performing certain types of teaching tasks, and repurposing and driving their professional development as teachers. This being said, GenAI also carries a number of benefits for students by fostering more inclusive, interactive and personalised learning processes. As outlined in the CRUE report (Cruz-Argudo et al., 2024), GenAI use (combined with AI) can improve the learning experience of students and the efficiency of teachers, in terms of:

- Automating certain administrative tasks and detecting fraudulent uses.
- Assisting in the design of exercises, content summaries and activities based on learning outcomes.
- Conducting assessments and giving feedback through the generation of assessment tests based on the class syllabus, or through rubric-based correction with constant and automated feedback.
- Adding value to active participation tools.
- Evolution of classic collaboration systems (videoconferencing) and LMS which, through the combination of learning analytics and GenAI technologies, allow student activity to be tracked in a much more personalised way, such as through the generation of learning paths.

This technology can, therefore, increase the personalisation of learning, increase educational accessibility and optimise the performance of repetitive teaching tasks, thereby favouring more creative and student-centred approaches. Nevertheless, a 'sine qua non condition' of its implementation must be that it is used critically and ethically. This will enable the laudable objectives of transforming higher education to be achieved.

GenAI Tools for Establishing New Teaching and Innovation Models in University Classrooms Through Co-Intelligence

Generative artificial intelligence is establishing itself as a key tool in education by taking over repetitive and administrative tasks. However, it is essential to recognise that the effectiveness of these technologies crucially depends on the human factor that teachers bring to the educational process. Although GenAI can personalise learning and optimise educational resources, the human element – empathy, understanding, and the ability to inspire and motivate – remains irreplaceable. Teachers instil values, foster critical thinking and model social skills that machines cannot replicate. Thus, as GenAI transforms education, the role of the teacher as a conscious human facilitator becomes even more vital, ensuring that technology serves as a complement to, and not a substitute for, genuine human interaction in learning.

While very useful AI tools exist, it is crucial that they be used as enhancers and not as substitutes for certain actions and functions inherent to educational processes. Mollick (2024) states that 'students who use GenAI as a "crutch" learn nothing. GENAI should enhance learning, not replace it: Co-intelligence with AI improves capabilities, but if misused, hampers learning'. Incorrect or superficial use of these technologies can lead to deterioration or stagnation of learning by preventing the student from actively participating in the knowledge-building process.

The real educational advantage of GenAI arises when a co-intelligence relationship is established, in which the student and AI interact collaboratively and intelligently. This intelligent interaction involves using GenAI, not just, as a source of quick answers or immediate solutions, but as a tool for solving complex problems. Practices based on co-intelligence are showing positive signs, especially in university settings, where GENAI is already being used to improve educational processes, promote the personalisation of learning and optimise assessment.

In terms of implementation based on intelligent collaboration, tools such as ChatGPT illustrate the way in which GenAI can be used for any aspect of the university teaching process, from content generation to support of personalised tutoring tasks. Microsoft's Office Suite, for example, now comprises Copilot, which assists in the creation and editing of documents by understanding the context underlying content and, consequently, more efficiently facilitating the drafting and organisation of complex ideas. Google Chrome extensions such as ScribeHow allow step-by-step tutorials to be recorded directly from the browser, while Print Friendly helps remove ads and unwanted elements prior to printing a web page. Further, AI assistants such as Monica, Veronica and Lucia on WhatsApp demonstrate the way in which AI adapts to everyday communication settings and offers real-time assistance for educational and communication tasks. All of the above examples underline the way in which GenAI can enhance the educational experience by facilitating the creation of accessible and personalised learning materials.

As an example, Cruz-Argudo et al. (2024, p. 9) summarise the capabilities of a number of these tools, amongst others, in terms of text creation in the context of university teaching:

- Text-to-text (Chatbots). Taking as a basis a text that specifies a series of instructions or requests (called a prompt), generate another type of text (for example, from a series of instructions, generate a text about a specific subject, or from a general text, generate a summary).
- Text-to-code (Copilot). This tool uses a descriptive text to generate source code (a function, a programme, etc.).
- Text-to-images (DALL-E, Midjourney, BlueWillow, etc.). Such tools use descriptive text to illustrate a desired image or elements that should form part of an image and, where relevant, outline the style and technical characteristics of a desired image, to generates an image based on the aforementioned input information.
- Text-to-video (Heygen, Synthesia, RunwayML, etc.). Following the input of prompts that illustrate a given theme to be addressed in a video and possible technical characteristics, these tools generate video media outputs.

- Text-to-presentation (Tome AI, Presentations.AI, etc.). Following the input of specific prompts, such tools generate a presentation in a digital format via PowerPoint, etc. Some such tools create questions for polling through AI (PrepAI, Quizgecko, Wooclap Quiz Wizard, etc.). These tools use specific texts and specific prompts that indicate the characteristics of questions (number of questions, number of answers, number of possible correct responses, question type [true or false, multiple choice, etc.], etc.) to generate a series of questions that can be answered online and that allow feedback to be provided in order to reflect participant knowledge or opinions. This functionality allows teachers to reduce their workload in terms of repetitive and management tasks, freeing up their time to interact with students.

In order to illustrate the specific application of these aforementioned tools in the context of higher education and, particularly, the elaboration of research papers, the role of GenAI tools can be discussed in accordance with the tasks specific to each phase of the research process: planning, development or fieldwork, and communication of results (see Figure 7).

Figure 7: GenAI tools and their application to different phases academic research paper elaboration: planning, development and communication
Source: Authors

Another pertinent application of GenAI pertains to simulations and virtual settings for fields such as medicine and engineering, where platforms such as

Osso VR and Labster offer detailed simulation scenarios that allow students to practice procedures and experiments in a controlled and safe environment. These tools, not only, enhance theoretical understanding, but, also, provide valuable practical experience without the risks associated with basic training in real environments.

In more advanced contexts, universities such as Massachusetts Institute of Technology (MIT) have developed GenAI systems that personalise adaptive learning by analysing individual student progress in order to tailor educational materials to their specific needs. These systems adapt to individual learning styles, at the same time as identifying areas in which students may need more support. This allows for more precise and timely educational interventions.

Debate surrounding the integration of GenAI into teaching design concerns the availability of resources. In this regard, it is important to bear in mind that many tools offer free versions that are limited in terms of functionality, requiring payment in order to access certain functions. This raises the question about whether all teachers and students have access to the most advanced versions of these tools. Clearly, the answer to this question is no. This is already leading to issues in terms of the democratisation of science and has been a major factor in widening the digital divide. It is also undeniable that many tools with applications in terms of academic paper elaboration, are also capable of actively collaborating in academic paper assessment.

For example, when analysing the impact of ChatGPT, as outlined in the guide by Torres-Salinas and Arroyo-Machado (2023), it can be observed that this tool has enormous potential when it comes to the process of conducting academic works. Firstly, it can assist in generating effective titles and summaries that capture the essence and contributions of the work. Secondly, it can help identify and suggest relevant keywords to ensure coherence and precision. Additionally, it can verify the appropriateness and formatting of bibliographic references. In terms of ideas and writing, it can propose short and concise sentences that enhance the clarity of the work. Finally, it can assist in drafting text and in terms of its presentation within the manuscript.

GenAI is transforming university education by identifying and responding to the specific needs of individual students through real-time analysis of performance and behavioural data. This analytical capability allows teachers to intervene in a timely fashion and adjust their pedagogical approaches to address any specific deficiencies or challenges, thus ensuring a more tailored and personal learning experience. Additionally, it facilitates attention to classroom diversity through algorithms that adapt educational materials to the individual abilities and preferences of students, allowing all students to progress at their own pace and, in this way, improving educational inclusion and equity. Similarly, adaptive platforms powered by GenAI provide resources and activities that challenge students according to their level of competence, which promotes autonomous and critical learning that is essential for ongoing professional and personal development. Collectively, GenAI relieves the mechanical burden associated with teaching and promotes a more innovative and personalised educational approach that is tailored to individual student needs and consistent with hybrid learning models. Although AI provides a powerful tool for the personalisation and betterment of educational outcomes, a methodical and regulated application is required to maximise its benefits and mitigate potential risks. Continuous adaptation of teachers and students to the nuances of AI is indispensable for achieving substantial advances in this booming field.

These tools offer significant improvements to the quality of academic studies (Crompton & Burke, 2023). However, it is crucial to address the ethical and regulatory challenges that accompany these technologies in order to maximise their burgeoning potential. Moving forward, the scientific community must ensure that the adoption of GenAI in teaching aligns with the principles of integrity, fairness and transparency. An equity dilemma also exists that must be considered, which is illustrated here through the teaching tool of the metaphor using the example of Michael Phelps' LZR swimsuit, which was banned for not complying with Olympic norms in terms of the principles of equality and equity. Another metaphor, the yo-yo metaphor, refers to the scenario in which somebody who knows nothing about a topic uses AI tools to garner enough information to get started, while somebody else, who is already an expert, uses AI tools to perform meta inferences. In both cases, the 'human touch' determines the course of the yo-yo.

In terms of all of the aspects discussed above, teachers may find that AI acts as a catalyst for innovation and teaching improvement by providing opportunities that have never previously been considered in terms of enhancing knowledge about AI(s), enhancing professional development and updating teacher knowledge regarding technology in order to successfully integrate such technology into the teaching and learning processes, and begin to find a new path towards teaching development and in teaching itself.

Elements for Reflection and Improvement: Opportunities for Innovation with GenAI

Given the opportunities presented by teaching innovation with GenAI, a promising horizon is envisioned for improving the quality of education making it more current and aligned with the realities and needs of the modern student. However, in order to fully leverage these opportunities, it is crucial that cautious and well-informed approaches are adopted. In this sense, core recommendations are proposed in several key areas.

Teacher training in the proper use of GenAI tools emerges, unanimously, as the starting point in the process of its application in higher education. To this end, continuous and up-to-date programmes must be offered on the implementation of such tools and the challenges that this may impose. This will require that greater resources are made available to fund innovation and research projects and to develop teaching materials that can lead to the effective integration of GenAI. The creation of joint calls and a repository of innovation projects would facilitate access to accumulated knowledge and foster collaborations amongst teachers, promoting an environment of collective and continuous learning. It is also fundamental that teachers are provided with the necessary training for protection of personal and sensitive data when working with GenAI tools, as well as to raise awareness about the responsible and ethical use of GenAI, as referred to by sustainable development goals (SDGs). Such tools also provide criteria and tools for the validation of learning outcomes, ensuring the quality and accuracy of education provision.

GenAI training in teachers should be incentivised in order to allow them to customise and adapt GenAI tools to the specific needs of their courses and students. The formation of working groups comprising teachers from related subjects would help to ensure that a collaborative and enriching approach is taken to GenAI training, which, in turn, would optimise resources and maximise educational benefits. Additionally, it is vital that the necessary computing resources are provided and that the effort of teachers involved in these initiatives is recognised. In this way, GenAI can be used to facilitate the design and planning of teaching through the curriculum, teaching guides, learning scenarios adjusted to specific contexts, educational needs, and development of personal and/or professional competencies in coordination with the real contexts of professional practice by:

- Providing ongoing and updated training to university teachers on GenAI.
- Encouraging and increasing the resources allocated to funding innovation and research projects, and developing teaching materials related to the application of GenAI.
- Creating a repository that illustrates innovation projects and their outcomes related to GenAI in order to facilitate knowledge generation around this topic and, also, enable collaboration between teachers.
- Increasing computing resources, such as specialised servers for training and GenAI use, and recognising the collaboration of teachers engaged in GenAI training.
- Raising awareness regarding responsible GenAI use in accordance with SDGs and providing training on data protection when working with GenAI tools.
- Educating about the nature of GenAI outputs in terms of potential issues.
- Providing criteria and tools for validating learning outcomes and conducting appropriate training.

It is also essential to allow teachers to train their own models by supporting coordination between coordinators of subjects that are related in content so that small groups of teachers who teach similar content in different subjects and degrees can be established, from which working groups can later be created to perform GenAI training tasks. This will ensure that reliable sources are on hand for training and that students receive better quality responses.

With regards to students, it is essential that they are encouraged to engage in critical reflection on the responses provided by GenAI. Students must be aware that these tools offer initial approximations that require further evaluation and critical consideration. Training on data protection and the nature of GenAI responses is crucial for students to adequately understand and manage the information and resources provided by these technologies.

Additionally, tools should be offered that facilitate the validation of learning outcomes for self-learning, thus promoting greater student independence and empowerment in relation to their own educational process. This may occur by:

- Raising student awareness about GenAI outputs as initial approximations that require critical reflection.
- Providing training on data protection when working with GenAI tools.
- Offering tools for validating self-learning outcomes and providing appropriate training.
- Educating about the nature of GenAI outputs in terms of related issues.
- Raising awareness about the responsible use of GenAI in accordance with SDGs.
- Developing general classroom standards for the entire university that regulate the way in which such materials should be obtained and processed in terms of respecting the privacy of teachers.

Student digital literacy regarding GenAI should be a curriculum priority from the beginning of university education. It is imperative that students are equipped to operate effectively in a digitalised environment. Additionally, specific competencies for content development through GenAI must be acquired in order to ensure that future professionals can actively contribute to the evolution of their field.

In the field of counselling and tutoring, GenAI helps to detect learning deficits and develop personalised learning activities for students with specific needs. Effective integration into this process depends on the appropriate training of teachers and the availability of suitable infrastructures.

GenAI assisted processes enable and facilitate the performance of activities related to the personal development of students in terms of their self-esteem and personal and student self-concept. This may occur through its impact on enhancing the use of different learning strategies and study techniques adapted to specific disciplines and specific knowledge, and improving social and professional skills in aspects such as professional image, entrepreneurship and lifelong professional development. This may be achieved by:

- Promoting the development of self-esteem, self-concept and emotional intelligence as people and as students by shaping a balanced and assertive personality.
- Diversifying learning strategies to build more meaningful, in-depth and applied learning.
- Enhancing the use of study techniques adapted to specific disciplines and knowledge.
- Improving general social skills for cooperative work and leading the transfer of knowledge to the social and business sphere.
- Developing professional competencies aligned with the needs of future workers.

An example of the aspects introduced above comes from the fact that even though GenAI itself cannot manage emotions directly, it can help improve the emotional intelligence of students through programmes designed to recognise and respond to emotional signals, in this way offering resources and activities that promote awareness and emotional regulation. Additionally, GenAI can be used to train students in communication and empathy skills through simulations and interactive exercises.

Use of GenAI facilitates the development and updating of the teaching process and application of Universal Design of Learning (UDL) for all people through active methodologies that promote participation and inspire students in real and virtual environments. This includes group critical reflection on outputs of GenAI application amongst teachers and students and generation of materials for the implementation of active methodologies in the classroom, such as flipped learning, project-based learning and service learning, amongst other examples within the framework of Universal Design for Learning (UDL).

The use of GenAI tools enables the tutoring of students to be improved by promoting their personal development, learning and personal/professional competency development. One particular benefit is its capacity to detect learning gaps in the tutoring of students and reliance on the generation of personalised activities that can serve as aids in the learning process, starting students out on the pathway towards 'precision education'. This is typically accompanied by complex personalised resources that enrichen student training.

In terms of assessment, GenAI helps assessment methodologies to be perfected by allowing for deeper critical reflection and personalisation of evaluative materials. Although it improves both the correction and self-correction of assessments, it is crucial to verify the authenticity and validity of content generated by GenAI and ensure that final evaluative decisions continue to be the responsibility of teachers. Also, it may contribute to increasing student motivation and engagement by personalising challenges and course content so that it aligns with the interests and skills of individual students.. Gamification systems and immediate feedback provision help keep students engaged and motivated as they are driven on by their own progress and achievements. Teachers and students must be fully informed about privacy clauses, especially in assessment contexts.

- Final assessment outcomes are always decided by the teacher even in cases when GenAI is used during the decision-making process.
- Teachers and students must be aware of the privacy clauses established by GenAI, especially when it comes to assessment.
- GenAI facilitates greater diversity of criteria, procedures and instruments, which supports adaptation of the assessment to meet individualised needs as a fundamental part of the training process.
- In the case of Bachelor's theses, Master's theses and Doctoral theses, a rubric should be created for students in which they indicate the scenarios in which they have used GenAI.

GenAI tools are used to improve assessment, better understand student learning outcomes, foster critical reflection, and transform teaching with the aim of improving the process of self-assessment and self-regulation pertaining to learning. Indeed, GenAI can help teachers generate generic material (exam questions of various types, topics for papers and projects, etc.) that can be used for student evaluation, at the same time as helping teachers produce personalised assessment material that is aligned to the needs and characteristics of students and implement knowledge self-management systems based on the intended outcomes established prior to the final evaluation given by the teacher.

The multidimensional approach to assessment of GenAI use in the context of education, not only, emboldens its use, but, also, ensures that its implementation is ethical, effective and aligned with the educational and personal needs of students, which will more effectively prepare them for a future in which technology and humanity converge harmoniously.

Conclusion

GenAI is transforming teaching practices and learning in higher education. However, at the same time it poses challenges that need to be carefully addressed in order to maximise its benefits. Ongoing teacher training on GenAI use, inclusion of digital literacy within curricula and a conscious focus on ethical regulation reflect essential steps towards integration of this technology in a way that complements and enrichens the educational experience, while always maintaining the indispensable human factor inherent to the teaching and learning process. In the face of these opportunities for teaching innovation, a horizon for potential improvement in the search for more current and relevant teaching emerges that rests on the cornerstone of the co-intelligent integration of GenAI and pertinent recommendations.

GenAI offers broad possibilities for fostering creativity in university classrooms by providing tools such as content generators, simulations and design platforms that allow students to experiment and create innovative projects. Such tools can inspire students to explore new ideas and approaches in a controlled and stimulating environment. Moreover, dynamic and participatory teaching methods are advocated for, both in physical and virtual settings, which are facilitated by the Universal Design for Learning and creation of adaptable educational materials. However, application of these active teaching methodologies requires continuous professional development for both teachers and students and introduces risks such as privacy breaches and identity impersonation. This necessitates the use of tools such as ChatGPT, in contingence with reliable fact-checking sources.

Statement on Use of AI

In the course of developing this work, the authors used ChatGPT 4.5 to create a preliminary structure regarding the state of the topic, without including literal or paraphrased texts. After using this tool, the authors carefully reviewed and modified the content and assume full responsibility for the contents of the publication.

Bibliography

Crompton, H., & Burke, D. (2023). Artificial intelligence in higher education: The state of the field. International Journal of Educational Technology in Higher Education, 20(1), 22.https://doi.org/10.1186/s41239-023-00392-8

Cruz-Argudo, F., et al. (2024). *La inteligencia artificial generative en la docencia universitaria.* Informe CRUE. Universidades Española: Madrid.

Educause (2023). *EDUCAUSE QuickPoll Results: Adopting and Adapting to Generative AI in Higher Ed Tech.* recuperado el 27-07-2023 de https://er.educause.edu/articles/2023/4/educause-quickpoll-results-adopting-and-adapting-to-generative-ai-in-higher-ed-tech

European Research Council (2023). Foresight: Use and impact of Artificial Intelligence in the scientific process. https://erc.europa.eu/sites/default/files/2023-12/AI_in_science.pdf

Olmedo-Moreno, E., Rakdani, F., Arenas-Carranza y S., Hortas-Aliaga, O. (2024). *Uso de herramientas IA la intervención socioeducativa,* AIDIPE. Universidad de Barcelona.

Olmedo-Moreno, E., Hortas-Aliaga, O. y Expósito-López, J. (2024). Percepción del plagio y uso de la Inteligencia Artificial en Educación Superior. *Actas de la VII Conferencia Inteligencia artificial y plagio inteligente: impacto pedagógico en la formación docente*. Pp: 321–329. Universidad A Coruña: A Coruña.

UNESCO (2022). *Recomendación sobre la ética de la inteligencia artificial.* UNESCO: Francia. https://unesdoc.unesco.org/ark:/48223/pf0000381137_spa

European Parliament and Council of the European Union. (2024, 13 June). Regulation (EU) 2024/1689, *Law on AI.* Official Journal of the European Union. https://eur-lex.europa.eu/

Mollick, E. (2024). *Cointeligencia. Vivir y trabajar con la IA*. Conecta: Barcelona.

Vivas, F. (2023). *Invisible: La inteligencia artificial en nuestra vida.* Ediciones Sudamericana.

Torres-Salinas y Arroyo-Machado (2023), *Guía Chat GPT V2*. InfluScience Ediciones. 10.5281/zenodo.10390816

The Impact of Generative AI on Academic Texts: Changes in Scholarly Communication and Integrity

Rubén Comas Forgas[1], Alex Glynn[2] and Carmen Touza Garma[3]

ABSTRACT

This book chapter explores the transformative impact of generative Artificial Intelligence (GAI) on academic communication, focusing on the changes it introduces to research derived publications. The work is informed by recent studies and evidence and highlights the dual-edged nature of GAI's role in academic writing. On the one hand, it improves accessibility, democratising academic communication by aiding researchers – especially non-native speakers – in creating polished academic texts that may improve visibility and engagement. On the other hand, the reliance on GAI risks standardising language use, diminishing originality and cultural distinctions, and potentially eroding the diversity of academic discourse. Additionally, ethical concerns arise from the lack of transparency regarding GAI involvement in academic texts generation, which could affect academic integrity.

The discussion extends to the implications of GAI on broader scholarly communication, emphasising the need for robust guidelines to govern its use. The authors advocate for transparency and ethical oversight, ensuring that GAI complements human creativity rather than replacing it.

Keywords: generative artificial intelligence, academic integrity, scholarly communication, AI in academic writing, ethics in publishing

Introduction: Academic Publishing, Setting a Definition

Science communication plays a central role in the dissemination of knowledge, ensuring that scientific discoveries are accessible, understandable, and beneficial to both the academic community and the broader society (Garvey, 2014). It includes a variety of channels and strategies aimed at facilitating the transmission of scientific knowledge, ranging from peer-reviewed journals to public engagement initiatives (Gregory & Miller, 1998).

1 University of Balearic Islands, Spain. https://orcid.org/0000-0002-8885-753X
2 University of Louisville, USA. https://orcid.org/0000-0002-3027-7276
3 University of Balearic Islands, Spain. https://orcid.org/0000-0001-9471-8221

Understanding the nature of science communication and its significance is fundamental to fostering informed societies and connecting research and practical applications.

Academic publishing refers to the system through which scholarly research is disseminated, validated, and archived within the academic community (Hyland, 2016). It serves as a mechanism for sharing peer-reviewed knowledge, enabling scholars to contribute to their fields while ensuring intellectual rigour and credibility (Fyfe et al., 2017). This system is deeply interconnected with institutional prestige, career progression, and research funding, making it a fundamental component of the higher education and research ecosystem.

Academic publishing has changed significantly over the past centuries, expanding from the domain of learned societies and independent scholars to a model dominated by commercial publishers and digital platforms. Despite its transformation, the primary objectives remain constant: to validate scientific knowledge through expert review, establish a record of scholarly contributions, and facilitate the global exchange of research findings (Fyfe et al., 2017).

The history of academic publishing is marked by three major phases:

Phase 1. Pre-1940s: Learned Societies and the Gentlemanly Ethos

Before the Second World War, academic publishing was largely controlled by learned societies, universities, and independent scholars. Publishing research was not a commercial endeavour; rather, it was motivated by the dissemination of knowledge and intellectual exchange. Many of the first scientific journals, such as the *Philosophical Transactions of the Royal Society* (1665), were established by these societies, providing a platform for scholars to share discoveries (Fyfe et al., 2022).

During this period, research publications were not financially profitable, as they relied on government sponsorships, university funding, or aristocratic patronage (Fyfe et al., 2017). Academic prestige was socially constructed, meaning that reputation was built through membership in elite institutions and scholarly circles, rather than through citation metrics or impact factors. The emphasis was on open intellectual exchange rather than financial viability (Graham & Diamond, 1997).

One significant limitation of this system was accessibility. Academic publishing was highly exclusive, with most researchers operating within limited networks of elite universities and societies. Print-based dissemination meant that only affluent institutions could afford access to scholarly works, restricting the circulation of knowledge (Arbuckle, 2021).

Phase 2. 1940s–1980s: Expansion, Professionalisation, and the Rise of Commercial Publishing

Following the Second World War, the academic publishing panorama experienced rapid transformation due to the growth of the global research community and expansion of higher education institutions. Government investments in research, particularly in science, technology, and medicine (STM), led to a surge in scholarly output (Fyfe et al., 2017).

This period saw the professionalisation of academia, where publication records became key indicators of career progression. The concept of '*publish or perish*' emerged, reinforcing the idea that scholarly publishing was essential for job security, tenure, and funding acquisition (Blackmore & Kandiko, 2011).

The increasing number of researchers and publications created new market opportunities for commercial publishers. British and Dutch companies, such as Pergamon Press and Elsevier, recognised the financial potential of academic journals, leading to a shift from mission-driven publishing to profit-oriented business models (Fyfe et al., 2017). These firms capitalised on library subscriptions, developing pricing models that prioritised institutional access over individual readership.

Another major development was the formalisation of peer review as a standard practice for evaluating research quality. While editorial review had existed in learned societies, the post-war expansion of academia necessitated a more structured system. By the 1960s and 1970s, commercial publishers integrated peer review as a value-added service, further solidifying their control over academic knowledge dissemination (Baldwin, 2015).

Phase 3. 1980s–Present: Digital Transformation, Open-access, and the Commercial Oligopoly

By the 1980s, the financial model of academic publishing began to shift dramatically. The rapid increase in publication volume, rising subscription costs, and shrinking university budgets led to what became known as the 'serials crisis' (Thompson, 2005). Libraries struggled to afford academic journals, as commercial publishers continued to increase subscription prices (Fyfe et al., 2017).

The arrival of digital technologies in the 1990s provided an opportunity for cheaper, faster, and more accessible dissemination of research. However, instead of reducing costs and improving access, large commercial publishers adapted their profit models to the online environment, creating paywalled journal databases such as Elsevier's Science Direct and Wiley Online Library (Lawson, et al., 2016).

At the same time, the open-access (OA) movement emerged as a counterbalance to commercial publishing dominance. Initiatives such as arXiv (for physics) and PubMed Central (for biomedical sciences) demonstrated the feasibility of freely accessible research repositories. The Budapest Open Access Initiative (2002) and the Berlin Declaration (2003) further advocated for public access to taxpayer-funded research (Eve, 2014).

Despite these advancements, commercial publishers continue to dominate the industry that generates high profits from publicly funded research. Researchers submit work for free, peer review is done without compensation, and universities pay substantial fees to access the same research (Mayoni, 2022). This model creates financial strain on institutions while limiting public access to knowledge. With profit margins exceeding 30%, publishers such as Elsevier and Springer Nature outperform major tech companies in profitability (Mayoni, 2022). Universities spend billions on journal subscriptions, diverting resources from research and education. In response, open-access initiatives like *Plan S* aim to make publicly funded research freely available. However, article processing charges (APCs) shift costs to researchers, maintaining financial barriers (Mayoni, 2022). The debate continues over how to balance fair pricing, accessibility, and sustainability in scholarly publishing (Larivière et al., 2015).

Ethics in Scientific Communication: A Historical Analysis

The ethical challenges in scientific communication have changed over time, reflecting broader shifts in academic practices, publishing standards, and institutional pressures. The history of ethical violations, ranging from disputed authorship to falsified data, illustrates how scientific dissemination has varied and adapted to emerging challenges. This section of the chapter explores ethical issues in scientific communication from the seventeenth century to the present, examining how different periods have dealt with concerns about research integrity, errors, and misconduct.

Seventeenth and Eighteenth Centuries: The Foundations of Scientific Publishing and Early Ethical Concerns

The seventeenth century saw the rise of scientific journals, marking a shift from private correspondence among scholars to more formalised methods of communication. The founding of Philosophical Transactions (1665) in England and Journal des Savants (1665) in France set the stage for peer-reviewed publishing (Morriello, 2024). However, the lack of standardised ethical guidelines led to disputes over credit and concerns about data reliability.

Isaac Newton and Robert Hooke's rivalry is an early example of ethical disputes in scientific publishing. Hooke accused Newton of failing to acknowledge his contributions to the theory of gravitation, sparking one of the first recorded conflicts over priority in scientific discovery (Johns, 2019). Such disputes became common as scientific institutions gained prestige, making recognition an increasingly valuable commodity.

The eighteenth century introduced more structured academic institutions, but misconduct persisted. Plagiarism was a frequent issue, with cases of scholars copying findings without proper attribution. The philosopher Gottfried Wilhelm Leibniz was accused of stealing Newton's calculus, leading to one of the most famous disputes in the history of mathematics (Morriello, 2024). While modern scholarship recognises that both developed calculus independently, the controversy illustrates the ethical ambiguities that arose when multiple researchers worked on similar problems in parallel.

Nineteenth Century: Institutionalisation of Science and Ethical Dilemmas

As universities and professional scientific societies gained influence in the nineteenth century, scientific publishing became more structured. However, this period also saw ethical challenges related to fraud, exaggerated claims, and manipulation of data. Charles Babbage, in his 1830 book *Reflections on the Decline of Science in England*, classified scientific misconduct into three categories: 'hoaxing' (deliberate fraud), 'forging' (falsification of data), and 'trimming' (selectively presenting results) (Franzen, 2021). These classifications remain relevant, as many modern cases of misconduct follow similar patterns.

During this period, honorary authorship became a growing concern. The practice of adding prominent scientists' names to papers they had not contributed increased in frequency, as institutional prestige became linked to publication records (Morriello, 2024). While such issues were largely ignored at the time, they laid the groundwork for later debates on proper attribution in scientific research.

Twentieth Century: Fraud, Conflicts of Interest, and Replication Crises

The twentieth century saw the expansion of scientific research as a profession, with increased funding, peer review, and specialisation. However, this growth also led to cases of research fraud that shaped later discussions on scientific integrity (Lafollette, 1992).

One notorious nineteenth-century fraud was the 'Piltdown Man' hoax, in which a supposed missing link between apes and humans was 'discovered' in England in 1912 but later exposed as a forgery (Gould, 1983). Though this case became widely known in the twentieth century, it reflects earlier traditions of presenting fabricated findings to support prevailing scientific narratives.

Another significant case was the work of Cyril Burt, a British psychologist who fabricated data in his studies on intelligence and heredity. His claims that intelligence was primarily inherited influenced education policies, despite later investigations revealing inconsistencies in his reported findings (Mackintosh, 1995). This case highlighted the risks of unchecked authority in scientific publishing and the need for external verification of data.

The mid-twentieth century also saw growing concerns over conflicts of interest. Pharmaceutical research, in particular, faced scrutiny as companies funded studies that favoured their products. The lack of transparency in funding sources led to calls for stricter disclosure requirements, setting the stage for modern ethical guidelines (Morriello, 2024).

The replication crisis became a major issue in psychology and biomedical sciences toward the end of the century. Many influential studies failed to be replicated, raising concerns about selective reporting and statistical manipulation (Ioannidis, 2005). This crisis exposed weaknesses in peer review and research design, demonstrating that ethical concerns extended beyond deliberate fraud to structural problems in how research was conducted and evaluated.

Twenty-first Century: Open Science, Retractions, and New Challenges

With the rise of digital publishing, ethical challenges in scientific communication have continued to advance. The ability to rapidly disseminate research has increased transparency but also introduced new concerns, such as the persistence of retracted studies in scientific literature (Da Silva & Vance, 2017).

One striking example is the 1998 study by Andrew Wakefield that falsely linked the MMR vaccine to autism. Although the paper was later retracted, it continues to be cited and used in anti-vaccine rhetoric, contributing to public health misinformation (Eggertson, 2010). This case illustrates how ethical breaches in scientific communication can have lasting consequences, even after official corrections are made.

Ethical guidelines have been strengthened in response to these challenges. Organisations such as the Committee on Publication Ethics (COPE) now provide frameworks for handling disputes over authorship, data integrity, and conflicts of interest. Open science initiatives, which promote data sharing and transparency, have been developed to address issues related to reproducibility and trust in research findings (Grant et al., 2022).

Despite these advancements, new ethical concerns have emerged. The pressure to publish frequently has led some researchers to engage in spurious research practices, such as 'p-hacking' (selectively reporting statistical analyses that yield significant results) and excessive self-citation to inflate academic impact (Fanelli, 2009). The expansion of global scientific collaboration has also revealed economic disparities, with researchers from lower-income institutions facing barriers to publishing in prestigious journals.

A New Era: Opportunities and Perils of AI in Academic Publishing

Artificial Intelligence (AI) has become an increasingly influential force in academic publishing, offering new opportunities while also raising significant ethical and epistemological concerns. AI-powered tools are now capable of assisting with writing, editing, peer review, and data analysis, creating an ecosystem where efficiency and accessibility are improved (Bearman et al., 2022). However, this transformation is not without challenges. Concerns about bias, misinformation, loss of human oversight, and the devaluation of expertise have led to discussions about the long-term implications of AI in scholarly communication (Lund et al., 2023). AI's growing presence necessitates a careful examination of its potential benefits and drawbacks, ensuring that its integration into academic publishing supports rather than undermines the integrity of research.

Opportunities in Academic Publishing

One of the most significant advantages of AI in academic publishing lies in its ability to improve the efficiency and accessibility of scholarly communication (Xu et al., 2021). AI-powered language models, such as ChatGPT, are particularly useful for researchers who are non-native English speakers, as they assist in refining grammar, enhancing clarity, and structuring manuscripts more effectively (Homolak, 2023). These tools enable researchers to focus more on the substantive contributions of their work rather than on linguistic accuracy. This is particularly relevant given the dominance of English in academic publishing, which has historically created barriers for scholars from non-English-speaking regions (Gendron et al., 2022).

Beyond language assistance, AI is also streamlining the peer review process. The traditional peer review system is often criticised for being slow, biased, and inefficient. AI has the potential to match manuscripts with appropriate reviewers based on their expertise, thereby reducing the time spent on finding suitable evaluators (Lund et al., 2023). Additionally, AI can assist in detecting potential conflicts of interest and identifying methodological flaws that may not be immediately obvious to human reviewers (Ray, 2023).

Another key benefit of AI is its role in democratising access to scientific knowledge. AI-driven translation technologies allow for greater dissemination of research across linguistic and cultural boundaries, making academic literature more accessible to diverse audiences (Shahmerdanova, 2025). AI is also improving metadata indexing and literature searches, ensuring that scholars can find relevant research more efficiently. By automating these processes, AI has the potential to break down traditional knowledge silos and create a more inclusive academic environment (Fyfe et al., 2017).

In addition to increase accessibility, AI can play an essential role in maintaining research integrity. Automated tools can analyse large datasets, identifying inconsistencies that may indicate errors or scientific misconduct. AI-driven software is capable of detecting statistical anomalies, image manipulation, and citation patterns that suggest unethical self-citation practices. Such technologies, if properly implemented, could serve as powerful safeguards against fraudulent research, ensuring that only high-quality, rigorously inspected work enters the academic record (Gendron et al., 2022).

Despite these advantages, the integration of AI into academic publishing is not without risk. The increasing reliance on AI raises critical questions about the future of scholarly communication, the role of human supervision, and the ethical considerations surrounding automated knowledge production. The challenges associated with AI require examination to prevent unintended negative consequences.

Perils of AI in Academic Publishing

One of the major concerns surrounding AI in academic publishing is the potential for deskilling and the devaluation of human expertise (Carobene et al., 2024). The ability of AI to generate coherent text, summarise research findings, and even suggest citations has led to fears that researchers may become overly reliant on automated systems, thereby diminishing their critical engagement with the writing and publishing process. If AI-driven writing tools become the norm, there is a risk that academic authors may develop a passive approach to knowledge creation, relying on machine-generated text rather than constructing their own original arguments (Gendron et al., 2022).

Additionally, the increasing role of AI in editorial decision-making could reduce the importance of human judgement in evaluating research quality (Shmueli & Ray, 2024). While AI can assist in identifying suitable reviewers and detecting potential biases in peer review, it cannot fully replicate the detailed decision-making processes that human editors and reviewers provide The peer review process is inherently qualitative, requiring evaluators to assess not only the technical soundness of a manuscript but also its originality, theoretical contribution, and broader impact on the field (Pontille & Torny, 2015). While these aspects may be difficult to quantify, they are not purely subjective, as they can be judged based on established academic standards and disciplinary expectations. However, as AI tools become more involved in academic writing and evaluation, concerns arise regarding their potential to homogenise scholarly discourse. AI is not inherently objective; rather, it reflects the biases embedded in its training data, which may inadvertently reinforce dominant paradigms while marginalising alternative perspectives. AI-driven decision-making systems risk prioritising quantifiable metrics over qualitative judgement, potentially leading to a homogenisation of academic research (Lund et al., 2023).

Another significant challenge is the issue of algorithmic bias and discrimination. AI systems are trained on existing datasets, which often reflect historical biases present in academic publishing. These biases can manifest in several ways, such as the reinforcement of gender and racial disparities, favouritism toward research from established institutions, and the perpetuation of citation practices that disproportionately benefit well-known scholars (Homolak, 2023). If AI algorithms are used to rank research output or determine the relevance of submissions, they may inadvertently marginalise voices from underrepresented regions and disciplines. The concern is that AI, rather than democratising knowledge production, could multiply existing hierarchies and exacerbate inequalities in academia (Lund et al., 2023).

The rise of AI-generated content also introduces ethical concerns regarding authorship, originality, and the validity of scientific findings. There have already been instances where AI-generated research papers have been submitted to academic journals, raising alarms about the potential for fabricated or misleading information to enter the scientific record. AI models have been found to produce plausible-sounding but incorrect or unverifiable claims, leading to concerns about misinformation and the integrity of academic discourse (Curtis, 2023).

In addition, the use of AI in academic publishing generates doubts about transparency and accountability. Unlike human reviewers and editors, AI typically operates as a black-box system (Von Eschenbach, 2021), making it impossible to understand how certain decisions are made. This opacity can be problematic when AI is used to assess manuscript quality, recommend citations, or even determine journal acceptance rates. If AI systems are not properly audited and regulated, they could introduce biases and inconsistencies that undermine the publishing process (Gendron et al., 2022).

Additionally, the increasing reliance on AI-driven systems could contribute to a homogenisation of academic publishing. Generative AI outputs tend to reflect the general trend of their input data, omitting outliers and edge cases (National Institute of Standards and Technology, 2024). Consequently, AI models often prioritise mainstream research topics and well-established methodologies, potentially relegating unconventional or interdisciplinary work that does not fit predefined patterns. This could lead to a narrowing of intellectual inquiry, where only research that aligns with algorithmic preferences receives visibility and recognition. The challenge, therefore, is to ensure that AI complements rather than constrains the diversity of academic thought (Lund et al., 2023).

The increasing incorporation of AI into academic publishing has led to significant discussions regarding its appropriate use. AI tools such as ChatGPT and other large language models are widely employed in research writing, peer review, and editorial processes (Lund & Naheem, 2023; Comas-Forgas et al., 2025). While these tools provide benefits such as improving writing quality and assisting with data analysis, their use has also introduced ethical and regulatory challenges. Concerns about authorship, accountability, transparency, and potential bias have prompted academic journals and publishers to establish guidelines to ensure responsible AI use (Tang et al., 2024). The following section explores the current policies, norms, and regulations that regulate AI-assisted academic writing and publishing, analysing how various stakeholders are addressing the challenges associated with these technologies.

Policies on AI Use in Academic Publishing

A key concern in AI use within academic publishing is determining whether AI can be listed as an author. Most academic publishers have established firm policies prohibiting AI from being credited as an author since it lacks accountability and the ability to take responsibility for the content it generates (Lund & Naheem, 2023; Ganjavi et al., 2024). Journals such as Nature and Science have explicitly stated that AI-generated content cannot be considered intellectual contributions, emphasising that authors must take full responsibility for any AI-assisted material (Ganjavi et al., 2024). Publishing associations such as the International Committee of Medical Journal Editors (ICMJE) have reinforced this stance, clarifying that AI does not meet the authorship criteria because it cannot be held accountable for research integrity (Teixeira da Silva & Tsigaris, 2023).

Transparency in AI use is another essential aspect addressed by publishers. The Cambridge University Press (2025), Elsevier (2025), Frontiers (2025), the Institute of Electrical and Electronics Engineers (Solomon, 2024), the Institute of Physics (2025), the Multidisciplinary Digital Publishing Institute (2025), the Public Library of Science (2025), Sage (2025), Science (2025), Springer (2025), Taylor & Francis (2025), and Wiley (2024) have published policies requiring that the use of artificial intelligence in submitted publications be disclosed. Frontiers, the Institute for Electrical and Electronics Engineers, the Public Library of Science, Science, and Taylor & Francis require specific details of the AI usage, such as the name of the software, the prompt used, or which sections of the text were affected.

Conversely, the Multidisciplinary Digital Publishing Institute, Sage, Springer, and Wiley make exceptions for text editing – as opposed to substantive content generation – but the distinction is far from clear-cut. It is most coherently explained by Sage, who distinguish 'assistive AI' – tools embedded in programmes such as Gmail that make suggestions for improvements – from 'generative AI', in which an AI tool is the 'primary creator' of the content. Only the latter must be declared; Sage characterises the former as an extension of spellcheckers or autocorrect. MDPI, Sage, and Wiley are far less specific as to what need or need not be declared.

Many leading journals have implemented disclosure policies requiring authors to explicitly state whether AI tools were used in any stage of manuscript preparation (Tang et al., 2024). According to a study analysing a sample of 300 academic journals, approximately 58.7% of journals have AI authorship policies, with 96.6% allowing AI assistance for manuscript improvement but prohibiting its inclusion as an author (Lund & Naheem, 2023). Disclosure is typically required in sections such as methods, acknowledgements, or in a dedicated AI declaration section (Ganjavi et al., 2024). However, there is still variability in how different publishers enforce these policies, leading to inconsistencies in disclosure practices (Bhavsar et al., 2025).

AI tools can inadvertently introduce ethical concerns such as data fabrication, bias, and plagiarism. AI-generated text may contain inaccurate or fictitious references, commonly referred to as 'hallucinations', which mislead readers and compromise research integrity (Tang et al., 2024). Some publishers have issued guidelines stating that AI-generated text must be carefully verified, and any fabricated content is subject to strict scrutiny (Ganjavi et al., 2024; Romero Moreno, 2024).

In general terms, publishers' AI policies present significant inconsistencies, based on a bibliometric analysis conducted by Ganjavi et al. (2024), as while 87% of top-ranked journals have developed AI-specific guidelines, only 24% of major publishers provide detailed policies on AI use in academic writing. This discrepancy creates confusion for authors and raises concerns about the lack of standardised AI acceptance in scholarly communication.

Norms and Guidelines for AI in Academic Publishing

Efforts are underway to standardise AI reporting in academic publishing. Two notable frameworks include CONSORT-AI (Consolidated Standards of Reporting Trials for Artificial Intelligence) and SPIRIT-AI (Standard Protocol Items for Interventional Trials – Artificial Intelligence), which provide structured recommendations for documenting AI involvement in randomised clinical trials (Tang et al., 2024). These guidelines encourage authors to describe the specific AI models used, their purpose, and any potential limitations that might affect the research outcomes.

Another relevant resource is the Committee on Publication Ethics (COPE) recommendations, which emphasise that AI tools cannot be listed as authors and that their contributions must be acknowledged transparently (Ganjavi et al., 2024). COPE also advises journals to include clear policies on AI usage in their author guidelines and ensure that peer reviewers and editors are aware of AI-related ethical concerns. Many journals affiliated with COPE have already adopted these recommendations to maintain ethical standards in publishing.

Additionally, several major publishers have introduced their own guidelines and principles regarding AI use:

- Elsevier mandates that authors take full responsibility for AI-assisted text (Bhavsar et al., 2025).
- Taylor & Francis has established a dedicated AI disclosure section in its author guidelines to ensure transparency (Ganjavi et al., 2024).
- Cambridge University Press emphasises that AI tools should be used ethically and that their impact on research quality must be assessed (Bhavsar et al., 2025).

Undeclared and Unethical Use of AI in Academic Publishing: Evidence and Research

This section of the manuscript examines the available evidence on the unreported and unethical use of AI in academic publishing, reviewing research on its prevalence, detection challenges, and implications for scholarly integrity.

Prevalence of Undeclared AI Use in Academic Publishing

Several recent studies provide evidence into the increasing presence of AI-generated content in academic literature. Gray (2024) estimates that at least 60,000 academic papers in 2023 (over 1% of all articles) contained AI-assisted writing without proper disclosure. This estimate was derived by analysing the prevalence of keywords and phrases disproportionately associated with AI-generated text. The study identified a sharp increase in such terms post-2022, contemporaneous with the release of ChatGPT-3.5 and other advanced large language models (LLMs).

A bibliometric study by Uribe and Maldupa (2024) focusing on dental research found a 177.2% increase in the usage of AI-generated phrases in research abstracts after the release of ChatGPT. The authors argue that this rise suggests widespread, yet unacknowledged, of AI-assisted content in scientific writing. This research also highlights concerns regarding linguistic homogenisation, where AI-driven text generation promotes uniform stylistic trends across disciplines (Uribe & Maldupa, 2024).

Further evidence from Comas-Forgas et al. (2025) supports these claims, showing a notable rise in AI-influenced language patterns in article titles. Their study focused on verb usage in research article titles suspected of AI authorship, revealed an unusual spike in certain verbs post-2022. These findings suggest that AI-driven content generation is subtly altering academic writing conventions, often without proper acknowledgement (Comas-Forgas et al., 2025).

Detection Challenges and AI-assisted Writing Patterns

One of the primary difficulties in identifying AI-generated text is the lack of clear linguistic markers. Casal and Kessler (2023) conducted a study evaluating whether experienced linguists and journal editors could distinguish between AI-generated and human-written abstracts. Their results showed that reviewers correctly identified AI-generated abstracts only 38.9% of the time, suggesting that AI-produced text is often indistinguishable from human writing. This low detection rate poses significant challenges for editors and reviewers aiming to ensure research authenticity (Casal & Kessler, 2023).

Gray (2024) further highlights that removing AI-generated 'hallucinations' and overly rigid language makes detection even more difficult. Unlike traditional forms of academic misconduct, such as plagiarism, which can be flagged through text-matching software (although not being 100% reliably), AI-generated content often bypasses existing detection mechanisms. This makes undeclared AI use a particularly insidious form of academic dishonesty.

Ethical Implications of Undeclared AI Use

The failure to disclose AI assistance raises serious concerns regarding authorship ethics and intellectual responsibility. Transparency in research is fundamental to scholarly communication, ensuring that readers and reviewers understand the methodologies and tools used in the writing process (Raman, 2023). When AI-generated content is introduced without acknowledgement, it blurs the line between original human creation and machine-assisted production.

Additionally, the undeclared use of AI in peer review has been flagged as a growing problem. Liang et al. (2024) found strong evidence that ChatGPT and similar tools are being used to generate peer reviews for conference papers, particularly in the artificial intelligence domain. While AI-assisted review writing could streamline the process, the lack of human critical judgement and potential for bias undermine the rigour of the peer review system (Liang et al., 2024).

Authorship in academic publishing is traditionally based on intellectual contribution, accountability, and responsibility. However, undeclared AI use challenges these principles. Stojanov (2025) highlights that AI-assisted writing is homogenising academic expression, making it difficult to differentiate individual writing styles and intellectual contributions. This trend risks diminishing the uniqueness of scholarly voices and could lead to standardised, AI-driven academic discourse (Stojanov, 2025).

The issue extends beyond authorship to scientific credibility. AI-generated content has been found to fabricate references, misinterpret data, and introduce errors that could mislead readers. AI 'hallucinations', particularly where the model produces non-existent citations, have been documented as a persistent issue (Buchanan et al., 2024). This raises concerns about the reliability of AI-assisted research outputs, especially when these inaccuracies go unnoticed. A particularly striking example was a study by Shoukat et al. (2024) published in *PLoS One*. Commenters on PubPeer noticed the appearance of the phrase 'Regenerate response', formerly a button on the ChatGPT interface, in the reference list. When the editors investigated, they were unable to verify eighteen of the seventy-six references in the article, suggesting that they may have been hallucinated (PLoS One Editors, 2024).

Commercial Exploitation and Paper Mills

Another dimension of unethical AI use involves the rise of paper mills – commercial enterprises that produce assisted AI-generated research articles for authors seeking easy publication (Byrne et al., 2024). Kendall & Teixeira da Silva (2024) argue that these third-party services often provide fraudulent academic content, undermining the integrity of peer-reviewed literature. The increasing sophistication of AI tools has made it easier for paper mills to produce seemingly legitimate research papers, flooding academic databases with unreliable or falsified information (Kendall & Teixeira da Silva, 2024).

Conclusions

The analysis of AI in academic publishing reveals a profound transformation in scholarly communication. As demonstrated in the preceding sections, AI has introduced significant shifts in research dissemination, linguistic patterns, and ethical considerations, requiring a recalibration of existing norms and policies. The findings in this chapter align with broader discussions in contemporary literature, which recognise both the benefits and risks associated with AI-driven text generation in academia (Adauto Medina et al., 2024; Dergaa et al., 2023).

AI tools, particularly large language models like ChatGPT, have been integrated into various stages of academic writing, from conceptualisation to final manuscript preparation. Their ability to refine grammar, structure arguments, and enrich coherence has enlarged access to high-quality academic communication, especially for non-native English speakers (Buruk, 2023). This potentiality is widely regarded as one of the major contributions of AI in academic writing, reducing barriers to participation in global scholarly discourse (Bom, 2023). However, the trade-off lies in the potential standardisation of academic language, which may inadvertently diminish the uniqueness of individual writing styles and cultural distinctions in scholarly communication (Comas-Forgas et al., 2025).

The growing reliance on AI raises fundamental ethical concerns regarding authorship, originality, and transparency. As highlighted in previous sections and stressed by various studies, the use of AI in writing necessitates clear disclosure to maintain academic integrity (Jarrah et al., 2023). Unacknowledged AI involvement in research papers has led to debates over the legitimacy of authorship claims and the responsibilities of scholars in ensuring proper attribution (Rahman et al., 2023). The findings of the existing corpus of evidence synthesised in this chapter emphasise the need for institutional policies that mandate explicit disclosure of AI-generated content in academic publications.

Several initiatives have emerged to monitor and regulate the use of AI in academic publishing, literature promoting greater transparency in scholarly work. The Problematic Paper Screener (https://dbrech.irit.fr/pls/apex/f?p=9999:1), developed to identify instances of 'tortured phrasing', has been used to identify phrasing characteristic of AI-generated content. Academ-AI (https://www.academ-ai.info) collects examples of suspected AI usage in the academic. These projects analyse text patterns, citation structures, and writing inconsistencies to flag potential AI involvement.

Major publishers, including Springer Nature and Elsevier, have introduced guidelines stipulating that AI-generated content must be explicitly acknowledged in research papers (Buruk, 2023). However, enforcement mechanisms remain inconsistent, highlighting the need for standardised regulatory frameworks across academic institutions (Jarrah et al., 2023).

Finally, one of the most significant implications of AI integration in academia is its impact on the peer review process. AI-assisted peer reviews have been increasingly utilised to streamline manuscript evaluations, potentially decreasing the depth of critique and introducing algorithmic bias (Rahman et al., 2023). While AI can improve efficiency by summarising key arguments and checking for inconsistencies, it lacks the proper understanding required for evaluating research contributions (Dergaa et al., 2023).

Looking ahead, the role of AI in academia will continue to progress, necessitating proactive policy interventions and ethical guidelines. Future research should focus on developing robust frameworks that balance the benefits of AI-enhanced writing with the preservation of scholarly integrity. Several key recommendations emerge from this analysis:

- Institutional policies on AI use: Universities, research centres, funding bodies and publishers should establish comprehensive guidelines detailing acceptable AI usage in academic writing. These policies should differentiate between AI-assisted editing and full-scale text generation, ensuring that transparency is maintained.
- AI disclosure standards: Mandatory AI disclosure sections should be integrated into research manuscripts, allowing reviewers and readers to assess and recognise the extent of AI involvement. This aligns with the principles of academic integrity and accountability (Jarrah et al., 2023).
- AI-detection and verification tools: The development of more sophisticated and reliable AI-detection mechanisms is essential to mitigate the risks associated with undisclosed AI use. Collaborations between academic institutions and AI research labs can improve the reliability of these tools (Bom, 2023).

- Ethical training for researchers: Incorporating AI ethics training into academic curricula can raise responsible AI use among researchers. By educating scholars on the ethical implications of AI in academic writing, institutions can promote a culture of integrity and accountability.
- Reevaluating research metrics: The impact of AI-generated content on citation practices and academic evaluations must be systematically studied. Alternative metrics that prioritise originality and human intellectual contributions should be explored.

AI Use Declaration

The authors acknowledge that ChatGPT-4.0 was utilised for proofreading purposes in the preparation of this book chapter. The AI assistance was limited to linguistic refinement, grammar correction, and clarity improvement, without altering the conceptual, analytical, or interpretative content of the manuscript.

All substantive content, including arguments, analyses, conclusions, and interpretations, remain solely the responsibility of the authors, who have thoroughly reviewed, validated, and approved the final version of the text. The use of AI does not imply any transfer of authorship or intellectual contribution beyond the stated scope.

Acknowledgements

Chapter elaborated within the framework of the: a) project PID2022-141031NB-I00, funded by MICIU/AEI/10.13039/501100011033/ and by ERDF A way of making Europe; b) 'Ibero-American Network of Research on Academic Integrity' funded by the AUIP (www.red-ia.org).

Bibliography

Adauto Medina, W. A., Velásquez, C. H. F., Zegarra, S. del R. O., Romero, G. P. M., Andía, A. Q., Bellido, I. E. A., Huaraca, C. R. P., Trejo, F. H. A., & Bravo, N. A. (2024). Using ChatGPT in University Academic Writing: A Bibliometric Review Study on the Implications for Writing Reports, Papers, Essays, and Theses. International Journal

of Learning, Teaching and Educational Research, 23(12), 360–381. https://doi.org/10.26803/ijlter.23.12.19
Arbuckle, A. (2021). Opening up scholarship in the humanities: digital publishing, knowledge translation, and public engagement (Doctoral dissertation). University of Victoria, Canada. https://dspace.library.uvic.ca/server/api/core/bitstreams/bf54fa89-c999-400c-96a2-73409f783bcb/content
Baldwin, M. (2015). Credibility, peer review, and Nature, 1945–1990. *Notes and Records of the Royal Society, 69*(3), 337–352. https://doi.org/10.1098/rsnr.2015.0029
Bearman, M., Ryan, J., & Ajjawi, R. (2022). Discourses of artificial intelligence in higher education: a critical literature review. *Higher Education, 86*(2), 369–385. https://doi.org/10.1007/s10734-022-00937-2
Bhavsar, D., Duffy, L., Jo, H., Lokker, C., Haynes, R. B., Iorio, A., Marusic, A., & Ng, J. Y. (2025). Policies on artificial intelligence chatbots among academic publishers: a cross-sectional audit. *Research Integrity and Peer Review, 10*(1). https://doi.org/10.1186/s41073-025-00158-y
Blackmore, P., & Kandiko, C. B. (2011). Motivation in academic life: A prestige economy. *Research in Post-Compulsory Education, 16*(4), 399–411. https://doi.org/10.1080/13596748.2011.626971
Bom, H.-S. H. (2023). Exploring the Opportunities and Challenges of ChatGPT in Academic Writing: a Roundtable Discussion. *Nuclear Medicine and Molecular Imaging, 57*(4), 165–167. https://doi.org/10.1007/s13139-023-00809-2
Buchanan, J., Hill, S., & Shapoval, O. (2023). ChatGPT Hallucinates Non-existent Citations: Evidence from Economics. *The American Economist, 69*(1), 80–87. https://doi.org/10.1177/05694345231218454
Buruk, O. (2023). Academic Writing with GPT-3.5 (ChatGPT): Reflections on Practices, Efficacy and Transparency. 26th International Academic Mindtrek Conference, 144–153. https://doi.org/10.1145/3616961.3616992
Byrne, J. A., Abalkina, A., Akinduro-Aje, O., Christopher, J., Eaton, S. E., Joshi, N., Scheffler, U., Wise, N. H., & Wright, J. (2024). A call for research to address the threat of paper mills. PLOS Biology, 22(11), e3002931. https://doi.org/10.1371/journal.pbio.3002931
Cambridge University Press. (2025). *Publishing ethics authorship and contributorship journals*. Cambridge Core. https://www.cambridge.org/core/services/publishing-ethics/authorship-and-contributorship-journals
Carobene, A., Padoan, A., Cabitza, F., Banfi, G., & Plebani, M. (2024). Rising adoption of artificial intelligence in scientific publishing:

evaluating the role, risks, and ethical implications in paper drafting and review process. *Clinical Chemistry and Laboratory Medicine, 62*(5), 835–843. https://doi.org/10.1515/cclm-2023-1136

Casal, J. E., & Kessler, M. (2023). Can linguists distinguish between ChatGPT/AI and human writing?: A study of research ethics and academic publishing. *Research Methods in Applied Linguistics, 2*(3), 100068. https://doi.org/10.1016/j.rmal.2023.100068

Chukwuere, J. E. (2024). Today's Academic Research: The Role of ChatGPT Writing. *Journal of Information Systems and Informatics, 6*(1), 30–46. https://doi.org/10.51519/journalisi.v6i1.639

Comas-Forgas, R., Koulouris, A., & Kouis, D. (2025). 'AI-navigating'or 'AI-sinking'? An analysis of verbs in research articles titles suspicious of containing AI-generated/assisted content. *Learned Publishing, 38*(1), e1647. https://doi.org/10.1002/leap.1647

Curtis, N. (2023). To ChatGPT or not to ChatGPT? The Impact of Artificial Intelligence on Academic Publishing. *Pediatric Infectious Disease Journal, 42*(4), 275–275. https://doi.org/10.1097/inf.0000000000003852

De Silva, P. U., & Vance, C. K. (2017). *Scientific scholarly communication*. Springer International Publishing.

Dergaa, I., Chamari, K., Zmijewski, P., & Ben Saad, H. (2023). From human writing to artificial intelligence generated text: examining the prospects and potential threats of ChatGPT in academic writing. Biology of Sport, 40(2), 615–622. https://doi.org/10.5114/biolsport.2023.125623

Eggertson, L. (2010). Lancet retracts 12-year-old article linking autism to MMR vaccines. *Canadian Medical Association Journal, 182*(4), E199–E200. https://doi.org/10.1503/cmaj.109-3179

Elsevier. (2025). *Generative AI policies for journals*. Elsevier. https://www.elsevier.com/about/policies-and-standards/generative-ai-policies-for-journals

vov Eschenbach, W. J. (2021). Transparency and the black box problem: Why we do not trust AI. *Philosophy & Technology, 34*(4), 1607–1622. https://doi.org/10.1007/s13347-021-00477-0

Eve, M. P. (2014). Open Access and the Humanities: Contexts, Controversies and the Future. Cambridge University Press. https://doi.org/10.1017/cbo9781316161012

Fanelli, D. (2009). How Many Scientists Fabricate and Falsify Research? A Systematic Review and Meta-Analysis of Survey Data. *PLoS ONE, 4*(5), e5738. https://doi.org/10.1371/journal.pone.0005738

Franzen, S. (2021). *University Responsibility for the Adjudication of Research Misconduct*. Springer International Publishing.

Frontiers. (2025). *Author guidelines*. Frontiers. https://www.frontiersin.org/guidelines/author-guidelines

Fyfe, A., Coate, K., Curry, S., Lawson, S., Moxham, N., & Røstvik, C. M. (2017). *Untangling academic publishing: A history of the relationship between commercial interests, academic prestige and the circulation of research.* Discussion Paper. University of St Andrews. https://eprints.bbk.ac.uk/id/eprint/19148/

Fyfe, A., Moxham, N., McDougall-Waters, J., & Røstvik, C. M. (2022). *A history of scientific journals*. UCL Press.

Ganjavi, C., Eppler, M. B., Pekcan, A., Biedermann, B., Abreu, A., Collins, G. S., Gill, I. S., & Cacciamani, G. E. (2024). Publishers' and journals' instructions to authors on use of generative artificial intelligence in academic and scientific publishing: bibliometric analysis. BMJ, e077192. https://doi.org/10.1136/bmj-2023-077192

Garvey, W. D. (2014). *Communication: the essence of science: facilitating information exchange among librarians, scientists, engineers and students*. Elsevier.

Gendron, Y., Andrew, J., & Cooper, C. (2022). The perils of artificial intelligence in academic publishing. *Critical Perspectives on Accounting, 87*, 102411. https://doi.org/10.1016/j.cpa.2021.102411

Gould, S. J. (1983). The Piltdown Conspiracy. Natural History.

Graham, H. D., & Diamond, N. (1997). *The rise of American research universities: Elites and challengers in the postwar era*. JHU Press.

Grant, S., Wendt, K. E., Leadbeater, B. J., Supplee, L. H., Mayo-Wilson, E., Gardner, F., & Bradshaw, C. P. (2022). Transparent, Open, and Reproducible Prevention Science. *Prevention Science, 23*(5), 701–722. https://doi.org/10.1007/s11121-022-01336-w

Gray, A. (2024). ChatGPT 'contamination': estimating the prevalence of LLMs in the scholarly literature. UCL Library Services. arXiv preprint arXiv:2403.16887

Gregory, J., & Miller, S. (1998). *Science in public: Communication, culture, and credibility*. Plenum Press.

Homolak, J. (2023). Opportunities and risks of ChatGPT in medicine, science, and academic publishing: a modern Promethean dilemma. *Croatian Medical Journal, 64*(1), 1–3. https://doi.org/10.3325/cmj.2023.64.1

Hyland, K. (2016). *Academic publishing: Issues and challenges in the construction of knowledge*. Oxford University Press

Institute of Physics. (2025). *Ethical policy for journals*. IOPscience – Publishing Support. https://publishingsupport.iopscience.iop.org/ethical-policy-journals/

Ioannidis, J. P. (2005). Why Most Published Research Findings Are False. *PLoS Medicine, 2*(8), e124. https://doi.org/10.1371/journal.pmed.0020124

Jarrah, A. M., Wardat, Y., & Fidalgo, P. (2023). Using ChatGPT in academic writing is (not) a form of plagiarism: What does the literature say? *Online Journal of Communication and Media Technologies*, 13(4), e202346. https://doi.org/10.30935/ojcmt/13572

Johns, A. (2019). Piracy: The intellectual property wars from Gutenberg to Gates. University of Chicago Press.

Kendall, G., & Teixeira da Silva, J. A. (2024). Risks of abuse of large language models, like ChatGPT, in scientific publishing: Authorship, predatory publishing, and paper mills. Learned Publishing, 37(1). https://doi.org/10.1002/leap.1578

LaFollette, M. C. (1992). *Stealing into print: Fraud, plagiarism, and misconduct in scientific publishing*. University of California Press.

Larivière, V., Haustein, S., & Mongeon, P. (2015). The Oligopoly of Academic Publishers in the Digital Era. *PLOS ONE, 10*(6), e0127502. https://doi.org/10.1371/journal.pone.0127502

Lawson, S., Gray, J., & Mauri, M. (2016). Opening the black box of scholarly communication funding: A public data infrastructure for financial flows in academic publishing. *Open Library of Humanities, 2*(1). https://doi.org/10.16995/olh.72

Liang, W., Izzo, Z., Zhang, Y., Lepp, H., Cao, H., Zhao, X., … & Zou, J. Y. (2024). Monitoring ai-modified content at scale: A case study on the impact of chatgpt on ai conference peer reviews. arXiv preprint arXiv:2403.07183.

Lund, B. D., & Naheem, K. T. (2023). Can ChatGPT be an author? A study of artificial intelligence authorship policies in top academic journals. *Learned Publishing, 37*(1), 13–21. https://doi.org/10.1002/leap.1582

Lund, B. D., Wang, T., Mannuru, N. R., Nie, B., Shimray, S., & Wang, Z. (2023). ChatGPT and a new academic reality: Artificial Intelligence-written research papers and the ethics of the large language models in scholarly publishing. Journal of the Association for Information Science and Technology, 74(5), 570–581. https://doi.org/10.1002/asi.24750

Mackintosh, N. J. E. (1995). *Cyril Burt: fraud or framed?.* Oxford University Press.

Mayoni, A. (2022). Scientific publishers are reaping huge profits from the work of researchers – and the universities are paying for it. *Uniavisen*. Retrieved from https://uniavisen.dk/en/scientific-publishers-are-reaping-huge-profits-from-the-work-of-researchers-and-the-universities-are-paying-for-it/

Morriello, R. (2024). *Dalla pirateria dei libri all'editoria predatoria: Un percorso tra storia della stampa ed etica della comunicazione scientifica*. Editrice Bibliografica.

Multidisciplinary Digital Publishing Institute. (2025). *Research and Publication Ethics*. MDPI. https://www.mdpi.com/ethics

National Institute of Standards and Technology. (2024). *Artificial Intelligence Risk Management Framework: Generative Artificial Intelligence Profile*. United States Department of Commerce. https://doi.org/10.6028/NIST. AI.600-1

PLoS One Editors. (2024) Retraction: A comparative analysis of blended learning and traditional instruction: Effects on academic motivation and learning outcomes. *PLoS One, 19*(4), e0302484. https://doi.org/10.1371/journal.pone.0302484

Pontille, D., & Torny, D. (2015). From manuscript evaluation to article valuation: The changing technologies of journal peer review. *Human Studies, 38, 57–79.* https://doi.org/10.1007/s10746-014-9335-z

Public Library of Science. (2025). *Ethical Publishing Practice*. PLoS One. https://journals.plos.org/plosone/s/ethical-publishing-practice

Rahman, M., Terano, H. J. R., Rahman, N., Salamzadeh, A., & Rahaman, S. (2023). ChatGPT and Academic Research: A Review and Recommendations Based on Practical Examples. *Journal of Education, Management and Development Studies, 3*(1), 1–12. https://doi.org/10.52631/jemds.v3i1.175

Raman, R. (2023). Transparency in research: An analysis of ChatGPT usage acknowledgment by authors across disciplines and geographies. Accountability in Research, 1–22. https://doi.org/10.1080/08989621.2023.2273377

Ray, P. P. (2023). ChatGPT: A comprehensive review on background, applications, key challenges, bias, ethics, limitations and future scope. *Internet of Things and Cyber-Physical Systems, 3*, 121–154. https://doi.org/10.1016/j.iotcps.2023.04.003

Romero Moreno, F. (2024). Generative AI and deepfakes: a human rights approach to tackling harmful content. International Review of Law,

Computers & Technology, 38(3), 297–326. https://doi.org/10.1080/13600869.2024.2324540

Sage. (2025). *Assistive and generative AI guidelines for authors | Policies & guidelines.* Sage Publishing. https://www.sagepub.com/about/policies/ai-author-guidelines

Science. (2025). *Science Journals: Editorial Policies.* Science. https://www.science.org/content/page/science-journals-editorial-policies

Shahmerdanova, R. (2025). Artificial Intelligence in Translation: Challenges and Opportunities. Acta Globalis Humanitatis et Linguarum, 2(1), 62–70. https://doi.org/10.69760/aghel.02500108

Shmueli, G., & Ray, S. (2024). Reimagining the Journal Editorial Process: An AI-Augmented Versus an AI-Driven Future. *Journal of the Association for Information Systems, 25*(1), 10. https://doi.org/10.17705/1jais.00864

Shoukat, R., Ismayil, I., Huang, Q., Oubibi, M., Younas, M., & Munir, R. (2024). A comparative analysis of blended learning and traditional instruction: Effects on academic motivation and learning outcomes. *PLoS One, 19*(3), e0298220. https://doi.org/10.1371/journal.pone.0298220

Solomon, D. (2024). Author guidelines for artificial intelligence (AI)-generated text. *IEEE Open*. https://open.ieee.org/author-guidelines-for-artificial-intelligence-ai-generated-text/

Springer. (2025). *Artificial intelligence (AI).* Springer. https://www.springer.com/us/editorial-policies/artificial-intelligence--ai-/25428500

Tang, A., Li, K. K., Kwok, K. O., Cao, L., Luong, S., & Tam, W. (2024). The importance of transparency: Declaring the use of generative artificial intelligence (AI) in academic writing. *Journal of nursing scholarship, 56*(2), 314–318. https://doi.org/10.1111/jnu.12938

Taylor & Francis. (2025). *AI policy.* Taylor & Francis. https://taylorandfrancis.com/our-policies/ai-policy/

Teixeira da Silva, J. A., & Tsigaris, P. (2023). Human-and AI-based authorship: Principles and ethics. *Learned Publishing, 36*(3). https://doi.org/10.1002/leap.1547

Thompson, J. B. (2005). *Books in the digital age: the transformation of academic and higher education publishing in Britain and the United States.* Polity.

Uribe, S. E., & Maldupa, I. (2024). Estimating the use of ChatGPT in dental research publications. Journal of Dentistry, 149, 105275. https://doi.org/10.1016/j.jdent.2024.105275

Wiley. (2024). *Best Practice Guidelines on Research Integrity and Publishing Ethics*. Wiley. https://authorservices.wiley.com/ethics-guidelines/index.html

Xu, Y., Liu, X., Cao, X., Huang, C., Liu, E., Qian, S., Liu, X., Wu, Y., Dong, F., Qiu, C.-W., Qiu, J., Hua, K., Su, W., Wu, J., Xu, H., Han, Y., Fu, C., Yin, Z., Liu, M., … Zhang, J. (2021). Artificial intelligence: A powerful paradigm for scientific research. *The Innovation, 2*(4), 100179. https://doi.org/10.1016/j.xinn.2021.100179

Criteria for Assessing the Impact of Generative AI on Students' Dissertation Defences

Cinta Gallent-Torres[1], Mercè Morey López[2] and Pilar Ezpeleta-Piorno[3]

ABSTRACT

This chapter explores the impact of Generative Artificial Intelligence (GAI) on students' oral discourse during the defence of Final Degree Projects (*Trabajo Fin de Título* or TFT, in Spanish). It addresses a significant gap in research by focusing on GAI's influence on spoken language, particularly in academic contexts like dissertation defences. The chapter also aims to establish criteria for evaluating oral defences in Spanish universities, with a special focus on GAI's role in their preparation.

Based on a review of literature from Scopus and Dialnet, and a comparison of evaluation criteria across fifteen Spanish universities, the chapter proposes key indicators for assessing these defences. It identifies six core competences for evaluation: communication skills, language use, structure and coherence, time management, use of visual aids, and handling questions. Also, it suggests specific GAI-related signs (e.g. impersonal language, repetitive sentences, or unclear use of sources) to detect AI-generated content that could affect the assessment of TFT.

The chapter emphasises the importance of ethical GAI use in oral presentations and concludes with proposals for the responsible integration of this technology into education to help students and educators reach their full potential.

Keywords: generative artificial intelligence, higher education, dissertation defences, oral academic discourse, academic integrity

Introduction

The growing presence of generative Artificial Intelligence (GAI) in everyday communication is transforming human language in both written and spoken forms. The way we create, interpret, and engage with text and speech has dramatically changed in the past few years (Ashour, 2020) – likely with no way back. Nowadays, chatbots respond to customer inquiries, avatars assist in job interviews, and news articles are automatically generated, blurring the lines between human and machine-produced content (Nguyen et al.,

[1] University of Valencia, Spain (https://orcid.org/0000-0002-4260-7594)
[2] University of the Balearic Islands, Spain (https://orcid.org/0000-0002-2050-6602)
[3] University Jaume I, Spain (https://orcid.org/0000-0002-4565-7183)

2024). In just a few years, GAI has had a significant impact on every sector of society, including higher education, where its increasing integration into educational practices has begun to affect linguistic norms, communication styles, and even the ways in which ideas are expressed in academic settings.

GAI also influences the nuances of expression in scholarly communication. In this context, research suggests that tools like ChatGPT, Mistral, Claude, and Jasper not only impact our choice of words and tone but also lead us to adopt 'language tics' that we may not be aware of (Gallent & Comas, 2025). The spread of these 'language tics' (commonly understood as repetitive words and structures) in our daily interactions with AI tools can be seen as a form of 'linguistic contagion' (Merminod, 2023). As certain words or phrases gain popularity through digital platforms and social media, AI now introduces new patterns into our speech, influencing the way we communicate. This shift mirrors what Trouillez (s.f., cited in Mongaillard, 2018) refers to as a 'mimetic effect', where linguistic changes spread like trends. Historically, these shifts were driven by media, celebrities, politicians or social movements, but today, AI has added a new layer to this dynamic.

Indeed, this tendency shows how language evolves in response to the tools we use. Certain words and phrases become so embedded in our speech that we fail to recognise them as products of our interactions with AI, yet we continue to assimilate them. This process aligns with Bourdieu's (1992) concept of the *circularity of language*, where language is not a neutral medium but a dynamic force that both reflects and constructs the reality in which we live. With the widespread use of AI systems, this circularisation of language is amplified. As we adopt these AI patterns, they become part of our communication, influencing the way we think, behave, and understand the world around us. In the context of higher education, where language is not only a tool for communication but also an essential vehicle for the construction and dissemination of knowledge, this shift could have important consequences. Thus, the use of AI language models may have a significant impact on how students, faculty, and scholars engage in critical discourse, disseminate knowledge, present results, and approach research.

This trend is becoming evident in academia, particularly in how AI is influencing scientific written discourse and the language used in research publications. Some researchers have analysed the linguistics of academic article titles (Comas et al., 2024; Teh & Uwasomba, 2024) and noticed a suspicious rise in the frequency of certain verbs, such as 'navigating', 'unveiling', 'unravelling', and 'deciphering', which have experienced an annual growth rate exceeding 200% in some cases. This 'questionable' increase clearly indicates AI's impact on academic writing, as the prevalence of these specific verbs suggests AI assistance rather than a simple stylistic choice by the authors.

There is no doubt that ChatGPT has its own written style, often robotic and awkward, but many choose to overlook this fact. This is particularly clear in the study conducted by Gao et al. (2023), where fifty ChatGPT-generated scientific abstracts were compared to fifty from high-impact journals. Four reviewers were asked to distinguish between AI-generated and authentic abstracts, correctly identifying 68% of the AI-generated abstracts and 86% of the authentic ones. Although the AI-generated abstracts looked like real scientific writing in terms of structure, grammar, and content, a closer analysis revealed significant weaknesses. These abstracts lacked depth and originality, used formulaic language, included irrelevant details, and demonstrated a surface-level understanding of the topic.

Cheng et al. (2023) also explored the capabilities of AI language models in generating scientific abstracts. They selected thirty research papers from *Nature*, *Genome Biology*, and *Biological Psychiatry*. Excluding the original abstracts, the full text of each paper was input into ChatPDF, which was prompted to generate abstracts mimicking the style of the original papers. A panel of eight experts was invited to evaluate the quality of these generated abstracts and to identify which ones were produced by ChatPDF, using a blind assessment approach. Among the thirty generated abstracts, three contained incorrect conclusions, and ten were correctly identified as AI-generated content. In line with this study, Geng and Trotta (2024) also conducted a statistical analysis on one million arXiv papers submitted between May 2018 and January 2024 to assess the textual density of ChatGPT's writing style in abstracts. Their model was calibrated and validated using a combination of real and ChatGPT-modified abstracts. The study found that large language models (LLMs), particularly ChatGPT, are increasingly influencing the style of arXiv abstracts, with an estimated 35% of abstracts in the computer science field reflecting the LLM writing style. As the authors noted, 'determining whether a given few sentences were generated by ChatGPT is difficult but determining that millions of sentences were influenced by ChatGPT is statistically feasible' (p. 1). In the coming years, research will likely focus on this issue, highlighting the need for clearer ethical guidelines regarding AI's role in academic writing, and a deeper reflection on the concepts of authorship and academic integrity.

While much of the recent research has focused on AI's impact on written discourse, particularly in academic and scientific articles (Rinaldy et al., 2023; Nguyen et al., 2024; Thasler-Kordonouri et al., 2024), its influence on spoken language, especially within educational contexts, remains underexplored. This research gap presents an opportunity to examine how AI tools – such as text-to-speech models, interactive pronunciation assistants, voice training apps, and real-time speech summarisers, among others – may be altering the way students approach public speaking and formal academic events, including the defence of final master's and bachelor's dissertations (known in Spanish as *Trabajo Fin de Título* or TFT). This event is a compulsory requirement for Spanish graduate and postgraduate students, as established by Royal Decree 822/2021, of 28 September. While universities may vary in their approaches (as regards the number of committee members, time allocated, defence format, (non)authorised use of AI, etc.), for many students, this experience serves as their first formal encounter with academic communication. In this sense, understanding how AI influences aspects such as delivery, word choice, lexical diversity, emotional tone, and speech clarity can provide valuable insights into both the opportunities and challenges these technologies present.

Based on the above, this work has two primary objectives: First, it aims to address a significant theoretical and knowledge research gap (Miles, 2017) by exploring a novel area of AI's influence: students' academic oral discourse. While existing studies on this particular field have focused on academic conferences held by scholars (Pérez-Colomé, 2024), there is limited research on how AI impacts students' oral discourse. Through a comprehensive literature review, this work will explore AI's impact on dissertation defences, examining factors such as its consequences, ethical implications and effects on academic integrity. The second objective is to establish a set of criteria for evaluating oral dissertation defences (as part of the TFT subjects), with particular emphasis on the role of GAI in their preparation.

Considering these objectives, we anticipate that analysing these criteria will lay the foundation for creating rubrics to assess dissertation defences in the future. As AI continues to shape academic practices, updated evaluation tools will be essential to ensure fair and effective assessment of oral presentations.

Literature Review

The study of AI's influence on students' oral discourse is still in its early stages, with limited empirical research to substantiate what may seem like a premature assumption to some. However, some authors argue that GAI is 'poised to fundamentally change how we communicate' (Hohenstein et al., 2023, p. 1), and AI tools such as ChatGPT are already being used 'to produce any kind of language, from text messages and social media posts to computer programs and speeches' (Ibid.). This growing integration of AI into communication has led researchers to explore its potential impact on oral language use, particularly in educational contexts.

For instance, Yakura et al. (2024) have investigated the role of AI systems in shaping human linguistic patterns. They argue that language, as a social phenomenon, constantly evolves through iterative processes of perception, internalisation, and reproduction – processes that individuals unconsciously adjust to in alignment with their social environments. This raises the possibility that spoken communication, too, may evolve under the influence of these AI models, either directly through text editing or indirectly via exposure to LLM-generated content.

Yakura et al. (2024) explore this phenomenon by analysing 280,000 video transcriptions from over 20,000 academic YouTube channels. Their study focuses on two key aspects: (i) changing trends in word frequency following the introduction of ChatGPT, and (ii) the correlation between these trends and word usage by ChatGPT. Their findings reveal that, after the release of ChatGPT, word frequencies in human spoken communication began to shift, highlighting the transformative impact of AI systems not only on written text but also on spoken language. These findings indicate that the relationship between human language and AI may be evolving, with humans starting to use language patterns generated by AI, while AI is also being shaped by human input. This change signals a shift in the role AI plays in academic and everyday communication, influencing both how we speak and write in different areas of life.

In connection with this, and from a linguistic perspective, research has introduced the concept of 'AI dialect'. Scholars like Martin and Jenkins (2024) have explored this idea, defining this term as the style or form of communication chosen by AI systems when interacting with users. Many AI systems are trained on data in standard English dialects and tend to respond in a similar way. However, the selection of a particular dialect raises concerns, especially regarding the risks of overestimating AI systems' capabilities and attributing human-like qualities to them. This can lead to misunderstandings, as users may expect a level of nuance or context that AI systems cannot replicate (Hohenstein et al., 2023). Such misconceptions create unrealistic expectations of AI's ability to understand cultural nuances, which can affect communication, particularly in sensitive or complex situations. Also, biases in AI training datasets could result in preferential treatment of certain dialects, reinforcing linguistic inequalities and marginalising minority or non-standard dialects (Hovy & Prabhumoye, 2021). This bias affects not only written language but also spoken language and may even be reflected in students' academic work and oral defences.

Relevant literature on this topic, such as the study by Helm et al. (2024), shows how AI-based language technologies – like large language models and machine translation systems – currently focus on only a small percentage of the world's most spoken and (financially and politically) supported languages (only 3%, according to the authors). Efforts to address this 'digital language gap' (or 'digital language divide' as defined by them) aim to extend these models to underserved languages. However, these efforts often have flaws as they tend to favour certain languages, leading to language modelling bias. This bias prioritises dominant languages and dialects, limiting the ability to express important cultural concepts for communities outside these dominant groups. As the authors note, the problem stems from a simplistic view of diversity by technology developers, which doesn't fully account for the deeper linguistic and cultural differences in languages. As a result, minority dialects are often marginalised, and the needs of underrepresented language communities are overlooked.

In educational settings, particularly in oral communication, AI bias can influence students' language use by reinforcing certain speech patterns while sidelining less represented dialects. This, combined with the English-centric perspective of AI technology (Wendler et al., 2024), may extend to human speech. In the context of this discussion, we already observe this effect on students' academic activities and presentations. While this observation is based on the authors' teaching experience, particularly when correcting students' short class presentations, it serves as an indication of an emerging trend that will undoubtedly lead to further reflection. For example, in one of the subjects taught by one of the authors of this chapter, *Communication in a Second Foreign Language for Tourism (French)*, some students mix informal English expressions and colloquial terms into their academic discourse. They use words like 'chill', 'trip', 'cool', or 'waffle', and even incorporate English verbs like *to jump* in constructions such as 'j'ai jumpé sur le bus'. This mixing of languages, combining formal vocabulary with problematic anglicisms, reflects a lack of fluency and over-reliance on English. Furthermore, some students' presentations reveal a lack of certain key features of oral communication, such as conversational pauses or filler words, which are essential for conveying emotion and meaning. The absence of these elements in AI-generated content can result in a lack of emotional depth and clarity, making communication feel less natural or authentic.

Given these observations, it is important to examine the role of AI in shaping students' oral discourse, particularly in longer, more complex activities that require extended speaking time, such as Final Degree Dissertation defences, which last approximately 15 minutes. These tasks offer a richer context for analysing language patterns, including the impact of AI-generated speech on communication skills. By focusing on these aspects, we aim to identify key criteria that faculty should monitor when assessing students' oral performance. Understanding these indicators is essential for both students and educators to recognise the role AI plays in shaping language use. This awareness can help guide students in using AI tools more effectively while encouraging them to remain mindful of the linguistic nuances and authentic communication required in academic settings. This approach, which we consider to be innovative, will contribute to a broader understanding of how AI interacts with language education and how it should be thoughtfully integrated into the classroom.

Study Approach and Methodological Framework

For this study, a bibliographic literature search was conducted using two databases, Scopus and Dialnet. The search focused on scientific articles published between 2022 and 2025 that were accessible in full text through institutional repositories. Research in English, Spanish, and French was included, with an emphasis on qualitative, quantitative, or mixed-method empirical studies relevant to higher education.

Various search strategies were employed, using keyword combinations in the TITLE-ABS-KEY field. These included terms like 'artificial intelligence AND speech', 'impact AND artificial intelligence AND language', 'generative AI AND speaking', 'artificial intelligence AND master dissertation', 'learning AND speaking AND AI AND language', 'artificial intelligence AND master AND defense', and 'AI AND oral discourse', among others. The goal was to identify studies related to the impact of AI, particularly generative AI, on language, communication, and educational processes, including its influence on thesis defences and academic work.

Although no articles specifically addressed the application of GAI in TFT defences, six studies that focused on the oral aspect of discourse were identified and used to support the ideas presented. Articles that centred on the influence of GAI on written discourse were excluded, as they did not specifically relate to the study's focus. However, some of these articles did offer insights that were indirectly relevant.

Additionally, sources such as official declarations (e.g. Bologna, Berlin, and Rome), academic studies (Mateo et al., 2009, 2012; Baron et al., 2023), teaching guides for TFT courses from fifteen public universities in Spain, and institutional recommendations (UNESCO, Conference of Rectors of Spanish Universities [CRUE], etc.) were examined. This analysis provided essential context for understanding how key educational reforms, particularly those initiated by the Bologna Declaration, have transformed higher education in Europe, with a specific focus on the importance of competence-based education, learning outcomes, and related shifts in educational frameworks. Also, the impact of digitalisation on education was considered, as technology continues to play an important role in shaping teaching and learning.

Some of the key reflections that helped shape the study are shared below, as they are important before presenting the proposed criteria for assessing students' oral defences.

Reflections and Rationale for Assessment Criteria

If we recall, the Bologna Declaration signed in 1999 set in motion a process of convergence in the European Higher Education Area (EHEA) that has radically transformed higher education. It implied a shift from content-oriented to learning-oriented pedagogical models. This new educational paradigm focused on student learning, placing more emphasis on competences and learning outcomes (Proyecto Tuning, 2003). Competence-based education introduced a profound change in the way we think about training, education, and teaching, as well as our approaches to assessment. In the Berlin Communiqué (Conference of Ministers Responsible for Higher Education, 2003), European ministers encouraged the member States to develop a framework of comparable and compatible qualifications for their higher education systems, aiming to describe qualifications in terms of workload, level, learning outcomes, competences, and profile. The importance of linking assessment processes to the development and enhancement of learning abilities was definitively established, with assessment seen as a tool for managing and ensuring the quality of learning (Mateo et al., 2009, 2012).

It is undeniable that the Bologna Process/EHEA has introduced substantial reforms. However, the enthusiasm of the early years has given way to more cautious optimism and, in some cases, a sense of disillusion (Bergan, 2019). As the process enters its third decade, it finds itself at a critical juncture, which requires the adaptation to new global and technological challenges, and major societal transformations to avoid irrelevance (Curaj et al., 2018). The 2020 Rome Ministerial Communiqué (EHEA, 2020) acknowledges the growing significance of GAI in higher education. It emphasises the necessity of ensuring that these technologies adhere to ethical standards and human rights, promoting inclusiveness in the educational sphere. The Council of the European Union's Recommendation on the key enabling factors for successful digital education and training (2023) emphasises that effective digital education is about creating more and better opportunities for learning and teaching in the digital age. Digital resources have the potential to bridge geographical divisions, and digital commons can offer substantial benefits such as strategic autonomy, reduced costs, and increased transparency. However, in this fast-developing world, it is vital to continuously improve the effectiveness and efficiency of education and training while supporting new teaching and learning methods, including those facilitated by existing and emerging digital solutions. Moreover, it is essential that learners gain a deep understanding of the technologies at play and develop the skills and competences necessary for the creative, safe, ethical, and responsible use of digital tools.

It is worth mentioning that the concept of competence is still evolving, with a variety of definitions in circulation. In line with Weinert's remarks (2001), Rychen and Salganik (2002) propose a demand-oriented approach, emphasising the prerequisites required to meet the demands of a professional position, social role, or personal project. They define competence as the ability to meet a complex demand successfully or carry out a complex task. As Hurtado (2007) notes, competence acquisition extends beyond mastering a discipline; it also involves regulating, monitoring, and taking initiative in the use and development of these skills. One of the most comprehensive definitions is put forward by Lasnier (2000), who describes competence as 'a complex know-how to act resulting from integration, mobilisation and organization of a combination of capabilities and skills (which can be cognitive, affective, psycho-motor or social) and knowledge (declarative knowledge) used efficiently in situations with common characteristics' (p. 32). Mateo et al. (2009, 2012) in their research on assessment and evaluation within the EHEA, define competences as a combination of knowledge skills and attitudes acquired by the learner. These competences are developed through integrative learning experiences, where knowledge and skills interact to effectively execute tasks.

Why is all the above important to consider? Because it forms the foundation for the criteria proposed to assess the impact of GAI on students' oral discourse, which will be discussed in the next section. Understanding this framework is essential for evaluating how these competences relate to the integration of emerging technologies, such as GAI, in academic settings.

Our Proposal

In the context of the EHEA, it has become standard and compulsory practice in Humanities and Social Science master's and bachelor's programmes to include a TFT project, which is regarded as the culminating learning experience of the degree. Although the characteristics of the TFT may vary across programmes, depending on their academic priorities and the professional profile they aim to develop in their students, the TFT generally requires students to integrate and apply the competences acquired throughout the degree (RD 822/2021, of 28 September). Students must also work with professional, creative, and innovative criteria, incorporating new competences specific to the TFT, such as autonomy, initiative, knowledge development, skills, strategies, and the ability to provide solutions to research problems that arise during the project.

In this context, the oral defence of the TFT project is a compulsory requirement for both graduate and postgraduate students. During the defence, all the students' communicative competences come into play. They must present their work orally to an expert audience, discussing the most essential, complex, or controversial aspects of their project contribution. This process requires, among other things, the internalisation of knowledge, expressiveness, emotional control, and quick thinking. Mateo et al. (2009, 2012) identified a list of seventeen competences associated with the TFT through the Dublin descriptors. Of these, the six that we consider most relevant to the oral defence are as follows:

- Present and defend in public the progress report to an evaluation committee
- Demonstrate ability to communicate in oral form
- Develop a correct and adequate report to be communicated orally
- Identify the most important aspect of the project
- Interpret rigorously the information obtained
- Respond to the demands of the expert audiences

The oral defence is considered a highly effective tool for assessing the student's oral communication competence and interactive skills (Ockey et al., 2019). However, to ensure its validity and reliability, the criteria and the issues addressed during the defence must be clear and known to the students. Assessment criteria not only define what must be done but also provide a framework for making judgements on the learning outcomes linked to the different competences. Setting clear assessment criteria in higher education projects is essential to ensure fair, transparent, and meaningful evaluation of students' work.

To establish the assessment criteria for the oral defence of the TFT, we began by considering six competencies and developed a list of criteria: communication skills; use of language; organisation, structure and coherence of the information presented; time management; use of visual aids; and handling of discussions and questions. We also outlined the specific aspects each criterion addresses. These criteria were then compared with those used for oral defences at fifteen different Spanish universities, specifically those related to degrees in Humanities and Social Sciences from public universities which were publicly available online. While a more in-depth analysis would be necessary, no major discrepancies were found, except for differences in organisation and levels of detail. In some cases, criteria were combined, while in others, certain criteria were omitted.

Table 11: Assessment criteria for the oral defence of the TFT

Criteria	Issues addressed
Communication skills	Oral expression and style Body language and voice register adjusted to the context (defence before an academic committee) Clarity and articulation Voice modulation, pace and emphasis to highlight Monotony
Use of language	Register adequacy Academic discourse Specialised vocabulary
Organisation, structure and coherence of the information presented	Clear and logical structure Topic transitions Objectives, research questions and relevance of findings stated and contextualised Depth of analysis Possible counterarguments and limitations
Time management	Pacing of the presentation Respect for the allocated time
Use of visual aids	Pertinence of the resources used Design and readability of the resources used (slides, videos, etc.) Effective use of graphs, images, or data
Discussion and questions handling	Engagement in academic discussion with the members of the tribunal Confidence and knowledge of the topic. Ability to clarify complex points Openness to constructive feedback Debating and argumentative skills

The general consensus in academic literature (Baron, 2023; Kasneci et al., 2023; Yakura et al., 2024) and institutional policies (CRUE, 2023; European Commission, 2022; UNESCO, 2023; US Department of Education, Office of Educational Technology, 2023) is that GAI tools can support students learning, However, their use without critical thinking, ethical decision-making, and personal engagement in academic work may be highly problematic for students' learning processes and cognitive development. Some of the challenges and risks associated with the application of LLM in education have been discussed by Kasneci et al. (2023). Those most directly related to TFT oral defences include: a) large language models can perpetuate and amplify existing biases towards certain groups of people and social injustices; b) the ease with which information is generated could negatively impact students' critical thinking and problem-solving abilities; c) while large language models can generate accurate and relevant information, they cannot replace creativity; d) it is becoming increasingly difficult to distinguish whether a text is machine-generated or written by humans; e) the ability of large language models to produce human-like text can make it difficult for students to differentiate between real knowledge and unverified information.

In this regard, Cotton et al. (2023), when discussing what chatbots can and cannot do, propose several methods for detecting work generated by LLMs, specifically ChatGPT. These methods include looking for patterns or irregularities in language, verifying sources and citations, checking for originality, identifying factual errors or inconsistencies, and evaluating the effectiveness and clarity of the writing. As they suggest, human writing tends to be more contextually aware and responsive to the audience's needs, while AI-generated writing tends to be more generic and less tailored to specific contexts. This difference can affect the overall effectiveness and clarity of the writing. Based on the literature review, and the six assessment criteria previously established for oral defences (Table 11), we propose the use of GAI signals (Table 12) to detect work generated by LLMs that may interfere with the criteria for assessing TFTs. It is important to consider these signals or indicators, as they will serve as the foundation for creating rubrics within the framework of these subjects.

Table 12: Signals for detecting AI use in the oral defence of the TFT based on the six assessment criteria

Criteria	**AI use signals**
Communication skills	Impersonal oral expression and style Lack of personal voice or style Lack of engagement, personal examples or reflection Social biases and fairness Monotonic or robotic tone in speech Lack of natural conversational flow
Use of language	Excessively general or vague language Overuse of unnatural phrasing (e.g. structures or terms that a native speaker wouldn't use) Repetitive sentence structures Inadequate register for the audience and context Generic discourse (e.g. statements or phrases that don't reflect an in-depth understanding of the topic) Non-specialised vocabulary (e.g. lack of discipline-specific terminology that demonstrates expertise in the subject matter) Lack of rhetorical devices that would usually be used in persuasive speech (e.g. rhetorical questions, analogies)
Organisation, structure and coherence of the information presented	Incoherent or inconsistent arguments Lack of clear signposting or transitions between sections Perfectly structured presentations without depth Listing and structured bullet points without previous or post-development Abrupt or poor topic transitions, which disrupt the flow of the presentation Inaccurate or unclear use of sources or references during the oral presentation, affecting the reliability of the arguments.
Time management	Lack of real-time adjustment during interaction (GAI can cause timing problems, giving long answers to simple questions or not shortening responses when time is short).
Use of visual aids	Over-designed presentations Inconsistent use of graphs, images, or data Lack of alignment between visual aids and oral content Inadequate or failure to reference visual aids.

Criteria	AI use signals
Discussion and questions handling	Excessively neutral or general arguments when responding to the committee board's question and feedback Limited ability to provide relevant examples or evidence to support arguments Clear positioning avoidance Lack of complexity Lack of nuanced discussion

The criteria and AI use signals presented in Table 12 are essential for ensuring that the assessment of oral TFT defences is fair, valid, and aligned with the competences that students are expected to demonstrate. Inappropriate use of AI tools can distort this evaluation, as it may lead to generic responses that lack deep reflection, creativity, or authentic communication skills, undermining the reliability of academic evaluation.

Beyond ensuring fair assessment, integrating these indicators also reflects a forward-thinking approach to education in a technological context. As GAI continues to evolve, it is essential to design evaluation systems that not only acknowledge the legitimate use of technology but also safeguard the authenticity of academic work. Adapting to this new reality requires balancing technological advancements with the preservation of meaningful human contributions.

All in all, ethical GAI use in academia means promoting transparency, academic integrity, and human oversight. As students increasingly rely on GAI tools, faculty may have no choice but to teach them how to use these tools appropriately and productively – not only to perform mechanical and repetitive tasks but also to develop strategies that enhance essential human competences such as critical thinking, strategic decision-making, creativity, personal reflection, and also the qualities that technology struggles to replicate: empathy and passion.

Discussion

The inappropriate use of GAI in education has been widely addressed and described by numerous authors (García-Peñalvo, 2024; Gallent-Torres &

Comas-Forgas, 2024; Sobral et al., 2024). This highlights the urgent need to emphasise the responsible use of these tools to guarantee ethics and academic honesty throughout the educational community.

However, the issues related to academic honesty are not the only ones being seriously violated. In fact, we believe that the ethical concerns arising from the generation of oral discourse content should be the main focus when analysing the results of this study. These concerns are in line with those of recent studies, such as those carried out by Yakura et al. (2024), who already identified a significant shift in the use of terms commonly associated with language generated by tools like ChatGPT. The authors also considered it particularly alarming that the widespread use of words in a standardised way could lead to the involuntary reduction of linguistic diversity through oral discourse. Indeed, one of the most serious consequences of reproducing decontextualised, non-native terms is the homogenisation of language. This is not only due to the 'denaturalisation' of the language itself but also because it reflects the key elements involved in cultural assimilationist processes (Malgesini & Giménez, 2000; Gordon, 1964), which are as follows:

- From the perspective of a culturally homogeneous dominant society, diversity is intrinsically questioned. As a result, language becomes standardised and the terms used are those that respond to that homogeneity, leading to the loss of specific meanings, senses and vocabulary.
- The acquisition of a common, homogeneous language becomes the ultimate goal. Interaction with what is considered to be a homogeneous standard (such as the responses provided by GAI) leads to the acquisition of that language, often at the expense of one's own.
- The unilateral nature of the process of change: in the assimilationist model, the burden of adaptation falls solely on the culturally diverse minority. GAI models do not 'learn' the specific terms unique to these minority groups.
- The perceived naturalness and inevitability of the assimilation process. In this case, the main axiom of this model is that it is a natural outcome. In fact, we could argue that it is 'naturalised' for the user of GAI, since it does not at any time take into account that the process itself is taking place.

It is unnecessary to repeat here the numerous reasons for the strong criticism that the assimilationist model has received as a theory of adaptation of the immigrant population in host contexts (Retortillo et al., 2006), but we do consider it essential to emphasise that we share the criticism of this approach, not only because of its fundamentally ethnocentric nature but also because from an ethical point of view it is absolutely unacceptable.

In fact, and continuing with the ethical aspects, although now focusing on GAI, the algorithms used by AI, given its rapid development over the last ten years, are already present in all areas (healthcare, administration, business, government, education). This represents progress in the elimination of automated tasks, but we cannot ignore that, in turn, and based on the results presented in this work, this automation comes at an excessively high cost: the parameters used in these algorithms are loaded with subjectivity (profiles, costs, allocations, prioritisations …).

Search engines, platform suggestions, browser routes, and texts generated by natural language processing models (NLPM) all provide biased answers (Palacios et al., 2023). This bias arises not only from statistics ignoring minorities or platforms that exclude diversity but also from disparities and inequality in hiring and promotion in both business and academia. In recent years, there has been talk of a 'diversity crisis in AI' (West et al., 2019). When this algorithmic bias is transferred to education, particularly in the academic discourse of future teachers, it leads to serious consequences, which we will summarise in two key points.

The first is directly related to learning (or the lack of it). Based on the results of the analysis conducted in this work, the indicators for assessing and recognising the use of GAI in shaping students' oral discourse prove to be essential. According to Freire's (1970) theory of dialogic action, dialogue – defined as a shared act of epistemological construction between learner and educator – is a fundamental part of the learning process. For Freire, the word embodies this dialogue, combining action and reflection, which he saw as continuously interacting. This interaction gives the word its transformative power. In our context, this transformation is learning. The process of evaluating oral discourse (the defence of the final degree project) aims, precisely, to assess the levels of achievement of the required competences and, thus, demonstrate the learning achieved by the student. If the student over relies on discourse provided by GAI, without any critical analysis or questioning, they are placing themselves at the opposite pole, which Freire also addressed: by sacrificing reflection (a core element of the word), the discourse loses its active dimension, becoming an 'inauthentic word'. This process, in turn, alienates the students, dulls their creative spirit and transforms them into a passive, disengaged individual (Freire, 1970). We consider it essential to provide teachers with a set of indicators to facilitate the identification of competency learning levels.

The second is the reproduction of inequalities (and the need to establish measures to avoid them). We must bear in mind that human cognitive processing tends to simplify information, a phenomenon that derives from the way we interpret messages. Fundamentally, we can distinguish between two systems of cognitive processing (Kahneman, 2012). The first (System 1), which is intuitive in nature, operates by filtering messages through a recognition protocol that minimises cognitive effort and responds quickly, without a sense of voluntary control; in short, it works automatically. The second (System 2) focuses attention on mental activities that require concentration, including complex calculations, and generally remains in a state of minimal effort, using only a fraction of its capacity. System 1 continuously generates suggestions to System 2, including impressions, intuitions, intentions and sensations. If System 2 approves them, these impressions and intuitions are transformed into beliefs, and impulses into voluntary actions. In most everyday situations, System 2 accepts System 1's suggestions with little or no modification, which means that we commonly give credence to our impressions and act according to our desires. Given that System 2 is characterised by requiring effort in its operations, and one of its distinctive properties is the tendency towards inertia, that is to say, a resistance to investing more effort than is strictly necessary, it is not generally activated unless System 1 does not recognise the situation or a problem is presented to it. Thus 'people who simultaneously face a demanding cognitive task and a temptation are more likely to give in to the temptation' (Kahneman, 2012, p. 42). Consequently, and following the analysis carried out and presented in this chapter, it is logical to infer that if students, given the ease offered by GAI tools in the configuration of their oral discourse, do not carry out a critical analysis of the content of that discourse, of the language and of the terms and expressions; therefore, the information that confirms their pre-existing mental schemas will tend to be accepted without question or, simply, as they do not have fully configured and organised previous mental schemas, they will be internalised and processed as valid (and will, in turn, validate the contents that may be the object of further study). Consequently, if the results of automated queries are not filtered by critical analysis and rigorously elaborated, they will once again present significant sexist, racist and classist biases, and reproduced in different academic contexts. In this sense, the definition and inclusion of indicators that allow for the concrete evaluation of aspects related to the use of concepts out of context and meaning, inappropriate terms or concepts with a strong discriminatory connotation are considered essential, since they will not only reveal the inappropriate use of GAI in oral discourse, but will also kerb the possible reproduction of discourses based on inequality and discrimination and will facilitate the critical analysis of the results of interaction with AI tools.

In view of all this, although there are no empirical studies yet to directly support the work presented here, we believe it raises a series of questions and scenarios that address some very relevant emerging needs. Therefore, we believe that we are setting out a line of research that can be widely studied and that will lay the foundations for avoiding the problems and future needs that have been discussed.

Conclusions and Prospective

The definition and establishment of a clear, dynamic, and holistic legal framework focused on guaranteeing human rights is seen as one of the primary solutions to counter the indiscriminate and unethical use of GAI (European Parliament, 2021; UNESCO, 2022). However, while essential, this approach must be complemented by other measures such as the exploration or creation of alternative models for the ownership of GAI (Moreno, 2025), which would enable a more equitable dissemination and use of GAI while helping to eliminate inherent biases and discrimination. Likewise, there is an increasing call for research into pedagogical approaches that can assess and analyse the specific impact of GAI in educational environments (De La Serna-Tuya et al., 2024).

Continuing with this last approach, while also considering the previous ones, we propose several strategies that can help strengthen faculty confidence in the management and use of GAI within the academic context.

Drawing from the principles of an inclusive perspective, it is essential to define and implement strategies that enhance learning environments – ones that address and mitigate the biases inherent in GAI. Rather than restricting GAI use altogether, which would be an ineffective and regressive approach, the focus should be on developing strategies that enhance the learning environment, enabling students to engage critically with the AI-generated content. Only through this lens – where AI's role is critically analysed and its biases understood – can we ensure the integrity and authenticity of oral defences and, more broadly, academic work. Therefore, we suggest several strategies to improve the use of GAI in academic settings, which we will outline below.

- The promotion of personalised learning, which in turn facilitates its evaluation through tools like Socratic debate between teacher and student (encouraging dialogue). For example, through questioning and challenging the knowledge that students believe they have acquired, followed by an iterative process of questions and answers, the teacher not only assesses the depth of competence gained but also helps the student become aware of and reflect on the learning process itself. GAI tools such as Poe can also been used for this task if considered more motivating.
- The promotion of collaborative work applied to ethics in research and in the preparation of academic work (UNESCO, 2017). Self-regulation based on validation and approval, both by the peer group and teachers, is also considered to be one of the key elements in avoiding the misuse of available GAI tools. This is only possible if it is grounded in a previously established and widely known code of ethics, which must be shared and collectively defined by the entire educational community.
- Deepening the understanding of the implications of GAI use in education. Research on the repercussions of GAI in education should be encouraged, focusing not only on students' use but also on its impact on the educational community as a whole, addressing the challenges it presents and, especially, its potential (Kanesci et al., 2023).
- Proposing Mock Defences: As part of defence training, students could participate in simulated defences in which they assume the role of

committee members and provide feedback to their peers. This exercise not only helps students develop their evaluation skills but also prepares them for their own defence by encouraging reflection on how GAI tools impact the authenticity and depth of academic discourse. This dynamic fosters critical thinking and promotes awareness of the ethical considerations related to the use of GAI in this particular context.

- Fostering an Interdisciplinary Approach to GAI Education: Encouraging collaboration between different faculties and programmes to explore the ethical, practical, and technological implications of GAI tools. This could involve joint projects across departments, enabling students to understand GAI from multiple perspectives and apply ethical considerations within their specific fields of study.

We believe the debate surrounding GAI should not be centred on whether it should be restricted or not. In fact, the focus should not be on the tool itself, either by demonising or glorifying it. The real issue lies in the misuse of GAI, not the technology itself. In this work, we have highlighted one of the consequences of such misuse: AI-generated oral discourse, which can have harmful effects that go beyond academic fraud. However, we are convinced that this issue can be addressed if faculty do not remain passive or resistant to the changes occurring in the educational context. By developing indicators that help us identify the problem clearly and interact directly with it, we can place students at the centre of their learning process. This, we believe, should be the foundation of all educational practices, and it represents an opportunity to move forward as a society.

Acknowledgements

This chapter was developed within the framework of Project IA-FIP (ref. PID2022-141031NB-I00), funded by MICIU/AEI/10.13039/501100011033 and the ERDF "A way of making Europe," as well as the Research Project CIAICO/2022/032 (2023–2025), funded by the Generalitat Valenciana (Spain). It also forms part of the initiatives of the Ibero-American Research Network on Academic Integrity (RED-IA), funded by AUIP; the Teaching Innovation

Project "*The Influence of GenAI on University Students' Discursive Production*" (ref. 3898146), funded by the SFPIE of the University of Valencia; the Instituto López Piñeiro of the Universitat Jaume I in Castelló; the Academic and Scientific Integrity Research Group (GRIAC, UIB); and the Teaching and Learning Languages in Multilingual Education Research Group (TeLL-ME, UV).

Bibliography

Ashour, S. (2020). How Technology has Shaped University Students' Perceptions and Expectations Around Higher Education: An Exploratory Study of the United Arab Emirates. *Studies in Higher Education, 45*(12), 2513–2525. https://doi.org/10.1080/03075079.2019.1617683

Baron, N. S. (2023). Who wrote this? How AI and the lure of efficiency threaten human writing. Stanford University Press.

Bergan, S. (2019). The European Higher Education Area: A Road to the Future or at way's End? *Tuning Journal for Higher Education, 6*(2), 23–49. https://doi.org/10.18543/tjhe-6(2)-2019pp23-49

Bourdieu, P. (1992). *Language and Symbolic Power.* Blackwell Publishers.

Cheng, S. L., Tsai, S. J., Bai, Y. M., Ko, C. H., Hsu, C. W., Yang, F. C., Tsai, C. K., Tu, Y. K., Yang, S. N., Tseng, P. T., Hsu, T. W., Liang, C. S, & Su, K. P. (2023). Comparisons of quality, correctness, and similarity between ChatGPT-generated and human-written abstracts for basic research: Cross-sectional study. *Journal of Medical Internet Research*, 25, e51229. https://www.doi.org/10.2196/51229

Comas-Forgas, R., Koulouris, A., & Kouis, D. (2024). 'AI-navigating' or 'AI-sinking'? An analysis of verbs in research articles titles suspicious of containing AI-generated/assisted content. *Learned Publishing*, 38, e1647. https://doi.org/10.1002/leap.1647

Conference of Ministers Responsible for Higher Education. (2003). Realising the European Higher Education Area: Communiqué of the Conference of Ministers Responsible for Higher Education in Berlin on 19 September 2003. European Higher Education Area.

Cotton, D. R. E., Cotton, P. A., & Shipway, J. R. (2023). Chatting and cheating: Ensuring academic integrity in the era of ChatGPT. *Innovations in Education and Teaching International*, *61*(2), 228–239. https://doi.org/10.1080/14703297.2023.2190148

Council of the European Union. (2023). *Council Recommendation of 23 November 2023 on the key enabling factors for successful digital*

education and training. Official Journal of the European Union, C 1115, 1–10. https://eur-lex.europa.eu/legal-content/EN/TXT/PDF/?uri=OJ%3AC_202401115
Conferencia de Rectores de las Universidades Españolas (CRUE) (2023). La inteligencia artificial generativa en la docencia universitaria: Oportunidades, desafíos y recomendaciones. https://www.crue.org/wp-content/uploads/2024/03/Crue-Digitalizacion_IA-Generativa.pdf
Curaj, A., Deca, L., & Pricopie, R. (Eds.) (2018). European Higher Education Area: The Impact of Past and Future Policies. Springer Cham.
De La Serna-Tuya, A. S., Sánchez, G., Gallardo, Y., & Jasso, E. (2024). Impacto de la Inteligencia Artificial: Ética, Educación y Desafíos Profesionales. In E. Ruiz-Velasco & J. Bárcenas (Coords.), *Argumentos y usos tecnopedagógicos de la Inteligencia Artificial* (pp. 143–150). Apoyo Editorial.
European Commission: Directorate-General for Education, Youth, Sport and Culture (2022). *Ethical guidelines on the use of artificial intelligence (AI) and data in teaching and learning for educators*. Publications Office of the European Union. https://data.europa.eu/doi/10.2766/153756
European Higher Education Area (EHEA). (2020). *Rome Ministerial Communiqué*. European Ministers of Higher Education. https://www.ehea.info/Upload/Rome_Ministerial_Communique.pdf
European Parliament (2021). *Artificial Intelligence Act*. https://www.europarl.europa.eu/RegData/etudes/BRIE/2021/698792/EPRS_BRI(2021)698792_EN.pdf
Freire, P. (1970). *Pedagogia do oprimido*. Siglo XXI.
Gallent-Torres, C. & Comas-Forgas, R. (2025). Speak like a robot. *The Linguist: Journal of the Institute of Linguistics*, *64*(1), 30–31. https://www.ciol.org.uk/sites/default/files/TheLinguist-64_1-download.pdf
Gallent-Torres, C., & Comas-Forgas, R. (2024). La llama de Prometeo: IA e integridad académica. *Cuadernos de Pedagogía, 549,* 16–27.
Gao, C. A., Howard, F. M., Markov, N. S., Dyer, E. C., Ramesh, S., Luo, Y. & Pearson, A. (2023). Comparing scientific abstracts generated by ChatGPT to real abstracts with detectors and blinded human reviewers. *Digital Medicine*, 6, 75. https://doi.org/10.1038/s41746-023-00819-6
García-Peñalvo, F. J. (2024). Inteligencia artificial generativa y educación: Un análisis desde múltiples perspectivas. *Education in the Knowledge Society (EKS), 25*, e31942-e31942. https://revistas.usal.es/tres/index.php/eks/article/download/31942/29746

Geng, M. & Trotta, R. (2024). Is ChatGPT Transforming Academic's Writing Style? arXiv:2404.08627v2. https://doi.org/10.48550/arXiv.2404.08627

Gordon, M. (1964). *Assimilation in american life. The role of race, religion and national origins*. Oxford University Press.

Hall, B. & López, M. I. (2011). Discurso académico: manuales universitarios y prácticas pedagógicas. *Literatura y Lingüística*, 23, 167–192. http://dx.doi.org/10.4067/S0716-58112011000100010

Helm, P., Bella, G., Koch, G., & Giunchjglia, F. (2024). Diversity and language technology: how language modeling bias causes epistemic injustice. *Ethics and Information Technology, 26*(8), 1–15. https://doi.org/10.1007/s10676-023-09742-6

Hohenstein, J., Kizilcec, R. F., DiFranzo, D., Aghajari, Z., Mieczkowski, H., Levy, K., Naaman, M., Hancock, J. & Jung, M. F. (2023). Artifcial intelligence in communication impacts language and social relationships. *Scientifc Reports*, 13, 5487. https://doi.org/10.1038/s41598-023-30938-9

Hovy, D., & Prabhumoye, S. (2021). Five sources of bias in natural language processing. *Language and Linguistics Compass, 15*(8), e12432. https://doi.org/10.1111/lnc3.12432

Hurtado Albir, A. (2007). Competence-based Curriculum Design for Training Translators. *The Interpreter and Translator Trainer, 1*(2), 163–195. https://doi.org/10.1080/1750399X.2007.10798757

Kahneman, D. (2012). *Pensar rápido, pensar despacio*. Penguin Random House.

Kasneci, E., Seßler, K., Küchemann, S., Bannert, M., Dementieva, D., Fischer, F., Gasser, U., Groh, G., Günnemann, S., Hüllermeier, E., Krusche, S., Kutyniok, G., Michaeli, T., Nerdel, C., Pfeffer, J., Poquet, O., Sailer, M., Schmidt, A., Seidel, T., Stadler, M., Weller, J. Kuhn, J., & Kasneci, G. (2023). ChatGPT for Good? On Opportunities and Challenges of Large Language Models for Education. Learning and Individual Differences, 103, 102274. https://doi.org/10.1016/j.lindif.2023.102274

Lasnier, F. (2000) *Réussir la formation par compétences*. Guérin.

Malgesini, G. & Giménez, C. (2000). *Guía de conceptos sobre migraciones, racismo e interculturalidad*. Catarata.

Martin, A. & Jenkins, K. (2024). Speaking your language: The psychological impact of dialect integration in artificial intelligence systems. *Current Opinion in Psychology*, 58, 101840. https://doi.org/10.1016/j.copsyc.2024.10184

Mateo, J., Escofet, A., Martínez, F. and Ventura, J. (2009). *Guía para la Evaluación de Competencias en el Trabajo de Fin de Grado en el Ámbito de las Ciencias sociales y jurídicas.* Generalitat de Catalunya. Agència per a la Qualitat del Sistema Universitari a Catalunya.

Mateo, J., Escofet, A., Martínez-Olmo, F., Ventura, J., & Vlachopoulos, D. (2012). Evaluation Tools in the European Higher Education Area (EHEA): an assessment for evaluating the competences of the Final Year Project in the social sciences. *European Journal of Education*, 47, 435–447. https://doi.org/10.1111/j.1465-3435.2012.01536.x

Merminod, G. (2023, 10 February). D'où viennent nos tics de langage ? Avis d'Expert.e.s [Podcast]. https://avisdexperts.ch/en/intervention/where-do-our-speech-tics-come

Miles, A. (2017). *Research Methods and Strategies Workshop: A Taxonomy of Research Gaps: Identifying and Defining the Seven Research Gaps*. [Doctoral Student Workshop]. https://tinyurl.com/y885tf36

Mongaillard, V. (2018). Ce que les tics de langage veulent dire. *Le Parisien*. https://www.leparisien.fr/societe/ce-que-les-tics-de-langage-veulent-dire-20-04-2018-7675581.php

Moreno, A. (2025). Riesgos sociotécnicos y códigos deontológicos en inteligencia artificial: ¿Hasta dónde llega la ética de la tecnología? *Niaiá. Revista Interdisciplinar sobre Formación y Resolución de Problemas Morales*, (3), 169–180. https://repository.tudelft.nl/file/File_d60b3020-fdd8-4f58-8706-de08292082de?preview=1

Nguyen, A., Hong, Y., Dang B., & Huang, X. (2024). Human-AI collaboration patterns in AI-assisted academic writing. *Studies in Higher Education*, *49*(5), 847–864, https://www.doi.org/10.1080/03075079.2024.2323593

Ockey, G. J., & Li, Z. (2019). New and not so new methods for assessing oral communication. *Language Value*, 7(1). https://doi.org/10.6035/LanguageV.2015.7.2

Palacios, M. A., Boeren, D., Ferreira, J. F. (2023). At the intersection of humanity and technology: a technofeminist intersectional critical discourse analysis of gender and race biases in the natural language processing model GPT-3. *AI & Society*. https://doi.org/10.1007/s00146-023-01804-z

Pérez-Colomé, J. (2024). Humans Are Already Repeating Words Learned from ChatGPT, such as 'Delve' and 'Meticulous'. *El País*. https://tinyurl.com/yeyt9e8e

Retortillo, A., Ovejero, A., Cruz, F. R., Arias, B., & Lucas, S. (2006). Inmigración y modelos de integración: entre la asimilación y el multiculturalismo. *Revista Universitaria de Ciencias del Trabajo, 7*, 123–139. http://uvadoc.uva.es/handle/10324/11345

Rinaldy Malik, A., Pratiwi, Y., Andajani, K., Numertayasa, I. W., Suharti, S., Darwis, A. & Marzuki (2023). Exploring Artificial Intelligence in Academic Essay: Higher Education Student's Perspective. *International Journal of Educational Research Open*, 5, 100296. https://doi.org/10.1016/j.ijedro.2023.100296

Rychen, D. S., & Salganik, S. L. (2002). DeSeCo Symposium [Discussion paper]. OECD/OCDE. https://tinyurl.com/a2m2b4cw

Sobral, S. R., Ferreira, M. J., Pereira, C. S., Durão, N., & Moreira, F. (2024). Exploring the Impact of Artificial Intelligence Generative Tools on Research in Higher Education Institutions: A Perspective from Portugal. *Proceedings of The 23rd European Conference on e-Learning.* Academic Conferences International. https://doi.org/10.34190/ecel.23.1.2512

Teh, P. L. & Uwasomba, C. F. (2024). Impacto f Large Language Models on Scholarly Publication Titles and Abstracts: A Comparative Analysis. *Journal of Social Computing*, 2(5), 105–121. https://www.doi.org/10.23919/JSC.2024.0011

Thasler-Kordonouri, S., Thurman, N., Schwertberger, U., & Stalph, F. (2024). Too many numbers and worse word choice: Why readers find data-driven news articles produced with automation harder to understand. *Journalism*, *0*(0), 1–21. https://doi.org/10.1177/146488492412622

U. S. Department of Education, Office of Educational Technology (2023). Artificial Intelligence and the Future of Teaching and Learning: Insights and Recommendations. Office of Educational Technology. https://www.ed.gov/sites/ed/files/documents/ai-report/ai-report.pdf

UNESCO (2017). Education for Sustainable Development Goals: learning objectives. UNESCO. https://doi.org/10.54675/CGBA9153

UNESCO (2022). *Recomendación sobre la Ética de la Inteligencia Artificial.* https://unesdoc.unesco.org/ark:/48223/pf0000381137_spa/PDF/381137spa.pdf.multi

UNESCO (2023). *Guidance for Generative AI in Education and Research.* https://unesdoc.unesco.org/ark:/48223/pf0000386693

Weinert, F. E. (2001). Concept of competence. A conceptual clarification. In D. Rychen & L. Salganik (Eds.), *Defining and Selecting Key Competencies* (pp. 45–66). Kirkland, Huber-Hogrefe Publishers.

Wendler, C., Veselovsky, V., Monea, G. & West, R. (2024). Do Llamas Work in English? On the Latent Language of Multilingual Transformers. arXiv:2402.10588. https://doi.org/10.48550/arXiv.2402.10588

West, S. M., Whittaker, M., & Crawford, K. (2019). *Discriminating Systems: Gender, Race and Power in AI.* AI Now Institute. https://ainowinstitute.org/discriminatingsystems.html

Yakura, H., López-López, E., Brinkmann, L., Serna, I., Gupta, P., & Rahwan, I. (2024). Empirical evidence of Large Language Model's influence on human spoken communication. arXiv:2409.01754. https://doi.org/10.48550/arXiv.2409.01754

Spanish Early Career Researchers and Research Integrity: Main Controversies and Artificial Intelligence

Blanca Rodríguez-Bravo[1] *and David Nicholas*[2]

ABSTRACT

The aim is to communicate information from Spanish Early Career Researchers participating in the Harbingers projects (2016–2023) through the seven rounds of interviews conducted with them. The overall goal is to learn about their perceptions of controversial behaviours and malpractices that undermine academic integrity in the research context. We made a sweep of the interviews to find out the main cracks in the science communication system and their implications for the integrity of science. To do so, we reviewed the sections on access to information, authorship, peer review, publication, metrics, open science, predatory journals and others. We paid attention to the repercussions of the pandemic and to the latest disruptor to appear, artificial intelligence. We introduced the voices of the interviewees.

Attitudes and practices have not remained unchanged. They have changed over the eight years of the project and greater pragmatism has been observed. Any activity that leads to passing the next evaluation and is aimed at obtaining a permanent position or the next contract is welcome. This approach has obvious risks for ethics and integrity. The still limited use of AI in 2023 does not imply that most of the interviewees do not give AI the importance it deserves. They all see a future for it, for some promising, and for others worrying.

Keywords: artificial intelligence, early career researchers, research integrity, scholarly communication, Spain

Introduction

The concept of academic reputation is hard to define but is mainly shaped by two notions (Herman, 2018): productivity in terms of quantity and quality; and impact in contribution to the state of knowledge of a field and achievements outside the academy. Thus, traditionally reputation has been associated exclusively with research, specifically with publications in

1 University of Leon, Spain. ORCID: 0000-0002-9476-7602

2 Ciber Research Ltd., UK. ORCID: 0000-0001-8046-2835

peer-reviewed journals and citations. However, new platforms are changing the way reputation is built, displayed and measured in the digital environment.

As Laudel & Gläser (2008) point out, the training phase is crucial in the careers of researchers because it allows them to move from the status of trainees to that of colleagues in the scientific community, while gaining recognition as independent researchers. It is the stage in which they have to make a name for themselves through innovative research while developing the skills necessary to contribute to knowledge in their field.

However, the situation in which early career researchers (ECRs), or researchers in the early stages of their research career, find themselves does not always allow them to enjoy this stage of training as they try to build a reputation in a precarious, competitive environment under great pressure. As Powell (2015) points out, they are not rewarded as they deserve and have difficulties to progress in academia. In fact, they complain that there is no clearly stated policy or pathway for them to follow that will lead to a stable job.

The main criterion by which they are evaluated is the quantity and positioning of publications, and they place their future mainly in publications indexed in the first quartiles of the JCRs. Along with this criterion, obtaining funding is also highly valued, a requirement that is not usually in the hands of this group, which is in a subordinate position (Rodríguez-Bravo & Nicholas, 2019).

Early Career Researchers consider that, although the evaluation to which they are subjected can be considered objective, because it is quantitative, it is not fair. They emphasise that in all fields data are not obtained at the same rate, and therefore the emphasis on the number of articles is not a fair measure.

The group has little autonomy to follow its own lines of research, depending on their mentors and the work of the group to obtain the desired optimal results. Those who feel little support say that large groups with a consolidated trajectory and funding are in a position of advantage over those working in small groups.

ECRs call for a more global evaluation that consider all scientific results, not only journal articles, but all the tasks performed, including teaching dedication, student tutoring, dissemination of research to other groups, among others. In recent times, communication to society and impact on sectors outside research have become more relevant and are being timidly introduced as complementary evaluation criteria. However, these evaluation criteria and their weighting are subject to constant change and this situation forces ECRs to try to anticipate and obtain all the merits that can be positively evaluated.

This competitive race in which they are immersed sometimes leads them to use and often to question and criticise practices that they consider unethical or that directly undermine research integrity. They blame the evaluation criteria for this situation and become pessimistic. They believe that these criteria largely mediate their behaviour and that their modification is a prerequisite for changing attitudes in the process of scientific communication.

Objectives and Methodology

This paper aims to report some of the results obtained in the framework of the Harbingers projects (https://ciber-research.com/) that have investigated the attitudes, behaviour and practices of junior researchers in relation to scientific communication in order to determine to what extent their millennial convictions – of openness, exchange and transparency – lead them to adopt new modes and platforms of communication.

ECRs is a concept that is far from unambiguous. In the Harbingers projects, the working definition was as follows: 'Researchers who are generally no older than 35 years, who are either PhDs and currently hold a research position, or have held research positions, and are pursuing their PhD. In no case are they researchers in stable positions'.

ECRs are not only a group of interest because of their youth and new way of thinking, but also because: 1. They are a considerably large group of researchers and constitute the present and the future of science and 2. They are a very active group that is at the forefront of the scientific communication process: they are authors, reviewers, sometimes lead research groups and are involved in all the fundamental tasks of the research process.

The Harbingers projects have had an international dimension with the participation of young researchers from several countries: China, Spain, United States, France, Malaysia, Poland, United Kingdom and Russia.

The two projects and one pilot so far have been developed within the framework of CIBER Research Ltd. (jointly with the University of Tennessee in the case of Harbingers-2) and have been funded by the Publishing Research Consortium (Harbingers-1) and the Alfred P. Sloan Foundation (Harbingers-2).

Both Harbingers-1 and Harbingers-2 consisted of semi-structured interviews – of about sixty questions and an hour and a half in length – repeated on three occasions to the same researchers followed by a survey to extend the data collection and to confirm or disconfirm the findings of the interviews. The interviews were directed to researchers in science and social science fields. Questionnaires arrived and were answered by scientists from all fields.

In the case of Harbingers-1 the interviews were unwound on an annual basis in 2016, 2017 and 2018. The survey was launched online in 2019. With respect to Harbingers-2, which aimed to analyse the change produced by the pandemic in the behaviour of novice researchers, the three interviews were conducted in 2021 and 2022 spaced six months apart. Likewise, this phase was completed with a survey using a questionnaire that made it possible to check the results obtained from the interviews in a larger number of ECRs and which was launched in the last four months of 2022.

Finally, a pilot study (Harbingers-3) was designed to determine the impact of generative artificial intelligence on the attitudes and habits of young researchers. A single round of interviews was used for this purpose in 2023. The complete results of the projects are available on the CIBER Research Ltd. website https://ciber-research.com/CIBER_projects.html

In this paper we had collected information from the Spanish ECRs participating in the three Harbingers projects and only from the interviews conducted with them, a total of 51: 18 in Harbingers-1, 23 in Harbingers-2 and 10 in Harbingers-3. In the selection of the interviewees, a balance between the participation of men and women was pursued and obtained. Also, the sample consisted of doctoral students and PhD students from different universities and research centres occupying various positions, but in no case stable positions. Moreover, it was distributed among several science and social science disciplines.

The overall goal is to learn about their perceptions of controversial behaviours and malpractices that undermine academic integrity in the research context. In the interviews of the three projects there were specific questions about novice researchers' knowledge and experience of unethical behaviours, bad science, and questionable practices in research and in the process of scientific communication.

However, we did not limit ourselves to the answers to these questions, but rather we made a sweep of the seven interviews to find out the main cracks in the science communication system and their implications for the integrity of science. To do so, we reviewed the sections on access to information, authorship, peer review, publication, metrics, open science, predatory journals and others. We alluded to the repercussions of the pandemic and the latest disruptor to appear, artificial intelligence. We introduced whenever possible the voices of the interviewees.

Results Analysis

To begin this section, we will include a brief summary of what Spanish ECRs understand by research integrity: to conduct research in an ethical way that allows colleagues or citizens to trust methods used and results obtained. The main concerns from Spanish ECRs among other ethical issues are: inappropriate authorship and the order of signatories, inappropriate citations, payment for publishing in open-access journals, publication in predatory and other questionable journals, salami slicing, peer review, misuse of data, as well as the current and feared consequences of the use of generative artificial intelligence applications. There are, therefore, many behaviours linked to the scientific communication process that ECRs question. Here, we will try to collect those aspects that are of most concern to the group studied.

Controversial Behaviours and Practices in the Process of Scientific Communication

To begin with, we consider it necessary to point out that as we have progressed through the Harbingers projects, there has been greater concern for ethical issues and greater awareness of fraudulent practices in research.

The scrutiny and transparency in all the processes developed in scientific communication are supported because they redound to the credibility of the scientists, which is essential for the public to support them. However, this does not always translate into daily practice due to the pressure to which the group is subjected. Thus, one researcher points out that 'extreme pressure can lead to fraud' and a female researcher underlines that 'researchers consciously or unconsciously seek the significant result they need'.

Most Spanish ECRs think that the pandemic may have boosted unethical or questionable practices, but they are not sure. They believe that they may simply be better known now because they are more widely publicised on social networks and because of the existence of platforms designed to bring these issues to light. All in all, the interviewees, except for one researcher, do not know of cases of malpractice at first hand and one researcher even states that 'young researchers are now more aware of ethical issues and try to abide by them'.

We will comment on some of the controversial practices most clearly identified by Spanish junior researchers following the order of the scientific communication cycle.

Access to Scientific Papers: Sci-Hub

Preferences for discovery and access platforms have not changed between Harbingers-1 and Harbingers-3: PubMed, WoS, Scopus, Google, Google Scholar and ResearchGate are the selected ones. Spanish scientists have wide access to electronic resources via these platforms or via electronic information 'big deals' such as Elsevier, Wiley, Springer and others. Despite this, more and more ECRs confess to using the pirate platform Sci-Hub when they cannot find what they are looking for through the usual channels. Most are aware of the characteristics of this platform, but it is a fast track, and they are always in a hurry (Rodríguez-Bravo & Nicholas, 2019).

Gardner & Inger in a 2018 report noted that between 5% and 13% of downloads by researchers come from Sci-Hub. In countries with fewer resources the percentage is higher than that observed in wealthier ones. Segado-Boj, Martín-Quevedo, & Prieto-Gutiérrez (2022) investigate this issue through an international survey with the objective to measure the willingness and motivations to use (or not use) scholarly piracy sites. Results told that more than 50% of the participants have used a scholarly piracy site at least once. They confirmed also the differences observed by Gardner & Inger (2018) between countries.

In Harbingers, differences between countries have also been noted. In some, its use may be related to unsatisfactory content provision by libraries, as in the case of Poland and Malaysia. In other countries, it rather derives from the need that researchers experience to obtain immediate access to the publication they require at a given moment. Novice researchers are aware that the service offered is not legitimate, however, many perceive it as morally acceptable since they consider that access to information should not be subject to barriers (Rodríguez-Bravo & Nicholas, 2022).

Authorship

Most of the Spanish ECRs interviewed are productive authors, some even prolific. The collective has an active participation in the research and often contributes to the whole process up to the final publication, not only to the experimental part. In theory, the order in which articles are signed derives from the contribution to the work, but this is not always the case, and this causes discomfort. The ECRs advocate that the criteria for establishing the order of signature should be clearly established.

The problem of establishing authorship criteria has become relevant due to the growth of collaboration in recent decades, which has led to a considerable increase in the number of authors of texts. In cases of multi-authorship, the sequence of authors is the only clue that allows credit to be given to the signatories.

ECRs pursue positions that count: first or last author and corresponding author. Recent doctoral students and PhDs are frequently listed as first author of the article because most of the results they publish are the result of their own doctoral thesis. As they gain experience and independence, they gain access to the ultimate position intended for senior researchers: 'I try to publish a lot and as high as possible as senior (last author or corresponding author)', says one researcher (Rodríguez-Bravo & Nicholas, 2020b). Another was critical of extending collaboration with other groups because 'collaborating extensively can cause you to lose senior positions: first author, last author or corresponding author' (Rodríguez-Bravo & Nicholas, 2021).

Logically, they are against giving authorships to colleagues who have not been involved in the research: 'I have done everything, the rest have signed', says one researcher. Thus, the discomfort stems from the assignment of undeserved authorships, from an order of authorship that does not reflect the work done, and from the fact that seniors occupy the top positions without enough contribution that justifies it. They advocate a stable policy that sets the order of authorship using always the same criteria and, failing that, a greater dialogue within the group to set the order (Rodríguez-Bravo & Nicholas, 2020b).

However, a greater pragmatism has been observed in some researchers since 2018 (Rodríguez-Bravo & Nicholas, 2019). In the early years they passionately defended that the order of authorship was strictly that deserved by the work invested in the research and/or in writing the article. Thus, a researcher points out: 'We help those who need a promotion by letting them appear as first author', 'this year I am first author in all the articles to obtain the next position (Miguel Servet), then I will move to last position and corresponding author'.

Peer Review

Authorship and arbitration are two sides of the same coin. On the one hand the production of content, and on the other the quality control of what is produced (Rodríguez-Bravo & Nicholas, 2020b).

Researchers usually have a conscious publication strategy that allows them to meet the requirements for evaluation and promotion. Their success will largely depend on the referees who evaluate their work. Peer review is crucial for publication and ECRs know that they are in the hands of the reviewers. One researcher underlines that peer review 'is a lottery!' (Rodríguez-Bravo et al., 2017). The main complaint of ECRs is that they believe that editors do not always choose appropriate reviewers for papers and as one researcher points out, 'The selection of reviewers is not transparent, and the results depend on this selection'. Another researcher points out (Rodríguez-Bravo & Nicholas, 2019), 'Reviewers should be revised based on feedback from authors'. They complain that reviewers are often not receptive to new ideas. As authors, likewise, they lament the slowness of the review process, although when they are reviewers, they ask for time and know that a serious review is not improvised.

In the peer review system, they favour the double-blind model, which they believe offers more opportunities for young people and women to obtain better results. In this sense, a female researcher argues that, although the research group to which she belongs is easy to identify in the peer review process, the reviewers will not be able to know 'whether I am the first author or my boss'.

The ECRs mostly advocate this system of closed identities, although they recognise that anonymity facilitates unethical actions on the part of the referees. Nor is review with open identities favourable to them as reviewers.

They find themselves in a weak position and are uncomfortable with being forced to speak out cautiously for fear of later reprisals (Rodríguez-Bravo & Nicholas, 2020b). The work by Segado-Boj, Martín-Quevedo & Prieto-Gutiérrez (2018) confirms the caution of this group with respect to open peer review, both as authors and in their role as reviewers. Nevertheless, some ECRs that are familiar with open peer review understand that this system can offer advantages: as reviewers it helps to detect self-plagiarism and as authors it avoids the arbitrariness of referees and serves as a control mechanism for reviewers, since it promotes accountability and thoroughness in the review.

Spanish ECRs also emphasise that selecting good reviewers and obtaining good reviews would be easier if the peer review work was recognised. One researcher sees an advance in the Publons platform: 'The truth is that it would be great, above all to be able to justify the reviews made in accreditations, promotions, etc'. The remuneration of reviewers is an increasingly frequent request. This is seen as the solution to the lack of availability of reviewers and the lack of seriousness with which the evaluation is sometimes carried out. They also emphasise the need for training and clear instructions from the journals. They believe that this would benefit refereeing. It is still too frequent to learn directly from seniors doing co-reviews or alone without having taken any course on the practice (Rodríguez-Bravo & Nicholas, 2020b). They have not had, apparently, bad experiences of ghostwriting – performing the work for their mentors anonymously – or at least, they do not mention them.

In recent years, following the pandemic, the number of publications has increased and with it the demand for peer review. In parallel, journals and authors have higher expectations about the quality of peer review and greater urgency in the review process. However, the number of reviewers has not increased accordingly. In addition, the more expert reviewers have limited time and energy to devote to review and reject many of the requests they receive due to saturation (Rodríguez-Bravo & Nicholas, 2024). One researcher emphasises: 'the system is on the verge of collapse. Too many articles and not enough reviewers with time available to perform a rigorous evaluation'.

Spanish ECRs consider that the quality of the reviews had declined before the pandemic and that the situation worsened with it. It is difficult to obtain competent and committed reviewers. They also continue to think that in traditional journals the system is slow and in some of the new journals the review periods are too short for their results to be reliable. One researcher adverts that she wants to trust the system but that it is difficult given that it is worse than ever: 'We are now pursuing immediacy and quality, but the two do not go hand in hand'.

ECRs link well-positioned journals with the quality of the refereeing. In fact, there are those who report submitting manuscripts to journals where they do not think they have a chance just to get the reviewers' opinion. In these post-pandemic times, researchers continue to advocate the double-blind system.

Research Results and Metrics

The longer they have been in academia, the more they feel the pressure to publish in prestigious journals because they are more aware of the evaluation policies and criteria to which they will have to submit, and they are aware that they are in a very competitive sector. The journals in which they publish are selected based on their impact factor and relevance in the scientific field, as well as the appropriateness of the research that has been carried out to the scope of the journal (Nicholas et al., 2022).

Spanish ECRs point out that since all scientists want to publish in a small number of journals, they generally must try their luck in more than one, which means that publication time is delayed and some results are never published, which is detrimental to science. One researcher points out: 'As all researchers cite the same journals, the distance between the best positioned and the rest increases. In addition, highly specialised journals never reach the top positions, even if they are excellent'.

Strategy is key and ECRs are increasingly clear that whoever publishes first and best will get the reward. Besides, as noted elsewhere (Rodríguez-Bravo & Nicholas, 2019), the importance of the number of publications has negative consequences for science as researchers are in too much of a hurry and this results in the research being presented losing coherence because it is fractioned to publish more papers (salami slicing). One researcher calls this practice 'papers engineering'. Another scientist says that she is thinking of fragmenting her research into blocks because it would be beneficial 'to have more publications, get feedback more quickly and motivate the students who work with her'. Another colleague adds: 'My strategy is to publish parts of the research without waiting to have all the data in order to gain presence in the field as soon as possible'. One researcher points out: 'if I had more time,

I would use it to finish my articles without such haste so that they would be more complete and better understood'.

ECRs are aware that the situation is not ideal: 'Focusing only on publishing is bad for science' says a researcher. In addition, the emphasis on getting publications can prevent new ideas from moving forward, given that starting from scratch requires more time to obtain publications. 'Researchers who start new lines of research should be valued positively because it requires more effort and time before they can publish'.

With regard to obtaining grants, the group does not find it easy: 'obtaining them is valued, but most young researchers are not given the freedom to request them'; 'Some colleagues have seen how projects that have been rejected have gone ahead when their bosses have requested them' and a researcher argues that 'projects should be awarded to those who have interesting ideas with applications in the industry instead of awarding grants based on the already established reputation of the groups'.

In summary, they consider that counting publications and grants is not the ideal solution. They advocate a comprehensive evaluation adapted to the researchers, their field of study and their group. As one researcher points out: 'working with plants is less complicated than with animals and working with animals less complicated than with humans. The greater difficulty implies more time to obtain results and to be able to publish'.

After the pandemic, the evaluation system focused on quantifying publications and citations no longer seems to convince anyone. Dissatisfaction has only increased. They want to do science without being so constrained by the publication of articles and, above all, by the publication of articles in journals in the first quartiles of the Journal Citation Reports. They are increasingly interested in disseminating their work in both academic and general social networks and in outreach and collaboration with society.

Spanish ECRs doubt the value of metrics and advocate a more complete evaluation of academic achievements. One researcher reminds that 'the reputation of a researcher is more than numbers; I don't believe in metrics'. The Spaniards are very critical of the current system since they emphasise that the ease of publishing and obtaining citations varies depending on the type of research being done and the group to which one belongs, as already pointed out in the introduction.

Journal metrics (JIF) are considered too dominant. As one researcher points out 'the impact factor controls our lives'. On the other hand, article-level metrics are of no interest. 'The number of citations of an article does not seem to me to be a valid indicator for its evaluation', notes a researcher who is also not very interested in personal metrics such as the h-index. This is explained by the fact that the brevity of the careers of junior researchers does not make it easy to increase the h-index. However, they do use it when required.

They also criticise the undeserved or forced citations of researchers from groups of friends that make them doubt the reliability of citation metrics. Nor do they trust altmetrics – they consider them easily manipulated – although some researchers welcome the use of complementary criteria in evaluation. Others do not. This is the case of one researcher who states: 'the thought of being evaluated by the number of followers on Twitter makes me tremble with fear'. Another researcher of the same opinion says: 'Metrics depend on the popularity of the researcher and his or her skill in the use of social networks, not only on the quality of the work'.

Open Science and Preprints

Open science should be welcomed by ECRs as it offers potential benefits to researchers in their position: a superior and wider audience as papers are not locked into subscription publications; can garner more reads, mentions and recommendations on social media, and, likely, more citations from a wider audience; increases opportunities for collaboration, accommodates millennials' preferences for research transfer, collaboration and seeking to level the playing field; provides more opportunities to publish by increasing the range of publications; and offers greater ease in increasing their visibility, which is connected to reputation, and is highly regarded by the new generations (Herman & Nicholas, 2019).

However, despite appreciating all the possibilities mentioned, ECRs do not practice open science as much as they would like to. The Harbingers-1 interviews showed that junior researchers in general, and Spanish researchers in particular, had little knowledge of open science. However, throughout the development of Harbingers projects this is an aspect in which a remarkable evolution has been observed. In Harbingers-1 it was found that researchers did not understand the concept of open science. They only had some knowledge of one of its dimensions: open access and more specifically open-access journals. The doctoral students do not know what it consists of and only a few ECRs in sciences that are already PhDs are aware of whether their research groups have a policy in this regard.

Many think that open access is the new business of publishers and do not understand that they demand to pay APCs (Article Processing Charges). At the beginning of Harbingers-1, in 2016, they distrust open-access journals, they are not sure of their quality and reliability. They doubt that their peer review was rigorous. They claimed not to use them because there are no well-positioned open-access journals in their areas and they are inclined to publish in journals with a proven track record, and, if anything, in hybrid journals. Impact factor, reputation and audience appropriateness are considered more relevant factors than openness or speed of publication during the early years of Harbingers. Both cost and the alleged lack of quality of journals are barriers pointed out in other works such as that of Segado-Boj, Martín-Quevedo, & Prieto-Gutiérrez (2018).

However, as other studies have pointed out (Ruiz-Pérez & Delgado López-Cozar, 2018) this perception is inherited from the early days of open access when these journals lacked the backing of large publishers or had not yet been placed in the rankings. The opinion about these journals has improved and so has their use, as we already appreciated in the interviews conducted in 2017 and 2018. More and more researchers consider that open-access journals offer advantages of access to content, greater dissemination and thus more possibilities of obtaining citations and increasing their visibility and reputation (Rodríguez-Bravo & Nicholas, 2021). One researcher mentions ethical reasons for publishing in open access: 'if the publication is financed with public money, it must be in open access for any interested party'.

Cost is the main obstacle to open publication in all the interviews conducted. Researchers cannot always afford it; hence these journals are changing the rules of the game. Young researchers depend on the money of their groups and the willingness of their mentors or the principal investigators of the projects to publish in gold open access. Strong groups can publish in open access, which can bring advantages to their members. And as one researcher points out: 'It is an advantage that is not based on the excellence of the work but only on money' (Rodríguez-Bravo & Nicholas, 2021).

Since 2020, open-access publishing has become standardised for most ECRs in Spain and the pandemic has helped (Rodríguez-Bravo & Nicholas, 2024). ECRs continue to believe that OA publication can boost their careers by promoting the impact of their work. Reaching more researchers can bring more citations. When they have project or grant money from their institutions, ECRs prefer to publish in open access because they believe in its benefits. As one researcher points out: 'The trend should be to publish in open access to allow access to all publications and facilitate international collaboration among scientists'. Another researcher states: 'The evaluation should take into account OA publications without considering only their impact factor. This will help to promote open science'. Another researcher points out: 'Lately, the evaluation criteria seem to be moving towards giving more importance to publishing in open access'. However, the amounts required to pay the APCs of the gold journals are increasing. And they do not always have specific grants for this purpose or project money to cover them. Some have made use of the Transformative Agreements signed at the national level to publish open access in hybrid journals (Rodríguez-Bravo & Nicholas, 2024).

ECRs do not mention diamond journals. Besides, thematic repositories or institutional repositories don't interest them as means of making their publications available. They are more favourable to academic networks and mainly to ResearchGate. Repositories are not always known and when their existence is known they are considered a responsibility of librarians who sometimes contact them and request their publications (Rodríguez-Bravo & Nicholas, 2019). This is, however, an aspect that has evolved in recent years since there is an obligation to deposit in the institutional repository the publications to be submitted for the six-year-research-evaluation in the call for 'sexenios'.

Likewise, they are unaware of the new open-access platforms and the preprint servers that became popular during the pandemic are of little interest to Spanish ECRs, and some even reject them. As one researcher comments 'it is naïve to think that the contents on these platforms can have the same value as a peer-reviewed article. I do not agree with the promotion that the European Union is making of these platforms in recent times'.

Some scientists are also wary of preprints because they fear that publishing preprints means giving up the possibility of publishing in a high-impact journal. As one researcher points out: 'Publishing preprints means burning my research before publishing it in journals'. Another researcher is of the same opinion: 'I do not publish preprints because many journals do not accept manuscripts previously published as preprints'.

Spanish ECRs do not agree with the fast publication routes brought about by COVID in some scientific areas. One researcher emphasises: 'some researchers have abused the publication of preprints in repositories' and 'I am concerned that scientists cannot distinguish between a preprint and a peer-reviewed article. Preprints are used as if they were a final product, and they are not'. Many researchers, therefore, do not consider that a product deposited in these platforms should have the consideration of a publication that has undergone a serious peer review process. They consider it a shortcut in the scientific career.

Haste is not a good adviser, and research is no exception. Some Spanish ECRs suggested that the need to quickly publish COVID-related findings led to inadequate quality of some of the research articles-or preprints-that saw the light of day.

However, not all scientists share this distrust. One researcher considers that 'the pandemic has stirred up the debate about the speed of science. We are more aware that we cannot wait months for the review process and that publishing unvalidated results may be necessary because society demands it'. Another scientist confirms this trend: 'the speed of publication has increased in importance'. Despite their favourable opinions, Spanish ECRs have not published preprints; they continue to focus on publishing in journals.

Regarding data sharing, most young researchers have a positive attitude. As can be seen from the survey conducted by Digital Science et al. (2020), researchers would like to share data under conditions that guarantee the security and privacy of them, privileges the publication of results and the recognition of the origin of the data. The Spanish ECRs express themselves along these lines (Rodríguez-Bravo & Nicholas, 2021). One researcher indicates: 'sharing data and software is important, science must be collaborative'. Another scientist points out the importance, confirmed by the pandemic, of publishing data quickly and openly to find solutions to urgent situations'. However, they are cautious: they want to exploit them in depth before making them openly available and, in addition, they do not practice much because they think that cleaning the data and preparing them for sharing takes time that they do not have.

Predatory and Questionable Journals

Questions about predatory journals were introduced in the 2018 interviews and retained in the Harbingers-2 and Harbingers-3 interviews. Curiously, neither predatory journals nor predatory conferences are mentioned in the sections dedicated to ethics and integrity. Nor in the sections on open science, which is odd given that open publication is linked to journal quality, especially during Harbingers-1 (Rodríguez-Bravo & Nicholas, 2020a).

It seems that the Spanish ECRs understand it is not in their interest to heed their calls. The main concerns were whether to publish in gold open-access journals in Harbingers-1 or the controversy of the value for their evaluation to publish in journals from certain publishers such as MDPI or Frontiers in Harbingers-2 (Nicholas et al., 2023a).

Contrary to expectations, predatory publishing turned out to be quite marginal to the scholarly pursuits of ECRs: it was little practiced and seen as an irritant rather than a danger to the scientific undertaking and its stakeholders. When alluded to at all, it was only in passing, not even as a problem in itself, but as part of the problems surrounding open-access publications and the possibility that predatory journals might bring about further deterioration in their quality.

It is true that the ECRs participants in our study were not generally inexperienced or naïve, came from good universities and were part of research groups of high-flying, knowledgeable researchers, so they were neither likely to fall prey to unscrupulous publishers nor come up with such low-quality research that their only option was publishing it in scam journals.

Less than half of Spanish ECRs said they were aware of policies, but even more (and some of the former) said they were directed where to publish and the WoS list is for most of them their 'Bible' when it comes to choosing journals. They also mentioned the guidelines of ANECA, the national agency for researchers' assessment, which in 2021 published a list of questionable journals because they exhibit 'anomalous behaviour'. ECRs were generally more uncomfortable about publishing with MDPI, a big publisher, because many of them are on ANECA's blacklist and for them that is bad news because they can publish in MDPI's journals which is relatively easy for them and pay the APCs with vouchers obtainable for peer reviewing for the publisher.

The ANECA report was highly controversial because not all the measurement criteria used were considered adequate. Indeed, ECRs feel confused, unable to understand why JCR's indexed journals are not suitable for obtaining a good assessment. To complicate matters even further, two years later, ANECA withdrew its report, claiming to justify the withdrawal on the grounds of a more overarching need to reform the research evaluation models in Spain, towards more qualitative and less bibliometric evaluation models. More specifically, this need is for evaluating of the quality of scientific articles, rather than the quality of the journals in which they are published only, and, in addition, to consider the impact of the research from a broader perspective (Nicholas et al., 2023b).

Artificial Intelligence (AI): The Last Disruptor

Generative artificial intelligence is the latest major disruptor of the science communication system and questions about its consideration, utility and use were introduced in Harbingers-3.

Wiley Publishing's survey (Naddaf, 2025) of nearly 5,000 researchers from more than seventy countries concludes that the actual use of AI is still limited. Only 45% of the first 1,043 respondents have employed AI in their work, mainly for translation, proofreading and copy editing. While 81% have used OpenAI's ChatGPT, only a third are aware of other tools such as Google's Gemini or Microsoft's Copilot. The data shows that usage varies by country and discipline, being more prevalent in China and Germany, as well as among researchers in computer science and medicine.

Despite this limited use of AI, a recent exploratory study (Hosseini et al., 2023) regarding the use of ChatGPT in education, research, and healthcare found that younger academics are more interested in using the technology than seniors, have more positive views, more interest, and most have already tried it. Similarly, a Nature survey (Nordling, 2023) of postdocs found that 31% said they used chatboxes. Of these, 43% used them on a weekly basis and 17% on a daily basis. However, more than half (67%) considered that AI had not changed their daily routine or their short-term career plans.

The data from the Harbingers set of countries showed that ECRs were thinking about, testing and, in some cases, experimenting with AI. There was a general acceptance that AI is going to be responsible for an increase in low-quality scientific articles, which could lead to a decrease in the credibility of science and research. Academic integrity and ethics are major concerns among which problems such as authenticity, plagiarism, copyright and lack of citations, or incorrect citations (hallucinations) stand out. It is widely believed that AI will be a transformative force that will exacerbate inequalities and disparities in academia (Clark et al. 2025, Nicholas et al., 2024).

From the results obtained from the Spanish researchers interviewed we can indicate that the use of AI tools is incipient in 2023, in line with the results obtained in other studies, but its possible impact on malpractice and inequality between some researchers and others can be perceived if its potential role in research is confirmed. Yet, although they consider it helpful, it has not yet saved them significant time or increased their productivity. However, they question whether in other areas its use may be having more weight and producing differences between researchers who use it and those who do not.

One researcher indicates that AI can have an impact on reputation: 'Yes, because it helps improve the quality of publications through deeper analysis. In addition, it can increase productivity – and decrease transparency'. Another researcher is clear that AI will be a transformative force: 'It will be a tremendously useful tool for research because it can process a lot of information quickly and provide useful results. For example, knowing the state of the art on a certain topic'.

Among all the researchers interviewed, only in one case was artificial intelligence her field of work. Interestingly, this researcher does not use generative artificial intelligence either in her work or in her daily life. However, she points out the following: 'The greatest interest of AI lies in its application to the medical environment because it allows to support doctors' diagnoses or even to anticipate them and consequently avoid major complications'.

The most widely used application is ChatGPT, and they use it mainly in the process of scientific communication. The main use they give it is to write texts in English and to correct language. It seems clear that in the field of scientific writing, AI has a promising future that goes beyond the automatic processes we know that correct words, complete them or translate texts.

Two researchers mention the usefulness of Research Rabbit for searching information and half a dozen researchers make use of AI to test code. One researcher stresses that the literature review traditionally requested in articles 'does not make sense since it can be done by artificial intelligence; it would be preferable to request short Letters-type articles'. Besides, one researcher has found it useful in teaching and outreach because it is so easy to make drawings, diagrams, etc.

No one uses generative AI to detect knowledge gaps in their fields, but they find it interesting to explore this avenue and some show special interest in it. On the other hand, none believe that generative AI applications can undertake peer review although they can be helpful in detecting plagiarism and self-plagiarism.

Ethical concerns are also reflected in the contributions of Spanish ECRs. They are worried about its use in the preparation of publications and most of them consider its use a manifestation of malpractice, mainly because of the lack of transparency it implies. One researcher indicates: 'I think there are researchers who are using AI to skip steps in research and publish AI-produced results as if they were their own. Researchers are behaving like students'. Another researcher emphasises: 'AI is filling journals with articles that are not original and do not contribute to science. Honestly, from my point of view they should be considered plagiarism'.

Another researcher warns of other dangers: 'Research is "frontier knowledge" and therefore current, not past knowledge which is what AI algorithms are based on. Therefore, there is a danger that all reviews follow the same model and that all articles go in the same direction. This is dangerous'.

One ECR points out that the main problem lies in the unethical use of AI: 'The only problem I see is that it is not used ethically. There are more and more applications of all kinds: photo editing, video, voice, etc., and if we don't use them correctly, in the end we won't be able to trust anything we see. However, I see more positive – and more important- consequences than negative ones. For example, its applications in the medical field or in saving time in repetitive jobs'.

Logically, ECRs who teach are also very concerned about their students' use of generative AI. They believe that as teachers they will not be able to detect its use in their assigned tasks and, therefore, to trust the output presented to them. Authenticity and plagiarism are concerns when it comes to the learning process.

The still limited use of AI in 2023 does not imply that most of the interviewees do not give AI the importance it deserves. They all see a future for it, for some promising and for others worrying, but they are all aware that 'it is not possible to put gates on the sea' and that AI will become increasingly relevant. Thus, another Nature survey answered by 1,600 international researchers reports that more than half of those interviewed consider that generative AI tools will be essential in their fields in the next decade (Van Noorden & Perkel, 2023).

Conclusion

Attitudes and practices have not remained unchanged. They have changed over the eight years of the project and greater pragmatism has been observed. Any activity that leads to passing the next evaluation and is aimed at obtaining a permanent position or the next contract is welcome (Rodríguez-Bravo & Nicholas, 2019). This approach has obvious risks for ethics and integrity.

One researcher stresses: 'Changing the evaluation criteria is the key to research integrity. If evaluation is no longer based on "weight" (the more you publish the greater your value is), the great concern to publish a lot will probably decrease. The current situation implies that sometimes the interest in the quality of what is published is abandoned'.

The need to occupy highly valued authorship positions can also make excessive collaboration look dangerous, a fact that does not favour science because they are very aware of its benefits since it allows them to make use of better techniques and obtain better research (Rodríguez-Bravo & Nicholas, 2019).

The system must rethink the pressure to which it subjects ECRs. The evaluation should be made more flexible and not only consider research merits, a recurrent complaint of the Spanish ECRs, and when these are evaluated, diversify the measures, also considering qualitative criteria. Outreach and open science activities should not only be requested from researchers but should also be considered in their assessment. Nowadays, as pointed out by one researcher they feel like 'monkeys in a fair' trying to obtain all kinds of merits that are not evaluated later.

There is also a need, for the sake of equity, to consider contextual factors in the recruitment and promotion of ECRs. It is necessary to achieve an integral evaluation adapted to the circumstances of the researchers, their field of study and their group. As we have seen, researchers complain that it does not take the same amount of time to obtain publishable results or citations in all fields.

Regarding the results related to AI, we must keep in mind that in 2023 many of the specialised AI tools we know were not yet available. The context was ChatGPT. The interviews that we will conduct in 2025 will surely provide richer results. However, the interviews revealed that novice researchers are not leaders in the new technology but rather critics who reflect on its possibilities and risks and sometimes experiment.

Bibliography

Clark, D., Nicholas, D., Swigon, M., Abrizah, A., Rodríguez-Bravo, B., Revez, J., Herman, E., Xu, J., & Watkinson, A. (2025). Authors, wordsmiths and twriters: early career researchers' responses to artificial intelligence. *Learned Publishing*, 38 (1). https://onlinelibrary.wiley.com/doi/epdf/10.1002/leap.1652

Digital Science, Hahnel, M., McIntosh, L. D., Hyndman, A., Baynes, G., Crosas, M., Nosek, B., Shearer, K., Selm, M. V., Goodey, G., & Nature research. (2020). The State of Open Data 2020. *Digital Science*. Report. https://doi.org/10.6084/m9.figshare.13227875.v2

Gardner, T., & Inger, S. (2018). How readers discover content in scholarly publications. Trends in reader behavior from 2005 to 2018. *Renew Training*.

Herman, E. (2018). Scholarly reputation. *FEMS Microbiology letters*, *365* (18), fny200. https://doi.org/10.1093/femsle/fny200

Herman, E., & Nicholas, D. (2019). Scholarly reputation building in the digital age. An activity-specific approach. Review article. *The information professional*, 8 (1). https://doi.org/10.3145/epi.2019.ene.02

Hosseini, M., Gao, C. A., Liebovitz, D. M., Carvalho, A. M., Ahmad, F. S., Luo, Y., MacDonald, N, Holmes, K. L., & Kho, A. (2023). An exploratory survey about using ChatGPT in education, healthcare, and research. *PLOS one*, 18 (10). https://doi.org/10.1371/journal.pone.0292216

Laudel, G., & Gläser, J. (2008). From apprentice to colleague: The metamorphosis of early career researchers. *Higher education*, *55*(3), 386–406. https://link.springer.com/article/10.1007/s10734-007-9063-7

Naddaf, M. (2025). How are researchers using AI? Survey reveals pros and cons for science. *Nature*, 2025 (4 February). https://doi.org//10.1038/d41586-025-00343-5.

Nicholas, D., Boukacem-Zeghmouri, C., Xu, J., Herman, E., Clark, D., Abrizah, A., Rodríguez-Bravo, B., & Swigon, M. (2018). Sci-Hub: The new and ultimate disruptor? View from the front. *Learned Publishing*, 32 (2): 147–153. https://doi.org/10.1002/leap.1206

Nicholas, D., Herman, E., Clark, D., Boukacem-Zeghmouri, C., Rodríguez-Bravo, B., Abrizah, A., Watkinson, A., Xu, J., Sims, D., Serbina, G., Swigon, M., Jamali, H. R., Tenopir, C., & Allard, S. (2022). Choosing the 'right' journal: Perceptions and practices of pandemic-era early career researchers. *Learned Publishing*, 35(4), 605–616. https://doi.org/10.1002/leap.1488

Nicholas, D., Herman, E., Abrizah, A., Rodríguez-Bravo, B., Boukacem-Zeghmouri, C., Watkinson, A., Swigon, M, Xu, J., Jamali, H. R., & Tenopir, C. (2023b). Never mind predatory publishers … what about 'grey' publishers? *Profesional de la información*, 32(5). https://doi.org/10.3145/epi.2023.sep.09

Nicholas, D.; Rodríguez-Bravo, B., Boukacem-Zeghmouri, C., Herman, E., Clark, D., Xu, J., Abrizah, A., Swigon, M., Watkinson, A., Sims, D., Jamali, H. R., Tenopir, C., & Allard, S. (2023a). Early career researchers and predatory journals during the Covid-19 pandemic. An international analysis. *Profesional de la información*, 32(1). https://doi.org/10.3145/epi.2023.ene.17

Nicholas, D., Swigon, M., Clark, D., Abrizah, A., Revez, J., Herman, E., Rodríguez-Bravo, B., Xu, J., & Watkinson, A. (2024). The impact of generative AI on the scholarly communications of early career researchers: An international, multi-disciplinary study. *Learned Publishing*, 37 (4). https://doi.org/10.1002/leap.1628

Nordling, L. (2023). How ChatGPT is transforming the postdoc experience. *Nature*, 622 (7983), 655–657. https://doi.org,10.1038/d41586-023-03235-8

Powell, K. (2015). The future of the postdoc. *Nature*, 520 (7546): 144–147. https://doi.org/10.1038/520144a

Rodríguez-Bravo, B., & Nicholas, D. (2019). Reputation and science communication: early-career Spanish researchers. *Profesional de la información*, 28 (2). https://doi.org//10.3145/epi.2019.mar.03

Rodríguez-Bravo, B., & Nicholas, D. (2020a). Discovering, reading, publishing sharing, and monitoring progress: behavior of Spanish researchers. *Profesional de la información*, 29 (5). https://doi.org/10.3145/epi.2020.sep.03

Rodríguez-Bravo, B., & Nicholas, D. (2020b). Co-authorship and peer review: practices and perceptions of Spanish junior researchers. *Revista General de Información y Documentación*, 30 (2), 379–399. http://dx.doi.org/10.5209/rgid.72817

Rodríguez-Bravo, B., & Nicholas, D. (2021). Spanish junior researchers and their involvement in open science. *Anales de Documentación*, 24 (2). http://dx.doi.org/10.6018/analesdoc.470671

Rodríguez-Bravo, B., & Nicholas, D. (2022). The relationship of junior researchers with university libraries. *AIB studi*, 62 (3). https://doi.org//10.2426/aibstudi-13788

Rodríguez-Bravo, B., & Nicholas, D. (2024). Disruptions and pandemic inheritance in the scientific communication of Spanish junior researchers. *Profesional de la Información*, 33 (2), https://doi.org/10.3145/epi.2024.0209

Rodríguez-Bravo, B., Nicholas, D., Herman, E., Boukacem-Zeghmouri, C., Watkinson, A., Xu, J., Abrizah, A., & Swigon, M. (2017). Peer review: the experience and views of early career researchers. *Learned Publishing*, 30(4). https://doi.org/10.1002/leap.1111

Ruiz-Pérez, S., & Delgado López-Cozar, E. (2018). Spanish researchers' opinions, attitudes and practices towards open access publishing. *Profesional de la información*, 26(4), 722–734. https://doi.org/10.3145/epi.2017.jul.16

Segado-Boj, F., Martín-Quevedo, J., & Prieto-Gutiérrez, J. J. (2018). Attitudes toward open access, open peer review, and almetrics among contributors to spanish scholarly journals'. *Journal of Scholarly Publishing*, 50 (1), 48–70. https://doi.org/10.3138/jsp.50.1.08

Segado-Boj, F., Martín-Quevedo, J., & Prieto-Gutiérrez, J. J. (2022). Jumping over the paywall: Strategies and motivations for scholarly piracy and other alternatives. *Information Development*, 40(3). https://doi.org/10.1177/02666669221144429

Artificial Intelligence in Higher Education: Limitations and Potential in the Teaching-Learning Process

Viviana Elizabeth Jiménez Chaves[1], Claudia Spinzi[2], Perla Sosa de Wood[3] and Andrea Paola Riego Esteche[4]

ABSTRACT
Artificial intelligence in higher education offers potential in the learning process, but like any phenomenon, it also presents limitations in its implementation. This research aims to describe the limitations and potential of AI in higher education in Paraguay. The study is descriptive in nature, and a questionnaire was implemented with ninety university-level teachers from both public and private universities in Paraguay. The main results indicate that the identified limitations include ethical concerns, data privacy, and students' technological dependence. Additionally, the potential benefits highlighted include improving content in the teaching-learning process, participation, timely feedback, and enhancing the quality and accessibility of higher education. It is a tool that improves teaching by helping evaluate tasks and providing personalised support to students.

Keywords: artificial intelligence, higher education, teaching process, learning, teacher

Introduction

The term Artificial Intelligence dates back to a publication by Alan Turing, who in 1941 introduced the concept of 'algorithm' in his work titled 'Computing Machinery and Intelligence'. The term AI was coined by John McCarthy, Marvin Minsky, and Claude Shannon in 1959, who defined it as 'The science and engineering of making intelligent machines through intelligent computational programs' (Granados Maguey & Cervantes Martínez, 2022; Inicio Flores, et.al.,2022; Sanabria-Navarro, Silveira-Pérezet al., 2023).

1 Universidad del Norte, Paraguay, https://orcid.org/0000-0002-9442-5039
2 Universidad del Norte, Paraguay, https://orcid.org/0000-0003-0106-8106
3 Universidad Nacional de Itapúa, Paraguay, https://orcid.org/0000-0003-3020-0188
4 Universidad de la Integración de las Americas, Paraguay, https://orcid.org/0000-0003-3203-3045

Artificial intelligence (AI) has emerged as a revolutionary tool in various fields, including higher education, and its impact on university professors is significant (Aranda-Corral et al., 2014). In higher education context, AI offers unprecedented opportunities to enhance the teaching-learning process, but it also presents significant challenges that must be addressed carefully.

UNESCO (2020), in the document 'Artificial Intelligence in Education', based on the approval of the Beijing Consensus on Artificial Intelligence and Education during the 'International Conference on Artificial Intelligence in Education' held in Beijing in 2019, identifies (from a humanistic approach) five areas: 1) AI in the service of education management and implementation; 2) AI in the service of empowering teachers and their teaching; 3) AI in the service of learning and evaluating outcomes; 4) The development of values and competencies necessary for life and work in the age of AI; and 5) AI as a means of providing lifelong learning opportunities for all.

AI also plays a key role in the optimisation of administrative tasks within the educational institutions (Popenici and Kerr, 2017). Tools such as chatbots and student management systems can automate repetitive students can automate repetitive processes, freeing up time for teachers to concentrate on more strategic and pedagogical activities (Piedra et al., 2023; Ferrada et al., 2020).

In recent years, the integration of AI technologies in the educational field has transformed teaching methodologies, offering new opportunities to personalise education and improve administrative efficiency (Brazdil and Jorge, 2001).

According to Vera (2023), AI enables the creation of adaptive learning environments that respond to the individual needs of students, promoting more effective and personalised learning.

Artificial intelligence can be harnessed in the field of education to improve student learning and performance. Various technologies can be employed to achieve this, such as virtual reality, augmented reality, games, among others (Castrillón et al., 2020).

AI-based applications for education have experienced rapid growth worldwide and have had an impact on higher education institutions in Latin America (Shrivastava, 2023). Some AI applications are being implemented to improve learning services, help teachers provide quality education, and support student learning (Chen et al., 2023).

According to Sánchez (2022), the analysis of Artificial Intelligence applied to education has been under international development for decades and has made significant progress in the last ten years thanks to the advancement of techniques such as machine learning, including educational data mining and learning analytics (González, 2023).

Artificial intelligence has enormous potential to transform education, offering the possibility of personalised and efficient learning experiences. However, it is crucial to be aware of the potential risks in education, such as bias and the possibility of job displacement (Gazquez et al., 2023).

According to Pérez-Ortega (2017), one of the main advantages is the ability of AI to provide instant and personalised feedback to students. This not only enhances learning and academic performance but also makes the work of teachers easier by allowing them to quickly identify areas where students need more support.

Tools such as chatbots and student management systems can handle queries and administrative tasks, allowing teachers to focus on teaching and professional development. Yang (2018) notes that the automation of administrative processes through AI can reduce teachers' workload and improve the accuracy and efficiency of educational operations. This not only benefits teachers but also enhances the quality of educational services for students (García-Peñalbo, 2023; Parra-Sánchez, 2022).

The growing dependence on artificial intelligence in the educational field presents both challenges and unique opportunities. On one hand, AI provides powerful tools to personalise teaching, offer instant feedback, and improve access to information. However, excessive use of these technologies could lead to negative effects, such as a decline in critical skills, reduced social interaction, and a lack of autonomy in learning. Therefore, it is essential that regulations address not only the implementation of AI but also crucial ethical and social issues, such as privacy, equity, and security (León Rodriguez & Viña Brito, 2017).

It is essential to critically analyse how the dependence on AI impacts student learning and their cognitive, emotional, and social development in higher education.

Ethical concerns related to privacy and data usage are another critical aspect in the implementation of AI in education (González-Calatayud et al., 2021; Sánchez Vila and Lama, 2007). The collection and analysis of large volumes of educational data raise issues about the protection of student privacy and the ethical use of information.

According to Fernández-Robles (2017), it is essential to establish clear and transparent policies regarding data management and to ensure that AI technologies are used ethically and responsibly. Trust in AI technologies and transparency in their use are crucial for their acceptance and success in the educational field (Forero-Corba and Negre-Bennasar, 2023; Riel and Polin, 2004).

Real-time feedback is a promising application of artificial intelligence in education. AI provides immediate and personalised feedback to students, which is essential for effective learning and has been shown to improve student performance in various contexts (D'Mello SK, Graesser AC, 2010). Additionally, real-time feedback benefits teachers, who can assess student performance, provide guidance and additional support, as well as monitor student progress and make adjustments to teaching in order to better address their needs.

Artificial intelligence would be highly supportive in education as it provides insights that allow for personalised learning for each student, ensuring better teaching and contributing to increased student engagement in their academic process. For this reason, Flores and García (2023) state that AI can become a great ally for both students and teachers, offering not only personalised pedagogical content but also personalised assistance and tutoring.

In the context of Paraguay, artificial intelligence in education is still in its early stages. In a study by Almada (2024) on the perception of the use of artificial intelligence by teachers in the field of computer science at the Centro Regional de Educación Saturio Ríos, conducted in 2024, it was found that one of the main challenges in implementing AI in the teaching-learning process is the lack of adequate technological resources. Many educational institutions do not have the necessary infrastructure to efficiently use AI, which limits their ability to implement AI tools and applications in the classroom. The lack of updated computer equipment, high-speed internet connections, and specialised software hinders access to the benefits that AI offers in education. This limitation prevents the personalisation of teaching, improves learning assessment, and provides adequate feedback to students (Fernández Batanero et al., 2024).

Ayuso and Gutiérrez (2022) argue that AI benefits learning environments within the framework of Higher Education and motivates students to make use of technologies in their future teaching practices.

For teachers, the incorporation of artificial intelligence tools represents a significant challenge, as discrepancies in their use can arise given the wide range of available resources (Lameras and Arnab, 2021). According to Loinaz (2021), artificial intelligence will change the traditional role of teachers, raising concerns about job losses and the quality of learning.

Another potential for increased teaching efficiency is seen through the automation of administrative tasks and the evaluation of assignments using AI algorithms (Minerva Project, 2023). This frees up time for teachers to focus more on direct interaction with students and on higher-value pedagogical activities.

Artificial Intelligence (AI) is experiencing growth in higher education. In Paraguay, although the adoption of AI in this field is still in its early stages, a promising future is seen with great transformative potential.

In Paraguay, there are initiatives that demonstrate the interest and potential of this technology. Some universities are beginning to explore the use of AI tools to improve teaching and learning, such as virtual tutoring platforms, personalised course recommendation systems, and data analysis tools to identify patterns in student performance using machine learning as the primary tool.

This research explores the potential and limitations of AI in higher education institutions in Paraguay, analysing its impact on learning personalisation, task automation, educational inclusion, and ethics in data use.2 Methodology

This is a descriptive research in nature. A questionnaire was administered to ninety university-level teachers from various public and private universities in Paraguay. The quantitative approach was used. The data collection procedure was carried out through a Google Forms questionnaire over a period of 4 weeks. The design was non-experimental. The teachers who participated in the questionnaire did so voluntarily. They teach undergraduate and graduate courses in various fields of science.

The variables studied were: Technological dependence of students; data privacy and security; educational content; technological infrastructure (Hernández Sampieri, 2010).

In Paraguay, there are fifty-four universities. 8 of these are public universities and forty-six are privately managed. Public universities are funded by the government and tend to have more affordable tuition fees, while private universities have their own sources of funding and may have higher costs.

Methodology

To achieve the objective of this research, it was decided to adopt a quantitative approach, descriptive in scope, with a non-experimental and cross-sectional design. A non-experimental design was chosen, since it was not desired to manipulate the variables, but to observe how teachers perceive the use of AI in the natural context (Hernández Sampieri et al., 2010).

Data collection was carried out through the application of a structured questionnaire, applied to ninety university teachers from different higher education institutions, both public and private, in Paraguay. The quantitative approach made it possible to obtain measurable and standardised information, enabling statistical analysis of perceptions and teaching practices.

Informants, Inclusion and Exclusion Criteria

The participant population consisted of teachers from both public and private universities throughout the country. There are currently fifty-four registered universities in the country, of which eight are public and forty-six are private. The public universities are financed by the Paraguayan government, while the private universities have their own funding.

The sample was non-probabilistic and consisted of ninety university professors from different universities in Paraguay, both public and private institutions. It should be noted that most of the participating professors teach in both public and private institutions, since it is common practice in the country for a professor to teach in different institutions. The technique used was chain or network sampling, teachers who were part of a database were invited to participate by email and were asked to share with their colleagues to increase the scope (Hernández Sampieri et al., 2007).

The inclusion criteria established were:

- Teachers working in undergraduate careers or graduate programmes.

- Teachers belonging to different areas of knowledge (Social Sciences, Health Sciences, Engineering, among others).
- Voluntary participation and prior informed consent.

Teachers who did not agree to participate voluntarily or who did not complete the questionnaire in its entirety were excluded from the study.

Data Collection Instrument

A structured questionnaire was used for data collection, designed specifically for this study, composed of closed and multiple-choice questions. The questionnaire consisted of an introductory section, which explained the purpose of the study, the importance of participation, approximate response time and guaranteed the confidentiality of the answers. Then, a section was included to identify the informant, requesting information on the institution of higher education, area of knowledge of the subjects taught and years of teaching experience at the institution. Finally, the questions corresponding to the study variables were presented, carefully formulated to obtain pertinent and precise information.

The variables analysed were:

- Technology dependence of students.
- Data privacy and security.
- Educational content.
- Technological infrastructure.

The definition and operationalisation of these variables was based on the proposal of Hernández Sampieri (2010).

Validation of the Instrument

The instrument was subjected to a content validation process through expert judgement. Specialists in the educational and technological areas were consulted and evaluated the relevance, clarity, coherence and wording of each item. They were also asked to comment on possible redundancies, the appropriateness of the order of the questions and the relevance of the response options. The suggestions were incorporated to ensure the validity and reliability of the questionnaire.

Data Collection Procedure

The questionnaire was applied virtually using the Google Forms platform over a period of four weeks. The invitation to participate was sent through institutional e-mails and professional networks, ensuring anonymity and confidentiality of the data. Informed consent was obtained from each participant before completing the questionnaire.

Data Analysis

The data collected were organised and processed using Microsoft Excel software. Descriptive statistical techniques were applied, such as the calculation of absolute frequencies, percentages and graphs, in order to identify patterns, trends and distributions in the teachers' responses. The analysis allowed interpreting the results in a clear and precise manner, facilitating the understanding of the observed phenomena (Guerrero-Bejarano, 2020).

Results Analysis

The findings are shown below, presenting some of the questions with their bar graphs representing the percentages of responses to each item. The first question presented is about the technological dependence of students, followed by privacy and data security issues, and finally whether AI can enrich educational content.

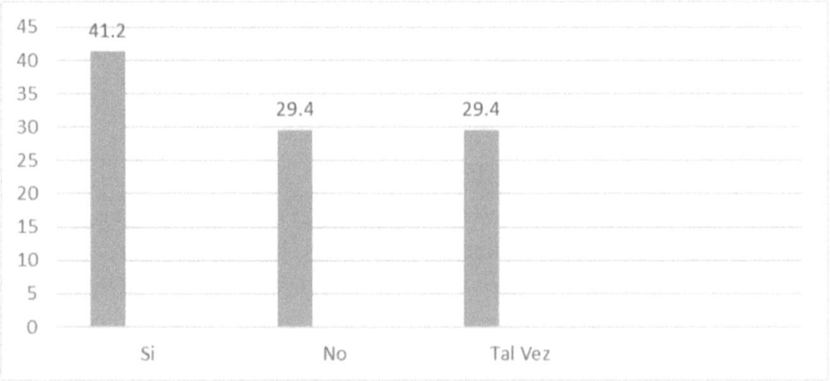

Figure 8: Do you think AI can create technological dependence in students?

41% state that AI could increase the likelihood of students becoming more dependent and passive. Additionally, 29.4% express doubts about this, suggesting that, under certain conditions, its use could foster dependency.

By offering quick and easy solutions without the student having to think much, it can reduce their ability to question and their critical thinking. To address these issues, it is crucial that educators, legislators, and society work together. Public policies and regulations are needed to protect data and promote equal access to technology. It is essential to foster educational practices that encourage students to think for themselves and actively engage in their learning. In this way, AI in education could be promoted as fair and beneficial for all (León Rodriguez & Viña Brito, 2017).

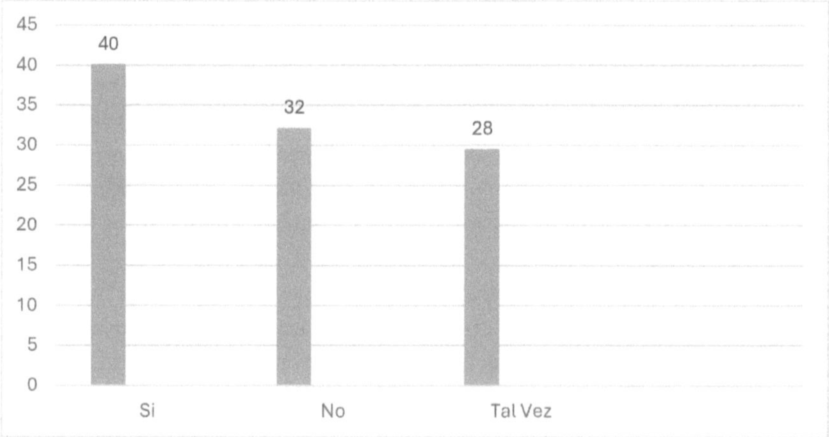

Figure 9: Do you think AI can create privacy and data security issues for students?

40% indicate that there is concern regarding the privacy and security of the data stored by AI. The privacy and security of students' data are critical aspects that must be carefully managed to prevent the misuse of personal information (Solove, 2006).

This concern among teachers about data privacy and the lack of updates in intelligent systems could create resistance to using this tool. Therefore, transparency regarding the use of AI data should be promoted to enhance trust and encourage its use in higher education (Forero-Corba and Negre-Bennasar, 2023; Riel and Polin, 2004).

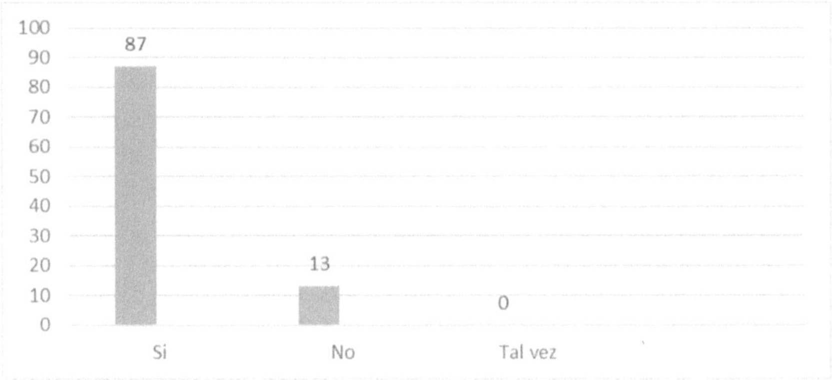

Figure 10: Do you think AI can enrich educational content and make it more interactive and engaging for students?

87% stated that AI enriches educational content and makes it more interactive and engaging for students. According to Almada (2024), AI in education presents numerous benefits. On one hand, it allows for the personalisation of the teaching process, adapting content and activities to the individual needs of each student. In this way, a more meaningful and motivating learning experience can be fostered.

Therefore, while there is a clear positive assessment regarding the ability of AI to dynamise and enrich content, legitimate concerns related to data privacy and the risk of fostering technological dependency in students also emerge. These findings underscore the need for an approach to the teaching and learning process, where the implementation of AI is accompanied by clear policies, critical pedagogical practices and an ethical commitment to ensure its responsible and beneficial use for the integral development of students.

Discussion and Conclusion

AI has strong potential to accelerate the achievement of global education goals by reducing learning access barriers, automating management processes, and optimising methods that improve learning outcomes (United Nations Educational, Scientific and Cultural Organization, 2019).

It also enhances the quality of content, making it more appealing to students by adapting it to mediums that currently pose a great challenge, such as smartphones.

The greater personalisation of learning for students is one of the main advantages of AI in higher education. AI systems can adapt to each student's learning pace, offering specific materials and instant feedback that promote more effective learning (European Digital Education Hub, 2022). Furthermore, accessibility is enhanced by providing digitised educational resources that are available anytime and anywhere (European Digital Education Hub, 2022). AI acts as support for teachers to identify areas of difficulty for students, allowing them to design more effective learning activities and provide personalised feedback.

In Paraguay, one of the main challenges is the lack of adequate technological infrastructure in many higher education institutions, which hinders the effective integration of AI into the teaching process. Additionally, limited access to devices and quality Internet connections can restrict student participation in AI-based educational activities, a situation prevalent in rural areas.

The integration of AI into higher education requires significant investment in technological infrastructure and educational resources (Osorio Umaña, 2022; Arabit-García et al., 2021). Educational institutions must be prepared to invest in AI technologies and in the training of their faculty. Martínez-Pérez and Fernández-Robles (2018) suggest that collaboration between governments, educational institutions, and the private sector is crucial to provide the necessary resources and support the implementation of AI technologies in higher education. The creation of networks and communities of practice can also facilitate the exchange of knowledge and experiences, promoting a more effective and equitable implementation of AI (Allaoua-Chelloug et al., 2023).

Another factor is the safeguarding of privacy and the protection of students' data, which are imperative and unavoidable. Higher education institutions must establish robust protocols and control mechanisms to ensure the integrity and confidentiality of information at all times, thus balancing the innovative potential of AI with respect for the fundamental rights of users in the educational environment (Salmerón et al., 2023).

The proliferation of algorithms can present significant challenges regarding information privacy and security, particularly if these algorithms are not developed and used ethically and responsibly (Faliero, 2021). Furthermore,

Moreno and Gutiérrez (2019) state that it is essential to prioritise the protection of personal data in any system that handles large volumes of information. The absence of clear and rigorous policies on the use and protection of data can lead to a decrease in user confidence in AI-based educational technologies. Therefore, it is crucial to implement strong security measures to safeguard personal data and ensure its ethical use. Similarly, Ramírez et al. (2023) underline the need for adequate regulation to oversee the use of AI in education, ensuring that algorithms are transparent and auditable. This would allow users to understand how their data is collected, stored, and used, and in turn, provides mechanisms for individuals to control and protect their personal information.

Challenges are also present among higher education students and faculty. Challenges are identified for institutions and in student learning when adopting AI for teaching, learning, student support, and administration (Popenici and Kerr, 2017). One of these challenges also centres on ethical issues to consider, as there are students who feel that when other students make use of AI, they are cheating the system and playing with some advantage over students who do not use it. More than half of U.S. college students believe that using AI tools to complete assignments or exams is cheating (Garrote et al. 2023).

Among the predominant factors influencing the difficulties faced by students in Paraguay is the need for most of them to work and study simultaneously, which significantly reduces their chances of succeeding in a professional career (Latitud, 2025). Likewise, digital inclusion in the country still faces major challenges, as there are rural areas and vulnerable populations where access to information technologies is limited (Manzanilla-Granados, et al., 2023).

According to Kroff et al. (2024), for universities to effectively implement AI, several aspects need to be addressed. First, training and continuous development programmes must be offered to enable teachers to acquire the necessary skills and knowledge to effectively integrate AI technologies into their pedagogical practices. In addition, clear and transparent policies must be established on the ethical and responsible use of AI in the educational context, addressing privacy and data protection issues.

According to Alvarez (2024) states that dependence on technology is another recurring problem. The use of AI requires an Internet connection and appropriate devices, which may not always be available in all educational settings. This technology dependency can create inequalities in access to educational resources and limit the use of AI in certain contexts. If we have been talking about the digital divide for some time now, the incorporation of AI into the educational environment creates a greater gap in this regard.

In the considerations to be taken into account regarding the challenge posed by the use of AI and the limitations that exist, we take into account what is expressed by Vera (2023), who states:

> ... the integration of AI in higher education is the access and equity gap. Although AI has the potential to democratise access to education, as it can offer online learning opportunities to a large number of students, there is a risk that only those with access to technology and adequate resources can fully benefit from it. This may increase the educational gap between students from different regions, socio-economic levels and technological capabilities (p. 19, 20).

According to Torres (2023) states that teachers require updated training in the use of technologies, thus overcoming the gap that often accompanies these changes. Only through adequate preparation will they be able to obtain positive results through AI if all the necessary steps are taken for its development. In short, overcoming these challenges is essential to fully harness the potential of AI in higher education. All of the above represents a worrying constraint that widens the educational gap, not only among teachers, but also among students themselves. Students clamour for changes in their training, but often do not find adequate answers to their demands.

In relation to ethics is a reason to be alert for any educational community, especially in the field of higher education in Paraguay, where the use of AI lacks regulation at the country level. For this reason it is appealed to the ethics that every professional should have, while the integration of these tools advances slowly in this area. It is expected that professionals acquire the necessary evaluation skills and develop classes that foster creativity as they rely on this type of AI-based tools. Likewise, the entire academic community is called upon to work on activities that allow students to gain experience in the use of these technologies during their careers. However, offering a course that works with AI is not an easy task and will continue to be a challenge in higher education (Torres, 2023).

Según kroff f.j. et al. (2024) manifiesta que las universidades deben asegurar que cuentan con la infraestructura y los recursos tecnológicos adecuados para implementar soluciones de IA de manera efectiva. Promover la colaboración entre universidades, gobierno y el sector privado para compartir conocimientos, recursos y mejores prácticas en la implementación de IA en la educación superior.

Artificial intelligence offers immense potential to transform university education, improving both the personalisation of learning and administrative efficiency (Soong and Ho, 2021). However, to fully leverage these advantages, it is essential to address challenges related to training, resistance to change, and ethical issues (Castillo-Gonzalez, 2022; Zawacki-Richter et al., 2019). Recent studies suggest that with proper implementation and adequate training, AI can become a powerful ally for university teachers in the coming years (Zambrano, 2024).

A study by Forero-Corba & Bennasar (2024) revealed that many students value the potential of AI to provide immediate feedback tailored to their learning needs, although some expressed concerns about privacy and fairness in the use of these technologies. In the same vein, some students expressed doubts about the accuracy of automated assessments and the risk of depersonalisation in the educational process, underscoring the importance of examining subjective experiences in the adoption of AI in academic settings.

Despite the benefits, some educators express concerns about over-reliance on AI-based systems. Hernández González et al. (2024) argues that some teachers fear that learning automation may reduce human contact and thus weaken students' social and interpersonal skills.

However, authors such as Sanabria-Navarro et al. (2023) argue that AI should not be seen as a replacement for teacher interaction, but as a complementary tool that allows educators to focus on more meaningful tasks, such as the development of critical and creative skills.

The impact of artificial intelligence on higher education is profound and multifaceted. While students and faculty value the opportunities for personalisation and efficiency that AI offers, they also emphasise the need to preserve a human-centred and ethical education. Institutions must carefully manage the integration of this technology, ensuring that it complements and enriches the educational experience rather than replacing human interaction and judgement (Ríos Hernández et al., 2024). The key to harnessing the potential of AI in higher education will be to find a balance that promotes innovation, respects privacy, and ensures that the technology serves as a support, not a substitute, for the essential elements of teaching and learning (Trejo-Quintana, 2023).

According to Ovando (2025), in order to achieve the incorporation of AI in higher education, it is essential to have a teacher training programme that allows them to take full advantage of computer systems that emulate human intelligence. It is of great relevance that the teaching staff of educational institutions participate in training activities where they comprehensively understand the benefits and disadvantages of the use of AI systems within the teaching processes. This will allow those responsible for bringing knowledge to students to have a vision that allows them to incorporate these new technologies through innovative teaching strategies.

On the other hand, it is important to understand that teaching methods change over time and that technology must function as a support for learning processes, so it does not make sense to go against its use, but rather to create evaluation methods where this type of tool does not replace the analytical and creative capacity of students. Although machines can replicate defined patterns of data, they still cannot surpass human creativity to develop new knowledge, and it is in this line where modifications must be made in the study programmes.

Supporting the creation of teaching materials: AI systems have the ability to generate teaching materials applicable to educational processes. The main advantage lies in the constant updating of the information contained in the databases that feed these systems, which guarantees access to up-to-date materials. This makes it possible to teach students based on global trends, thus offering quality education aligned with global events. In this context, tools like ChatGPT are emerging as resources with great potential for teaching.

Finally, while the significant potential benefits of AI in teaching and learning processes in higher education are recognised, there are obstacles that could hinder its effective implementation. The distrust among teachers regarding data privacy and the lack of knowledge on effective strategies to use this tool without affecting students' independence and critical thinking represent challenges. Additionally, the lack of public and institutional policies regulating this technology, along with structural factors in the country that restrict its use, such as access and infrastructure, could hinder progress in the proper use of AI. Overcoming these challenges is essential to capitalise on the potential of Artificial Intelligence in transforming higher education in Paraguay. Potential of Artificial Intelligence in transforming higher education in Paraguay.

Bibliography

Almada-Barrios, B. A. (2024). Percepción sobre el uso de inteligencia artificial por parte de docentes del área de informática en el Centro Regional de Educación Saturio Ríos 2024. *Revista UNIDA Científica, 8*, 58–67. https://doi.org/10.69940/ruc.20241203

Allaoua-Chelloug, S., Ashfaq, H., Alsuhibany, S., Shorfuzzaman, M., Alsufyani, A., Jalal, A. y Park, J. (2023). Real objects understanding using 3D haptic virtual reality for e-learning education. *Computers, Materials & Continua, 74*, 1607–1624. https://doi.org/10.32604/cmc.2023.032245

Arabit-García, J., García-Tudela, P. A. & Prendes-Espinosa, M. P. (2021). Uso de tecnologías avanzadas para la educación científica. *Revista Iberoamericana De Educación, 87*, 173–194. https://doi.org/10.35362/rie8714591

Aranda-Corral, G. A., Calmet, J., & Martín-Mateos, F. J. (Eds.). (2014). *Artificial Intelligence and Symbolic Computation*. Cham: Springer International Publishing. https://doi.org/10.1007/978-3-319-13770-4

Ayuso, D., & Gutiérrez, P. (2022). La Inteligencia Artificial como recurso educativo durante la formación inicial del profesorado. *RIED-Revista Iberoamericana de Educación a distancia, 25*, 347–362. https://doi.org/10.5944/ried.25.2.32332

Brazdil, P., & Jorge, A. (Eds.). (2001). *Progress in Artificial Intelligence: Knowledge Extraction, Multi-agent Systems, Logic Programming, and Constraint Solving.* Springer Berlin Heidelberg. https://doi.org/10.1007/3-540-45329-6

Castrillón, O. D., Sarache, W., & Ruiz-Herrera, S. (2020). Predicción del rendimiento académico por medio de técnicas de inteligencia artificial. *Formación Universitaria, 13*, 93–102. https://doi.org/10.4067/s0718-50062020000100093

Chen, K., Cao, F., Hao, L., Xiang, M., & Kamruzzaman, M. M. (2023). Application Analysis of Digital Neural Network-Based Data Mining Method in Maximizing the Performance of Sports Training. *Revista Brasileira de Medicina Do Esporte, 29*, 1–4. https://doi.org/10.1590/1517-8692202329012022_0152

D'Mello, S. K., & Graesser, A. C. (2010). Multimodal semi-automated affect detection from conversational cues, gross body language, and facial features. *User Model User-Adap Inter, 20*,147–87 https://doi.org/10.1007/s11257-010-9074-4

European Digital Education Hub. (2022). *Teaching with AI – Assessment, Feedback and Personalisation (Briefing Report No. 7).* European Digital

Education Hub's squad on artificial intelligence in education https://www.indire.it/wp-content/uploads/2023/06/Teaching-with-AI-%E2%80%93-Assessment-Feedback-and-Personalisation-7.pdf

Faliero, J. (2021). Limitar la dependencia algorítmica. Impactos de la Inteligencia Artificial y sesgos algorítmicos. *Nueva Sociedad, 294*, 120–129. https://biblat.unam.mx/es/revista/nueva-sociedad/articulo/limitar-la-dependencia-algoritmica-impactos-de-la-inteligencia-artificial-y-sesgos-algoritmicos

Fernández-Robles, B. (2017). La utilización de objetos de aprendizaje de realidad aumentada en la enseñanza universitaria de Educación Primaria. *IJERI: International Journal of Educational Research and Innovation, 9*, 90–104. https://www.upo.es/revistas/index.php/IJERI/article/view/2599

Forero-Corba, W., & Bennasar, F. N. (2024). Techniques and applications of Machine Learning and Artificial Intelligence in education: A systematic review; [Técnicas y aplicaciones del Machine Learning e Inteligencia Artificial en educación: Una revisión sistemática]. R*IED-Revista Iberoamericana de Educacion a Distancia 1*, 209–253. Ibero-American Association for Distance Higher Education (AIESAD).

Flores-Vivar, J., & García-Peñalvo, F. (2023). Reflections on the ethics, potential, and challenges of artificial intelligence in the framework of quality education (SDG4). [Reflexiones sobre la ética, potencialidades y retos de la Inteligencia Artificial en el Marco de la Educación de Calidad (ODS4)]. *Comunicar, 74*, 37–47. https://doi.org/10.3916/C74-2023-03

García-Peñalbo, F. (2023). La percepción de la Inteligencia Artificial en contextos educativos tras el lanzamiento de ChatGPT: Disrupción o Pánico. *Education in the Knowledge Society, 24*, 1–9. https://doi.org/10.14201/eks.31279

Garrote Jurado, R., Pettersson, T. & Zwierewicz, M. (2023). *Students' attitudes to the use of Artificial Intelligence*. ICERI2023 Proceedings. https://doi.org/10.21125/iceri.2023.0191

Gazquez, J. J., Pérez, M. del C., & Suazo, I. (2023). *Aprovechando el Potencial de la Inteligencia Artificial en la Educación: Equilibrando Beneficios y Riesgos*. https://doi.org/10.32457/ejep.v16i1.2205

Granados Maguey, D. A., & Cervantes Martínez, M. d. (2022). La Inteligencia Artificial y su Repercusión en la Educación Superior. *Academia Journals, 14*, 395–399.

González, C. S. (2023). El impacto de la inteligencia artificial en la educación: transformación de la forma de enseñar y de aprender. *Revista Qurriculum, 36*, 51–60. https://doi.org/10.25145/j.qurricul.2023.36.03

Guevara Alban, G. P., Verdesoto Arguello, A. E., & Castro Molina, N. E. (2020). Metodologías de investigación educativa (descriptivas, experimentales, participativas, y de investigación-acción). *RECIMUNDO*, *4*(3), 163–173. https://doi.org/10.26820/recimundo/4.

Hernández Sampieri, R; Fernández Collado, C., & Baptista Lucio, P (2010). *Metodología de la Investigación*. Mc Graw Hill.

Hernández Sampieri, R; Fernández Collado, C., & Baptista Lucio, P (2007). *Fundamentos de Metodología de la Investigación*. Mc Graw Hill.

Incio Flores, F. A., Capuñay Sanchez, D. L., Estela Urbina, R. O., Valles Coral, M. Ángel, Vergara Medrano, S. E., & Elera Gonzales, D. G. (2021). Inteligencia artificial en educación: una revisión de la literatura en revistas científicas internacionales. *Apuntes Universitarios, 12*, 353–372. https://doi.org/10.17162/au.v12i1.974

Lameras, P., & Arnab, S. (2022). Power to the Teachers: An Exploratory Review on Artificial Intelligence in Education. *Information, 13*(1), 14. https://doi.org/10.3390/info13010014

Latitud 25. (2025). Noticias sobre inteligencia artificial y educación. *Latitud 25*, https://enlatitud25.com/news/author/nnews-uss00/

León Rodriguez, G. de la C., & Viña Brito, S. M. (2017). La inteligencia artificial en la educación superior. Oportunidades y amenazas. *INNOVA Research Journal, 2*, 412–422. https://doi.org/10.33890/innova.v2.n8.1.2017.399

Loinaz, M. (2021). Sistemas Inteligentes en el ámbito de la Educación. *Inteligencia Artificial. Revista Iberoamericana de Inteligencia Artificial 5(12), 5–12*. https://www.redalyc.org/articulo.oa?id=92551202

Manzanilla-Granados, H. M., Navarrete-Cazales, Z., & López-Hernández, P. A. (2023). Políticas educativas para la innovación, inclusión y TIC en Bolivia, Paraguay y Uruguay. *Educação & Sociedade*, *44*, 1–18. https://doi.org/10.1590/ES.261474

Marcayata, C. (2023, 25 de marzo). La brecha digital es la gran deuda pendiente en Ecuador, más en la ruralidad. *Gestión digital*: https://revistagestion.ec/analisis-sociedad/la-brecha-digital-es-la-gran-deuda-pendiente-en-ecuador-mas-en-la-ruralidad/#:~:text=A%20nivel%20nacional%2C%20a%20partir,2%25%20en%20julio%20del%202022.

Martínez-Pérez, S., & Fernández-Robles, B. (2018). Objetos de Realidad Aumentada: Percepciones del alumnado de pedagogía. Pixel-Bit. *Revista de Medios y Educación, 53*, 207–220. https://doi.org/10.12795/pixelbit.2018.i53.14

Minerva Project. (2023). Integrating Artificial Intelligence: Key Strategies for Higher Education. Url: https://www.minervaproject.com/white-paper/integrating-artificial-intelligence

Morocho Cevallos, R. A., Cartuche Gualán, A. P., Tipan Llanos, A. M., Guevara Guevara, A. M., y Ríos Quiñónez, M. B. (2023). Integración de la Inteligencia Artificial en la Educación. *Ciencia Latina Revista Científica Multidisciplinar, 7,* 2032–2053. https://ciencialatina.org/index.php/cienciala/article

Organización de las Naciones Unidas para la Educación, la Ciencia y la Cultura. (2019). *¿Cómo la inteligencia artificial puede reforzar la educación?* UNESCO. https://es.unesco.org/news/como-inteligencia-artificial-puede-reforzar-educacion

Osorio Umaña, F. (2022). Inteligencia artificial y derecho de autor: un estudio sobre la regulación británica. *Revista Justicia & Derecho, 5,* 1–15. https://doi.org/10.32457/rjyd.v5i1.1833

Obando Zambrano, B. S., Vega Alvarado, C. A., & Bermúdez Carrillo, L. A. (2025). Implicaciones académicas del uso de inteligencia artificial en la educación superior: Caso Universidad de Costa Rica. *Sede de Guanacaste. InterSedes, 26,* 1–11. https://doi.org/10.15517/isucr.v26i53.56102

Pérez-Ortega, I. (2017). Creación de Recursos Educativos Digitales: Reflexiones sobre Innovación Educativa con TIC. *Revista Internacional de Sociología de la Educación, 6,* 243–268. https://doi.org/10.17583/rise.2017.2544

Popenici, S. & Kerr, S. (2017). Exploring the impact of artificial intelligence on teaching and learning in higher education. *Research and Practice in Technology Enhanced Learning, 12*. https://doi.org/10.1186/s41039-017-0062-8

Salmerón Moreira, Yinis Migdalia, Luna Alvarez, Heriberto Enrique, Murillo Encarnación, Wilvir Gary, & Pacheco Gómez, Víctor Alejandro. (2023). El futuro de la Inteligencia Artificial para la educación en las instituciones de Educación Superior. *Conrado, 19*(93), 27–34. http://scielo.sld.cu/scielo.php?script=sci_arttext&pid=S1990-86442023000400027&lng=es&tlng=es.

Sanabria-Navarro, J.-R., Silveira-Pérez., Pérez-Bravo, D.-D., & de-Jesús-Cortina-Núñez, M. (2023). Incidences of artificial intelligence in contemporary education. *Comunicar, 31*(77). https://doi.org/10.3916/c77-2023-08

Sánchez López, L. A. (2022). Inteligencia artificial y visión por computadora aplicada a la educación. *Revista Odigos, 3*, 61–73. https://doi.org/10.35290/ro.v3n2.2022.587

Sánchez Vila, E. M., & Lama Penín, M. (2007). Técnicas de la Inteligencia Artificial Aplicadas a la Educación. Inteligencia Artificial. *Revista Iberoamericana de Inteligencia Artificial, 11*(33), 7–12. https://www.redalyc.org/pdf/925/92503302.pdf

Shrivastava, R. (2023). Role of Artificial Intelligence in Future of Education. International *Journal of Professional Business Review, 8*(1), e0840. https://doi.org/10.26668/businessreview/2023.v8i1.840

Soong, T. K., & Ho, C.-M. (2021). Artificial intelligence in medical OSCEs: Reflections and future developments. *Advances in Medical Education and Practice, 12*, 167–173. https://doi.org/10.2147/AMEP.S287926

Solove, D. (2006). *A Taxonomy of Privacy. University of Pennsylvania Law Review*, 154(3), 477–560. https://scholarship.law.upenn.edu/cgi/viewcontent.cgi?article=1376&context=penn_law_review

UNESCO. (2020). *La Inteligencia Artificial en la Educación*. UNESCO. https://es.unesco.org/themes/tic-educacion/inteligencia-artificial

Trejo-Quintana, J. (2023). Más preguntas que respuestas La inteligencia artificial y la educación. *Perfiles Educativos, 45*, 43–55. https://doi.org/10.22201/iisue.24486167e.2023.Especial.61690

Vera, F. (2023). Integración de la Inteligencia Artificial en la Educación superior: Desafíos y oportunidades. *Transformar, 4*, 17–34. https://www.revistatransformar.cl/index.php/transformar/article/view/84

Yang, F. (2018). Study on student performance estimation, student progress analysis, and student potential prediction based on data mining. *Computers & Education, 123*, 97-108. https://doi.org/10.1016/j.compedu.2018.04.006

Artificial Intelligence in Music Composition: Ethical and Academic Challenges in the Classroom

Rocío Chao Fernández[1] *and Vicente Castro Alonso*[2]

ABSTRACT
This chapter explores the impact of artificial intelligence (AI) on music composition and music education in the perception of future secondary school teachers. It is highlighted that AI provides educational and creative applications, including the capacity to generate musical compositions and personalise learning. However, the educational implications of AI also give rise to ethical challenges, including issues of authorship, technological dependence and the possible devaluation of human creativity itself. The chapter employs a qualitative study design, examining the perceptions of a sample of trainee teachers following an educational intervention. The participants identified potential benefits, such as enhanced personalisation of performance-based teaching processes, but also expressed concerns about the devaluation of the art form and possible job displacement. Furthermore, the importance of commensurate digital literacy for responsible use by adolescents is emphasised. In conclusion, it is asserted that, with careful integration and ethical considerations, AI has the potential to enhance music education, promoting both technological learning and human creativity.

Keywords: artificial intelligence, music composition, education, creativity, ethics

Theoretical Framework

Technologies have burst forcefully into all areas of our society, including education, where their integration, although not a recent phenomenon, is advancing at a rapid pace (Vázquez-Sánchez, 2024). In this scenario, teachers have taken on an increasingly active role in the incorporation and use of Information and Communication Technologies (ICT) in teaching and learning processes (Tejada & Pozos, 2018). Without doubt, digital environments constitute a teaching resource that is increasingly used by teachers, even in the field of music education (Dammers, 2019; Torrado, 2020), with the aim of optimising the learning of their students (Giráldez, 2015).

1 University of A Coruña. Galicia-Spain. https://orcid.org/0000-0002-6584-0049
2 University of A Coruña. Galicia-Spain. https://orcid.org/0000-0001-9817-3783

Initially, its use was limited to the introduction of tools such as computers, digital whiteboards and the internet into the classroom (Felpeto-Guerrero et al., 2020), but as technological advances are made in the industry, its innovations are adapted and applied to existing cultures and education systems (Schmidt & Tang, 2020).

In recent times, Artificial Intelligence (hereinafter AI) has had a significant impact in various fields, including education. Such is its imprint that Vivar & Peñalvo (2023) point out that it has been considered the fourth revolution since it gradually transforms society and its behaviours. But what is AI? Authors such as Alvarado-Rojas (2015) and Rouhiainen (2018) define it as the ability of machines to learn and use what they have learned to make decisions as a human being would, or even better. For their part, Delgado de Frutos et al. (2024) specify that it is a system's ability to correctly interpret environmental data and use this knowledge to efficiently, adaptively and autonomously achieve specific goals.

In the field of education, AI has also established itself as a tool with great potential, capable of performing tasks that would normally require human intelligence (De Haro, 2024), and very useful as a support in all areas (Cukurova et al., 2020). However, its implementation generates both benefits and challenges, so it is necessary to understand its pedagogical usefulness for it to be considered by teachers and students. In terms of benefits, Beaulac & Rosenthal (2019) and Xu et al. (2019) point out that it is advantageous for predicting the academic success of students based on their behaviour. Murtaza et al. (2022) and Chen et al. (2020) highlight its contribution to the search for personalised learning, as it helps to analyse the characteristics of each learner to be able to programme personalised learning pathways for them. Along these lines, Kabudi et al. (2021) posit a theory that emphasises the advantages of optimising and adapting pedagogical approaches to enhance academic outcomes. For their part, Mousavinasab et al. (2021) indicate that it has enabled the development of intelligent tutorials that offer guidance and explanations to students in real time. Wang et al. (2018) emphasise that it speeds up the correction of assessable tasks and helps to detect plagiarism, while Chen et al. (2020) point out its usefulness when analysing large volumes of data to improve teaching and academic performance.

However, the implementation of AI in education also has drawbacks and limitations. In this regard, Grace et al. (2023), Muñoz-Cantero et al.

(2024) and Reiss (2021) highlight that one problem posed by AI is related to the responsible use of student data and ethical and privacy issues. Another limitation is the loss of human interaction because, although as indicated, AI can provide personalised tutoring and explanations, it lacks the human touch (empathy, intuition, ability to establish connections with students, etc.) that can be crucial when addressing certain aspects (Ahmad et al., 2021; Aparicio, 2023; Reiss, 2021). Korteling et al. (2021) point out that AI does not always achieve adequate contextual understanding, as it does not interpret emotions, does not capture nuances and is not capable of adapting to unexpected situations, which can make it difficult to use in literature, the arts and the social sciences.

But one of the main drawbacks of its incorporation as an educational tool is that it can generate excessive dependence (both among learners and teachers) and consequently impoverish critical thinking and problem-solving skills, which would hinder their academic and professional growth in the long term (Jara & Ochoa, 2020). Finally, we cannot forget the technological barriers, which must be reduced to guarantee an equitable distribution of resources (Botelho, 2021; Vinuesa et al., 2020), as well as guaranteeing adequate teacher training for its effective implementation (Córica, 2020).

Focusing on music teaching, Gisbert & Vela (2024) point out that 'current affairs in the classroom are marked by an increase in resources linked to Artificial Intelligence (AI), and music education is no exception' (p. 97). According to Merchán Sánchez-Jara et al. (2024), the use of AI has been quietly transforming music teaching, emerging as an innovative tool capable of transforming the teaching-learning process. To its potential and limitations, in addition to those already mentioned, we must add those intrinsic to the subject itself, where AI can be used to provide real-time feedback on musical practice, to work on auditory training (Agarwal & Greer, 2023; Cruz et al., 2018), to evaluate performance practice, both in the expressive and technical fields (Burrows et al., 2018; Giraldo et al., 2018), although where it has had the greatest impact is as an aid to composition (Kang, 2018; Yu and Ding, 2020; Zulić, 2019).

In this respect, it is necessary to point out that musical composition is one of the curricular aspects to which teachers have traditionally paid less attention (Botella Nicolás & Escorihuela Carbonell, 2021; Kladder & Lee, 2019), mainly because of the lack of training of teachers in this area (Zaragozá, 2009), as well as the widespread association with musical processes of greater scope and complexity, considered only within the reach of those who possess a specific conceptual and/or technical mastery (Castro-Alonso & Chao-Fernández, 2024). In this sense, Randles & Muhonen (2015) point out that teachers are less comfortable when it comes to teaching composition, as well as having little confidence in their abilities to compose their own music: 'in order for teachers to feel comfortable introducing students to music composition, they should first learn to create music themselves, thus establishing a creative identity themselves' (Randles & Muhonen, 2015, p. 63). This not only shows a lack of confidence in their abilities, but also the conviction that their students are not capable of doing it either (Bautista, 2020).

However, the use of AI to carry out a compositional process raises many questions about authenticity and authorship (Elgammal et al., 2017) emphasise that it does not replace artists, but that working together can generate innovative and surprising works. In contrast, McCormack et al. (2020) warn that the use of AI for composition could lead to dehumanisation and challenges the traditional conception of creativity and authorship.

Furthermore, it is not without certain limitations, since the teacher who promotes it will have to receive specific training in the use of these technological tools and their pedagogical implications (Alam, 2024) and they will have to accept that their role changes from being the only source of knowledge to becoming a guide capable of promoting critical reflection on the application of AI and guiding their students in its ethical and creative use (Kuok Ho, 2024).

The truth is that AI offers numerous possibilities for music creation. One of the most popular tools is the Doodle Bach platform, created by Google to commemorate the 334th birthday of Johann Sebastian Bach (Huang et al., 2019; Zhang & Cheng, 2023; Zhang et al., 2024; Choi, 2023). This software specialises in the composition of Baroque chorales through the realisation of contrapuntal harmonisations using Western musical notation: the user can create a monophonic melody that will be harmonised automatically following the Baroque structure of a four-part chorale.

For his part, Gómez García (2023) highlights the tool generated by the Meta team, Audiocraft, an application made up of two main components: AudioGen, focused on the generation of sound effects through detailed descriptions made by the user; and MusicGen, focused on musical composition based on textual indications and parameters established by the consumer. Gómez García (2023) also advocates the use of the Soundful platform as a compositional and monetisation tool for content creators and musical artists, as well as mentioning others such as EcrettMusic, Flowmachines, iZotope, Landr Magenta, MuseNet, Soundraw and SUNO.

In short, there are many compositional tools available that can be used to support the creative process. Other AI platforms for composition, which are in constant development and collaboration with users, are AIVA, Amper Music, Amazon's Deep Composer, Chrome Music Lab, DeepBach, Deep Composer, EvoM, FlowComposer, Google's Magenta Project, Hyperscore, JukeDeck, Magenta.js, MySong and Soundtrap. However, in no case should they be a substitute for the creative work of the human mind, because as Gioti (2021) points out, human imperfections, unlike the precision of computers, are essential to music, giving it unique character and emotional depth that would otherwise be lost in a generic and mechanical sound.

Objectives

The overall objective of this study is to explore the perception and potential use of artificial intelligence in music composition among future music teachers, both in their role as musicians and in their future teaching work.

This is subdivided into the following specific objectives:

i. To explore how trainee teachers perceive the presence of AI in music composition and what implications they consider it may have for creativity and in the workplace.
ii. To investigate the experiences and reflections of trainee teachers on the use of AI in music learning and teaching.
iii. To examine the concerns in the debate that arises around the role of creativity and digital literacy in the educational context in the face of the advance of AI.

Methodology

Research Approach and Design

This qualitative study seeks to gain an in-depth understanding of the perceptions, applications and challenges of AI in teaching and musical composition among future teachers following an educational intervention. The research is therefore exploratory and descriptive in nature, oriented towards discursive collection originating from the subjective perspectives of participation (Flick, 2015). The research design is structured in the three phases shown in Figure 11.

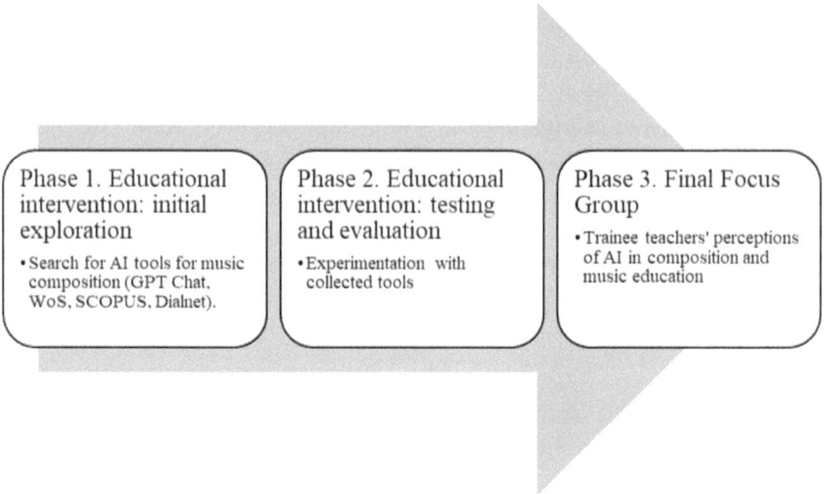

Figure 11: Research design

Phases 1 and 2 of the study correspond to the implementation of an educational intervention designed ad hoc by the authors of this chapter, arranged in the master's degree in Secondary Education Teaching (Music itinerary) in January 2025. Through an initial exploration, the participants establish a search for AI tools for musical composition: 1) discussing in a small group the suggestions generated by ChatGPT; and 2) refining and contrasting the search through published sources indexed in databases such as SCOPUS, Web of Science and Dialnet. A subsequent stage includes the testing and evaluation of the results obtained, prioritising those applications and free software, to recognise the main potentialities and/or hypothetical uses in a secondary education classroom.

This training and professionalisation period is followed by a final phase, aimed at obtaining perceptions about AI in line with the research objectives, which is the subject of this chapter. This design therefore makes it possible to gather theoretically and practically based opinions through the experiential contact of participating with AI tools with applications towards the generation of musical content.

Instrument

Following Krueger and Casey (2000), the line of questioning starts with an easy beginning, continues in a sequential manner and moves from the general to the specific.

The questions are grouped into two main blocks, the first being questions aimed at assessing the participants in their capacity as musicians and artists, and the second in their role as future secondary school teachers. Opening questions are posed such as 'Can you imagine using AI tools in your future music classes?' and open questions such as 'In what situations have you found AI useful for composing?' or 'For what specific aspects would you find AI useful as future teachers?'.

The data collection process is moderated by the second author, who tries to encourage the participation of all members as a manager of the production of a discourse in terms of homogeneity and heterogeneity within the group (Callejo, 2001). The generation of a comfortable and permissive environment is favoured (Krueger & Casey, 2000), developing the focus group requesting sincere opinions, and declaring the voluntary nature and the research purpose of the collection of information, without having any kind of repercussion on the qualification of the subject, as reflected in the informed consent distributed among the participants.

Participation

The selection of participants for the Focus Group is intentional, being established with the pre-existing group of students on the itinerary: this considerably reduces recruitment efforts, while encouraging a feeling of cohesion as opposed to groups of strangers, favouring a natural flow in the conversation (Bloom et al., 2001).

The ten trainee teachers (TT) have the sociodemographic characteristics included in Table 13, being mostly men (60%) and having initial training rooted in the field of Music Performance (70%). With an average age of 26.8 years, 60% of the participants claim to have worked as music teachers, although in most cases in the field of instrument teaching in music schools or conservatories. It should be noted that none of the participants had professional experience as a secondary school teacher at the time of this study.

Table 13: Description of the sample of participants

	Gender	Age (years)	Education	Teaching Experience
TT1	Female	27	Music Pedagogy	Yes (Music School)
TT2	Female	24	Performance (classical)	No
TT3	Female	23	Performance (classical)	No
TT4	Male	22	Composition	No
TT5	Male	25	Performance (classical)	Yes (Music School)
TT6	Male	26	Performance (classical)	Yes (Music School)
TT7	Male	29	Performance (jazz)	Sí (Academy)
TT8	Male	29	Performance (jazz)	Sí (Conservatory)
TT9	Male	25	Performance (classical) & Musicology	No
TT10	Female	38	Musicology	Yes (Non-formal)

Data Processing and Analysis

The data collection was audio-recorded, with prior authorisation, for subsequent transcription. Subsequently, the transcripts were manually coded to assign codes to quotes from the text, grouping all the information collected into categories that emerged inductively from the data collected. The refinement of the final codes (Figure 12) is the result of a conceptual specification through a double coding cycle, first descriptive and second focused (Saldaña, 2009)

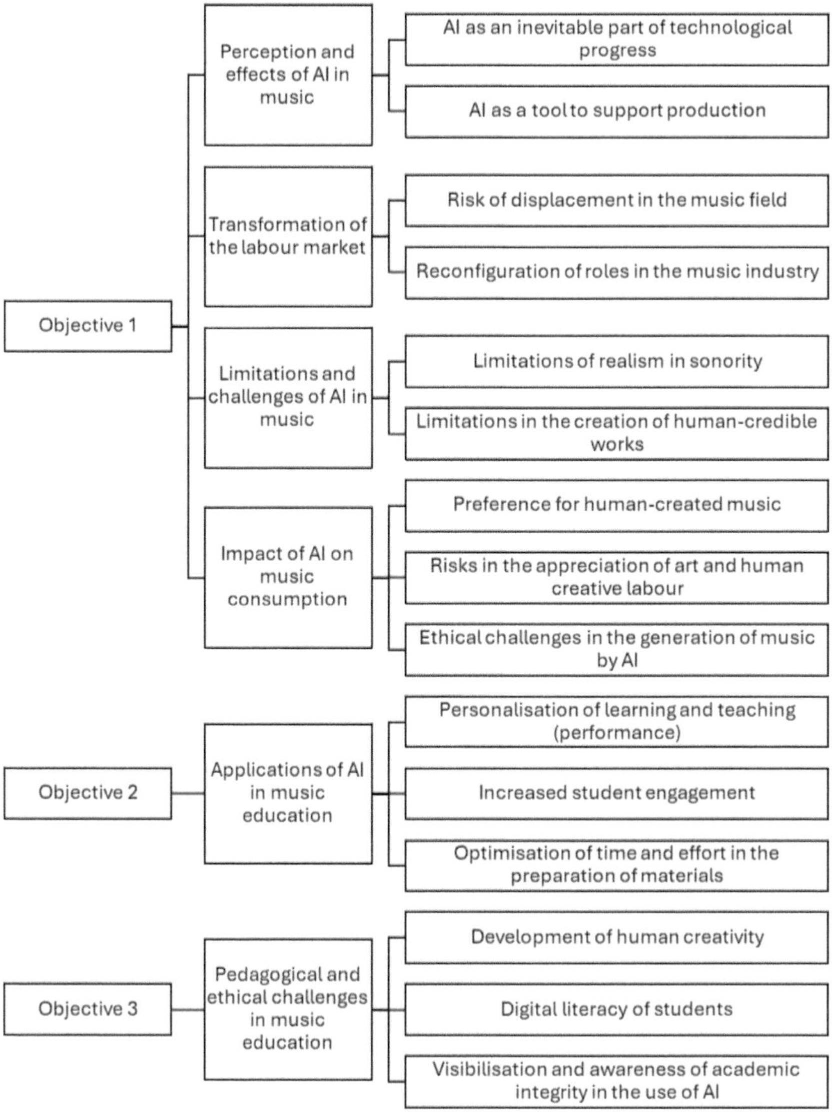

Figure 12: Alignment of content analysis categories and codes

Results

The report with the results of the content analysis of the Focus Group is presented below, grouping the main ideas into three subsections linked to each specific objective of the study. Also included are representative textual fragments for each code from the discourse of each participant, all of which are translations from the original Spanish and Galician.

Perceptions and Challenges of AI in Musical Composition

Certain trainee teachers accept the emergence of AI in musical composition as part of technological progress, as an inevitable side effect that will affect different professional sectors: 'it's the law of life, it's called the law of evolution: when baguettes arrived in the supermarket, the same thing happened to bakers; life evolves and it affects different sectors, and now it's happening to us more' (TT1).

In their role as practising musicians, some teachers express their fear of a perceived risk of job displacement as a direct result of AI: 'it's happening […] in other classes like Fine Arts there were already two girls [future teachers] who complained that they would be out of work because it was better to have an AI' (TT2). Others, however, relativise the threat to the production and composition specifically of commercial electronic genres, arguing their simplicity in terms of means of production:

> If you're a reggaeton composer working in a studio […] you must hire a singer and spend hours producing a track, when an AI can do it the same in five minutes. Why is it the same? Because the artistic quality is very low. But [AI] can compete against that (TT7).

In any case, the trainee teachers point to the existence of certain current technical limitations in the use of AI for musical composition, mainly due to the relatively artificial sound of its output, or because they consider that its results are not very credible from a human point of view, or lacking in deep musical meaning:

> For bassoon there are still no [realistically created] AI sounds, they're not there, they're not there (TT3).

> Artificial intelligence creates something for you, but what it creates is like a first idea; but really that can't go anywhere because it has no form, no sheet music, nothing (TT1).

Because of this, these same teachers express a certain tranquillity regarding the musical consumption preferences of the public, as expressed in the following dialogue that takes up the metaphor previously initiated:

> TT5: I prefer the baker's bread to the supermarket baguette, so I buy it from the baker, you know?
>
> TT1: Yes, just as there will be audiences who prefer to go to a concert rather than listen to some AI at home.

Despite everything, other teachers such as TT6 express a less optimistic view, saying that technological development could dilute the sound distinctions between musical productions made by humans and those generated with AI, especially for those less trained ears: 'you [TT1] have training and know how to distinguish, but for many people they don't'. In addition, the participant adds the social devaluation of art among the public, indicating that 'the problem is that people perceive it as the same result', because of how society values 'artistic activity itself, how people perceive creation' (TT6).

Educational Applications of AI in Music Teaching

Although there are concerns about the impact of AI on human creativity and the labour market, trainee teachers also recognise its potential as a support tool in the educational context. The research experience in the search for AI tools for composition allows trainee teachers to glimpse its potential applications in the field of music education, with a specific focus on the secondary stage.

Most of the participants mention the advantages that AI provides in facilitating the process of reading, understanding and interpreting musical pieces. Testing certain applications allows them to recognise their potential, highlighting their degree of optimisation in areas such as the sonorisation of scores from a photograph and the identification of chords:

> I found an app where [...] you take a photo of the score, and it plays it for you. Well, it's not something you can take to a performance [by itself], but imagine, you want to try and see what the sonata sounds like with the accompaniment, and it really shines, to be honest (TT2).
>
> We came across an [app] that recognised chords, which was very good and can be used as an educational tool. And the truth is that we started playing the piano

> and it recognised absolutely everything. And it was instantaneous, what's more, you could add [audio] from YouTube and a lot of other sites. It's pretty good (TT5).

Another teacher also highlights the existence of software that allows you to adjust the speed to the stage of study of a musical work, allowing for personalisation of the accompaniment during rehearsals:

> There's an app that lets you modify the tempo of the [instrumental] backing track. So, if you include a piano backing track at a standard tempo, imagine you download the backing track from the internet […] and you're practising it at a different speed, you can download it to practise at that tempo (TT3).

On the other hand, from a less technical point of view, some participating teachers highlight the motivational contribution that AI could imply in certain dynamics of the music classroom:

> TT8: [AI applications] to put a base: you put some harmonies on it and say, 'make it have the piano, the drums, the bass; and make it in classic rock style, in cumbia style …'. And let the students play.
>
> Interviewer: That they play over that.
>
> TT8: Sure, that they play over it or sing it.
>
> Interviewer: To make […] those performance activities more dynamic.
>
> TT8: Yes, so that it's also more attractive to them [the students]. I mean, if you're going to put them […] there with the xylophones. But if you put a backing track behind it … 'look, try this style'. Maybe [the student] will say how cool does this sound over this.

Teacher TT1, for her part, mentions an implication of AI as an assistant in song composition: 'the children create the lyrics and then you put it into applications like SUNO and a song comes out […]. I find it very useful. The children are really excited about it' (TT1). Both contributions, therefore, agree on the use of technology as a complement to the musical practices already carried out in the classroom (musical interpretation or composition of lyrics), alluding to the versatility of AI in achieving more professional results in encouraging student engagement.

The last group of educational AI applications affect the optimisation of the teacher's own time and effort in the elaboration of didactic materials, expanding the innate possibilities in the music classroom. In this sense, to the uses mentioned by TT8 and TT1, the following should be added:

> There are also [AI applications] for people who produce: programmes for sampling, which extract the voice of a song or the percussion ... And that's quite useful (TT4).

> [AI applications] that you can put a link [URL] into, and they give you the chords, some basic instruments on the piano, guitar, violin ... and you can transpose it up and down, and change [the tempo] (TT3).

However, despite the advantages that AI could offer to music teaching, its incorporation into the educational sphere is not without dilemmas in terms of the development of students' creativity and the need for adequate digital literacy for its responsible use. The following section explores these questions.

Challenges and Dilemmas in Music Education: Creativity and Digital Literacy

The prevailing position between participation weighs up the validity of providing literacy for a responsible and ethical use of AI, although in no case ignoring the promotion of creativity as a fundamental part of the human development of the individual:

> I think the most important and interesting thing is to enhance their [the students'] creativity; but even so, an explanation of this [satisfactory handling of AI tools] wouldn't hurt either (TT2).

> At a certain level, yes, teaching how to use it [AI tools], because I think it's very useful and can be used. But it can't interfere with the personal development of the kids, I think (TT5).

Certain trainee teachers prioritise the provision of spaces for the development of human creativity through education, both from an early age and in adolescence itself: 'when we talk about creativity, it's how children are guided, it's creativity in childhood, creativity in primary school [...], but adolescents and adults can also be creative' (TT6). Their main argument alludes to the plausible lethargy of human ability to develop their own ideas in a self-reflective way:

> I can compare it to the ability to write by hand. There are primary schools where students no longer write by hand: they have computers and write absolutely everything on the computer (TT5).

> I think creativity should be encouraged […] I think it's very important […] to encourage imagination and to look inside yourself; that we all have something there and to listen to the voice we all have inside. Because if you run out of ideas, you go looking for ChatGPT […] I feel that nowadays we are bombarded with a lot of stimuli from TikTok, Instagram, watching videos. But you stop and think and say 'I have half an hour here for me, to listen to myself, to listen to my thoughts', and I don't think that's encouraged much these days (TT7).

On the other hand, other trainee teachers postpone this emphasis on the creative development of the individual, prioritising new needs resulting from the incursion of AI into everyday life. In some cases, this leads to a rejection of the time spent in the classroom on creative processes of a self-reflective nature, such as those described above: 'OK, let's not get them to use ChatGPT in class, let's try to boost their creativity in class: but they're all going to go home and none of them are going to be creative' (TT3). This, the teacher clarifies, reflects how society (and the participant herself) uses AI indiscriminately: 'I tell ChatGPT to make me the weekly menu, I tell it 'I have this in the fridge, tell me what I can eat', because I don't know how to cook'.

Almost all the participating teachers expressed the need for a commitment on the part of educational institutions to offer digital literacy that is up to date and useful for the student's life. This applies even in the case of the students present in the classrooms today, in their capacity as digital natives:

> There are students who don't know how to attach a PDF to an email. I mean, being a digital native is no guarantee of that [knowing how to use AI tools satisfactorily] (TT6).

> There is no such thing as 'well, they know how to use them'. No. I think many don't know how to use them well (TT10).

Added to this is the lack of awareness of copyright infringement and academically dishonest behaviour:

> This is like when they told you that you couldn't use Wikipedia and what you did was look for the information on Wikipedia on another blog so that when you cited it wouldn't be Wikipedia (TT3).

> In the end, if you are using resources, those resources are not born by 'spontaneous generation': they come from somewhere, you are using something that is valid for your work; it is only fair that you know where you are getting it from and, if it is from someone, that you cite it […] We are talking about tools that are proving to be very controversial, that violate intellectual property and are not regulated and have a rather dubious practice (TT6).

This scenario gives rise to new educational needs, challenges of which the trainee teachers taking part are aware: 'it is necessary to talk about current tools, analyse them and see how to use them […] compare information […] know how [things] were done without them' (TT10).

Discussion and Conclusions

The findings of this study reveal that trainee teachers have differing perceptions of AI in music composition. Some consider it an inevitable technological evolution, comparable to other advances in other sectors, reflecting an acceptance of technological progress as a constant phenomenon in professional life, coinciding with the studies of De Haro (2024). However, there is great fear about the possible labour and creative displacement, especially when it comes to those musical genres whose simplicity allows AI to replicate them with relative ease, in line with Cukurova et al. (2020).

In addition, teachers recognise the current technical limitations of AI, such as the artificiality of sound and the lack of musical depth, which suggests that, although AI can generate compositions, these lack the authenticity and deep meaning that characterises music created by humans (Korteling et al., 2021). Despite these concerns, some teachers are confident that audiences will continue to value music created by human beings, although others fear that sonic distinctions will be diluted as technology advances, which could contribute to the social devaluation of art (Ahmad et al., 2021; Aparicio, 2023).

On the other hand, the interviewees recognise the potential of AI as an educational tool, emphasising its usefulness in the reading, understanding and interpretation of musical pieces. The tools that allow the sonorisation of scores from a photograph and the identification of chords are considered valuable resources that can facilitate the teaching and learning process, in accordance with the research of Murtaza et al. (2022) and Kabudi et al. (2021), among others. In addition, applications that adjust the speed of music to suit the needs of the student reinforce the idea of intelligent and personalised tutoring (Mousavinasab et al., 2021).

The motivational potential of AI in the classroom is also emphasised, as it allows students to interact with AI-generated musical bases, which can increase engagement and make musical activities more attractive. This aligns with the idea that AI can enrich the educational experience by providing new ways to explore music and foster creativity (Cruz et al., 2018).

In addition, trainee teachers emphasise the importance of fostering human creativity and providing adequate digital literacy. This is crucial to avoid excessive dependence on technology and to ensure that students develop critical and creative skills (Jara & Ochoa, 2020). Some informants emphasise the need for spaces for creative development from early childhood to adolescence, arguing that creativity should not be limited to childhood but should be encouraged throughout the educational life (Castro-Alonso & Chao-Fernández, 2024).

Another recurring theme in this study is the need for adequate digital literacy, as many of the participants point out that being digitally native does not guarantee effective handling of AI tools. In addition, the importance of raising students' awareness of intellectual property and honest academic practices is emphasised, reflecting theoretical concerns about the responsible use of data and ethical and privacy issues (Grace et al., 2023; Muñoz-Cantero et al., 2024; Reiss, 2021). This scenario gives rise to new educational needs, challenges that trainee teachers are aware of and willing to address (Botelho, 2021; Vinuesa et al., 2020).

Finally, it is concluded that, although artificial intelligence represents a powerful educational resource, its use could lead to the emergence of scenarios that are difficult for teachers to manage. In this sense, it is essential that teachers have adequate training that allows them to develop a critical view of its use, its benefits and its limitations. that allows them to stimulate reflection and critical thinking in their students: only in this way will they be able to encourage reflection and critical thinking in their students (Aparicio, 2023). In this way, it will be possible to construct an ethical, upright and balanced educational environment, in which artificial intelligence is integrated harmoniously, allowing learners to take advantage of both human and artificial intelligence (Cukurova et al., 2020).

In short, this research has highlighted a highly relevant and scarcely explored issue that will undoubtedly continue to be the subject of study by other researchers. Aware of the limitations identified, such as the small size of the sample and its delimitation to a specific geographical and cultural context, we remain committed to deepening this line of research. For future studies, it would be essential to include trainee teachers from diverse geographical and cultural contexts to obtain more representative results. In addition, it would be pertinent to explore the impact of artificial intelligence on musical composition and teaching at different educational levels, identifying differences and similarities in its application. Through longitudinal studies, it would be possible to analyse the evolution of perceptions and the use of AI over time. Likewise, it is considered relevant to evaluate the effectiveness of various AI tools used in music creation, as well as to examine their ethical implications, with special attention to the intellectual property of compositions generated by artificial intelligence. Finally, delving into students' perceptions and experiences regarding the use of AI in music teaching and composition would provide a more complete view of its impact in the educational field.

Bibliography

Agarwal, M. & Greer, R. (2023). Spectrogram-Based Deep Learning for Flute Audition Assessment and Intelligent Feedback. In Proceedings of the 2023 IEEE International Symposium on Multimedia (ISM), Laguna Hills, CA, USA, 11–13 pp. 238–242. 10.1109/ISM59092.2023.00045.

Ahmad, S. F., Rahmat, M. K., Mubarik, M. S., Alam, M. M. & Hyder, S. I. (2021). Artificial Intelligence and Its Role in Education. *Sustainability, 13*(22), 12902.https://doi.org/10.3390/su132212902

Alam, M. D. (2024). Future Skills and Artificial Intelligence (AI) Literacy for Teachers: An Analysis. 10.13140/RG.2.2.20639.16801.

Alvarado-Rojas, M. E. (2015). Una mirada a la inteligencia artificial. *Revista de Ingeniería, Matemáticas y Ciencias de la Información, 2*(3), 27–31. http://ojs.urepublicana.edu.co/index.php/ingenieria/article/view/234/213

Aparicio, W. O. (2023). La inteligencia artificial y su incidencia en la educación: transformando el aprendizaje para el siglo XXI. *Revista Internacional de Pedagogía e -Innovación Educativa, 3*(2), 217–230. http://dx.doi.org/10.51660/ripie.v3i2.133

Bautista, A. (2020). Formación y desarrollo profesional en docentes de interpretación musical: propuestas para cambiar concepciones y prácticas. En J. I. Pozo, M. P. Pérez Echeverría, J. A. Torrado y G.

López-Íñiguez (Coords.), *Aprender y enseñar música. Un enfoque centrado en los alumnos* (pp. 381–410). Morata.

Beaulac, C. & Rosenthal, J. S. (2019). Predicting University Students' Academic Success and Major Using Random Forests. *Research in Higher Education, 60*, 1048–1064. https://doi.org/10.1007/s11162-019-09546-y

Bloor, M., Frankland, J., Thomas, M. y Robson, K. (2001). *Focus Groups in Social Research*. Sage.

Botelho, F. H. F. (2021). Accessibility to digital technology: Virtual barriers, real opportunities. *Assistive Technology, 33*(sup1), 27–34. https://doi.org/10.1080/10400435.2021.1945705

Botella Nicolás, A. M. y Escorihuela Carbonell, G. (2021). Educación performativa musical: herramientas para la investigación. *Revista de Comunicación de la SEECI, 54*, 1–19. https://doi.org/10.15198/seeci.2021.54.e614

Burrows, J., Kumar, V., Kinshuk & Dewan, A. (2018). Assessing a music student's progress. *In Proceedings of the IEEE 18th International Conference on Advanced Learning Technologies (ICALT)*, pp. 202–206. 10.1109/ICALT.2018.00055

Callejo, J. (2001). *El grupo de discusión: introducción a una práctica de investigación*. Ariel.

Castro-Alonso, V. & Chao-Fernández, R. (2024). Knowing 'how to create' in order to know 'how to teach'? Perceptions and conditioning of Spanish music teachers in secondary education. *British Journal of Music Education*, 1–17. 10.1017/S0265051724000342

Chen, L., Chen, P. & Lin, Z. (2020). Artificial Intelligence in Education: A Review. *IEEE Access, 8*, 75264–75278. https://doi.org/10.1109/ACCESS.2020.2988510

Choi, M. (2023). Design, Implementation, and Effects of Elementary Music Creation Class Using an AI-Based Music Program, Doodle Bach. *Korean Journal of Research in Music Education,52*(4), 211–237. [CrossRef]

Córica, J. L. (2020). Resistencia docente al cambio: Caracterización y estrategias para un problema no resuelto. *RIED. Revista Iberoamericana de Educación a Distancia, 23*(2), 255–272. https://doi.org/10.5944/ried.23.2.26578

Cukurova, M., Luckin, R. & Kent, C. (2020). Impact of an Artificial Intelligence Research Frame on the Perceived Credibility of Educational Research Evidence. *International Journal of Artificial Intelligence in Education, 30*(2), 205–235. https://doi.org/10.1007/s40593-019-00188-w

Cruz, L., Rolla, V., Kestenberg, J. & Velho, L. (2018). Visual Representations for Music Understanding Improvement. In Aramaki, M., Davies, M., Kronland-Martinet, R., Ystad, S. (Eds.). *Music Technology with Swing*, Springer, pp. 468–476. https://doi.org/10.1007/978-3-030-01692-0_31

Dammers, R. J. (2019). The role of technology in music teacher education. En: Conway, Colleen; Pellegrino, Kristen; Santaley, Ann Marie; West, Chad (Eds.). *The Oxford handbook of preservice music teacher education in the United States*, pp. 365–376. Oxford University Press.

De Haro, J. J. (2024). *Inteligencia artificial en educación*. Centro Nacional de Desarrollo Curricular en Sistemas no Propietarios (Cedec). https://doi.org/10.4438/2695-4192_PEePub154_2023_847-19-137-X

Delgado de Frutos, N., Campo-Carrasco, L., Sainz de la Maza, M. & Extabe-Urbieta. J. M. (2024). Aplicación de la Inteligencia Artificial (IA) en Educación: Los beneficios y limitaciones de la IA percibidos por el profesorado de educación primaria, educación secundaria y educación superior. *Revista Electrónica Interuniversitaria de Formación del Profesorado, 27*(1), 207–224. https://doi.org/10.6018/reifop.577211

Elgammal, A., Liu, B., Elhoseiny, M. & Mazzone, M. (2017). CAN: Creative Adversarial Networks, Generating 'Art' by Learning About Styles and Deviating from Style Norms. *International Conference on Innovative Computing and Cloud Computing.* https://acortar.link/7YnddZ

Felpeto-Guerrero, A., Sánchez-Vázquez, R., Chao-Fernández, R. & Chao-Fernández, A. (2020). Use of Arduino Microcontroller in Education: Creation of 'The Musical Stairs'. *Proceedings*, *54*(1), 6. https://doi.org/10.3390/proceedings2020054006.

Flick, U. (2015). *El diseño de Investigación Cualitativa*. Ediciones Morata.

Grace, E. G., Vidhyavathi, P. & Malathi, P. (2023). A study on 'AI in education: opportunities and challenges for personalized learning'. *Industrial Engineering Journal, 52*(05), 750–759. https://doi.org/10.36893/IEJ.2023.V52I05.750-759

Gioti, A. M. (2021). Artificial intelligence for music composition. Handbook of Artificial Intelligence for Music: Foundations, Advanced Approaches, and Developments for Creativity, 53–73. *HAL Open Science,* 03287663. https://inria.hal.science/hal-03287663/document

Giráldez, A. (2015). *De los ordenadores a los dispositivos móviles: propuestas de creación musical y audiovisual.* Graó.

Giraldo, S., Ortega, A., Perez, A., Ramirez, R., Waddell, G. & Williamon, A. (2018). Automatic assessment of violin performance using dynamic time warping classification. In Proceedings of the 26th IEEE Signal Processing and Communications Applications Conference (SIU), pp. 1–3. 10.1109/SIU.2018.8404556

Gisbert, V. & Vela, M. (2024). Inteligencia Artificial en el aula de música: Experiencia y percepción del profesorado especialista en Educación Secundaria. *Educatio Siglo XXI, 42*(3), 97–114. https://doi.org/10.6018/educatio. 623181

Gómez García, J. (2023). *Composición en la era digital: la integración de inteligencias artificiales en la composición para cine y medios.* [Trabajo fin de Grado]. Universidad de Los Andes. https://hdl.handle.net/1992/73476

Huang, C.-Z. A., Hawthorne, C., Roberts, A., Dinculescu, M., Wexler, J., Hong, L. & Howcroft, J. (2019). The Bach Doodle: Approachable music composition with machine learning at scale. *20th International Society for Music Information Retrieval Conference,* Delft, The Netherlands. https://acortar.link/0L4P7Y

Jara, I. & Ochoa, J. M. (2020). Usos y efectos de la inteligencia artificial en educación. https://doi.org/10.18235/0002380

Kabudi, T., Pappas, I. & Olsen, D. H. (2021). AI-enabled adaptive learning systems: A systematic mapping of the literature. *Computers and Education: Artificial Intelligence, 2,* 100017. https://doi.org/10.1016/j.caeai.2021.100017

Kang, J. (2018). *Development of a music composition program using scratch.* Master's thesis, College of Education, Konkuk University, Seoul.

Kladder, J. & Lee, W. (2019). Music Teachers Perceptions of Creativity: A Preliminary Investigation. *Creativity Research Journal, 31*(4), 395–407.

Korteling, J. E., van de Boer-Visschedijk, G. C., Blankendaal, R. A. M., Boonekamp, R. C. & Eikelboom, A. R. (2021). Human- versus Artificial Intelligence. *Frontiers in Artificial Intelligence, 4.* https://www.frontiersin.org/articles/10.3389/frai.2021.622364

Krueger, R. A. y Casey, M. A. (2000). *Focus Groups. A Practical Guide For Applied Research.* Sage.

Kuok Ho, D. T. (2024). Implications of Artificial Intelligence for Teaching and Learning. *Acta Pedagogia Asiana.* 3. 65–79. 10.53623/apga.v3i2.404.

McCormack J., Hutchings P., Gifford T., Yee King M., Llano M. T. & D'inverno, M. (2020). Design Considerations for Real-Time Collaboration with Creative Artificial Intelligence. *Organised Sound, 25*(1), 41–52. 10.1017/s1355771819000451

Merchán Sánchez-Jara, J. F., González Gutiérrez, S., Cruz Rodríguez, J. & Syroyid Syroyid, B. (2024). Artificial Intelligence-Assisted Music

Education: A Critical Synthesis of Challenges and Opportunities. *Education Sciences*, *14*(11), 1171. https://doi.org/10.3390/educsci14111171
Mousavinasab, E., Zarifsanaiey, N., Niakan Kalhori, S. R., Rakhshan, M., Keikha, L. & Ghazi Saeedi, M. (2021). Intelligent tutoring systems: A systematic review of characteristics, applications, and evaluation methods. *Interactive Learning Environments*, *29*(1), 142–163. https://doi.org/10.1080/10494820.2018.1558257
Muñoz-Cantero, J.-M., Pérez Crego, M.-C. & Espiñeira-Bellón, E.-M. (2024). Desarrollo de la integridad académica como oportunidad de justicia. *Revista Electrónica Interuniversitaria de Formación del Profesorado*, *27*(3), 153–169. https://doi.org/10.6018/reifop.615081
Murtaza, M., Ahmed, Y., Shamsi, J. A., Sherwani, F. & Usman, M. (2022). AI-Based Personalized E-Learning Systems: Issues, Challenges, and Solutions. *IEEE Access*, *10*, 81323–81342. https://doi.org/10.1109/ACCESS.2022.3193938
Randles, C. & Muhonen, S. (2015). Validation and further validation of a measure of creative identity among USA and Finland pre-service music teachers. *British Journal of Music Education*, *32*(1), 51–70. 10.1017/S0265051714000151
Reiss, M. J. (2021). The use of AI in education: Practicalities and ethical considerations. *London Review of Education*, *19*(1). https://doi.org/10.14324/LRE.19.1.05
Rouhiainen, L. (2018). *Inteligencia Artificial. 101 cosas que debes saber hoy sobre nuestro futuro*. Alienta Editorial.
Saldaña, J. (2009). *The Coding Manual for Qualitative Researchers*. Sage.
Schmidt, J. T. & Tang, M. (2020). Digitalization in Education: Challenges, Trends and Transformative Potential. En M. Harwardt, P. F.-J. Niermann, A. M. Schmutte y A. Steuernagel (Eds.), *Führen und Managen in der digitalen Transformation* (pp. 287–312). Springer Gabler. https://doi.org/10.1007/978-3-658-28670-5_16
Tejada, J. & Pozos, K. V. (2018). Nuevos escenarios y competencias digitales docentes: hacia la profesionalización docente con TIC. Profesorado, Revista de Currículum y Formación del Profesorado, 22(1), 25–51. https://recyt.fecyt.es/index.php/profesorado/article/view/63620/
Torrado, J. A., Pérez Echeverría, M. P. & Pozo, J. I. (2020). Aprendiendo música por medio de las TIC. En: J. I. Pozo; M. P. Pérez Echeverría; J. A. Torrado; G. López-Íñiguez (Coords.). *Aprender y enseñar música: Un enfoque centrado en los alumnos*. Morata, pp. 291–305.

Vázquez-Sánchez, R. (2024). Percepciones del alumnado de Música sobre el uso de recursos didácticos basados en la Inteligencia Artificial [Music students' perceptions of the use of Artificial Intelligence-based teaching resources]. *European Public & Social Innovation Review, 9,* 1-18. https://doi.org/10.31637/epsir-2024-912.

Vinuesa, R., Azizpour, H., Leite, I., Balaam, M., Dignum, V., Domisch, S., Felländer, A., Langhans, S. D., Tegmark, M. & Fuso Nerini, F. (2020). The role of artificial intelligence in achieving the Sustainable Development Goals. *Nature Communications, 11*(1), 233. https://doi.org/10.1038/s41467-019-14108-y

Vivar, J. M. F. & Peñalvo, F. J. G. (2023). Reflexiones sobre la ética, potencialidades y retos de la Inteligencia Artificial en el marco de la Educación de Calidad (ODS4). *Comunicar, 74,* 37–47. https://doi.org/10.3916/C74-2023-03

Wang, Z., Liu, J. & Dong, R. (2018). Intelligent Auto-grading System. *2018 5th IEEE International Conference on Cloud Computing and Intelligence Systems (CCIS),* 430–435. https://doi.org/10.1109/CCIS.2018.8691244

Xu, X., Wang, J., Peng, H. & Wu, R. (2019). Prediction of academic performance associated with internet usage behaviors using machine learning algorithms. *Computers in Human Behavior, 98*, 166–173. https://doi.org/10.1016/j.chb.2019.04.015

Yu, L. & Ding, J. (2020). Application of music artificial intelligence in preschool music education. IOP Conference Series. *Materials Science and Engineering, 750*(1), 12101. DOI 10.1088/1757-899X/750/1/012101

Zaragozá, J. L. (2009). *Didáctica de la música en la educación secundaria. Competencias docentes y aprendizaje*. Graó.

Zhang, Y. & Cheng, L. (2023). Artificial intelligence-assisted music education: A critical synthesis of challenges and opportunities. *Education Sciences, 14*(11), 1171. https://doi.org/10.3390/educsci14111171

Zhang, S., Lu, X. & Liu, X. (2024). Study on the Influence of AI Composition Software on Students' Creative Ability in Music Education. *Journal of Educational Technology and Innovation, 6(2)*. https://www.jeti.thewsu.org/index.php/cieti/article/view/190

Zulić, H. (2019). How AI can change/improve/influence music composition, Performance and Education: Three Case Studies. *INSAM, I*(2), 100–114.

Academic Integrity or Artificial Intelligence? Towards a Preventive Culture in Sweden

Christophe Premat[1]

ABSTRACT

Academic integrity remains a critical pillar of higher education, yet the emergence of artificial intelligence (AI) presents new challenges and opportunities for universities. This study examines how Swedish higher education institutions, particularly Stockholm University, navigate the evolving relationship between academic integrity and AI technologies such as chatbots. While traditional concerns about plagiarism persist, the study highlights a shift towards preventive strategies rather than punitive measures, aligning with broader institutional efforts to foster a culture of integrity. Through a mixed-methods approach, this research draws upon survey data from students who participated in an online academic integrity course, as well as written reflections from students discussing the ethical implications of AI-assisted learning. The findings reveal that students largely recognise the importance of academic integrity, yet they grapple with the role of AI in academic work. Some view AI tools as valuable aids for writing and research, while others express concerns about ethical boundaries and citation practices. The study employs a phenomenographic perspective to explore students' reasoning and evolving attitudes towards AI and integrity. The results indicate a pragmatic approach within Swedish universities, balancing AI's integration with ethical guidelines. The study also underscores the limitations of AI-detection tools and the necessity of clear policies regarding AI usage. Additionally, it suggests that fostering academic integrity should involve collaboration between students, educators, and writing centres, rather than relying solely on rule enforcement. Ultimately, this research argues for a redefinition of academic integrity in the digital age – one that embraces AI's potential while maintaining rigorous academic standards. By promoting AI literacy, transparent guidelines, and ethical discussions, universities can equip students with the critical skills needed to navigate AI-assisted education responsibly.

Keywords: academic integrity, artificial intelligence, higher education, AI chatbots, plagiarism, ethics, Stockholm University, preventive strategies

Introduction

Academic integrity remains a cornerstone of higher education (Bretag, 2016), ensuring that learning and research maintain ethical standards. In recent years, concerns over plagiarism and academic dishonesty have

---

[1] Stockholm University. https://orcid.org/0000-0001-6107-735X

intensified due to the increased accessibility of digital resources and the emergence of generative artificial intelligence (AI). However, recent data from Swedish higher education institutions indicate a notable decline in disciplinary cases related to academic misconduct. This trend provides a valuable opportunity to assess the effectiveness of preventive measures and the evolving academic culture (Premat, 2019a). According to the Swedish Higher Education Authority (2024), the number of students who faced disciplinary action, including suspensions and warnings, decreased by 14% from 2,671 cases in 2022 to 2,306 in 2023. This accounts for approximately 0.72% of all full-time students. The most significant decrease was observed in plagiarism-related cases, which fell from 1,783 in 2022 to 1,483 in 2023. Notably, while suspensions decreased by approximately 18%, warnings increased by 10%, suggesting a shift towards corrective rather than punitive measures (Karlsson, 2019). At the same time, the emergence of AI-assisted misconduct has become a new concern. Reports from twenty-seven Swedish higher education institutions indicate that they have handled disciplinary cases related to misleading use of AI tools, while seven institutions reported no such cases. In total, 221 disciplinary cases involving AI-related misconduct were recorded. Of these, eighty-two students faced suspension, while twenty-six received warnings. Interestingly, in eighty-three cases, no action was taken against the student due to unclear institutional guidelines or insufficient evidence. These figures highlight the challenges universities face in addressing AI-related misconduct, particularly in establishing clear policies and ensuring sufficient proof in disciplinary cases.

The relationship between academic integrity and artificial intelligence has evolved rapidly, as AI tools are now widely accessible to students and educators alike. Recent research highlights both the potential benefits and ethical concerns surrounding AI in academia. Studies suggest that AI can assist students in generating ideas, improving writing skills, and enhancing learning experiences when used ethically (Bendixen et al., 2024). However, concerns have been raised about the misuse of AI for deceptive purposes, such as generating unoriginal work or fabricating citations (Bonn & Pinxten, 2019). Research has also examined the impact of AI-detection tools in mitigating academic misconduct. While some universities have adopted AI-detection software, its reliability remains a subject of debate (Leib et al., 2023). Haghighi, Saqalaksari, and Johnson (2023: 9) argue that AI's integration into education must be accompanied by clear ethical guidelines to prevent ambiguity and misuse as the overuse of these tools have a deep impact on the environment. Additionally, recent studies suggest that institutional culture plays a significant role in shaping students' attitudes toward AI use in academia. Universities that emphasise proactive education on academic integrity tend to have lower rates of misconduct, while those relying primarily on punitive measures struggle to adapt to the evolving landscape of AI-assisted learning (Premat, 2023). As AI continues to develop, higher education institutions face a fundamental dilemma: should they integrate AI as a legitimate academic tool while emphasising responsible use, or should they impose stricter controls to maintain traditional academic standards? Scholars such as Cerdà-Navarro et al. (2022) advocate for a balanced approach, arguing that AI literacy must be integrated into university curricula to ensure ethical usage while maintaining rigorous academic expectations. Some other researchers analyse the role of Centres for academic writing in Sweden. While these centres act as language brokers helping students navigate academic writing, their work is constrained by institutional monolingualism, assessment-focused teaching, and limited agency in university policies (Kaufhold & Yencken, 2021: 7). There is space for working on learning strategies and academic integrity but it requires collaborative strategies between teachers, students and these centres (Hellman & Thorsten, 2021).

This chapter explores these issues within the framework of academic integrity at Stockholm University. By examining institutional responses to AI-generated content, evolving policies, and student perceptions, this study aims to shed light on how universities can cultivate a culture of integrity that aligns with contemporary digital realities. Through an analysis of an online course on academic integrity at a Swedish university, this chapter evaluates students' understanding of plagiarism and their attitudes toward ethical academic practices. Ultimately, the key question is whether universities should focus on reinforcing traditional values of integrity or embrace new technological paradigms while maintaining rigorous academic standards. The response to AI in academic integrity discourse can be viewed through two contrasting perspectives: a pragmatic approach that acknowledges AI as an inevitable part of academic development and seeks to integrate it within ethical guidelines, and an ideological stance that views AI as a threat to traditional educational values and emphasises strict regulation. While pragmatic attitudes may encourage adaptation and responsible AI use, ideological positions may insist on preserving conventional assessment methods, potentially resisting innovation.

Background

Sweden has a long-standing commitment to academic integrity, with national regulations and university policies designed to promote ethical scholarship. Academic institutions emphasise preventive measures such as early education on proper referencing, plagiarism detection software, and fostering a culture of integrity within academic communities. The *Stockholm University Handbook on Academic Integrity* (Bendixen et al., 2024) highlights the evolving challenges posed by AI chatbots in student assessments. It categorises AI involvement into different levels, ranging from learning support and brainstorming to outright plagiarism through unedited AI-generated text. The handbook underscores the importance of transparency, requiring students who use AI tools to disclose their usage explicitly. University guidelines equate submitting AI-generated work as one's own with ghostwriting, a serious academic offence.

A recent legal case in Sweden further illustrates the complexities of AI and academic integrity (*Kammarätten i Göteborg*, 14 July 2023). A student was accused of cheating after submitting an essay suspected to be AI-generated. The university's disciplinary committee initially ruled against the student, citing deceptive intent. However, the appeals court overturned the decision, arguing that the institution lacked clear guidelines on AI use at the time. The ruling emphasised the need for universities to establish explicit policies on AI tools in academic work, as regulatory ambiguity can lead to unfair disciplinary measures:

'No other conclusion can be drawn than that, after conducting a ChatGPT search, the student neglected to further verify the accuracy of the citations and, due to carelessness, ended up submitting an academic work containing three fabricated citations. In the absence of clear guidelines and information from the university regarding the permissibility or impermissibility of different approaches to ChatGPT or other forms of AI, the administrative court finds that it is not evident that the student attempted to mislead in their academic work by using unauthorised aids or in any other way as specified in Chapter 10, Section 1 of the Higher Education Ordinance nor that they were aware that their actions would have been considered impermissible (cf., for example, the ruling by the Administrative Court in Växjö on 20 June 2023, in case no. 1998-23). Under such circumstances, the student's incorrect citations in the take-home exam are instead a matter for the relevant faculty's substantive assessment of the quality of the academic work. Based on these considerations, the administrative court finds that the evidence in the case does not clearly demonstrate that the student has committed a disciplinary offence under the Higher Education Ordinance. The appealed decision should therefore be annulled' (*Kammarätten i Göteborg*, 14 July 2023)[2].

This case set a precedent for how Swedish universities handle AI-related academic misconduct, reinforcing the importance of updating institutional policies to reflect technological advancements. Stockholm University has developed detailed guidelines for teachers, researchers, and decision-makers regarding AI chatbot usage. The university acknowledges that AI tools like ChatGPT present both opportunities and risks, emphasising the need for careful judgement in their application. The guidelines distinguish between acceptable and unacceptable uses, stating that 'letting an AI chatbot write a text that is more or less unedited and submitting it as the student's own in an attempt to mislead the examiner' (Stockholm University, 2024, 15 October) is equivalent to ghostwriting or plagiarism and is typically considered cheating. However, students are permitted to use AI for tasks such as refining their writing, identifying errors, and synthesising information – provided they 'clearly explain how the AI chatbot has been used' (Stockholm University, 2024, 15 October). This approach reflects a pragmatic balance, allowing for AI integration while maintaining academic accountability.

The university also recommends adapting assessment methods to mitigate AI-related misconduct. Strategies include 'avoiding unsupervised home examinations' (Stockholm University, 2024, 15 October), introducing oral components, and requiring incremental submissions that track a student's writing process. Additionally, the university advises caution when using AI-detection tools, acknowledging that 'tools that assess the probability of AI-generated text are unlikely to be fully reliable and must be supplemented with other evidence in disciplinary cases' (Stockholm University, 2024, 15 October). Stockholm University's regulatory approach blends pragmatic

---

2 Our translation. The name of the student was anonymised.

and ideological elements. The emphasis on 'accountability, transparency', and 'explicit acknowledgement' (Stockholm University, 2024, 15 October) demonstrates an effort to adapt to AI's role in education, while phrases like 'ensuring academic trustworthiness' and 'upholding the core values of scholarship' reinforce a traditional commitment to human authorship. This duality reflects the broader challenge institutions face in integrating AI while preserving academic integrity. Sweden's academic integrity policies also seek to balance regulation with educational support. Institutions are encouraged to collaborate with students to foster ethical academic practices rather than relying solely on punitive measures. The *Stockholm University Handbook* (Bendixen et al., 2024) suggests that educators should incorporate AI literacy into coursework, guiding students on responsible AI use while designing assessments that minimise the risks of AI-facilitated dishonesty (Farnese et al., 2011).

The handbook is based on current research into the difficulties of detecting AI-generated text:

> So far, although several attempts have been made by researchers, there is not much optimism about creating accurate and effective systems that can detect AI-generated text. Furthermore, teachers and academic staff seem to also not be able to determine whether a text has been generated by a student (Bendixen et al., 2024: 24).

In other words, despite ongoing efforts, there is little confidence in the effectiveness of AI-detection systems, as distinguishing AI-generated text from human writing remains a significant challenge. Educators struggle to determine whether students have written their work, and existing detection tools often produce unreliable results. This raises concerns about the fairness and accuracy of academic integrity enforcement. Rather than relying on flawed detection methods, institutions may need to prioritise transparency, critical thinking (Davies, 2013), and alternative assessment strategies such as process-based evaluation and oral discussions. As AI technology evolves, the focus should shift from detection to responsible integration, ensuring that students understand how to use AI ethically while maintaining academic standards. This awareness reflects a pragmatic and inclusive approach: rather than imposing highly restrictive and punitive measures that may fail to detect AI-generated content, the handbook advocates for integrating AI tools in a way that encourages students to engage with them critically. AI chatbots can assist in refining language in academic papers, allow students to double-check their writing, and help them gain a more objective perspective on their work.

The handbook mentions some of the chatbots that may be used by students if they explicitly mention it:

> Several tools can be used by students when being assessed in written form, such as AI chatbots (i.e. ChatGPT), Digital Writing Assistants (i.e. Grammarly) and Automated Paraphrasing Tools (i.e. Quilbot) [sic] which are often also integrated into Microsoft Office package (provided to students by the university). It is therefore significant to support students in using such tools in a way that is beneficial for their learning, does not violate academic integrity and follows each department's, programme and course standards (Bendixen et al., 2024: 25).

Rather than viewing these tools as threats, institutions must focus on guiding students in their responsible use. Simply banning AI-driven writing aids is neither practical nor beneficial, as they are already embedded in everyday academic and professional environments. Instead, universities should establish clear expectations about how these technologies can be used to support learning without compromising originality. This means distinguishing between acceptable uses – such as improving structure and correcting language – and practices that violate academic integrity, like submitting unedited AI-generated work. By naming specific chatbots, the handbook ultimately suggests making them allies rather than enemies, reflecting the Swedish philosophy on academic integrity. Recommendations always take precedence over punishments, a principle that was also evident in the way the Swedish government responded to the pandemic (Norberg, 2023: 3; Premat, 2024: 441).

Previous Studies and Theoretical Framework

Recent research on AI integration in education has focused on its impact on academic integrity, student agency, and the evolving interaction between learners and digital tools. While AI-powered systems like ChatGPT can enhance learning efficiency, they also raise concerns regarding ethics, authorship, and critical thinking. Wang et al. (2025: 294) examined graduate students' engagement with GPT-based tools, finding that while overall usage was limited, unethical practices emerged, particularly under high academic pressure. Their study further revealed that after experimenting with a GPT platform, students' intention to use AI in research increased, though their self-efficacy, course satisfaction, and perceptions of AI remained unchanged. These findings underscore the necessity of institutional policies, AI literacy training, and faculty engagement to promote ethical AI use in academia. Academic integrity concerns are further highlighted by Coetzer and van Aardt (2024: 174), who studied AI-generated texts in a South African university writing centre. Their research found that students increasingly submitted ChatGPT-generated work as their own, struggling to justify their arguments when questioned. Identifying generic phrasing, unreliable citations, and formulaic structures as common features of AI-generated texts, they warned that AI risks erasing students' voices in academic writing. To counter this, they proposed Socratic questioning and academic literacy interventions to encourage students to critically engage with AI rather than rely on it passively. These findings align with broader concerns about how AI standardisation may undermine originality and independent thought in academic discourse.

Beyond academic ethics, studies have also examined the factors influencing students' adoption of AI in education. Güner et al. (2024) applied the Technology Acceptance Model (TAM) to explore students' attitudes toward ChatGPT, identifying key determinants such as perceived usefulness, enjoyment, privacy concerns, and social influence. Their findings reveal a tension between AI's benefits – such as efficiency and accessibility – and concerns over ethics, authorship, and privacy risks. This reflects a broader debate about how digital systems shape student agency and responsibility in learning environments. While many studies focus on AI's ethical and attitudinal dimensions, others investigate how learners interact with digital tools. Gonçalves et al. (2024) provide a systematic review of enactive interaction in technology-based learning environments, emphasising how embodied learning principles intersect with digital tools. Their study highlights key technologies such as sensors, tangible interfaces, wearable devices, and robotics, which facilitate enactive learning through full-body, gesture-based, and motion-driven interactions. However, they identify challenges such as the lack of a unified vocabulary, the absence of a structured framework, and the underexplored social dimensions of enactive learning. Notably, concepts like autonomy and emergence remain insufficiently addressed, raising questions about how AI-driven learning environments can better integrate social and cognitive dimensions.

These findings align with cognitive ecology (Petitot et al., 1999), which frames the interaction between learners and digital systems as central to shaping autonomy in learning. Rather than viewing human cognition as separate from technological tools, this perspective emphasises the complex interdependencies between technological affordances, ethical considerations, and pedagogical strategies. As AI continues to transform education, it necessitates a rethinking of learning ethics – ensuring that students remain active participants rather than passive recipients of AI-generated content. Current research assumes that artificial intelligence not only challenges academic integrity but also calls for a clarification of ethical assumptions within epistemology. Francisco Varela demonstrated how studies on machines and artificial intelligence systems have established the principle of the inaccessibility of mental processes. He writes:

> Computationalism insists on the existence of mental processes that cannot be brought to consciousness at all. Thus it is not that we are simply unaware of the rules that govern visual processing; we cannot in principle ever be aware of these rules. One computationalist account asserts that these processes cannot be brought to consciousness without ceasing to function, because by its very nature consciousness is slow and deliberate, not fast and automatic as, say, vision must be to function properly (Varela, 1999: 37).

The computationalist view suggests that certain cognitive processes, like vision, operate unconsciously and cannot be brought to awareness without disrupting their function. However, enactivist and embodied cognition perspectives challenge this, arguing that cognition emerges from interaction with the environment rather than from purely internal computations. While some neural processes may remain inaccessible, perception is shaped by bodily action and experience, suggesting that learning is not purely symbolic but deeply intertwined with movement and engagement with the world. Moreover, consciousness is not necessarily slow and deliberate – expert skill performance and pre-reflective awareness demonstrate that cognition can be immediate and fluid. Alternative frameworks like enactivism and dynamical systems theory advocate for an integrated understanding of cognition, where perception, action, and consciousness continuously interact rather than existing in separate domains.

These insights into cognition and AI's epistemological implications connect with Bernhard Rieder's *Engines of Order*, which explores how algorithmic techniques originally designed for document retrieval have evolved into powerful digital infrastructures shaping knowledge, social structures, and decision-making. Rieder argues:

> Rather than simply organizing information, these algorithms intervene in how content is filtered, categorized, and prioritized, reinforcing patterns of visibility and influence in an increasingly complex and fragmented world. By blending statistical pragmatism with large-scale computation, these systems do not just reflect reality but actively construct it, making them engines of order that shape contemporary digital life in profound ways (Rieder, 2020: 28).

This perspective highlights how AI is not a neutral tool but an active force that influences what knowledge is made visible, accessible, and valued. Simondon's theory of technogenesis further expands this discussion by proposing that technical objects are not static tools subordinated to human control but evolving entities with their own trajectories. He critiques the traditional division between culture and technology, emphasising that technical objects develop through internal coherence and historical progression. According to Simondon:

> Technical objects should be understood as evolving entities that develop through a process of technogenesis, rather than as static tools subordinated to human use. He critiques the traditional division between culture and technology, proposing that technical objects possess their own mode of existence, shaped by their internal coherence and historical progression. Simondon advocates for a deeper engagement with technology, emphasizing that understanding its evolution and inherent logic can bridge the gap between humans and machines, fostering a more integrated relationship between society and technological development (Simondon, 2017).

Taken together, these perspectives challenge simplistic views of AI and digital tools as mere extensions of human agency. Instead, they suggest that AI not only influences academic integrity but actively shapes epistemology, cognitive engagement, and the way knowledge is structured in digital environments. As AI continues to redefine education, a critical, interdisciplinary approach is necessary to ensure that students and educators navigate these transformations responsibly, ethically, and with an awareness of the deeper cognitive and technological forces at play.

Data and Method

The corpus for this empirical investigation consists of two sets of data collected from students at Stockholm University. The first dataset comprises survey responses from 100 anonymous students or teachers who tested the videos in pedagogical workshops and participated in an online self-study course on academic integrity. The data were collected online using the application Survey & Report between 1 February 2023, and 8 March 2025 and have a length of 5,619 words. This course was structured around three short instructional videos[3], each less than ten minutes long, covering key topics such as the definition and importance of academic integrity, the consequences of plagiarism, and study techniques to uphold ethical academic practices. Following the completion of the course, students responded to a survey designed to assess their understanding and engagement with the material. The survey included questions regarding their perception of academic integrity after watching the videos, the effectiveness of the course content, and the study strategies they employ to maintain integrity in their academic work. Responses provide insight into the extent to which the course influenced their awareness of academic integrity principles. In compliance with the General Data Protection Regulation (GDPR), the survey was accessible via a link without recording any metadata for the participants. Following Article 6A of GDPR, participants had to give their consent before filling out the survey. As the self-study course was created in 2022, just a few weeks before the launch of ChatGPT in November 2022, participants could reflect on chatbots, but the focus of the questions remained on their understanding of the principles of academic integrity. All the participants had taken a course in social sciences or in humanities.

Most of the participants came from two introductory courses, an introduction course on Canadian studies (29 participants) and an introduction course on quantitative methods (18 participants). The other respondents took courses in applied social research, business ethics, philosophy courses or cultural studies (East Asian studies). 10 participants were teachers that tested the self-study course in the framework of a pedagogical workshop. The participants had to watch three videos and fill out quiz before answering two questions ('After

3 https://www.su.se/centre-for-the-advancement-of-university-teaching/resources-and-support/assessing-and-grading/teaching-to-avoid-plagiarism-1.782901 (Last visit, 13 March 2025).

watching the three short movies, do you have a clear idea of what is expected of you as a student?'; 'can you share the best learning strategy that you use?').

The second dataset consists of written reflections from forty-two students who attended a course on academic integrity in modern languages at Stockholm University on 6 September 2024. The length of the answers corresponds to a text of 2,626 words. These students were prompted to respond to the question: 'Should I mention that I have used ChatGPT to solve an academic assignment?' The written responses capture individual perspectives on the role of artificial intelligence in academic writing and whether its usage should be explicitly acknowledged in academic work. The students answered anonymously via a Padlet (online collaborative board) with the question. The data presents a range of opinions on the necessity of transparency and the ethical implications of using AI in student assignments. The collection of these written reflections offers an opportunity to document student viewpoints regarding the evolving landscape of digital tools in academic contexts. Unlike the self-study course, this dataset specifically addresses the intersection of chatbots and academic integrity, encouraging students to analyse the implications of AI-assisted learning. The answers were translated from Swedish to English for the purpose of the present study.

The two datasets together provide a foundation for assessing how students engage with academic integrity principles and how they perceive the role of AI in their studies. They offer insight into both general understanding following structured instruction and personal reflections on the application of integrity in academic work. The data supports the ongoing discussion on how universities can guide students in ethical scholarship while adapting policies to contemporary digital challenges. These data complement each other as the self-study course on academic integrity was created in 2022, just a few weeks before the launch of ChatGPT in November 2022. While the participants of the self-study course reflected on chatbots within the framework of academic integrity principles, the second dataset originates from a course where students had to consider the relationship between chatbots and academic integrity explicitly.

The methodological approach is partially based on a phenomenographic perspective, allowing students to react and express their emotions and feelings regarding their relationship with artificial intelligence. A key question explored in this study is: What questions arise for students when working with language while potentially benefiting from chatbots without compromising their academic integrity? Phenomenography is a qualitative method that helps identify recurring social representations and reasoning patterns among participants. As Bauman (2000: 56) states, 'The way human beings understand the world tends to be at all times praxeomorphic: it is always shaped by the know-how of the day, by what people can do and how they usually go about doing it'. Both surveys were analysed using Tropes software, which specialises in text analysis, particularly semantic analysis, linguistic processing, and discourse exploration (Puebla et al., 2012). For the purposes of this study, a mixed-method approach was chosen, as *Tropes* software provided quantified results on the frequency of associations in students' responses.

Findings

The survey results show that the vast majority of participants found the short movies useful (97 answered yes to the question), indicating a strong need to discuss academic integrity at the university level. Even though the students have heard about plagiarism, the act of proposing a self-study course on academic integrity contributes to officialise it, which explains the strong consensus on these introductory courses.

Table 14 summarises the most ten frequent nouns, adjectives and verbs among the participants.

Table 14: Frequent words for the answers on the question of the utility of the self-study course

Nouns (number of occurrences)	Adjectives (number of occurrences)	Verbs (number of occurrences)
Student (16)	Academic (25)	Be (34)
Cheating (8)	Good (12)	Have (17)
Knowledge (7)	Clear (7)	Expect (10)
Understanding (7)	Relevant (6)	Shall (9)
Writing (6)	New (6)	Avoid (7)
Video (6)	Very (5)	Do (7)
Time (6)	Important (5)	Can (6)
Information (5)	Scientific (4)	Use (6)
Source (5)	Own (3)	Keep (5)
Work (5)	Easy (3)	Think (4)

The high frequency of the words 'student' (16 occurrences), 'cheating' (8), and 'knowledge' (7) suggests that students are aware of the risks of academic dishonesty while also valuing knowledge as a fundamental part of their academic journey. Additionally, the presence of words such as 'understanding' (7 occurrences) and 'writing' (6 occurrences) highlights that students recognise the importance of academic integrity in their written work. This aligns with several survey responses that emphasise the need for proper referencing, scientific methodology, and transparency in academic writing. The most frequent adjectives, particularly 'academic' (25 occurrences), 'good' (12), and 'clear' (7), reflect students' perception of the self-study course as an important, structured, and effective tool. Many responses praised the clarity of the movies and their usefulness in outlining expectations. The adjective 'relevant' (6 occurrences) further supports this, indicating that students see academic integrity as an important and applicable topic. Interestingly, 'scientific' (4 occurrences) suggests that only a few students view academic integrity not just as an ethical requirement but as an integral part of the research process. This reinforces the notion that proper citation and methodology contribute to the reliability of academic work. The relatively low frequency of this term may be explained by the fact that the self-study course is often taken by students at the basic level of university education. The predominance of objective adjectives (61.5%) in students' responses suggests a focus on factual descriptions, while the presence of subjective adjectives (34.2%) indicates personal engagement, and the low occurrence of numeral adjectives (4.3%) highlights that quantification played a minor role in their reflections.

The most frequent verbs provide insight into how students perceive their role in maintaining academic integrity. The most common verb, 'be' (34 occurrences), suggests that students recognise academic integrity as an intrinsic part of their identity as students. One comment particularly highlights this perspective: 'Keep in mind the attitude one should have towards academic integrity and keep track of good habits that help not to fall into the easy path of plagiarism' (Comment A, survey on academic integrity). This statement is formulated as a piece of advice that the student wishes to share with others, reinforcing the idea that maintaining integrity requires active effort and awareness. Words like 'have' (17), 'expect' (10), and 'shall' (9) indicate that students are not only aware of what is expected of them but also acknowledge their responsibility in upholding these standards. Some concrete comments further illustrate this point: 'I have a clear idea of what is expected from me regarding academic writing and the risks of plagiarising' (Comment B, survey on academic integrity). 'After watching the three short movies, I now have a clear understanding of what is expected of me as a student, especially regarding academic integrity. The emphasis on honesty, trust, and openness in academic work resonated with me. It's clear that academic integrity isn't just about avoiding cheating or plagiarism but about building trust within the academic community' (Comment C, survey on academic integrity). Additionally, verbs like 'avoid' (7 occurrences) and 'keep' (5 occurrences) highlight students' recognition of the importance of avoiding plagiarism and maintaining integrity throughout their academic journey. The presence of 'use' (6 occurrences) further emphasises the significance of proper citation and reliance on credible sources. The frequency of pronouns in students' responses provides insight into their perspective on academic integrity.

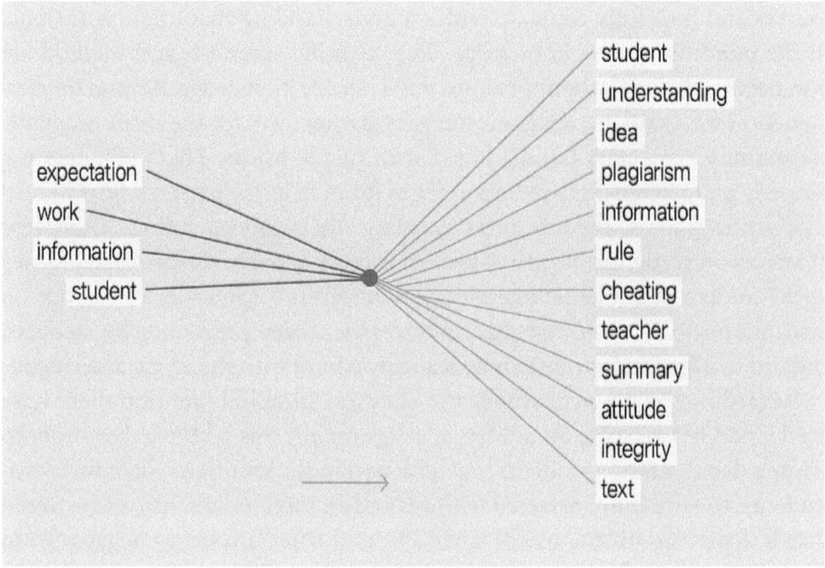

Figure 13: Frequent word associations with the pronoun 'I'
Source: Results from the Tropes software

The predominance of 'I' (59.5%) suggests that students view academic integrity as a personal responsibility and an individual commitment (see the word associations in Figure 13). This aligns with their acknowledgement of expectations and their role in maintaining ethical standards. The presence of 'you' (10.7%) indicates that some responses are framed as advice or guidance directed towards others, reinforcing a sense of peer awareness and collective responsibility. The lower occurrences of 'we' (8.3%) and 'they' (8.3%) suggest that while students recognise academic integrity as a shared value within the academic community, they primarily see it as an individual duty rather than a collective effort. This reflects a strong personal engagement with the topic but may also highlight a potential gap in viewing academic integrity as a collaborative practice within their educational environment. It is reflected in the following comment: 'Prior to these three videos, I had a good understanding of what academic integrity was, but those were a good summary. As a student, you are expected to be a true academic. In other words, you should be able to read and study the academic texts in a way that allows you to develop your own understanding and personal opinions. To build knowledge, you need to draw from legitimate academic sources and hopefully come up with an understanding that might contribute to the building of new knowledge. The scientific approach and method are non-negotiable, as it is the only way to build reliable knowledge. Beyond the consequences for a student, academic integrity is important for the entire academic community – we can't build a house with fragile bricks. That's why quoting properly and referencing are important as it can help the person who will read your writings to use the references to enlarge their understanding' (Comment D, survey on academic integrity). Here, it is possible to see the personal journey of the student in academic integrity, moving from 'I' (previous knowledge on academic integrity), 'you' (the expectations of the academy regarding the students) and 'we' as a final reflection on how academy is built with these tacit agreements.

Regarding the use of chatbots, the question 'Should I mention that I have used ChatGPT to solve an academic assignment?' was addressed in order to create a debate among students that took part in the seminar. Out of forty-two students, twenty-four answered with yes and an explanation, fifteen answered that it depended on the use of ChatGPT and three answered negatively. In fact, the answers showed a lot of nuances and conditions when it comes to the use of ChatGPT. Table 15 gives the most frequent nouns, adjectives and verbs that were extracted from the students' answers.

Table 15: Frequent words for the answers of the students reflecting on the use of ChatGPT

Nouns (number of occurrences)	**Adjectives (number of occurrences)**	**Verbs (number of occurrences)**
Source (48)	Academic (21)	Use (97)
Assignment (24)	Other (16)	Shall (59)
Text (23)	Important (7)	Be (52)
Information (23)	All (7)	Mention (43)
Tool (20)	Same (5)	Cite (20)
One (14)	Original (5)	Reference (16)
Work (9)	Like (5)	Can (14)
Reference (7)	Specific (4)	Do (12)
Idea (7)	Similar (3)	Find (11)
Search engine (6)	Factual (3)	Write (9)

Source: Tropes software

The students' responses highlight a strong focus on *ethical considerations* in using ChatGPT, as reflected in the frequent verbs 'use' (97 occurrences) and 'shall' (59 occurrences), which emphasise the need for proper usage and academic responsibility. The prominence of 'source' (48 occurrences) indicates concerns about *credibility and verification*, with many students stressing that ChatGPT should not replace primary sources but rather support academic writing. The frequent adjectives, such as 'academic' (21 occurrences) and 'important' (7 occurrences), suggest that students recognise ChatGPT's role within structured academic standards but remain cautious about its reliability. The diversity of opinions, with some students advocating for full transparency while others see it as a mere tool, underscores the complexity of integrating AI into academic work. For instance, one student commented the unnecessity of quoting ChatGPT as a chatbot if it was only used to check the spelling of a text: 'Yes, if the text is produced by ChatGPT, but not if ChatGPT has been used to find facts (which one then verifies, just like other search engines), to correct spelling errors (just like Google Translate, Word), etc'. (Student A, 6 September 2024). The comparison with other chatbots like Google Translate and Word is here interesting as it suggests a general approach of these supportive tools. Another student answered to the question in the following way: 'ChatGPT can be used as a so-called tool when studying, but it is not a scientific source, which means that it cannot be referenced in the bibliography. When it comes to ChatGPT, one should not use it as the primary tool for writing, for example, a text; however, it can be an additional aid'. This response underscores the distinction between using ChatGPT as a *study aid* versus a *scientific source*, reinforcing the idea that while it can nouns academic work, it should not replace primary references. The emphasis on ChatGPT as a supplementary tool highlights students' awareness of its limitations and the importance of relying on credible sources in scholarly writing.

Tropes software provides data on references, organising the main substantives of the analysed text into equivalent classes to represent the broader context. In this graph, each reference is represented as a sphere, with its size corresponding to the number of words it contains (see Figure 14). The distance between the central class and the surrounding classes reflects the number of relationships linking them: the closer two classes are, the more connections they share, whereas greater distance indicates fewer shared relationships.

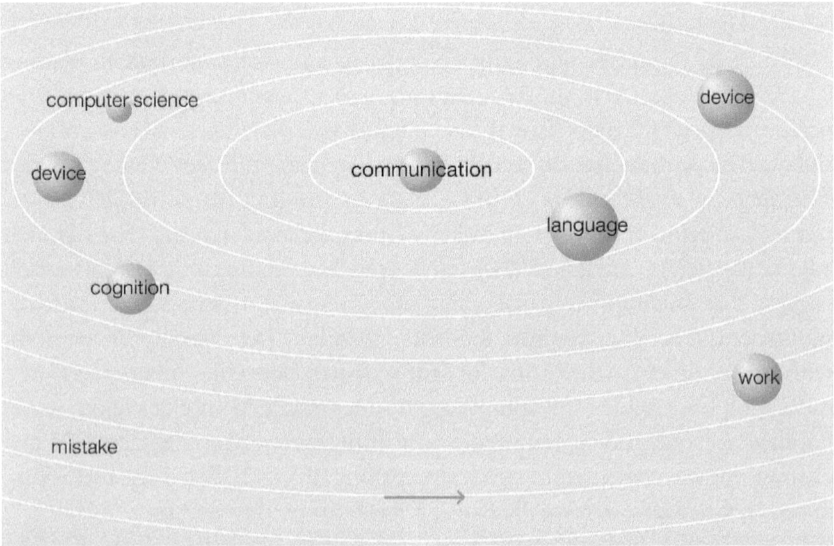

Figure 14: Relationships between key concepts in students' answers regarding the use of ChatGPT

Source: Results from the Tropes software

Figure 14 visually represents the key concepts extracted from students' responses regarding ChatGPT, with 'communication' positioned at the centre, indicating its strong relevance to the discussion. The surrounding terms, such as 'language', 'device', 'work', and 'computer science', suggest that students associate ChatGPT with linguistic processing, digital tools, and professional or academic tasks. On the left side of the graph, terms like 'cognition' and 'mistake' highlight concerns about the cognitive impact of AI and potential errors, reflecting students' caution about ChatGPT's reliability. The presence of 'device' on both sides suggests a dual perspective – while some see ChatGPT as a useful tool, others emphasise the risks of over-reliance on technology. The organisation of concepts aligns with the diverse opinions found in the students' responses. The graph's structure reinforces the idea that students perceive ChatGPT as both an aid in communication and knowledge-building and a potential source of academic integrity concerns. This supports the findings that students emphasise responsible usage, verification of sources, and the need for clear ethical guidelines in integrating AI into academic work.

Many responses use factive verbs such as 'should be mentioned' and 'must be cited' to express clear directives about academic integrity, aligning with an emphasis on actions and requirements within the responses. In contrast, stative verbs like 'depends', 'is' and 'believe' indicate uncertainty and subjectivity, reflecting the varied perspectives of respondents on when citation is necessary. The presence of reflexive verbs suggests an emphasis on individual involvement in decision-making, as seen in expressions like 'I think', 'I consider', and 'I should mention'. Performative verbs, which express actions through language, appear rarely, with examples such as 'I declare' and 'I confirm' being infrequent. This indicates that respondents do not impose strong authoritative statements but rather discuss possibilities. The frequent use of condition connectors such as 'if' and 'depends' reinforces the idea that the necessity of citation is situational. Comparison connectors like 'similarly' and 'just like' are used to compare ChatGPT with other tools such as Google Translate and Wikipedia. Opposition connectors such as 'however' and 'but' highlight the contrast between those who argue for mandatory citation and those who see it as unnecessary. Addition connectors like 'also' and 'in addition' suggest that respondents often provide multiple reasons to support their stance. Manner adverbs such as 'clearly' and 'transparently'

Table 16: Linguistic patterns in responses on ChatGPT citation practices

Types of verbs (proportions)	**Types of connectors (proportions)**	**Modalities (proportions) (= Adverbs enabling the narrator to involve in what he says)**	**Types of adjectives (proportions)**	**Use of pronouns (proportions)**
Factive (Verbs expressing actions) (47.3%)	Condition (31.5%)	Manner (27%)	Objective (existence or absence of a property) (73.4%)	I (23.5%)
Stative (states of concepts of possession) (20.1%)	Comparison (17.8%)	Negation (21.9%)	Subjective (judgement on something or an emotional reaction) (22%)	We (0.5%)
Reflexive (32.1%)	Opposition (15.4%)	Time (16.8%)	Numeral (4.6%)	You (9.8%)
Performative 0.5%	Addition (15.4%)	Intensity (14.3%)		They (0.5%)
	Disjunction (12.4%)	Assertion (12.8%)		
	Time (5.4%)			
	Cause (1.2%)			
	Goal (0.8%)			

Source: results from the Tropes software

emphasise how ChatGPT should be cited, while negation adverbs like 'not necessary' and 'should not be mentioned' appear in responses from those who argue against mandatory citation. Time adverbs such as 'before', 'when', and 'after' appear in statements discussing the moments in the research process when ChatGPT should be cited. Objective adjectives, such as 'important', 'necessary', and 'academic', indicate factual descriptions of citation practices, whereas subjective adjectives such as 'questionable' and 'credible' reflect the respondents' opinions about the reliability of ChatGPT. The relatively high use of 'I' aligns with the frequent presence of personal opinions in responses, as seen in expressions like 'I think it should be mentioned' or 'I don't believe it's necessary'. The low occurrence of 'we' and 'they' suggests that respondents speak individually rather than collectively. The presence of 'you' indicates that some responses address the reader directly, offering advice on best practices. The linguistic features in Table 16 provide a structural and stylistic analysis of the responses, highlighting that the text is predominantly objective, directive, and conditional. The responses mainly focus on factual descriptions and individual opinions, using factive verbs, conditional connectors, and objective adjectives. The limited use of performative verbs and collective pronouns suggests a lack of authoritative or universal consensus, reinforcing that opinions on ChatGPT citation vary. In fact, students exercise caution when using these chatbots because they are aware of the potential risk of violating academic integrity principles. Most of them remain pragmatic, recognising that they can benefit from chatbots for text verification while avoiding the generation of sources or information. This latter precaution illustrates a commitment to academic honesty. For instance, a student proposed a difference between 'tool' and 'source' to indicate the best manner to use ChatGPT:

> One should only use ChatGPT when solving an academic assignment if it can be done with academic integrity. It is more advantageous as a tool than as a source in most cases. If it is used as a source, one must, of course, cite it correctly. If it is used as a tool, I think it should be mentioned if it is relevant to the context (Student B, 6 September 2024).

All the comments were about the choice of discerning what can be automatised and what can be cited as a part of a scientific approach, the other aspects of ChatGPT like creativity or enjoyment (Güner et al., 2024: 389-90) were not dealt with by the participants.

Discussion

The first result highlights the importance of training on academic integrity in a Swedish context, emphasising the need to protect the very essence of university studies. It presents the Academy as a space for developing knowledge and scientific methods. The responses revealed that students did not see academic integrity merely as a trap but rather as a set of fundamental values essential for preserving the scientific approach. This result aligns with a previous study (Farnese et al., 2011: 358) which, well before the emergence of ChatGPT, actually showed that issues of academic honesty similarly affected researchers, teachers, and students. This has the merit of placing them in the same position regarding cheating and plagiarism. According to Farnese and colleagues, fostering a culture of academic integrity requires combating scientific fraud among researchers to create the conditions for an inclusive academic integrity culture, with researchers setting a good example for their students (Farnese et al., 2011: 362). Students can help researchers and academics to question the principles of transmission of knowledge, as AI devices and chatbots are a considerable challenge for the research community. Duffy (2020: 79) deepens the question of 'knowledgeable peers' that share the same core of values and that can push forward 'cowriting agencies' (Duffy, 2020: 85). These agencies can put students and researchers in collaborative tasks with the same desire to coproduce knowledge and question the outlines of the scientific method. If Duffy does not directly mention academic integrity, there is this fundamental idea that collaboration is something that needs to be explored and studied in details. The collective aspect of a research is not something natural and teachers should primarily focus on this practice in order to empower research communities (Premat, 2022b: 270; Redman & Merz, 2008: 775). Coetzer & van Aardt argue that students' voices should not be neglected when it comes to discussions on sources and AI tools as most of them could be tempted to rely on these devices to facilitate their learning processes (Coetzer & van Aardt, 2024: 153). Developing a culture of academic integrity requires an adaptation of core values to the elaboration of new digital tools, but the discussions were similar in the past with the emergence of internet (Granitz & Loewy, 2006: 294) and the development of Wikipedia (Premat, 2020). The challenges that AI devices pose to higher education systems present an opportunity to redefine knowledge and discuss science in a more generalist way (Davies, 2013: 535). When discussing critical thinking in higher education, Davies examines the opposition between generic approaches (where thinking is seen as a universal category) and specific approaches (where critical thinking is embedded in field-specific methodologies). He argues that critical thinking should be concretised in teaching so that students can recognise its value (Davies, 2013: 537). In this context, academic integrity can be introduced as a code of values that manifests critical thinking in concrete ways – through source criticism (Chankova, 2017), diversification of theories, and an understanding of paradoxes and academic disputes. In the Swedish context, the discussion of academic integrity has been proposed as a possible introduction to what science and knowledge are (Premat, 2022a). There is a distinction made between academic dishonesty with the purpose of misleading the readers (Parry, 2001) and plagiarism which sometimes could be caused by students who do not pay attention to academic standards:

> Unfortunately, there are also examples of students who have bought texts or copied other's work, or in other ways forged that they have submitted as their own academic work. This is a deliberate attempt to deceive and is therefore considered to be academic dishonesty. Stockholm University takes this seriously. By academic dishonesty is also meant when students collaborate in an authorised manner, carry unauthorised aids such as cheat sheets, unauthorised notes or mobile phones, or otherwise try to mislead during examinations or in the production of graded material (Bendixen et al., 2024: 13).

In a previous study, Mahon emphasises that deception is necessarily intentional, as it requires the deceived person to acquire or maintain a false belief (Mahon, 2007: 194). Applied to the context of academic integrity, deception is also evident when no corrective measures are taken to restore the truth.

Stockholm University's approach to academic integrity is not to impose a universal standard with ethical rules to follow but rather to encourage students to reflect on their own practices so that they can identify learning techniques that may be problematic in terms of integrity, such as the improper use of AI tools. Stockholm University's pragmatic approach to integrity seeks to make critical thinking a more tangible concern, responding not only to ethical scandals in Sweden – such as the Macchiarini case (Asplund, 2021) – but also to broader discussions on fake news and the manipulation of ideological discourses (Wikforss, 2017, Premat, 2019b). Bonn and Pixten (2019) highlighted a mismatch between our understanding of academic integrity and the standards applied to uphold it. As they state,

> our findings add to this perspective by highlighting that this imbalance also reveals a mismatch between what we know may predispose to inadequate research practices

> and the approaches to target misconduct that are discussed in the empirical literature (Bonn & Pixten, 2019: 350).

This suggests that existing integrity policies may not be fully aligned with research on the root causes of misconduct, potentially limiting their effectiveness. This is why Stockholm University's anti-plagiarism manual was developed using studies that incorporate not only teachers' perspectives but, more importantly, those of students.

The second finding highlights the importance of considering students as allies in defining academic integrity standards. Their perspective is valuable, as it reveals their awareness of ethical dilemmas related to the originality of scientific work. Through reflection, students come to understand that AI tools can act as adversaries to science when they are perceived as automatically generating texts with a seemingly scientific appearance. These deceptive outputs cannot replace the pursuit of truth (Boyle et al., 2018: 349) through well-established research protocols, such as data collection. At the same time, AI provides significant support for writing and aligns with other chatbots that enhance communication around research findings. Thus, when given the opportunity, students develop a pragmatic approach that concretely embodies the challenges of academic integrity. This demonstrates that, regardless of their level, they apply the principles of enactive ethics by learning to navigate academic work autonomously – neither conforming to absolute and authoritarian standards nor engaging in predatory practices of academic dishonesty. In comparison with recent studies on academic dishonesty in a Chinese context, which involved twenty-one participants (Wang et al., 2024: 297), this study demonstrates that academic seminars provide an effective framework for fostering a shared culture of academic integrity. Students' unconscious adoption of an enactive approach to integrity can be understood in light of Francisco Varela's interpretation of Mencius, a Confucian philosopher (fourth century BC) who emphasised innate moral dispositions and the spontaneous enactment of ethical behaviour. As Varela explains, Mencius believed that true virtue arises from an activated disposition, where moral judgement and action emerge naturally from a person's cultivated ethical awareness:

> For Mencius, only truly virtuous people attend to their nature sufficiently well to understand an event in terms of their experience and thus ensure that the

> appropriate extension follows easily. For the truly virtuous then, moral judgment that results in immediate and spontaneous moral action is not different from true description (Varela, 1999: 29).

Similarly, students engaging with academic integrity do not merely follow imposed rules but progressively embody ethical conduct as they reflect on the challenges posed by AI-generated content. Just as Mencius distinguishes between actions that are merely correct and those that are truly virtuous – requiring genuine motivation – students move beyond superficial compliance with academic integrity policies. Instead, they develop an internalised ethical framework that guides their autonomous navigation of research and writing. This spontaneous yet informed engagement with integrity (Premat, 2023: 12) aligns with enactive ethics, where ethical behaviour is not dictated but emerges dynamically from experience and participation in the academic community. It does not mean that students already solve the problems surrounding academic integrity and chatbots, but it would be possible to define a situated ethics from the experience of the forty-two participants to the seminar on academic integrity which could be: *Act in a way that preserves your autonomy in defining scientific problems and reflects on the rightful role that digital tools can play.* This maxim raises other dilemmas, notably a cognitive dilemma: if students are no longer accustomed to sufficiently working on their ability to construct a text, this may be detrimental to them in the long term, as noted by Skaar and Hammer in a Norwegian context (Skaar & Hammer, 2013: 31). These studies confirm the idea of an enactive ethics characterised by an approach that considers AI and academic integrity from the perspective of literacy. In reality, students must both understand how academic integrity can be realised and how digital tools function. Starting a course with discussions about chatbots, their mechanisms, and their influence puts into practice what Simondon advocated: a better culture of the technical objects that surround us (Simondon, 2017; Rieder, 2020; Gonçalves et al., 2024). The results illustrate the fact that universities may test diverse strategies to reinforce academic integrity at the age of AI devices, it presupposes an alliance between what Howlett called the 'thin learning' (technical-strategic learning) that focuses on improving policy effectiveness through better data, evaluation, and technical adjustments and 'thick learning' (political-experiential learning) that involves understanding broader political and social contexts, recognising patterns of failure, and adapting strategies to avoid blame (Howlett, 2012: 540). Working concretely on these issues in collaboration with academic writing centres (Karlsson, 2019: Hellman & Thorsten, 2021), students, and teachers/researchers would help strengthen both a culture of academic integrity and a digital literacy that goes beyond mere technical knowledge of how AI tools function. Broader discussions on digital competence have a risk of missing the necessity of empowering digital literacy among students and researchers (Hanell, 2018: 149). An enactive ethics must be able to challenge top-down agendas that impose non-scientific objectives on academia while neglecting how student-teacher interactions sustain living traditions of critical thinking in the age of automated thought systems (Gayá, 2017: 38; Coetzer & van Aardt, 2024).

Limitations of the Study

The study has several limitations. The small sample size of 100 survey responses and forty-two written reflections from students at Stockholm University limits its generalizability to broader populations. Additionally, reliance on self-reported data may introduce social desirability bias, as students might present ethically aligned responses rather than their actual behaviours. The study also faces a temporal limitation, as the self-study course on academic integrity was designed before the widespread use of AI chatbots like ChatGPT, making it less reflective of evolving AI interactions in academic settings. Nevertheless, the updates on AI in the last version of the handbook on academic integrity (Bendixen et al., 2024) show that academic integrity was questioned in the era of a massive use of AI tools.

Conclusion

Academic integrity is undergoing a profound transformation in the era of artificial intelligence, requiring universities to rethink traditional standards and adapt to new ethical challenges. This study highlights the need to move beyond punitive measures and instead foster a preventive culture that encourages students to engage with integrity as an evolving practice. The findings suggest that students do not merely conform to imposed rules but actively navigate the ethical complexities of academic work, particularly in relation to AI tools. Through reflective engagement, they develop a pragmatic understanding of integrity that aligns with the principles of enactive ethics, where ethical behaviour emerges from active participation rather than external enforcement. Stockholm University's approach illustrates a shift from rigid, top-down regulations to a more dynamic model of academic integrity, where students and educators collaboratively define ethical standards. In this regard, the study suggests that students unconsciously adopt an enactive approach by integrating critical thinking and ethical reasoning into their academic practices. Rather than viewing AI tools as threats, they assess their appropriate use, distinguishing between legitimate support for writing and practices that undermine originality. This nuanced perspective challenges binary conceptions of academic dishonesty and instead encourages a situated understanding of integrity that adapts to technological change. Ultimately, the findings advocate for a redefinition of academic integrity that acknowledges both the risks and opportunities of AI in higher education. By embracing a preventive, collaborative, and enactive approach, universities can ensure that integrity remains a core academic value while equipping students with the ethical awareness needed to navigate the digital age. The implementation of an enactive ethics has the advantage of facilitating the understanding of the scientific approach and the nature of academic integrity. The study proposes a new alliance (Prigogine & Stengers, 1979) between students, teachers, and researchers to foster both an inclusive and critical culture of academic integrity, as well as digital literacy skills that enable a deeper understanding of the implications of using AI tools.

Bibliography

Asplund, K. (2021). *Fuskarna: Om Macchiarini och andras svek mot vetenskapen.* Lidingö: Fri Tanke förlag.

Bauman, Z. (2000). *Liquid Modernity.* Cambridge: Polity Press.

Bendixen, C., Premat, C., Gunnerstad, A., & Farazouli, A. (2024). *Preventing plagiarism: Handbook for Stockholm University staff* (2nd ed.). Stockholm University. https://doi.org/10.17045/sthlmuni.27826344.v1

Bonn, N. A., & Pinxten, W. (2019). A Decade of Empirical Research on Research Integrity: What Have We (Not) Looked At? *Journal of*

Empirical Research on Human Research Ethics: An International Journal, 14(4), 338–352. https://www.jstor.org/stable/26973914

Boyle, R. J., Clements, J. A., Proudfoot, J. G. (2018). Measuring Deception: A Look at Antecedents to Deceptive Intent. *The American Journal of Psychology*, 131, 3, 347–367.

Bretag, T. (2016). *Handbook of Academic Integrity*. Singapore: Springer. https://doi.org/10.1007/978-981-287-098-8

Cerdà-Navarro, A., Touza, C., Morey-López, M., & Curiel, E. (2022). Academic integrity policies against assessment fraud in postgraduate studies: An analysis of the situation in Spanish universities. *Heliyon*, *8*(3), e09170. https://doi.org/10.1016/j.heliyon.2022.e09170

Cilesiz, S. (2011). A phenomenological approach to experiences with technology: current state, promise, and future directions for research. *Educational Technology Research and Development*, 59(4), 487–510. http://www.jstor.org/stable/41414955

Chankova, M. (2017). Dealing with Students' Plagiarism Pre-Emptively Through Teaching Proper Information Exploitation. *International Journal for the Scholarship of Teaching and Learning*, 11(2). https://doi.org/10.20429/ijsotl.2017.110204

Coetzer, Z., & van Aardt, P. (2024). Unsilencing the Student Voice: Detecting and Addressing ChatGPT-Generated Texts Presented as Student-Authored Texts at a University Writing Centre. *International Journal of Critical Diversity Studies*, 6(2), 151–179. https://www.jstor.org/stable/48811033

Davies, M. (2013). Critical thinking and the disciplines reconsidered. *Higher Education Research & Development*, 32 (4), 529–544. https://doi.org/10.1080/07294360.2012.697878

Duffy, W. (2020). Cowriting Agency. In: *Beyond Conversation: Collaboration and the Production of Writing* (pp. 71–98). University Press of Colorado. http://www.jstor.org/stable/j.ctv19fvx77.7

Farnese, M. L., Tramontano, C., Fida, R., & Paciello, M. (2011). Cheating behaviors in academic context: Does academic moral disengagement matter? *Procedia: Social and Behavioral Sciences*, 29, 356–365, https://doi.org/10.1016/j.sbspro.2011.11.250

Gayá, P., & Brydon-Miller, M. (2017). Carpe the academy: Dismantling higher education and prefiguring critical utopias through action research. *Futures*, 94, 34–44. https://doi.org/10.1016/j.futures.2016.10.005

Gonçalves, D. A., Caceffo, R., Valente, J. A., Bonacin, R., dos Reis, J. C., & Baranauskas, M. C. C. (2024). Enactive interaction in technology-based

learning environments: A systematic literature review. *Educational Technology & Society*, 27(2), 87–113. https://www.jstor.org/stable/48766165
Granitz, N., & Loewy, D. (2007). Applying Ethical Theories: Interpreting and Responding to Student Plagiarism. *Journal of Business Ethics*, 72(3), 293–306. http://www.jstor.org/stable/25075380
Güner, H., Er, E., Akçapinar, G., & Khalil, M. (2024). From chalkboards to AI-powered learning: Students' attitudes and perspectives on use of ChatGPT in educational settings. *Educational Technology & Society*, 27(2), 386–404. https://www.jstor.org/stable/48766180
Haghighi, S. R., Saqalaksari, M. P., & Johnson, S. N. (2023). Artificial Intelligence in Ecology: A Commentary on a Chatbot's Perspective. *Bulletin of the Ecological Society of America*, 104(4), 1–14. https://www.jstor.org/stable/48744438
Hanell, F. (2018). What is the 'problem' that digital competence in Swedish teacher education is meant to solve? *Nordic Journal of Digital Literacy*. Retrieved 11 March, 2025, from https://www.idunn.no/doi/full/10.18261/issn.1891-943x-2018-03-02
Hellman, J., & Thorsten, A. (2021). Plagiera eller referera vetenskapligt? En studie om vad studenter behöver lära sig för att bli bättre på referathantering. *Högre Utbildning*, 11 (1), 41–55, https://doi.org/10.23865/hu.v11.273
Howlett, M. (2012). The lessons of failure: learning and blame avoidance in public policy-making. *International Political Science Review*, 33(5), 539–555. http://www.jstor.org/stable/23353158
Kammarrätten i Göteborg. (2023, 14 July). *Disciplinnämnden vid Göteborgs universitet v. Martin Nordlund*, Case No. 4285-23.
Karlsson, T. S. (2019). När blir det plagiat? – En tvärsnittsstudie av studenters färdigheter och förmågor gällande fusk i form av plagiat. *Högre utbildning*, 9(2), 32–47. https://doi.org/10.23865/hu.v9.1645
Kaufhold, K., & Yencken, D. E. (2021). Academic writing centres in multilingual settings: Intermediary agents of higher education language policy? *Linguistics and Education*, 64, 100950. https://doi.org/10.1016/j.linged.2021.100950
Leib, M., Köbis, N., Rilke, R. M., Hagens, M., & Irlenbusch, B. (2023). Corrupted by Algorithms?: How AI-Generated and Human-Written Advice Shape (Dis)Honesty. IZA – Institute of Labor Economics. http://www.jstor.org/stable/resrep57648
Mahon, J. (2007). A definition of deceiving. *International Journal of Applied Philosophy*, 21, 181–194.

Norberg, J. (2023). Sweden during the Pandemic: Pariah or Paragon? Cato Institute. http://www.jstor.org/stable/resrep52975

Parry, H. (2001). Academic Dishonesty. In: Janice Newton, Jerry Ginsburg, Jan Rehner, Pat Rogers, Susan Sbrizzi, John Spencer (eds.), *Reflections on Teaching and Learning in Higher Education* (pp. 163–165). University of Toronto Press.

Petitot, J., Varela, F. J., Pachoud, B., Roy, J.-M. (eds.) (1999). *Naturalizing phenomenology. Issues in contemporary phenomenology and cognitive science.* Stanford: Stanford University Press.

Premat, C. (2019a). Hur kan man lära studenter att undvika plagiering? Stockholm University. Preprint. https://doi.org/10.17045/sthlmuni.7850993.v2

Premat, C. (2019b). Quick facts and plagiarism in higher education. Stockholm University. Educational resource. https://doi.org/10.17045/sthlmuni.9944180.v1

Premat, C. E. (2020). Wikipedia Practices, Quick Facts, and Plagiarism in Higher Education: In: E.-S. Y. Ezza & T. Drid (Eds.), *Advances in Higher Education and Professional Development* (pp. 199–221). IGI Global. https://doi.org/10.4018/978-1-7998-2265-3.ch009

Premat, C., Fagerlind, C., Collin, J. (2022a). Att presentera akademisk integritet. Stockholm University Design Patterns. Presentation. https://doi.org/10.17045/sthlmuni.19746493.v1

Premat, C. (2022b). 'Effektivt grupparbete – en pedagogisk ateljé för universitetslärare'. In: V. Alfredsson et al. (eds.), *Använd rummet, Högskolepedagogiska metoder för aktiva lärosalar* (pp. 267–273). Lund: Studentlitteratur.

Premat, C. (2023). Engaging upper secondary school pupils with integrity and source criticism. *International Journal for Educational Integrity.* https://doi.org/10.1007/s40979-023-00127-2

Premat, C. (2024). Le rôle de l'expertise dans la construction du consensus suédois face à la pandémie. In: Premat, C., et al. (eds.), Comparing the place of experts during the first waves of the COVID-19 pandemic. Stockholm: Stockholm University Press. DOI: https://doi.org/10.16993/bco.j.

Prigogine, I, & Stengers, I. (1979). *La Nouvelle Alliance. Métamorphose de la science.* Paris: Gallimard.

Puebla, C. A. C., & Davidson, J. (2012). Qualitative Computing and Qualitative Research: Addressing the Challenges of Technology and Globalization. Historical Social Research/Historische Sozialforschung, 37(4 (142)), 237–248. http://www.jstor.org/stable/41756484

Redman, B. K., & Merz, J. F. (2008). Scientific Misconduct: Do the Punishments Fit the Crime? *Science*, *321*(5890), 775–775. http://www.jstor.org/stable/20144537

Rieder, B. (2020). *Engines of Order. In Engines of Order: A Mechanology of Algorithmic Techniques* (pp. 25–50). Amsterdam University Press. https://doi.org/10.2307/j.ctv12sdvf1.5

Simondon, G. (2017). *On the mode of existence of technical objects.* Minneapolis: Univocal.

Skaar, H., & Hammer, H. (2013). Why students plagiarise from the internet: The views and practices in three Norwegian upper secondary classrooms. *International Journal for Educational Integrity*, 9(2). https://doi.org/10.21913/IJEI.v9i2.889

Stockholm University (2024, 15 October). *Guidelines on using AI-powered chatbots in education and research.* Retrieved from https://medarbetare.su.se/en/our-su/communicate-su/communication-support/guidelines-on-using-ai-powered-chatbots-in-education-and-research

Swedish Higher Education Authority (2024). Disciplinärenden 2023 vid universitet och högskolor, Rapport 2024:4. Universitetskanslersämbetet. https://www.uka.se/

Varela, F. (1999). *Ethical Know-How. Action, Wisdom, and Cognition*. Stanford: Stanford University Press.

Wang, Z., Yin, Z., Zheng, Y., Li, X., & Zhang, L. (2025). Will graduate students engage in unethical uses of GPT? An exploratory study to understand their perceptions. *Educational Technology & Society*, 28(1), 286–300. https://www.jstor.org/stable/48810720

Wikforss, Å. (2017). *Alternativa fakta om kunskapen och dess fiender.* Fri Tanke förlag.

AI-assisted University Training for Educators: Plagiarism, Ethics, and Research Skills Development

José Sánchez-Santamaría[1]*, María José Galván-Bovaira*[2]*,*
Natalia Hipólito-Ruiz[3] *and Carmen Carmona-Rodríguez*[4]

Deciding more wisely when, how, and for what purpose to use technology. Only then will we be in a position to determine what we can and cannot do with it
(MORDUCHOWICZ, 2023, P. 14)

ABSTRACT

No educational decision should be made without being evidence-informed. Particularly when the decision holds significant importance. Professional competences, such as research skills, play a crucial role in bridging scientific evidence within educational practice. This approach is driven by the need to provide rigorous and contextually appropriate responses to the complex challenges facing education today – responses that have a tangible and measurable impact. The importance of this competence is increasingly prominent in higher education, as it entails fostering critical thinking skills necessary to prepare professionals capable of analysing and enhancing educational processes. Despite multiple efforts – such as the Gorard pathway – the gap between educational theory and professional practice remains significant, often hindering informed decision-making in the field. In this context, the emergence of AI presents new opportunities not only to strengthen the development of research skills but also to enhance the planning, management, and dissemination of educational research.

This chapter examines the meaning and function of AI in developing research skills in Higher Education, considering its ethical implications. The starting point is to consider AI as essential tools for fostering research skills through an ethical and critical approach, aimed at preparing professionals who ground their practice in available scientific evidence. It also analyses how current skill frameworks, such as the ResearchComp of the

[1] GRIOCE. University of Castilla-La Mancha (RoR: 05r78ng1), Spain (https://orcid.org/0000-0002-5179-4555)

[2] GRIOCE. University of Castilla-La Mancha (RoR: 05r78ng1), Spain (https://orcid.org/0000-0001-7442-6029)

[3] University of Castilla-La Mancha (RoR: 05r78ng1), Spain (https://orcid.org/0000-0002-9255-9201) mailto: natalia.hipolito@uclm.es

[4] University of Valencia (RoR: 043nxc105), Spain (https://orcid.org/0000-0002-9276-0984)

European Commission (2023), can serve as a reference for integrating AI-driven research skill development into university education, with a strong focus on academic integrity and professional ethics. Finally, It further addresses plagiarism as a major pedagogical and ethical challenge in the training of educators when developing AI-supported research skills.

Keywords: research skills, generative artificial intelligence, higher education, evidence-informed practice, academic integrity

Introduction

All professional practice should be grounded in evidence, and such evidence must, in turn, meet specific quality standards that guide sound decision-making (Gorard, 2020). This need becomes even more pressing in today's context of digital transformation, where challenges are increasingly dynamic and complex, demanding responses that are as precise, adaptive, and coherent as possible (Ciraso-Calí et al., 2022). Therefore, the goal is for interventions to generate a real and verifiable impact on improving the educational environment. Scoping reviews (Vanlommel & van den Boom-Muilenburg, 2024) indicate that the link between theory – understood as an evidence base – and professional practice remains weak in the field of education. A significant gap persists, affecting both the quality and the impact of educational interventions. This raises a crucial question: What scientific basis truly supports decision-making in educational practice? In many cases, the answer is concerning – very little, if any at all. This highlights the urgent need to bridge these gaps, which currently hinder meaningful and sustained improvements in education, and to strengthen initial educator training with a focus on soft skills.

One of the most important sets of skills for supporting evidence-informed professional practice is research skills. Their role is essential in strengthening educators' ability to respond to the challenges they face in their professional environments. Providing education professionals with the skills to investigate, analyse, and make evidence-based decisions helps foster a more equitable and higher-quality education. This not only raises the level of quality and rigour in educational practices and interventions, but also supports professional growth by empowering educators to generate explanatory, interpretive, and critical knowledge about the educational realities they work in (Sánchez-Santamaría et al., 2024). In this sense, initial training in research skills has a positive impact on each educator's professional performance and helps foster critical and participatory citizenship by promoting the use of scientific knowledge to solve educational problems (Brown & Ion, 2022).

Artificial intelligence (AI) is increasingly becoming a key support tool in initial educator training, particularly in the development of research skills. However, its integration into educational practice remains limited (Sánchez-Santamaría et al., 2025), largely due to ongoing resistance and uncertainty surrounding its use. Despite these barriers, AI demonstrates significant potential across all phases and tasks within the educational research process: from problem definition and question formulation to mapping and reviewing scientific literature, refining research designs, collecting and analysing large datasets, comparing with qualitative data, and supporting the dissemination and communication of research findings (Wilder & Calderone, 2025). This wide range of applications offers new opportunities to address persistent shortcomings in initial training and to foster innovative forms of learning aimed at strengthening the research skills of future educators. Nevertheless, the adoption of AI is not without risk. Ethical challenges and the psychopedagogical implications for skills-based learning must be critically examined. In this context, the integration of AI into skill development must be grounded in a strong ethical framework, making it essential to ensure that its use genuinely enhances professional practice in education in the face of ongoing digital transformation (Sánchez-Santamaría & Olmedo, 2023). Such an approach requires the cultivation of critical and creative thinking, alongside the promotion of autonomy and ethical responsibility. This is vital in addressing potential dependencies or biases that could compromise the quality of learning (Yousaf, 2025) and, by extension, diminish the capacity of research skills to effectively inform and improve educational practice.

These considerations lead to two fundamental questions. First, how should research skills be conceptualised and developed in initial educator training, particularly in light of new skills-based frameworks? Second, what are the opportunities and limitations – ethical, pedagogical, and related to academic integrity – of integrating AI as a didactic tool in the development of these skills? And what role do we, as human agents, play in the research process amidst the growing presence of AI?

This chapter examines the meaning and role of AI in the development of research skills in higher education, with particular attention to its ethical implications and the challenges posed by plagiarism. It begins by framing AI as a fundamental tool for fostering these skills through an ethical and critical approach, with the aim of preparing professionals in the field of education whose teaching practice is grounded in scientific evidence. It also analyses how current skills frameworks, such as ResearchComp (European Commission, 2023), can serve as a guide for integrating AI-supported research skills into university education, with a special focus on academic integrity and professional ethics. Furthermore, it addresses plagiarism as one of the most pressing pedagogical and ethical challenges in the process of training educators to develop research skills using AI tools.

Working Hypotheses, Research Questions, and Objectives

This study analyses the pedagogical and ethical implications of training university-level educators in research skills with the support of AI. It explores the relationship between ResearchComp (European Commission, 2023) and the opportunities and limitations presented by generative AI. Table 17 presents the working hypotheses, as well as the research questions and objectives that guide the analysis and proposed uses of AI in the development of research skills within initial educator training (Table 17).

Method

This study employs a descriptive-exploratory methodology grounded in a reflective analytical approach, following the framework proposed by Creswell and Creswell (2017). Its aim is to examine emerging educational phenomena shaped by ongoing processes of digital transformation – particularly those involving AI. Rather than seeking to produce generalisations, the objective is to build a comprehensive frame of reference that clarifies the meaning, function, and implications of AI within the context of initial educator training in research skills. The increasing integration of AI tools into university education – often employed unconsciously and without adequate safeguards, as has previously been noted – raises significant ethical and pedagogical challenges that demand careful attention.

Table 17: Working hypotheses, research questions, and objectives

Working hypotheses	Research questions	Objectives
Initial educator training incorporates the development of research skills in its curricula, either as part of one or more methodology-related courses, or through the integration of some of its components into various subjects not necessarily focused on research	How are research skills integrated into the curricula of initial educator training? How are their purpose and role understood within teacher education?	To analyse the presence of research skills in the curricula of educator training programmes, and to identify their role and intended purpose
A wide range of AI tools can be used throughout all phases and tasks of the research process, provided their use is guided by a critical perspective that makes both their potential and limitations visible	Which AI tools support the various stages of the research process, and is it possible to ensure safe and conscious use in educator training?	To identify AI tools applicable to educational research and to establish possibilities for critical use in university contexts, specifically in initial educator training
The ResearchComp framework offers a coherent and transferable foundation that can effectively guide initial educator training in research skills	To what extent can the ResearchComp framework serve as a guide for the design and evaluation of training programmes in research skills?	To analyse the potential of the ResearchComp framework as a reference for guiding and improving research skills development in future educators
Ethical and pedagogical use of AI can enhance the development of research skills in initial educator training by providing meaningful support for a range of learning and application needs related to this soft skill	How does the ethical and pedagogical use of AI contribute to the development of research skills in initial educator training?	To propose ethical and pedagogically sound approaches for integrating AI into the development of research skills in initial teacher education, guided by the ResearchComp framework

It adopts a structured and reflective strategy, combining documentary and conceptual analysis with empirical insights from two recent studies on AI, plagiarism, and research skills development in university contexts (Ref.: SBPLY/23/180225/000216 and Code: OTR0424). The analysis draws on multiple sources: curriculum plans, academic publications on the educational uses of AI, the European ResearchComp framework (European Commission, 2023), and a critical review of AI tools, grounded in both prior research and the authors' own experimentation and practical experience. Using this approach, the chapter analyses the potential and limitations of these tools, along with their pedagogical and ethical implications for strengthening research skills through the use of AI.

This study identifies at least three limitations: (i) the literature review was not conducted through a systematic process but rather through a narrative approach, highlighting arguments and evidence related to the proposed hypotheses; (ii) the study combines evidence with reflective and practical proposals, which means it does not provide concrete evidence of the impact of these proposals; and (iii) its aim is not to produce generalisable results but to establish the context and clarify the meaning and role of AI in the development of research skills within initial educator training, while addressing ethical considerations and issues related to plagiarism

Results

Research Skills in Initial Educator Training

In the current educational context, the development of research skills has become a fundamental pillar in the training of education professionals. This includes not only future teachers but also other key actors such as social educators, pedagogues, and academic staff across various educational domains. The increasing emphasis on evidence-informed practice demands that these professionals not only master pedagogical techniques but also acquire the capacity to interpret, produce, and apply scientific knowledge in their educational environments (Böttcher-Oschmann et al., 2021). The integration of research skills into initial training programmes enhances educational decision-making and contributes significantly to the professionalisation of education. Nevertheless, previous studies have highlighted persistent challenges in this area, particularly the difficulty many education students face in establishing a robust link between theoretical knowledge and practical application. This gap undermines the effective use of research principles in authentic educational contexts (Salmento et al., 2021).

One of the main challenges faced by universities in developing research skills lies in the lack of alignment and coherence within teacher education programmes, which creates inequalities in both access to and development of key skills. Several studies have identified that communication skills and the ability to conduct literature reviews are among the least developed areas in education curricula (Duche-Pérez et al., 2024; Mercer-Mapstone & Matthews, 2017). This gap negatively affects future educators' ability to ground their practice in empirical evidence (Ciraso-Calí et al., 2022). Many students struggle to grasp key research concepts such as theory, methodological design, and the interpretation of results (Salmento et al., 2021). Recent findings by Sánchez-Santamaría et al. (2025) show that while training programmes for educators include skills and abilities related to research, these are typically framed in terms of analytical, methodological, and technological capacities. A chi-square test ($\chi^2 = 24.91$, $df = 24$, $p = 0.411$) revealed no statistically significant differences in the distribution of key terms related to research skills across the universities analysed. Moreover, 85% of the study plans reviewed – from a total of forty Spanish universities – explicitly recognise the importance of developing research skills. However, their implementation is limited and fragmented in terms of content and approach. The most frequently emphasised elements include designing, implementing, and evaluating research projects, conducting critical data analysis, and producing scientific reports. These are often accompanied by the inclusion of different research methodologies – mainly quantitative and qualitative, and, to a lesser extent, mixed methods. The use of digital tools, particularly statistical software, is reported in 60% of institutions, while ethical considerations in research appear in 40%. Among the most prominent skills are cognitive abilities, whereas areas such as self-management, innovation, and publication of results receive comparatively less attention in the curricula.

Teaching educational research has emphasised the importance of using active methodologies and blended learning environments to foster the development of research skills in teacher education (Sánchez-Santamaría &

Morales Calvo, 2014). These approaches encourage reflection on teaching practice and the generation of knowledge based on lived experience. In this context, research-learning projects (RLPs) have been shown to provide a suitable framework for students to develop key abilities such as formulating research questions, selecting appropriate methods, collecting and analysing data, and communicating and disseminating findings (Ciraso-Calí et al., 2022). Practice-based approaches such as reflective practice and action research have proven to be effective strategies for preparing educators with strong research skills. These methods promote the construction of knowledge from practice, enabling educators to identify problems in their own contexts, design interventions, gather data, and evaluate the impact of their actions (Ciraso-Calí et al., 2022). However, for these methodologies to be truly effective, it is essential to have institutional infrastructure that supports educational research and provides opportunities for teachers to engage in learning and research communities (Sabariego et al., 2020).

The integration of AI tools undoubtedly offers a promising opportunity to enhance research training, as long as it takes into account the contextual conditions, as well as the meaning and purpose of research skills within initial educator preparation (Sánchez-Santamaría et al., 2024). Nonetheless, important challenges remain in this area – challenges that may be further intensified by the use of AI in the absence of sound ethical and pedagogical guidance.

The European Framework for Researchers: ResearchComp

The advancement of competence-based higher education has gone hand in hand with the development of skills reference frameworks, one of which is ResearchComp. Developed by the European Commission, ResearchComp (2023) is a reference tool aligned with the European classification of skills, competences, and occupations (ESCO). The framework for research skills is structured around seven core areas, which are further divided into thirty-eight specific skills (see Figure 15). For each skill, the framework defines expected learning outcomes across four performance levels, ranging from foundational to expert. In addition, it provides example activities and exercises designed to support the development of each skill.

Figure 15: The European Competence Framework for Researchers
Note: Image generated with GAI support, https://chatgpt.com/c/67e682bc-8c3c-8010-b1c8-f95e3a44249b Source: http://bit.ly/43ArSSZ

Thus, each of the thirty-eight specific skills included in the ResearchComp framework is clearly defined and structured in the form of a rubric. One example is the skill area 'cognitive abilities' and the specific skill 'abstract thinking' (Table 18).

Table 18: Example of abstract thinking

Definition: Demonstrate the ability to use concepts in order to make and understand generalisations, and relate or connect them to other items, events, or experiences

Foundational	Intermediate	Advanced	Expert
Assimilates concepts from own discipline Establishes relationships with own knowledge	Elaborates concepts independently Identifies and understands complex trends and patterns	Uses with confidence concepts from other disciplines Provides insights beyond the obvious	Connects unrelated ideas and concepts to elaborate theories Contributes outstanding insights pushing the frontiers of knowledge

Source: http://bit.ly/43ArSSZ

As shown, the framework provides a clear and detailed structure for acquiring and developing specific research skills, offering precise definitions for each. It also outlines performance indicators across various levels, helping to assess both theoretical understanding and practical application. This contributes to more effective learning processes. As the next section will demonstrate, the framework opens up numerous possibilities for promoting meaningful and coherent professional development in research skills, particularly when supported by AI.

The inclusion of this framework in the initial training of future education professionals is essential (Sánchez-Santamaría et al., 2024). It promotes a consistent approach to developing this transversal skill within the context of subject content and practical coursework, ensuring that activities are aligned with intended learning outcomes. Rather than adding a separate course dedicated to research skills, the objective is to embed them throughout the academic curriculum. This approach allows educators to incorporate research-related components naturally and coherently when planning lessons and designing assessments. Such an approach makes it easier for research skills to be developed in a continuous and context-sensitive way across different areas of study. It also enhances students' ability to understand and apply their learning. With regular exposure to research-oriented tasks in varied contexts, students become better equipped to apply knowledge in real and complex situations.

Educators can also bring research skills into their own teaching practice. This enriches their day-to-day work and supports innovation and improvement in education, grounded in evidence. Drawing on research-based methods and strategies, they can refine and adapt their pedagogical practices to meet evolving educational needs – benefiting not only themselves but also the wider educational community. Therefore, incorporating research skills into the academic programme is not an added burden, but rather an essential tool for the professional development of both students and educators, promoting high-quality, evidence-based education. Moreover, the framework also paves the way for the integration of AI into educational contexts. By clearly outlining where and how AI can be used, new methodologies and tools can be explored to enhance the teaching and learning process, offering innovative solutions adapted to the current needs of education.

Proposals of AI-driven Research Skills in University Training

The development of research skills in education can be supported by the potential offered by AI tools (European Research Council, 2023), as long as both students and researchers ensure their competent and ethical use. In this regard, UNESCO (2023) encouraged countries and institutions to develop policies related to AI, while universities around the world began implementing plans to incorporate AI tools into research practices (Cedeño-Tapia, 2023).

As noted earlier, and based on current evidence, Solís (2024) highlights several advantages in his study on the impact of AI on postgraduate students' research skills. According to his findings, AI can support learners in identifying and formulating clear, relevant research questions; simplifying the search for information and its critical and reliable analysis; analysing large datasets to extract meaningful insights; and communicating results clearly and precisely. Similarly, studies on the use of AI in research training report a positive impact on doctoral students' skill development.

In particular, the experimental group showed significant improvements in the substantive, design-related, procedural, optional, and communication dimensions (Oliinyk et al., 2024). Moreover, AI allows for personalised learning and task automation, although institutional policies and safeguards are required to prevent unethical use (Pokotylo & Sylkina, 2023). To address these challenges, a range of pedagogical strategies has been proposed to strengthen research skills within teacher education programmes. These include project-based learning, collaborative approaches, the use of digital technologies for data collection and analysis, and connections with practical experiences in real educational settings (Böttcher-Oschmann et al., 2021).

For all these reasons, it is essential to examine both the potential and limitations of developing research skills in initial educator training through the use of AI tools. The following section presents, first, a selection of AI tools designed to support research processes, and second, a set of proposals for using AI across the seven dimensions of the ResearchComp framework (European Commission, 2023).

AI Tools for Research Training in Education

The possibilities offered by AI tools are wide-ranging and relate to key aspects such as access to, management of, and the production of scientific knowledge. A broad array of tools exists in this domain, and what we aim to highlight is that these resources can make a significant contribution to addressing specific needs in research contexts (Sánchez-Santamaría & Olmedo, 2023). However, caution is needed. These tools are intended to support – not replace – ethical decision-making (Ortega-Bolaños et al., 2024), and any use of AI in research tasks requires human oversight.

The following section presents a representative selection of AI tools, organised into three main areas: (i) scientific literature review and analysis; (ii) research design and data analysis; and (iii) scientific communication, dissemination, and collaboration. Each table provides a brief description of the tool's function, its potential applications, identified limitations, and the expected impact on the development of research skills.

Table 19 shows a selection of AI tools that can support the review and analysis phase of scientific literature, particularly in tasks such as formulating research questions, conducting scoping reviews, and performing systematic reviews. AI-based tools such as ChatGPT, Scholarcy, and Research Rabbit provide different forms of support during this phase, each with its own specific features. For instance, ChatGPT is a language-based AI model that can help generate ideas, synthesise information, or rephrase research questions. These tools can significantly enhance the processes of searching, selecting, and evaluating bibliographic sources.

Table 19: Selection of AI tools for literature review and formulating research questions

AI/GAI tool	Potential uses	Expected impact	Limitations: ethics, plagiarism, and equity
Chatbots (e.g. ChatGPT, Mistral), AI search (e.g. Perplexity, DeepSeek), or AI assistants (e.g. Copilot)	Natural language processing Speeds up the analysis of scientific articles	Supports literature review and analysis Formulating research questions	Limited understanding of highly technical or domain-specific contexts Source verification required; risk of ghost authorship Paid version/free version
ChatGPT PDF, Humata, Scholarcy, Scite, Consensus, SciSpace, Semantic Scholar	Analysis of scientific articles, citations, and source relationships Streamlines the review process	Increases efficiency	Difficulty interpreting complex visuals or non-standard formats Risk of automatic extraction without deep reading; inaccurate citation Paid version/free version
Rayyan, Scite, Inciteful, Consensus	Support for systematic reviews Facilitates systematic review processes	Enhances quality and speed	Potential inaccuracies in results Algorithmic bias Paid version/free version

(Continued)

Table 19: *(Continued)*

AI/GAI tool	Potential uses	Expected impact	Limitations: ethics, plagiarism, and equity
Research Rabbit	Exploration of authorship and collaboration networks Identifies collaboration patterns	Helps visualise and understand research networks	Accuracy depends on data availability Risk of overinterpretation Paid version/free version
Trinka	Documentation and citation organisation Supports academic writing	Improves information management and scientific communication	Limited features in free versions Risk of automated content being accepted uncritically Paid version/free version
DeepL, Copilot	AI-powered automatic translation Accelerates translation of scientific documents	Improves accessibility and research dissemination	Difficulty with highly technical terminology Risk of presenting translated work as original Paid version/free version
Extensions: Monica, Sider,	Web-based information processing Enhances online workflow for specific tasks	Supports online research management	Browser compatibility issues Risk of idea appropriation without attribution Paid version/free version

Another set of AI tools can make a significant contribution to the design and analysis of both qualitative and quantitative data. This range of resources supports diverse tasks such as scenario simulation, image generation, statistical analysis – with the inherent limitations of language-only AI models – and discourse analysis. In addition, several tools have been specifically developed to assist in these processes and already incorporate AI functionalities, such as SPSS, Excel, or ATLAS.ti. Together, these applications expand the possibilities for hypothesis exploration, data visualisation, and the automation of analytical procedures (Table 20).

Table 20: A selection of AI tools for methodological design and data analysis

AI/GAI tool	Potential uses	Expected impact	Limitations: ethics, plagiarism, and equity
Chatbots (e.g. ChatGPT, Mistral), AI search (e.g. Perplexity, DeepSeek), or AI assistants (e.g. Copilot)	Compare, simulate, or revise research questions, objectives, or hypotheses; support research design, data analysis, and image generation Facilitates the review and refinement of key research elements	Improves planning and research design processes	May generate content that reflects others' work without proper attribution; lacks source verification Risk of misattributed content; unverified sources Paid version/free version
Tableau, Data Analyst GPT	Data visualisation and analysis	Enhances data communication	Complex and time-consuming to master May display fictitious or misinterpreted data
HeyGen, Sora, DALL·E	Automated generation of images and text-to-image outputs	Enables fast, high-quality visual production	Image quality and relevance may not always meet expectations Potential bias in generated content; copyright issues Paid version
ATLAS.ti, SPSS, Excel, IBM Watson	Automated functions for data analysis and simulations	Increases efficiency and reduces errors	Often requires paid access; steep learning curve Risk of methodological errors or data manipulation Paid version

AI tools designed to support scientific communication and dissemination, as well as the strengthening of collaboration networks, make use of the potential of both social and academic platforms to develop AI-driven functionalities. Their value lies in their ability to increase the visibility of research outcomes, strengthen researchers' digital identities, and foster exchange and collaboration within the scientific community. Notable examples include tools such as AMiner and Dimensions AI, which – despite their different purposes – make a significant contribution to improving scientific communication processes, promoting transparency, and advancing the principles of open science (Table 21).

Table 21: A selection of AI tools for dissemination and communication and collaboration

AI/GAI tool	Potential uses	Expected impact	Limitations: ethics, plagiarism, and equity
AI-based functions in Meta, Google Scholar, Web of Science, Scopus	Dissemination and communication of research findings Increased visibility and reach	Sharing results and building connections within the scientific community	Challenges in filtering and validating information Free version Author verification concerns Paid version/free version
Dimensions	Digital identity and open data sharing Contributes to open science	Fosters collaboration and transparency	Requires awareness and acceptance by the scientific community for widespread adoption Security and privacy risks; potential for bias and selection errors Paid version/free version
AMiner	Extraction of relevant information about researchers, institutions, and publications Improves efficiency in locating research-related information	Trend analysis, identification of collaborations, and assessment of academic influence	Issues related to data accuracy, updates, and quality Risk of selection bias Paid version

Applications of AI Tools Under ResearchComp

The development of the ResearchComp framework (European Commission, 2023), together with the increasing potential of AI as a valuable resource for supporting the development of research skills, represents a significant opportunity within the field of initial educator training. These opportunities, presented below, are intended as illustrative rather than exhaustive examples of how the European reference framework can inform the design of new curricula while also promoting the responsible incorporation of AI tools into educational and academic practice.

Tables 22 and 23 outline possible applications of AI tools aligned with the seven key dimensions of the ResearchComp framework (European Commission, 2023) – from cognitive abilities to managing research tools. Each dimension includes concrete examples of AI-supported resources, along with associated ethical dilemmas or risks such as ghost authorship, manipulation of research results, or the inappropriate use of automated systems. This comprehensive perspective highlights the importance of integrating AI technologies in educator preparation through a critical and ethically informed lens. Upholding the integrity, transparency, and quality of research processes in education remains a fundamental priority.

Table 22: AI tools and their relation to ResearchComp (I)

Dimension	Aligned university skills	Definition
Cognitive abilities	Critical thinking, problem-solving, creativity, analytical skills	Mental capacities used to process, analyse, generate, and connect complex ideas that enable innovative research
Working with others	Teamwork, communication, leadership, interpersonal skills	Collaborative and interpersonal skills that support constructive interaction and inclusive environments in research contexts
Self-management	Autonomy, responsibility, time management, adaptability	Skills related to self-directed learning, work-life balance, and proactive adaptation to challenges

Source: Based on European Commission (2023)

Practical Experiences of the Use of AI in ResearchComp (I)

- Research concepts and questions. An innovative way to engage students with key concepts in research competence involves integrating GAI as a support tool in the learning process. For instance, when addressing the concept of *educational research* or another relevant term, the process begins with definitions drawn from current scholarly literature. From there, students are encouraged to use GAI tools to explore various formulations or applications of the chosen concept. What makes this approach particularly valuable is that it goes beyond simply repeating definitions: It fosters comparison and discussion of their similarities, differences, and potential limitations. This not only activates critical thinking but also stimulates enriching conversations about how knowledge is constructed in the field of education. In our experience, this approach aligns well with the learning goals we pursue in the training of future educators. By reflecting on the uses of GAI in real teaching contexts, students develop a deeper and more contextualised understanding of the concept of research.
- Research questions and references. One of the most important aspects of educational research is knowing how to ask questions and how to base them on existing literature. Therefore, one of the experiences developed in the framework of the educational innovation group ProSkillsForLife was to learn how to formulate questions and search for references with the support of AI. This activity addresses the three dimensions of ResearchComp (I) and was focused on the use of screens and their impact on student learning in primary and secondary education. It uses two AI tools: ChatGPT dimensions to locate relevant articles and Perplexity to formulate questions. The education students work in groups and then share their proposals with the class. The process has to be evidenced and a reflective record is made of the ethical implications of the work carried out. All this makes it possible to work on the three competences involved in ResearchComp (I): cognitive abilities, working with others, and self-management.
- 'Stakebot'. Another innovative teaching proposal for developing students' research competence involves creating a chatbot based on the contributions of influential authors, such as Robert Stake. This

'Stakebot' would serve as an interactive resource specifically designed to support learning in the ResearchComp (I) and (II) courses. There is even the possibility of contacting the author or his foundation to request permission, using his key works on case study research as a foundation. The idea is for the 'Stakebot' to function as a conversational simulator of Stake himself, enabling students to interact with a virtual version of this theoretical reference. Through this interaction, students are expected to practice essential skills: formulating questions, defining research objects, and receiving guidance on essential literature, particularly related to case study methodology. What makes this tool especially valuable is not only its innovative nature, but also the opportunity it offers for real-time feedback as students test out decisions and approaches related to research content. This dynamic can transform the learning process into a more personalised, critical, and engaging experience. The ethical issue is not compromised, as the activity is based on the author's publications while respecting copyright.

Table 23: AI tools and their relation to ResearchComp (II)

Dimension	Aligned university skills	Definition
Making an impact	Communication, social engagement, innovation, digital literacy	Ability to communicate and apply research beyond academia, promoting societal, educational, and economic value
Managing research	Project management, strategic planning, evaluation, negotiation	Skills for leading and managing research processes strategically, from funding applications to dissemination
Doing research	Scientific reasoning, methodological skills, academic writing, ethics	Practical and theoretical engagement in the production of original scientific knowledge in accordance with ethical standards
Managing research tools	Digital skills, data management, legal awareness, technical proficiency	Capacity to manage digital and technical tools that ensure high-quality, transparent, and open research

Source: Based on European Commission (2023)

Practical Experiences of the Use of AI in ResearchComp (II)

To support the development of dimensions associated with ResearchComp (II), several learning proposals and activities can be implemented:

- Research results. This can be addressed in class through methodologies such as challenge-based learning or service learning, which connect academic learning with real-world contexts. Activities can also focus on communicating a project, process, or research outcome. For example, students may be asked to create an infographic or a short text generated with AI, combining tools like ChatGPT or Copilot to draft, refine, and discuss their ideas. Jasper AI is also useful for producing accessible or easy-to-read content. Additionally, AI-powered presentation tools such as Canva AI or Mistral can support the design of visual materials.
- Research planning. Students plan and design a research project proposal by defining the topic, objectives, methodology, roles, expected outcomes, and timeline. To support this process, they can use tools like ChatGPT, Writefull, or Trinka AI to draft key sections and organise tasks. The proposal is presented in the format of a research call, including a visual timeline. This activity promotes the development of scientific reasoning, academic writing, and research ethics, and is evaluated based on internal coherence, feasibility, appropriate integration of AI, and ethical justification for its use.
- Case study. Students explore the case study approach based on the contributions of Robert Stake, using the 'Stakebot' as a tool. In this activity, they formulate questions and reflect on the design of a qualitative case study. The outcome includes a structured methodological design and an ethical statement regarding the use of generative AI.
- Cleaning and analysing data. Students are provided with a disorganised dataset, without knowing whether it is real or synthetic, and are informed that it is part of a research study. They may use Excel with GAI functions, GitHub Copilot, or data-analysis-oriented chatbots – though these tools have limitations. Generally, chatbots are more effective when used to clarify concepts, analyses, or interpretations. The objective is for students to carry out a technical and critical analysis of the results, assessing the capabilities and limitations of the GAI tool used, as well as its potential support in data interpretation.

Ethical and Plagiarism Implications of the Use of AI in Research Skills Training

The unprecedented ease with which AI-generated written, visual, or oral content can now be presented as original work significantly increases the risk of dishonest practices. At the same time, it can undermine creativity as a fundamental means of generating diverse and innovative solutions to new challenges. And, as previously shown, the development of AI tools – including large language models (LLMs) and chatbots – is significantly transforming research processes related to information search, production, and communication in higher education. These tools offer numerous opportunities to enrich the teaching and learning of research skills, but they also pose clear risks related to academic misconduct (Moya & Eaton, 2023). In this context, new forms of plagiarism have emerged, complicating detection and demanding deeper study to understand their specific manifestations and underlying causes. Chan (2023) introduced the concept of 'AI-giarism', referring to AI-mediated plagiarism characterised by the production of texts, images, or information synthesis without citing original sources or without disclosing the intervention of AI itself – raising serious ethical concerns.

In this scenario, the initial training of educators in research skills, when supported by AI, must address at least two essential aspects. First, it is necessary to provide learning experiences that promote responsible and ethical use of AI. Second, it is crucial to offer meaningful training opportunities that enable future educators to develop critical and creative capacities to understand the limitations of AI and its implications for maintaining academic integrity. Developing research skills without simultaneously fostering ethical competence is not only a pedagogical error but also a significant risk, as it reduces the ability to recognise and prevent academic dishonesty. Dishonest practices, moreover, tend to be reproduced and, in this case, could even become normalised and integrated into future professional practice.

Among the most common forms of academic dishonesty associated with AI use in research skills training (an adaptation from Alcaide-González et al., 2019) are:

- Literal copying. Copying and pasting content, even when cited, without reworking it or conducting critical analysis. It is common for students to use chatbots to generate entire paragraphs and insert them into academic work without transformation or personal reflection. This can be prevented by reformulating content, integrating it into original contributions, and adding critical analysis based on personal understanding.

- Honorary authorship. Signing a work without having genuinely contributed to its creation. This occurs, for example, when an AI-generated article is presented without the author's active involvement. To avoid this, it is essential to participate in content creation and explicitly acknowledge any AI support.
- Content plagiarism. Copying significant portions of AI-generated content without citing its origin, as might occur when using AI to draft a methodology section based on previous studies. Preventing this behaviour requires proper citation and a well-founded personal interpretation.
- Ghost authorship. Presenting a project or article generated entirely by AI as one's own. For instance, submitting a report created by AI without acknowledging its contribution, knowing that AI cannot be considered an author due to the absence of legal responsibility. This can be avoided by clearly declaring AI involvement and ensuring that human input is not entirely replaced, especially in significant reports or publications.
- Simulated data. Intentionally inventing or altering data. Some AI tools allow the generation of false data or the manipulation of results, for example, to adjust sample responses to a normal distribution or to create results from non-existent surveys. This practice can be prevented by using appropriate statistical methods and ensuring the collection of real, verifiable data supported by solid evidence.
- Salami slicing. Fragmenting a larger work into smaller parts presented as independent studies, without genuine original contributions in each. AI can facilitate this by easily breaking down complex texts. This can be avoided by using AI to assess whether each part provides distinct and novel elements that justify separate publication.
- Citation errors. AI may produce 'hallucinations', meaning invented or incorrect citations. This technical limitation is due to AI's lack of

reasoning or interpretation, relying instead on instructions and potentially incomplete or outdated sources. Preventing these errors requires human supervision, the use of specialised tools like reference managers or verified academic databases, and careful validation of all citations.

Practical Experiences with AI Use from an Ethical Perspective

When designing activities that integrate GAI into the development of research competence from ResearchComp, it is essential to address four key objectives: identify, understand, reflect, and prevent the inappropriate use of these digital tools. Below are six proposals with concrete pedagogical guidelines for implementation in the classroom:

- Case analysis of inappropriate or unethical GAI use.
  Students work in small groups to analyse real or simulated cases involving the misuse of GAI in educational research (e.g. using AI-generated texts without citation, including false data, etc.). They receive brief case descriptions and must determine what went wrong, why, and how it could have been avoided. Ethical reasoning and group discussion are encouraged, fostering critical debate. This activity strengthens the ethical dimension of research competence.
- Create, compare, and learn: critical rewriting of AI-generated texts.
  Students use a GAI tool to generate a short text on a topic related to educational research. They then rewrite it, integrating real academic sources and adding their own analysis. The activity can be organised as a workshop in three steps: generating the initial text with AI, researching and analysing academic sources, and rewriting the content critically. Finally, both versions are compared and discussed in terms of depth, academic rigour, and reliability. This allows students to contrast automatic production with informed reflection.
- Comparative analysis: identifying authorship. Two texts on the same topic are presented – one entirely generated by GAI and the other written by a human. Students must identify which is which and justify their reasoning.
  Working in groups, they apply criteria such as argumentative coherence, academic style, use of sources, and conceptual depth. Once they reach a

conclusion, each group shares their analysis with the class. This activity promotes critical reading and analytical thinking.

- Mapping ethical risks of AI in research. Students create conceptual maps to represent potential ethical risks associated with the use of GAI in research. The activity begins with a guided brainstorming session on common risks (e.g. bias, privacy, lack of transparency). Then, in groups, students build conceptual maps connecting these risks to real-world examples and proposing preventive strategies. This strengthens ethical awareness and contextual analytical skills.
- False citations and source evaluation. The phenomenon of hallucinations in GAI – fabricated or unreliable references – is addressed. Students request references from a GAI tool on a research topic and then verify the accuracy, relevance, and reliability of the sources provided.

  As part of the analysis, the concept of predatory journals is introduced, along with validation strategies. The activity can conclude with the creation of a shared rubric for evaluating academic sources.
- Quantitative or qualitative analysis with GAI. The use of AI-powered tools for qualitative data analysis is explored, focusing on their usefulness and risks when students lack sufficient methodological training. A specific tool (e.g. a platform that categorises open-ended responses) is introduced. Students analyse a simple dataset manually and then with GAI, comparing the outcomes. The session concludes with a discussion on the limitations, biases, and ethical responsibilities involved in using technology for qualitative research.

It is essential to remember that neither authorship nor responsibility for dishonest practices can be attributed to AI. These tools are not designed to produce fraud nor do they include functions aimed at promoting dishonesty. However, irresponsible use can facilitate such practices, severely limiting the quality and impact of research skills development. Understanding, analysing, and reflecting on these traditional forms of plagiarism – now adapted through AI – is key to prevention and to ensuring that research skills training results in ethical, high-quality learning, aimed at educational improvement and transformation.

Conclusions

The rise of artificial intelligence in education brings with it a persistent concern: Could machines eventually replace human educators? This anxiety, often rooted in the disorientation caused by a rapidly evolving technological landscape (Fullan et al., 2023), is not unfounded if we reduce education to mechanical reproduction rather than the creative and reflective construction of knowledge. Whether researchers delegate all research tasks to AI raises important ethical questions. While AI may foster productivity and support researchers in tasks like data analysis or literature review, it should not replace critical thinking, creativity, or ethical judgement. The key is transparency and responsibility in how and in which moment of the research process we use these tools. However, current evidence suggests that AI is not suited to perform such a role fully. Therefore, it is imperative to reinforce critical, reflective, and creative capacities, alongside the crucial role of human judgement in validating decisions. Despite AI's remarkable outputs, especially in the generation of written content, these tasks remain fundamentally human. We believe that AI will not replace researchers; however, it has already transformed how we do research. We need to take into account that human insight, curiosity, and ethical reflection remain irreplaceable.

It is impossible to learn how to do research without a deep and meaningful knowledge base, just as it is impossible to use AI responsibly without a minimum level of digital competence. The ability to ask meaningful questions, critically question educational realities, interpret findings within specific contexts, and evaluate the quality and impact of results are non-negotiable skills for future educators. Only by nurturing these abilities can teachers develop into competent and ethical researchers who can respond effectively to the challenges of evidence-informed education. Throughout this chapter, we have seen how AI can enhance educational practice. Yet, its benefits and limitations configure an open, complex, and ethically charged scenario – one that calls for educators capable of integrating AI critically, responsibly, and humanely.

Therefore, the use of AI in research tasks and in the learning of research skills is acceptable, as long as it functions as a support tool rather than a substitute for human engagement. As highlighted by authors such as

Gallent-Torres et al. (2023), the real problem emerges when AI is used without transparency and without being subject to critical human supervision, which jeopardises both the academic integrity of the learning process and the quality of the outcomes derived from AI use. As discussed throughout this chapter, ethics plays a central role in guiding the responsible use of AI. This calls for students and educators to commit to responsible practices and to avoid dishonest behaviours that deviate from an ethical and creative approach to knowledge production (Masbernat et al., 2024). There is no doubt that institutional policies play a decisive role in promoting responsible, honest, and reflective uses of AI in developing educators' research competence. However, these policies must be complemented by pedagogical approaches explicitly designed to foster such values and practices (Avello-Sáez et al., 2024).

Regarding the first working hypothesis, the results obtained allow us to conclude that, although research competence is present in all the curricula analysed, its inclusion is uneven and lacks a structured framework. It is mainly associated with methodological courses or with those that reinforce the scientific foundations of each discipline, while its presence in other subjects is limited and scattered, without a clear pedagogical definition (Sánchez-Santamaría et al., 2025). This situation highlights the urgent need to rethink and strengthen its didactic approach and to ensure the coherence of the competency framework, especially in the current context of curricular reforms (Herrera-Pavo et al., 2023).

The purpose and meaning of research competence in the curricula, despite addressing critical aspects of the research process, reveals a clear gap between theory, practice, and, above all, the professional profile. This underscores the need to advance towards a training model based on evidence-informed research. In this scenario, it is essential to design systematic and well-grounded strategies for the effective development of this competence during initial teacher education. Only in this way will future educators be able to adopt a critical and reflective stance in their professional practice, oriented towards continuous improvement and grounded in scientific evidence. In this regard, the incorporation of active methodologies, project-based learning, and the use of the digital environment stand out as key resources for strengthening these skills (Goenechea & Valero-Franco, 2024). However, all these elements require a firm institutional and pedagogical commitment to ensure the effective integration of research into teacher training, ultimately contributing to higher-quality, more ethical, and evidence-based education.

Concerning the second and third hypotheses, the findings confirm the existence of a wide variety of digital tools, both AI-powered and AI-specific, applicable to each phase and task of the research process. Furthermore, the value of ResearchComp (European Commission, 2023) as an adaptable tool for structuring and assessing research competence in higher education is particularly noteworthy. Its potential is enhanced when combined with AI tools, opening new avenues for improving initial educator training in this area. The utility of ResearchComp (European Commission, 2023) lies in providing a pedagogical foundation for AI, giving it an educational purpose and integrating transversal competences into research learning. Thus, ResearchComp (European Commission, 2023) establishes learning to do research as an itinerary that must be adapted to the professional profile and contextualised according to the needs of evidence-informed educational interventions, following a competence-based approach with varying levels of complexity. Initial teacher education must therefore incorporate systematic and well-structured strategies to develop these competences, enabling future teachers to adopt a critical and reflective stance based on evidence and oriented towards continuous improvement.

Regarding the fourth hypothesis, the findings indicate that AI is transforming higher education, facilitating research processes and optimising both initial and postgraduate training (Jafari & Keykha, 2024). This transformation is not free from ethical challenges, such as the risk of plagiarism or excessive reliance on automated tools (Spivakovsky et al., 2023). Training in research skills thus faces ethical tensions and dishonest practices that will become increasingly difficult to detect. There are serious ethical concerns, centred around the idea that AI can assist researchers, but it should not be used to fabricate data, write entire papers without oversight, or replace human reasoning. The role of ethics in AI use for training in educational settings is central. Students and researchers must learn not just how to use AI, but when and why it is appropriate – or not. These dishonest behaviours may manifest, for example, in the production of systematic reviews or scoping reviews, which could cease to be formative tasks if fully performed by AI. The lack of ethics in producing these types of work not only deteriorates the quality of the evidence supporting educational practice but also severely limits the ethical development of future educators (UNESCO, 2023; European Union, 2022). Therefore, in order to guarantee responsible and reflective use of AI in research training, we need clear guidelines, ongoing discussions about its impact, and the inclusion of digital ethics in the curricula. This needs to be aligned with teachers and students adopting a critical approach towards the use of AI and the evaluation of AI outputs. Thus, plagiarism also needs to be included as a key factor in the curricula of future educators. It is essential to prioritise prevention over punishment, understanding that, although the latter may sometimes be necessary, it is itself a symptom of educational failure.

The changes are not only refining what we already do well and addressing areas for improvement, but also prompting us to engage more consciously and critically with the ways we design and foster learning. This opportunity allows us to articulate what we know, do, and aspire to achieve, based on what we need to contribute to a more just, democratic, and fully committed society with human rights. While we cannot know for sure what the future holds with AI, we do know that its impact will be profound and transformative.

Bibliography

Alcaide-González, D., et al. (2019). *Plagio en trabajos académicos: diagnóstico y prevención*. https://www.uv.es/plagio/crditos.html

Avello-Sáez, D., Lucero-González, N., & Villagrán, I. (2024). Desarrollo de una declaración de uso de inteligencia artificial con una perspectiva de integridad académica en educación médica y ciencias de la salud. *Revista Médica Clínica las Condes*, 35(6). https://doi.org/10.1016/j.rmclc.2024.06.003

Böttcher-Oschmann, F., Groß Ophoff, J., & Thiel, F. (2021). Preparing teacher training students for evidence-based practice: Promoting students' research competencies in research-learning projects. *Frontiers in Education*, 6, 642107. https://doi.org/10.3389/feduc.2021.642107

Brown, C. & Ion, G. (2022). Práctica educativa informada por la investigación: cómo ayudar a los educadores a comprometerse con la investigación para el bien común. *Revista de Educación*, *397*, 239–260. https://doi.org/10.4438/1988-592X-RE-2022-397-546

Cedeño-Tapia, S. J. (2023). La inteligencia artificial como herramienta complementaria en la investigación y educación: responsabilidad ética y humana. *Revista Unidad Sanitaria XXI*, 2(7), 6–10. https://cerac.unlpam.edu.ar/index.php/usanitariaXXI/article/view/8172

Chan, C. K. Y. (2023). Is AI changing the rules of academic misconduct? An in-depth look at students' perceptions of «AI-giarism». *arXiv (Cornell University)*. https://doi.org/10.48550/arxiv.2306.03358

Ciraso-Calí, A., Martínez-Fernández, J. R., París-Mañas, G., Sánchez-Martí, A., & García-Ravidá, L. B. (2022). The research competence: Acquisition and development among undergraduates in education sciences. *Frontiers in Education*, 7, Article 836165. https://doi.org/10.3389/feduc.2022.836165

Creswell, J. W. & Creswell, J. D. (2017). *Research design: qualitative, quantitative, and mixed methods approaches* (4th Ed.). Sage.

Duche-Pérez, A. B., Plata, A. R. M. R., Grundy-López, R. E., & Flores, V. A. R. (2024). Research Competencies and Skills in Universities: A Systematic Literature Review. *Revista De Gestão Social E Ambiental, 18*(5), e07747. https://doi.org/10.24857/rgsa.v18n5-176

European Commission (2023). *ResearchComp: The European Competence Framework for Researchers*. https://research-and-innovation.ec.europa.eu/jobs-research/researchcomp-european-competence-framework-researchers_en

European Research Council (2023). *Foresight: Use and impact of Artificial Intelligence in the scientific process.* https://erc.europa.eu/sites/default/files/2023-12/AI_in_science.pdf

European Union (2022). *Ethical guidelines on the use of artificial intelligence (AI) and data in teaching and learning for educators.* https://op.europa.eu/es/publication-detail/-/publication/d81a0d54-5348-11ed-92ed-01aa75ed71a1

Fullan, M., Azorin, C., Harris, A., & Jones, M. (2023) Artificial intelligence and school leadership: challenges, opportunities and implications. *School Leadership & Management*, 20, 1-20. https://doi.org/10.1080/13632434.2023.2246856

Gallent-Torres, C., Zapata-González, A., & Ortego-Hernando, J. L. (2023). El impacto de la inteligencia artificial generativa en educación superior: una mirada desde la ética y la integridad académica. *RELIEVE – Revista Electrónica de Investigación y Evaluación Educativa*, 29(2). https://doi.org/10.30827/relieve.v29i2.29134

Goenechea, C., & Valero-Franco, C. (2024). Educación e inteligencia artificial: un análisis desde la perspectiva de los docentes en formación.

REICE Revista Iberoamericana sobre Calidad, Eficacia y Cambio en Educación, 22(2), 33–50. https://doi.org/10.15366/reice2024.22.2.002
Gorard, S. (2020). *Getting evidence into education.* Routledge. https://doi.org/10. 4324/9780429290343
Herrera-Pavo, M. Á., Orellana-Navarrete, V., Jaramillo Baquerizo, C. P., & Balladares Burgos, J. A. (2023). Hacia los nuevos escenarios en la Educación: 2º Congreso internacional de la innovación y la tecnología en educación. *Revista Andina de Educación*, 6(2), 000620. https://doi.org/10.32719/26312816.2022.6.2.0
Jafari, F., & Keykha, A. (2024). Identifying the opportunities and challenges of artificial intelligence in higher education: A qualitative study. *Journal of Applied Research in Higher Education*, 16(4), 1228–1245. https://doi.org/10.1108/JARHE-09-2023-0426
Masbernat, P., Cornejo-Plaza, I., & Cippitani, R. (2024). La integridad científica en la formación universitaria en el contexto de la inteligencia artificial. *Revista de Educación y Derecho*, (2-extraordinario), 207–248. https://doi.org/10.1344/reyd2024.2-extraordinario.49189
Mercer-Mapstone, L. D., & Matthews, K. E. (2017). Student perceptions of communication skills in undergraduate science at an Australian research-intensive university. *Assessment & Evaluation in Higher Education, 42*(1), 98–114. https://doi.org/10.1080/02602938.2015.1084492
Morduchowicz, R. (2023). *La inteligencia artificial ¿Necesitamos una nueva educación? UNESCO.* https://unesdoc.unesco.org/ark:/48223/pf0000386262
Moya, B. A., & Eaton, S. E. (2023). Examinando recomendaciones para el Uso de la IAGenerativa con integridad desde un lente de enseñanza y Aprendizaje. *RELIEVE – Revista Electrónica de Investigación y Evaluación Educativa 29*(2). https://doi.org/10.30827/relieve.v29i2.29295
Oliinyk, I., Bulavina, O., Romanenko, T., Tatarnikova, A., & Smirnov, A. (2024). The role of artificial intelligence in building the research competence of future doctors of philosophy. *Revista de la Universidad del Zulia, 15*(43), 377–396. https://doi.org/10.46925//rdluz.43.22
OpenAI. (2025). *ChatGPT* (28 de octubre). Second revision of the English translation. https://chat.openai.com/chat
Ortega-Bolaños, R., Bernal-Salcedo, J., Germán Ortiz, M., et al. (2024). Applying the ethics of AI: A systematic review of tools for developing and assessing AI-based systems. *Artificial Intelligence Review, 57*(100). https://doi.org/10.1007/s10462-024-10740-3

Pokotylo, K. M., & Sylkina, S. O. (2023). Academic culture and integrity in the educational process in the conditions of military realities. *Slobozhan Scientific Bulletin, 3*, 144–149. https://doi.org/10.46502/issn.1856-7576/2024.18.03.22

Sabariego Puig, M., Cano Hila, A. B., Gros Salvat, B., & Piqué Simón, B. (2020). Competencia investigadora e investigación formativa en la formación inicial del docente. *Contextos Educativos. Revista de Educación*, (26), 239–259. https://doi.org/10.18172/con.4326

Salmento, H., Murtonen, M., & Kiley, M. (2021). Understanding teacher education students' research competence through their conceptions of theory. *Frontiers in Education, 6*, 763803. https://doi.org/10.3389/feduc.2021.763803

Sánchez-Santamaría, J. & Olmedo, E. (2023). El despertar de la inteligencia artificial: Implicaciones para la competencia investigadora en Educación. *Aula Magna 2.0.* https://cuedespyd.hypotheses.org/13719

Sánchez-Santamaría, J., & Morales Calvo, S. (2014). Desarrollando competencias de investigación a través de metodologías activas en un entorno B-learning. Contextos Educativos. *Revista de Educación, 17*, 23–44. https://doi.org/10.18172/con.2591

Sánchez-Santamaría, J., Bovaira, M. J. G., & Carro, L. (2025, 3 February). Research skills in Social Education in Spain: Update the training or stay out of professional practice. *EdArXiv.* https://doi.org/10.35542/osf.io/jc6et_v1

Sánchez-Santamaría, J., Olmedo, E., Ballester-Vial, Mª.G., & Boroel, Brenda. (2024). Práctica educativa informada por la evidencia: La competencia investigadora con apoyo de la Inteligencia Artificial desde el *up-skilling. Teaching and Technology.* (3), e3907, 145–155. https://doi.org/10.17345/ute.2024.3907

Solís, J. L. (2024) Impacto de la IA en las competencias investigativas de los estudiantes de la ESGE: un estudio innovador. *Revista Científica de la Escuela Superior de Guerra del Ejército* 3(1), 35–43. https://doi.org/10.60029/rcesge.v3i1art3

Spivakovsky, O. V., Omelchuk, S. A., Kobets, V. V., Valko, N. V., & Malchykova, D. S. (2023). Institutional policies on artificial intelligence in university learning, teaching and research. *Information Technologies and Learning Tools, 97*(5), 181–202. https://doi.org/10.33407/itlt.v97i5.5395

UNESCO (2023). *Oportunidades y desafíos de la era de la inteligencia artificial para la educación superior: una introducción para los actores de la educación superior.* https://unesdoc.unesco.org/ark:/48223/pf0000386670_spa/PDF/386670spa.pdf.multi

Vanlommel K., & van den Boom-Muilenburg, S. N. (2024). How can we understand and stimulate evidence-informed educational change? A scoping review from a systems perspective. *Journal of Educational Change, 25*(4), 605–634. https://doi.org/10.1007/s10833-024-09506-z

Wilder, C., & Calderone, S. (2025). Empowering educational leadership research with generative AI: Insights and innovations from a qualitative EdD dissertation. *Impacting Education: Journal on Transforming Professional Practice*, 10(1), 18–26. https://doi.org/10.5195/ie.2025.489

Yousaf, M. N. (2025). Practical considerations and ethical implications of using artificial intelligence in writing scientific manuscripts. *ACG Case Reports Journal, 12*(2), e01629. https://doi.org/10.14309/crj.0000000000001629

www.ingramcontent.com/pod-product-compliance
Ingram Content Group UK Ltd.
Pitfield, Milton Keynes, MK11 3LW, UK
UKHW041824100926
8556IPUK00002B/18

9 783631 941263